Contemporary Perspectives on Cognition and Writing

PERSPECTIVES ON WRITING
Series Editors: Susan H. McLeod and Rich Rice

The Perspectives on Writing series addresses writing studies in a broad sense. Consistent with the wide ranging approaches characteristic of teaching and scholarship in writing across the curriculum, the series presents works that take divergent perspectives on working as a writer, teaching writing, administering writing programs, and studying writing in its various forms.

The WAC Clearinghouse, Colorado State University Open Press, and University Press of Colorado are collaborating so that these books will be widely available through free digital distribution and low-cost print editions. The publishers and the Series editors are committed to the principle that knowledge should freely circulate. We see the opportunities that new technologies have for further democratizing knowledge. And we see that to share the power of writing is to share the means for all to articulate their needs, interest, and learning into the great experiment of literacy.

Recent Books in the Series

Douglas M. Walls and Stephanie Vie (Eds.), *Social Writing/Social Media: Publics, Presentations, and Pedagogies* (2017)

Laura R. Micciche, *Acknowledging Writing Partners* (2017)

Susan H. McLeod, Dave Stock, and Bradley T. Hughes (Eds.), *Two WPA Pioneers: Ednah Shepherd Thomas and Joyce Steward* (2017)

Seth Kahn, William B. Lalicker, and Amy Lynch-Biniek (Eds.), *Contingency, Exploitation, and Solidarity: Labor and Action in English Composition* (2017)

Barbara J. D'Angelo, Sandra Jamieson, Barry Maid, and Janice R. Walker (Eds.), *Information Literacy: Research and Collaboration across Disciplines* (2017)

Justin Everett and Cristina Hanganu-Bresch (Eds.), *A Minefield of Dreams: Triumphs and Travails of Independent Writing Programs* (2016)

Chris M. Anson and Jessie L. Moore (Eds.), *Critical Transitions: Writing and the Questions of Transfer* (2016)

Joanne Addison and Sharon James McGee, *Writing and School Reform: Writing Instruction in the Age of Common Core and Standardized Testing* (2016)

Lisa Emerson, *The Forgotten Tribe: Scientists as Writers* (2016)

Jacob S. Blumner and Pamela B. Childers, *WAC Partnerships Between Secondary and Postsecondary Institutions* (2015)

CONTEMPORARY PERSPECTIVES ON COGNITION AND WRITING

Edited by Patricia Portanova, J. Michael Rifenburg, and Duane Roen

The WAC Clearinghouse
wac.colostate.edu
Fort Collins, Colorado

University Press of Colorado
upcolorado.com
Boulder, Colorado

The WAC Clearinghouse, Fort Collins, Colorado 80523–1040

University Press of Colorado, Boulder, Colorado 80303

© 2017 by Patricia Portanova, J. Michael Rifenburg, and Duane Roen. This work is licensed under a Creative Commons Attribution-NonCommercial-NoDerivatives 4.0 International.

ISBN 978-1-64215-003-2 (PDF) | 978-1-64215-004-9 (ePub) | 978-1-60732-858-2 (pbk.)

Library of Congress Cataloging-in-Publication Data

Names: Portanova, Patricia, 1989– editor. | Rifenburg, J. Michael, 1982– editor. | Roen, Duane H., editor.
Title: Contemporary perspectives on cognition and writing / edited by Patricia Portanova, J. Michael Rifenburg, and Duane Roen.
Description: Fort Collins, Colorado : The WAC Clearinghouse, 2018. | Series: Perspectives on writing | Includes bibliographical references.
Identifiers: LCCN 2017059422| ISBN 9781607328582 (pbk. : alk. paper) | ISBN 9781642150049 (epub)
Subjects: LCSH: Language and languages—Style—Psychological aspects. | Rhetoric and psychology. | Written communication—Psychological aspects. | Cognition.
Classification: LCC P301.5.P75 C66 2018 | DDC 808.001/9—dc23 LC record available at https://lccn.loc.gov/2017059422

Copyeditor: Don Donahue
Designer: Mike Palmquist
Series Editors: Susan H. McLeod and Rich Rice

The WAC Clearinghouse supports teachers of writing across the disciplines. Hosted by Colorado State University, and supported by the Colorado State University Open Press, it brings together scholarly journals and book series as well as resources for teachers who use writing in their courses. This book is available in digital formats for free download at wac.colostate.edu.

Founded in 1965, the University Press of Colorado is a nonprofit cooperative publishing enterprise supported, in part, by Adams State University, Colorado State University, Fort Lewis College, Metropolitan State University of Denver, Regis University, University of Colorado, University of Northern Colorado, Utah State University, and Western State Colorado University. For more information, visit upcolorado.com. The Press partners with the Clearinghouse to make its books available in print.

CONTENTS

Foreword. Are Cognitive Studies in Writing Really Passé?............ vii
    John R. Hayes

Introduction... 3
    Patricia Portanova, J. Michael Rifenburg, and Duane Roen

Section I: Historical Context

Chapter 1. The Psychology of Writing Situated within Social Action: An Empirical and Theoretical Program........................... 21
    Charles Bazerman

Chapter 2. The Evolving Relationship Between Composition and Cognitive Studies: Gaining Some Historical Perspective on our Contemporary Moment... 39
    Ellen C. Carillo

Chapter 3. Attending to Phenomenology: Rethinking Cognition and Reflection in North American Writing Studies 57
    Dylan B. Dryer and David R. Russell

Section II: Reconsidering Approaches to Teaching and Learning

Chapter 4. Neuroscience of Reading: Developing Expertise in Reading and Writing 79
    Alice S. Horning

Chapter 5. Language Attachment Theory: The Possibilities of Cross-Language Relationships 95
    Bonnie Vidrine-Isbell

Chapter 6. Meaningful Practice: Adaptive Learning, Writing Instruction, and Writing Research 115
    Gwen Gorzelsky, Carol Hayes, Joseph Paszek,
    Edmund Jones, and Dana Lynn Driscoll

Section III: Neuroscientific Discoveries and Applicability

Chapter 7. Neural Implications for Narrative in Multimodal Persuasive Messages 135
    Dirk Remley

Contents

Chapter 8. Pedagogy and the Hermeneutic Dance: Mirroring, Plasticity, and the Situated Writing Subject 153
    Jen Talbot

Chapter 9. Neuroplasticity, Genre, and Identity: Possibilities and Complications 169
    Irene Clark

SECTION IV: WRITING-RELATED TRANSFER AND IMPLEMENTING THE HABITS OF MIND

Chapter 10. Teaching Metacognition to Reinforce Agency and Transfer in Course-Linked First-Year Courses. 191
    Dianna Winslow and Phil Shaw

Chapter 11. Metacognition and the Reflective Writing Practitioner: An Integrated Knowledge Approach. 211
    Kara Taczak and Liane Robertson

Chapter 12. Seeing is Believing: Re-presentation, Cognition, and Transfer in Writing Classes. 231
    Marcus Meade

Chapter 13. "Did You Ever Take that Test Yourself?" Failed Knowledge Transfer, Peer-to-Peer Pedagogies, and the *Framework* Habits of Mind as Two-Way Street 247
    Steven J. Corbett with Jeremy Kunkel

SECTION V: STUDENT VOICES: RESEARCHING SELF-PERCEPTIONS, DISPOSITIONS, AND PRIOR KNOWLEDGE

Chapter 14. Researching Habits-of-Mind Self-Efficacy in First-Year College Writers. 271
    Peter H. Khost

Chapter 15. Defining Dispositions: Mapping Student Attitudes and Strategies in College Composition. 291
    E. Shelley Reid

Chapter 16. Mapping the Prior: A Beginning Typology and Its Impact on Writing. 313
    Kathleen Blake Yancey

Afterword. Reflection: What Can Cognitive Rhetoric Offer Us?. 331
    Linda Flower

Contributors 347

FOREWORD
ARE COGNITIVE STUDIES IN WRITING REALLY PASSÉ?

John R. Hayes
Carnegie Mellon University

Over the past few decades, a number of influential voices within the Conference on College Composition and Communication have discouraged researchers' interest in cognitive approaches to writing. The cognitive approach has been accused of many sins—including being scientific, failing to resist dominant ideologies (e.g., serving corporate masters), and being anti-feminist (see Charney [1996, 1998] for excellent critiques and reviews). Other critics have asserted that cognitive approaches to writing are ineffective and have, in fact, disappeared. As recently as 2006, Martin Nystrand and Paul Prior, in separate articles in the *Handbook of Writing Research*, made these comments:

> By the 1980s, this new social perspective gathered momentum within writing studies. Challenging the Flower and Hayes (1981) cognitive model of writing processes, Nystrand (1982) argued that "the special relations that define written language functioning and promote its meaningful use . . . are wholly circumscribed by the systematic relations that obtain in the speech community of the writer" (p. 17). Bizzell (1982), also challenging Flower and Hayes's cognitive model, argued that "what's missing here is a connection to social context afforded by the recognition of the dialectic relationship between thought and language . . ." (Nystrand, 2006, p. 19)
>
> Research on writing processes in the United States initially settled on cognitive processing theory (i.e., Flower & Hayes, 1981); however, that paradigm was soon critiqued as too narrow in its understanding of context and was eclipsed by studies that attended to social, historical, and political contexts of writing. (Prior, 2006, p. 54)

From these quotes, one might easily infer (1) that cognitive writing research was briefly popular in the early 1980s but was soon abandoned and (2) that it was abandoned because it failed to take adequate account of social, political, and historical contexts. In this foreword, I will address these two issues.

HAVE WRITING RESEARCHERS REALLY LOST INTEREST IN COGNITION?

The best evidence to answer the question as to whether cognitive studies have been abandoned would be provided by a broad survey of the literature to find how many cognitively oriented articles about writing were published in the years from 1980 to the present in all manner of journals worldwide. To carry out such a survey would require an enormous effort; so I decided instead to ask the more limited question, "Are people still citing cognitive models of writing?" I reasoned that if interest in cognition had died in the 1980s, citations of cognitive models should be scarce, certainly in the last few decades.

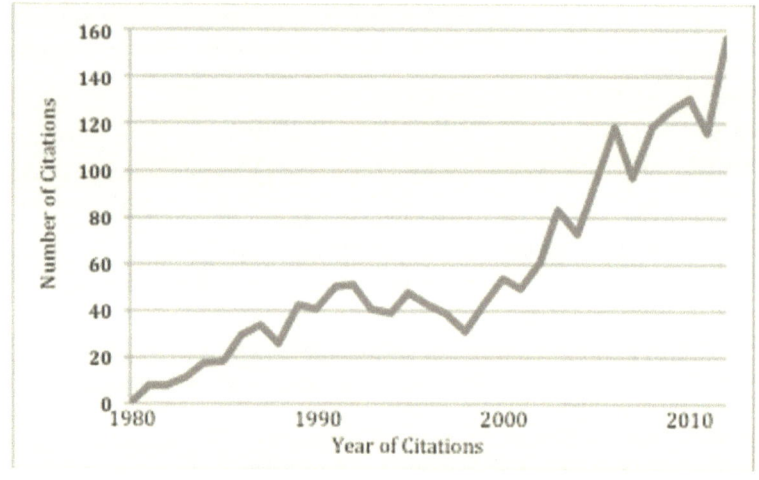

Figure 1. Citations per year of Hayes' and Flower's (1980) cognitive model between 1980 and 2012.

I obtained the citations for Figures 1 through 4 by consulting Google Scholar in March, 2014. Figure 1 shows yearly citations of the Hayes-Flower (1980) model. Rather than fading into the twilight, interest in that model appears to have grown fairly steadily since 1980 with the exception of a dip in the late 1990s. Figures 2 and 3 show yearly citations for Ronald T. Kellogg's (1996) model and Hayes' (1996) revision of the 1980 model. Because these models were introduced well after the early 1980s, one would predict, according to the account of Nystrand and Prior, that there would not have been much interest in these models. However, as with the Hayes and Flower (1980) model, researcher's interest in both of these models has been substantial and growing.

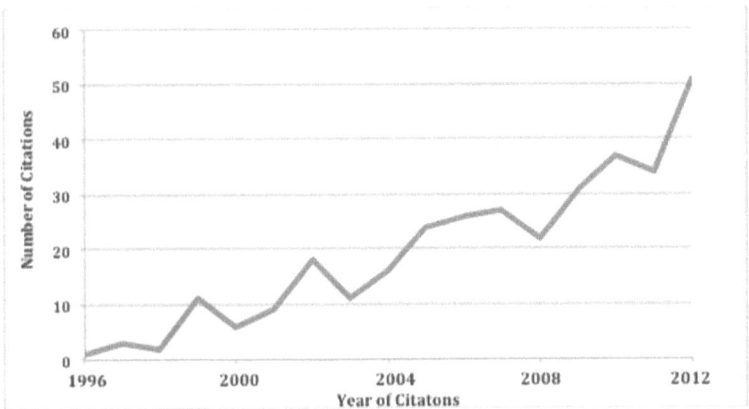

Figure 2. Citations per year of Kellogg's (1996) model between 1996 and 2012.

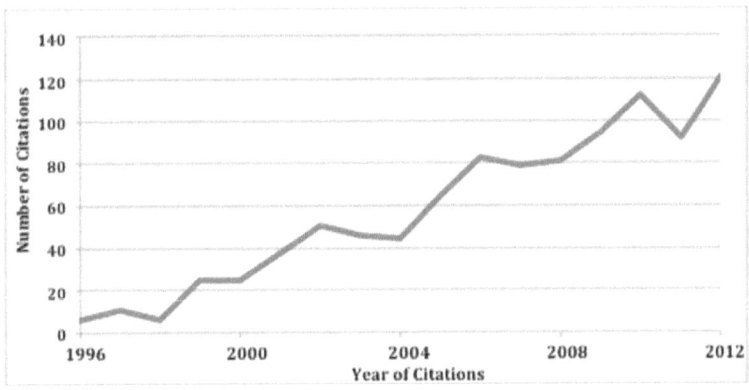

Figure 3. Citations per year of Hayes' (1996) model between 1996 and 2012.

Why would Nystrand and Prior declare the death of interest in cognitive processes in writing when clearly that interest has not died? Perhaps they had focused primarily on the North American environment, but that the sustained interest in cognition in writing was really a European or Asian phenomenon. To explore this possibility, I divided the citations for the Hayes and Flower (1980) model into U.S./Canadian versus non-U.S./Canadian citations and plotted them separately, as shown in Figure 4.

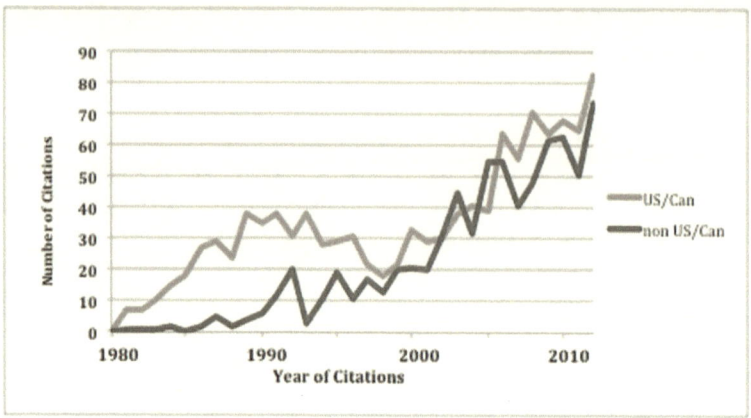

Figure 4. U.S./Canadian and non-U.S./Canadian citations per year of the Hayes-Flower (1980) writing model.

It is clear that the dip in citations seen in Figure 1 in the late 1990s is a U.S./Canadian phenomenon. However, after 2000, citations by both groups increase steadily and rather dramatically.

To summarize, it is clear that contrary to Nystrand's and Prior's claims, interest in cognition in writing appears to have increased substantially since the 1980s. In fact, cognitive writing studies are very much alive and well both in North America and abroad. These studies have had impact in many fields including writing instruction for adults (Penrose & Sitko, 1993) and children (Boscolo, 2008; McCutchen, 2006), writing to learn (Klein, 1999), second language writing (Devine, Railey & Boshoff, 1993), writing by individuals with disabilities (Arfe, Dockrell & Berninger, 2014; Ellis, 1993), writing for mental health (Lepore & Greenberg, 2002), writing and technology (Pea & Kurland, 1987), and professional communication (Schriver, 2012).

Although Nystrand's and Prior's claims that interest in cognitive writing research had vanished were clearly mistaken when applied to the research community generally, they may have accurately reflected attitudes common in North American English departments. Perhaps it was specifically members of English departments who had rejected cognitive writing research.

To explore this possibility, I surveyed all of the articles in *Written Communication* published in the years from 1984 to 1988 and from 2010 to 2014. I divided the articles into three groups, according to the department of the first author. In the first group were articles by authors who identified their department either as English, rhetoric, literacy, literature, or composition. In the second group, the authors were from departments of education, psychology, or instruction. In the third group, the authors came from all other sources. I noted whether each of the articles in the first two groups referenced any of the following cognitive theorists: Berninger, Bereiter, Flower, Hayes, Kellogg, Scardamalia. This was my measure of the author's interest in cognition. Figure 5 shows a sharp decline over time in articles that reference cognitive theorists in the English/rhetoric group but not in the education/psychology group.

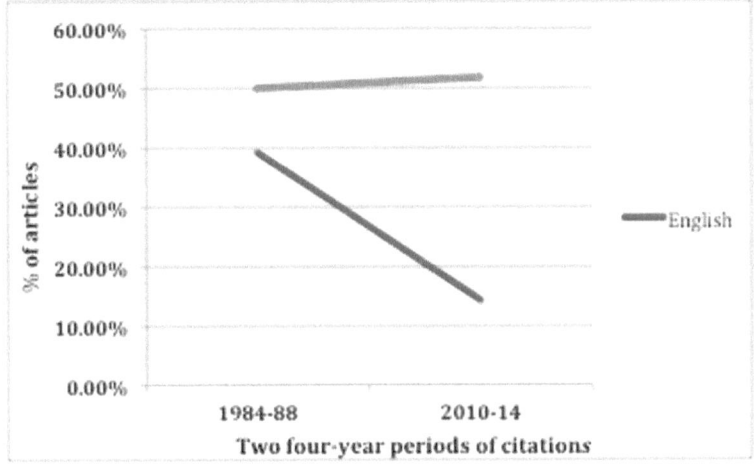

Figure 5. Percent of articles referencing selected cognitive theorists during two periods in Written Communication.

Although some members of English departments still create high quality studies of cognitive writing processes, the number of such studies appears to have declined in English Departments in sharp contrast to the writing research community more generally.

DO COGNITIVE STUDIES HAVE TOO NARROW AN UNDERSTANDING OF CONTEXT?

Why would English and related departments reject cognitive research about writing? Prior (2006) claimed that writing researchers recognized that the field of cognitive studies was "too narrow in its understanding of context . . ." (p. 54). In particular, he highlights social, historical, and political contexts. This might mean that the writing researchers that Prior was referring to were more interested in social, historical, and political factors than cognitive ones. Probably true, but I don't think that was the essence of the criticism. I think the critique is really that cognitive researchers uniquely ignored context. To clarify the issue, we need to discuss the relation between research and context.

To start, we should recognize that both social/cultural and cognitive factors are essential for understanding writing. Written language is a cultural product. Language would be impossible without the conventions that have been created through social interaction. Further, the purpose of most writing is social: to communicate with others. But cognitive factors are essential, too. Individuals must learn and remember the socially created linguistic conventions if they are to have any effect. Indeed, without cognitive processes, such as long-term memory, working memory, and perception, one can neither write nor read.

Those readers who have relatives or friends with senile dementia know the importance of cognitive functioning for successful social relations. I have observed this in my own family. My mother and my aunt took care of my aging grandmother. Grandmother had no idea who I was but one day she confided in me that "these two ladies" (her daughters) were keeping her captive, but that one day her husband (long since dead) would come to rescue her. A healthy cognitive system is important for social functioning. Even life-long relationships can be erased when memory fails.

Given that both cognitive and social/cultural factors are essential for a full understanding of writing, what are the implications that concern for attention to context has for carrying out writing research? Does it mean that a study focused on a cognitive factor must take all relevant historical, social and political factors into account to be worth doing? Or that a study focused on an historical factor must take all relevant social, political, and cognitive factors into account to be worth doing? If that were so, we would need to know what all the relevant contextual factors are. But we don't! We can guess what some of them are and take them into account when we design a study. But we can't know them all. Finding out what they are is an important part of what research is about. For example, the use of control groups, common among cognitive researchers, is an effective way to discover important contextual factors. The argument that cognitive writing research pays insufficient attention to context is plainly a red herring.

To illustrate the situation that researchers face in trying to take context into account, I will recount an incident that I experienced some years ago. I was preparing to do a study about creativity in musical composers. Herbert Simon and William Chase (1973) had published a study showing that if chess players were to become grand masters, they needed at least 10 years of intensive practice. I wondered if composers needed a similar period of intensive practice before they created the works for which they became famous. I decided to study the musical preparation of as many composers about whom I could find adequate biographical material. My sample included 76 composers covering a time period of more than two centuries, starting with Vivaldi and ending with Stravinsky.

To get expert advice, I described my study to a musicologist on campus. His advice, which he presented in a kindly way, could be summarized as, "You're wasting your time." He explained that the esthetic goals of musicians who composed in different centuries and in different artistic traditions were so diverse that there could be nothing in common among them. Therefore, I couldn't expect to find any consistent results. This wasn't an implausible argument. Social and historical factors might have overwhelmed the effects of practice.

But in this case, they didn't. I found that 73 of the 76 composers I studied had had ten or more years of practice before they wrote the works for which they became famous and the remaining three had either eight or nine years. In a second study (Hayes, 1989), I found similar results for painters. Nina Wishbow (1988) found parallel results for poets. Practice, then, clearly has an impact on creative performance even though cultural and historical factors must surely have been operating as well.

My point is not that cognitive factors are more important than social or historical ones. Rather, my point is that whether cognitive, social, historical, or political factors have a significant impact in a given situation is a matter to be decided by observation, and not by assumption.

Given that the argument about context is a red herring, why then might English Departments shun cognition? Richard Haswell (2005) suggested it might be a matter of pursuing fads. Every few years, a hot new topic may be required to replace the once hot old topic. Perhaps, but I believe that the underlying cause is that many of the people who become members of English departments dislike science and math. The tradition of empirical argument that is central to cognitive writing research may not fit comfortably with the professional styles of English professors. In an article entitled, "Finding a Comfortable Identity," William Irmsher (1987) wrote, "What we know is that scholars in the humanities characteristically distrust quantitative measures, even for linguistic or stylistic studies" (p. 85). He advises writing scholars to "prefer case-study and ethnographic inquiry to controlled group studies involving comparisons" (1987, p. 86). Finally, he complains "must we continue to be plagued by the scientific nemesis? By the specters of averages and standard deviations?" (1987, p. 87). Irmsher clearly did not like science or statistics, and in these quotes, he foreshadowed the strange valorization of qualitative over quantitative methods that is popular in English departments today.

Although many writing researchers in English departments have divorced themselves from cognitively oriented studies, the present volume gives hope of a reconciliation. The authors in this volume do not dispute the importance of social, political, and historical influences, but they do embrace the importance of cognition and neuroscience for understanding writing. Many of the authors cite the importance of transfer and metacognition for teaching and learning writing; others express interest in attention and knowledge. The phenomena of plasticity and mirroring receive special attention from authors interested in the implications of neuroscience for writing.

If these authors in this book and like-minded colleagues can garner attention from an audience within English departments and beyond, perhaps they can reduce the bias against cognitive writing studies. Perhaps, in coming decades, researchers in English departments will integrate cognitive science and neuroscience in their studies of writing to design more effective research programs and more effective writing instruction. Let's hope!

REFERENCES

Arfe, B., Dockrell, J. & Berninger, V. (2014). *Writing development in children with hearing loss, dyslexia, or oral language problems*. New York: Oxford.

Bizzell, P. (1982). Cognition, convention, and certainty: What we need to know about writing. *PRE/TEXT, 3*(3), 213–243.

Boscolo, P. (2008). Writing in primary school. In C. Bazerman (Ed.), *Handbook of research on writing* (pp. 289–305). Mahwah, NJ: Lawrence Erlbaum.

Charney, D. (1996). Empiricism is not a four-letter word. *College Composition and Communication, 47*(4), 567–593.

Charney, D. (1998). From logocentrism to ethnocentrism: Historicizing critiques of writing research. *Technical Communication Quarterly, 7*(1), 9–32.

Devine, J., Railey, K. & Boshoff, P. (1993) The implications of cognitive models in L1 and L2 writing. *Journal of Second Language Writing, 2*(3), 181–291.

Ellis, A. W. (1993) *Reading, writing and dyslexia: A cognitive analysis* (2nd ed.). Hillsdale, NJ: Lawrence Erlbaum.

Flower, L. S. & Hayes, J. R. (1981). A cognitive process theory of writing. *College Composition and Communication, 32*(4), 365–387.

Haswell, R. H. (2005). NCTE/CCCC's recent war on scholarship. *Written Communication, 22*(2), 198–223.

Hayes, J. R. (1985). Three problems in teaching general skills. In S. F. Chipman, J. W. Segal & R. Glaser (Eds.), *Thinking and learning skills, Vol. 2*. Hillsdale, NJ: Lawrence Erlbaum.

Hayes, J. R. (1989). *The complete problem solver* (2nd ed.). Hillsdale, NJ: Lawrence Erlbaum.

Hayes, J. R. (1996). A new framework for understanding cognition and affect in writing. In C. M. Levy & S. Randall (Eds.), *The science of writing: Theories, methods, individual differences, and applications* (pp. 1–27). Mahwah, NJ: Lawrence Erlbaum.

Hayes, J. R. & Flower, L. S. (1980). Identifying the organization of writing processes. In L. W. Gregg & E. R. Steinberg (Eds.), *Cognitive processes in writing* (pp. 3–30). Hillsdale, NJ: Lawrence Erlbaum.

Irmscher, W. F. (1987). Finding a comfortable identity. *College Composition and Communication, 38*(1), 81–87.

Kellogg, R. T. (1996). A model of working memory in writing. In C. M. Levy & S. Ransdell (Eds.), *The science of writing: Theories, methods, individual differences, and applications* (pp. 57–72). Mahwah, NJ: Lawrence Erlbaum.

Klein, P. D. (1999). Reopening inquiry into cognitive processes in writing-to-learn. *Educational Psychology Review, 11*(3), 203–270.

Lepore, S. J. & Greenberg, M. A. (2002). Mending broken hearts: Effects of expressive writing on mood, cognitive processing, social adjustment and health following a relationship breakup. *Psychology and Health, 17*(5), 547–560.

McCutchen, D. (2006). Cognitive factors in the development of children's writing. In C. A. MacArthur, S. Graham & J. Fitzgerald (Eds.) *Handbook of writing research* (pp. 115–130). New York: Guilford Press.

Nystrand, M. (1982). *What writers know: The language, process, and structure of written discourse.* New York: Academic Press

Nystrand, M. (2006). The social and historical context for writing research. In C.A. MacArthur, S. Graham & J. Fitzgerald (Eds.), *Handbook of writing research* (pp. 11–27). New York: Guilford Press.

Pea, R. D. & Kurland, D. M. (1987). Cognitive technologies for writing development. In L. Frase (Ed.), *Review of Research in Education,* Vol. 14 (pp. 277–326). Washington, DC: AERA Press.

Penrose, A. M. & Sitko, B. M. (1993). *Hearing ourselves think: Cognitive research in the college writing classroom.* New York: Oxford University Press.

Prior, P. (2006). A sociocultural theory of writing. In C. A. MacArthur, S. Graham & J. Fitzgerald (Eds.) *Handbook of writing research* (pp. 54–66). New York: Guilford Press.

Schriver, K. A. (2012). What we know about expertise in professional communication. In V. W. Berninger (Ed.), *Past, present, and future contributions of cognitive writing research to cognitive psychology* (pp. 275–312). New York: Psychology Press.

Simon H. A. & Chase W. G. (1973). Skill in chess. *American Scientist 61*(4), 394–40.

Wishbow, N. (1988). *Studies of creativity in poets.* (Unpublished doctoral dissertation). Carnegie Mellon University, Pittsburgh.

Contemporary Perspectives on Cognition and Writing

INTRODUCTION

Patricia Portanova
Northern Essex Community College

J. Michael Rifenburg
University of North Georgia

Duane Roen
Arizona State University

In 2013, a search through the Conference on College Composition and Communication program for the term "cognition" yielded few results. In fact, the term "cognition" has not appeared as a category for submissions to Cs in several years. As Carol Berkenkotter and Thomas Huckin's (1995) analysis of CCCC program topics has shown, the current topics of interest are defined *for* participants by conference leadership and their selected theme and, to be fair, may not encompass *all* interests of *all* members of the field. Yet this search (and the omission of the term *cognition* from any of the CFP language) gave the perception that few, if any, attendees of that year's CCCC were sharing ideas, theories, or research related to writing and cognition. Of course, this is false: there has been and continues to be significant interest in the mind, how we learn, how we process information, and how this all relates to writing. Rather, there has been a decline in the use of the term *cognition* to describe our scholarship in writing studies because, as Ellen Carillo, Dylan Dryer and David Russell show in this collection, the word is fraught with contention.

Although writing research grew in large part out of the U.S. history and culture of first-year composition courses in higher education, the international community of writing research scholars continues to embrace *cognition,* using cognitive principles to inform writing research in multiple disciplines. Yet, studies building upon the history of writing and cognition research within composition studies have rapidly decreased in the US since the 1980s. An aggregation of data collected by Jonathan Goodwin (2012) indicates a steady decline in published scholarship on cognition and writing. Goodwin's data were derived from an algorithm that compiled all references in the digital library JSTOR to the following keywords: *composing strategies, invention research, heuristic, discovery, revision, discourse researchers, rhetorical writer,* Flower, process, Lee, stages, and *explore*.

The data show a steady increase in scholarship on these topics, which peaked in the early 1980s only to decline through the 1990s and the early aughts. This trajectory aligns with a familiar narrative in composition history: the rise and fall of cognitive research on writing. (To frame this volume, Carillo offers a rich and detailed account of this narrative in her chapter).

In response to what appeared to be a decline in scholarship in this area, we organized a Special Interest Group on Cognition and Writing at the 2014 CCCC in Indianapolis. Our first featured speaker was John R. Hayes, the well-known cognitive psychologist, who shared his research on the supposed death of cognition and writing research. As he discusses further in the foreword to this collection, Hayes complicated the rise and fall myth of cognitive studies by examining citations of his well-known article he co-authored with Linda Flower in 1981. Citations steadily increased in published journal articles over the past 25 years—with the most citations of his work since its publication appearing in 2012. However, as he shows, while writing research informed by cognitive science has increased steadily internationally, and domestically in other disciplines, such published research has fizzled out in U.S. English departments where the majority of compositionists are employed.

Hayes' presentation in 2014 spurred a lively discussion among SIG members. The Special Interest Group identified several potential reasons for the decline in cognitive research within English departments. Cognitive research frequently hinges upon interdisciplinary collaboration. Advances in cognitive research and new technologies for research may be best understood by experts in fields such as in neuroscience, psychology, and special education, but interdisciplinary collaboration is still infrequent in the field where tenure decisions are often based on "publish or perish" expectations; co-authored work may not receive the same value as individual scholarship. With teaching, service, and other administrative responsibilities, it is often difficult to arrange interdisciplinary research projects logistically. However, interdisciplinary projects may mean access to new technology such as eye-tracking software, fMRI imaging, statistical analysis software, and other useful empirical research tools to expand our understanding of the mind at work while writing.

Despite the recent decline of published articles citing the work of Flower and Hayes, it is clear that there is significant interest and ongoing research in cognition and writing by compositionists in English departments that adopt cognitive principles. We look to the national consensus document, the *Framework for Success in Postsecondary Writing* (2011), as one such example of this interest. A joint venture between the Council of Writing Program Administrators, the National Council of Teachers of English, and the National Writing Project, the *Framework* operates from several key assumptions, according to Peggy O'Neill, Linda

Adler-Kassner, Cathy Fleischer, and Anne-Marie Hall (2012), who worked on the *Framework* and authored an article on their work for a symposium published in *College English*. The first assumption was that writing instruction is a shared enterprise between K-16 educators; the second is that college readiness is also a shared enterprise between secondary and postsecondary teachers; and finally, they believed the *Framework* should be guided by the CWPA Outcomes Statement for First-Year Composition, a national consensus document offering clear direction for thousands upon thousands of compulsory postsecondary writing classes offered in the US.

As Nicholas Behm, Sherry Rankins-Robertson, and Duane Roen (2017) note in the "Introduction" to their recent collection on the *Framework*, the document represents a thread in a national discussion about what writing teachers can do to help students be more successful. Although the Framework reflects one form of consensus (as defined by the CWPA/NCTE/NWP task force that crafted the document), it also is a response to other views of what constitutes success in the writing classroom. The *Framework* contributes to the conversation, but it will not end debates about which instructional approaches will help students write more effectively. Those debates will rage on long after all readers of this collection have ended their careers.

Unique to the *Framework*, and where this edited collection enters into the conversation, is the addition of eight habits of mind believed essential for college readiness and college writing success. The executive summary of the *Framework* offers the HOM as "ways of approaching learning that are both intellectual and practical and will support students' success in a variety of fields and disciplines" (Behm, Rankins-Robertson & Roen, 2017, p. 1). The eight are curiosity, openness, engagement, creativity, persistence, responsibility, flexibility, and metacognition. Particularly helpful for the wide readership of the *Framework*, immediately following the introduction of the HOM, the executive summary leads into briefly capturing how teacher can foster the HOM through "writing, reading, and critical analysis" (Behm, Rankins-Robertson & Roen, 2017, p. 1). Thus with the emphasis on developing the HOM in conjunction with, for example, rhetorical knowledge, the *Framework* in general and the HOM in specific are one entry into these important conversations on cognition and writing.

Kathleen Blake Yancey, Liane Roberston, and Kara Taczak's (2014) award-winning *Writing Across Contexts: Transfer, Composition, and Sites of Writing* offers an additional entry into the conversations animating this collection. Yancey, Robertson, and Taczak build on the HOM by highlighting the role of the eighth HOM, metacognition, in facilitating writing-related transfer and introducing students to threshold concepts, which, in brief, are central definitive concepts that mark a discipline. Finally, Adler-Kassner and Elizabeth Wardle's (2015) edited collection *What We Know: Threshold Concepts of Writing Studies* is a crowd-sourced and expansive, but at the same time focused, offering of five threshold concepts. The fifth is "Writing Is (Also Always) a Cognitive Activity" and Dylan Dryer, Charles Bazerman, Howard Tinberg, Chris Anson, and Kara Taczak explicate this concept with their contributions. Three of these voices continue their thinking in chapters for this collection.

In the wake of this scholarship and many more individual articles populating our journals and conversations driving our listservs, our Special Interest Group of eighty-two members increases membership each year. The goal of *Contemporary Perspectives on Cognition and Writing*, then, is to bridge the publishing gap between the work of the 1980s and the diverse contemporary research by U.S.-based compositionists.

All of the chapters included in this collection are authored or co-authored by faculty from English departments and/or independent writing programs, and represent a variety of perspectives such as using the history of cognitive research in composition to inform our inquiry (Bazerman; Carillo; and Dryer & Russell); theory-building that bridges neuroscience and rhetoric (Remley); neuroplasticity, genre, and identity (Clark); the neuroscience of reading (Horning); and using the HOM to facilitate writing-related transfer (Corbett; Khost; Meade; and Reid). We believe this collection will appeal to scholars interested in a diverse range of research methods and methodologies, as well as composition pedagogy grounded in cognitive principles. This collection is appropriate for advanced undergraduate or graduate courses and it is particularly suited to an introduction to composition studies course. It is a useful supplement to the popular anthologies *Cross-Talk in Comp Theory*, edited by Victor Villanueva and Kristin Arola (2011) and the Susan Miller (2009) edited *Norton Anthology of Composition* with our focus on the transfer of writing knowledge and the habits of mind outlined in the *Framework* (2011).

DEFINING TERMS

Given the range of research interests represented in this book, as well as the diverse perspectives shared through the Cognition and Writing SIG, we found it restrictive to impose a narrow definition of the term *cognition* on individual scholars. Each chapter in this collection explores the intersection of research on cognition and writing through a contemporary lens, drawing upon shared scholarship in the field. Rather than force one particular view, we asked individual authors to define the term within the context of their own work, thus creating a more collaborative and inclusive community of cognition and writing scholars.

As a result, our understanding of the term *cognition* is developed throughout the collection and represents several different research interests. In this section, we explore some of those definitions by exploring how scholars have used terms in the past. We hope this brief survey of the literature will serve as a foundation for the chapters that follow.

Cognition and Metacognition

As Peter Khost notes in this collection, "*cognition* can be a mystifying term. At times the word just seems to mean *thinking*; at other times it entails emotions, non-emotional affect . . . and even assimilated social influences. So this word that denotes the thinking of a single person can also paradoxically connote the opposite of thinking and involvement of other people." Khost points to the principles undergirding discussions of cognition the field: is it individual or social? In common usage, *cognition* is "the mental action or process of acquiring knowledge and understanding through thought, experience, and the senses" ("Cognition"). The word itself derives from the Latin word *cognosco-con* ("with") and *gnōscō* "know). The Latin form comes from the Greek verb γι(γ)νώσκω *gi(g)nósko* ("I know, I perceive"). The noun form is γνῶσις *gnósis* ("knowledge"), which means "to conceptualize" or to recognize" (Franchi & Bianchini, 2011, p. xiv). This definition—to perceive, conceptualize, or recognize—Khost notes, appears to mean *thinking* in broad terms.

Likewise, the term *metacognition* is often broadly defined as *thinking about thinking*. The *Framework* defines metacognition as "the ability to reflect on one's thinking as well as on the individual and cultural processes and systems used to structure knowledge" (Behm, Rankins-Robertson & Roen, 2017, p. 5). In this collection, Carillo shows the complexity of metacognition—distinguishing it from cognition. She borrows Howard Tinberg's distinction between cognition and metacognition:

> cognition refers to the acquisition and application of knowledge through complex mental processes . . . but the effective accomplishment of writing tasks over time requires even more. It calls upon metacognition, or the ability to perceive the very steps by which success occurs and to articulate the various qualities and components that contribute in significant ways to the production of successful writing.

Both Carillo's ideas and Tinberg's definitions align with the definition of metacognition offered in the *Framework,* which is "the ability to reflect on one's own thinking as well as on the individual and cultural processes used to structure knowledge" (Behm, Rankins-Robertson & Roen, 2017, p. 1) and with the work of Dianna Winslow and Phil Shaw as well as that of Taczak and Robertson in this collection. Dryer and Russell, in this collection, integrate Bazerman's social perspective by describing research on social metacognition that "examines people's 'complex determinations about the reliability of our own thoughts, feelings, and beliefs as well as attributions about the thoughts, feelings, and beliefs of others around us'" (Jost et al., 1998, p. 137). Here, it becomes evident that contemporary perspectives on cognition and metacognition include a decidedly social perspective.

Lev Vygotsky (1986) uses the term *consciousness* rather than *cognition*. In reflecting on work of Jean Piaget (1974) and Edouard Claparede (1974), Vygotsky comments on the relationship among action, thought, and language: "To become conscious of a mental operation means to transfer it from the plane of action to that of language, i.e., to recreate it in the imagination so that it can be expressed in words" (1986, pp. 163–164). Vygotsky clarifies his use of to the term by noting, "we want clarify the term *consciousness* as we use it in speaking of nonconscious functions becoming conscious. . . . This model implies that the child's thought is not fully conscious; it contains conscious as well as unconscious elements" (1986, p. 169). He further notes that "becoming conscious of our operations and viewing each as a process of a certain *kind* [emphasis in original]—such as remembering or imagining—leads to their mastery" (1986, p. 171). Vygotsky also observes that "Written speech is considerably more conscious, and it is produced more deliberately than oral speech" (1986, p. 182). Additionally, notes Vygotsky, "Signs of writing and methods of their use are acquired consciously. Writing, in its turn, enhances the intellectuality of the child's actions" (1986, p. 183). Vygotsky concludes that "the essential difference between written and oral speech reflects the difference between two types of activity, one of which is spontaneous, involuntary, and nonconscious, while the other is abstract, voluntary, and conscious" (1986, p. 183).

SOCIAL AND SITUATED COGNITION

In social cognitive theory (Bandura, 1985) the three components of influence (individual, behavior, and environment) are equally valued though exert different degrees of influence dependent on context. Thus, a social cognitive theory is also situated (see below). According to Albert Bandura, in the social cognitive view people are neither driven by inner forces nor automatically shaped and controlled by external stimuli. Rather, human functioning is explained in terms of a model of triadic reciprocality in which behavior, cognitive and other personal factors, and environmental events all operate as interacting determinants of each other. The nature of persons is defined within this perspective in terms of a number of basic capabilities (Bandura, 1985, p. 18).

Unlike one-sided determinism (e.g., behavior is determined by environment) or one-sided interactionism (persons and situations are treated as independent entities), social cognitive theory "favors a conception of interaction based on triadic reciprocality. In this model of reciprocal determinism . . . behavior, cognitive and other personal factors, and environmental influences all operate interactively as determinants of each other. In this triadic reciprocal determinism, the term reciprocal refers to the mutual action between causal factors" (p. 23), what Bandura defines as "triadic reciprocality" (Bandura, 1985, p. 23). For Bandura, people learn by observing others' behavior, attitudes, and outcomes of those behaviors. As outlined above, learning is explained in terms of a continuous reciprocal interaction between cognitive, behavioral, and environmental factors. The conditions for effective modeling include attention, retention, reproduction, and motivation.

Early in their introduction to their edited collection *Situated Cognition: Social, Semiotic, and Psychological Perspectives*, David Kirshner and James Whitson (1997) outline the exigence driving the work of social cognitionists: "We are engaged not as individuals, but as *socii*, and we are engaged in the worlds of each other and of ourselves and of things that surround us in concrete social and material situations: worlds that necessarily include us and are in formation with us as we form ourselves in part through cognitive/transformative engagement with each other, our surroundings, ourselves" (p. 2). Pulling strongly from Soviet sociohistoric theories of Vygotsky and Alexsei Leont'ev, social cognition shifts the focus of the unit of analysis from the individual to sociocultural and sociohistoric conditions in which cognitive activities, such as writing, are embedded. Descrates' long valorized singular *cogito* no longer holds up under the broad weight of understanding how the self-interactions with a multitude of external influencers during activity. As Mike Rose (2004) offers in his account of workplace literacies in *Mind at Work*, "individuals [act] in concert with each other and with tools, symbols, and conventions delivered by the culture" (p. 218).

Situated cognition is the larger umbrella term for theories which acknowledge how external objects share the work of cognitive activity. Under this umbrella one finds externalist views of cognition such as distributed cognition and extended cognition. According to Kristopher M. Lotier (2016), externalism posits that "no cognitive action can occur without the contribution of human or nonhuman others, including language and various technological artifacts" (p. 362) "thus blur[ring] the distinctions between body and mind, mind and world" (p. 366). For example, Edwin Hutchins (1995) details the highly complex process of docking a ship and shows this cognitive activity is not solely located in the head of the pilot but distributed across various states of representational and external media: a nautical slide rule, maps, landmarks. Andy Clark and David Chambers (1998), working more from the extended cognition subfield of situated cognition, offer an example of an Alzheimer's patient they name Otto, who, in an attempt to navigate New York City, writes down directions on a notepad thereby offloading internal cognitive data to an external surface for later retrieval. They open their article with a pithy, powerful question: "Where does the mind stop, and the rest of the world begin?" (Clark & Chambers, 1998, p. 7).

A strong thread woven into the fabric of social cognition is schooling. Indeed, the Kirshner and Whitson (1997) collection grew out of an American Educational Research Association symposium. Social cognitionists offer a commitment to learning, generally, curricular learning, specifically. Jean Lave and Etienne Wenger (1991) explored situated cognition through, what they term, *legitimate peripheral participation*, a model of apprenticeship. Lave and Wenger borrow from Vygotsky's zone of proximal development to dispute common misinterpretations of the internalization of learning as unproblematic. They summarize a theory of social practice as "the relational interdependency of agent and world, activity, meaning, cognition, learning and knowing" (Lave & Wenger, 1991, p. 50) and "emphasize the inherently socially negotiated character of meaning and the interested, concerned character of the thought and action of persons-in activity" (p. 50). The words "relational" and "negotiated" suggest that knowledge is in flux rather than static—changing over time. Lave and Wenger hope that they have expanded our notion of learning to include "the interconnections of activity and activity systems, and of activity systems and communities, culture, and political economy" (1991, p. 121). They claim that in transforming terms such as *person, situated learning activity, knowing,* and *social world*, we can understand the world, and learning, as experienced.

Echoing Lave and Wenger, Barbara Rogoff (1990) argues "children's cognitive development is an apprenticeship—it occurs through guided participation in social activity with companions who support and stretch children's understanding of and skill in using the tools of culture" (p. vii) Rogoff further develops her definition in "Observing sociocultural activity on three planes: Participatory appropriation, guided participation, and apprenticeship" emphasizing that "the individual and the environment are often considered separate entities when, in fact, they are "being mutually defined and interdependent in ways that preclude their separation as units or elements" (1990, p. 139). Focusing specifically on an individual's literate development, Paul Prior (1998) draws heavily from situated cognition and sociohistoric theory to map the writing development of graduate students in sociology.

Returning back to this collection, Gwen Gorzelsky, Carol Hayes, Joseph Paszek, Ed Jones, and Dana Lynn Driscoll define situated cognition as "a theoretical framework positing that cognition is fundamentally shaped by both bodily experience (as distinct from strictly mental experience) and by emotional, socio-cultural, physical, and other environmental factors" (p. 140) and, drawing from Bandura, argue "situated cognition theorists have defined knowledge as dynamically constructed, remembered, and reinterpreted in social contexts. Through interactions among brain, body, and environment, individuals actively build knowledge, rather than passively receiving it" (p. 140).

No matter the discipline from which one approaches social cognition, the focus remains the same, which, returning to Kirshner and Whitson (1997), asks us to remember that "we are engaged in the worlds of each other and of ourselves and of things that surround us in concrete social and material situations" (p. 2).

Embodied Cognition

In her pivotal book *Wealth of Reality: An Ecology of Composition*, Margaret Syverson (1999) calls upon research on complex systems and ecologies to ask a question still resonating with composition scholars almost two decades later: "can the concepts currently emerging in diverse fields on the nature of complex systems provide us with a new understanding of composing as an ecological system" (p. 5). At the sake of diluting these fecund concepts for the purposes of brevity, complex systems and ecologies return us to the ideas offered by social cognitionists, namely that cognitive activities, like writing, occur not just within the individual mind and body but within a larger network of culture, external animate and inanimate objects, and spatial and temporal influencers. For Syverson's purposes, an ecology is a "kind of meta-complex system composed of interrelated and interdependent complex systems and their environmental structures and processes" (1999, p. 5). Further, and here is where we get to embodied cognition, she holds an ecological system of composition has four attributes, one of which is embodiment. "Writers, readers, and texts have physical bodies," Syverson posits, "and consequently not only the content but the process of their interaction is dependent on, and reflective of, physical experience" (1999, p. 12). If situated cognition illuminates the role of the external during cognitive activity, embodied cognition illuminates the role of the muscles, the heartbeat, the inhalations, and exhalations during cognitive activity.

Embodied cognition seeks to unravel the pernicious mind/body dualism that has woven its way into the fabric of western education. In a sense, embodied cognition is a return to Hellenic education just as Isocrates, the progenitor of the liberal arts curriculum, offered a pedagogy pairing training in gymnastics with philosophy as the two were "twin arts" (Syverson, 1999, p. 289). As Debra Hawhee (2004) has persuasively illustrated in *Bodily Arts*, ancient western rhetorics were refined physically and theoretically through rhetorical performances and wrestling contests. Hawhee offers us the concept of the "sophist-athlete," and, indeed, we believe Gorgias wrote a handbook on rhetoric and a handbook on wrestling as the two are chiefly concerned with reading and countering an opponent's moves. Historian of education H. I. Marrou (1982) details how the Romans, after conquering the Greeks, adopting much of the Greek education system but did away with athletics. And we feel these repercussions today, as physical education is often skipped over in favor of more scholastic activities. Embodied cognition reminds us of the role of the body during writing, a point Kristie Fleckenstein (1999) succinctly makes when she asserts, "We are writing bodies" (p. 297). In the wake of Fleckenstein's argument, composition studies pulled from interdisciplinary research to begin crafting bodily pedagogies and theories for how our skin and bones, breath and heartbeat shape our written words. Abby Knoblauch (2012) offers a helpful categorization of this research, breaking it into three camps: embodied language, embodied knowledge, and embodied rhetoric. In this collection, both Steven Corbett and Bonnie Vidrine-Isabelle engage with this term.

COLLECTION OVERVIEW

Contemporary Perspectives on Cognition and Writing unfolds in five related sections. In the first, we offer historical context for studying the intersection of cognition and writing and chart the rising interest in cognition and writing in the 1980s, most notably with the work of Linda Flower and John R. Hayes. Taken together these chapters ask: What cognitive principles and theories influence our current teaching, research, and theory-building? Charles Bazerman, in our lead chapter, offers a rich, personal reflection on how he grew to understand how psychological issues of writing operated within his empirical and theoretical projects. Like Bazerman, Ellen Carillo sketches a broad historical picture of composition studies with attention to relationship between composition and cognitive studies. Carillo uses the current interest in metacognition within composition studies to anchor her survey and argues studies of individual cognition will enrich current discussions of transfer. Dylan Dryer and David Russell anchor their survey of the field to current interest in reflection. Dryer and Russell investigate how research in phenomenology and neuro-phenomenology speaks to notions of reflection, and, ultimately, how reconceiving reflection phenomenologically carries implications for writing teachers and programs as it may provide a way to operationalize national consensus documents like the WPA Outcomes

Statement for First-Year Composition (OS). The practical implications Dryer and Russell sketch foreshadow the final two sections of this collection, which bring to bear the theory-building of the opening sections on the classroom and national consensus documents, such as the OS and the *Framework for Success in Postsecondary Writing*.

The second section reconsiders our approaches to student learning in light of recent studies and neuroscience. Alice Horning opens this section with a discussion on the psycholinguistic features of the reading process and how adhering to these features suggests a redefinition of academic critical literacy. Bonnie Vidrine-Isbell draws from her experience working in the University of Washington's Language and Rhetoric program and the Institute for Learning Brain Sciences to articulate how primary language acquisition studies aid how we understand secondary language acquisition. Gwen Gorzelsky, Carol Hayes, Joseph Paszek, Ed Jones, and Dana Lynn Driscoll call our attention to educational data mining and learning analytics research. Despite justifiable concerns with adaptive learning technologies, the co-authors specifically illustrate three adaptive learning prototypes they are developing to teach genre, source use, and metacognitive knowledge. They ask readers to view these technologies as a means for helping students develop structured writing practices and cognitive habits crucial for writing development and intellectual growth.

Our third section contains three chapters on neuroscientific discoveries and applicability and asks how advances in neuroscience research impact our understanding of what writing is and how it works. Dirk Remley synthesizes work in neuroscience, narrative, and multimodality. He calls our attention to multimodal commercial messages—such as the marketing materials of a law firm in Cleveland, Ohio—and shows how neurobiological dynamics of the mirror neurons and reward neurons enhance development of these messages. Jen Talbot describes how the neurological concepts of plasticity and mirroring demonstrate the co-constitutive dimension of cognition and affect. She ends by arguing affective neuroscience connects with writing pedagogies, particularly postprocess pedagogy. Irene Clark ends this section by also calling upon recent research on neuroplasticity. Clark urges us to see this recent research as complicated, problematizing the interconnection between genre and identity.

Curricular writing spaces and writing instruction figure more prominently in our fourth and fifth section. The jointly authored *Framework for Success in Postsecondary Writing* (2011) forwards explicit awareness of the role of cognition during literate development. In this national consensus document, students are given eight habits of mind for success and writing teachers are given ways to facilitate a student's growth in these habits of mind. Our remaining seven chapters draw—sometimes directly, sometimes indirectly—from the *Framework* and provide productive conversations on what these sometimes abstract and seemingly unteachable habits look like in a curricular writing space. Additionally, many of the remaining chapters ground their discussion in writing-related transfer, as recent developments in transfer research (e.g., Nowacek, 2011; Yancey, Robertson & Taczak, 2014) call attention to the importance of metacognition, a habit of mind in the *Framework*. Dianna Winslow and Phil Shaw open our fourth section by introducing readers to the efficacy of a linked course—one in FYC and one in STEM. This linked course served first-generation students and deaf and hard-of-hearing students at Rochester Institute of Technology. Using a mixed-method research design, Winslow and Shaw report on how this linked course introduced students to the importance of metacognition and how metacognitive principles positioned the students well for future writing and learning contexts. Kara Taczak and Liane Robertson continue their award-winning research on transfer by highlighting the importance of metacognition. They delineate between metacognition and reflection—although both are vital components of successful writing transfer—and urge readers to see cognition, metacognition, and reflection as separate but interrelated components of literate development. Marcus Meade expands our conversation on how explicit focus on cognition aids in transfer by turning to Guy Debord's well-known concept of the spectacle. Meade specifically holds that writing classes often overvalue that which is observable and evaluable; therefore, writing classes focus on more observable foci of knowledge and practice and elide the habits of mind. Steven Corbett opens his chapter with a scene from the 1982 sci-fi film *Blade Runner* as a way to offer an important question: are writing instructors applying the habits of mind to their writing lives? Corbett then sketches an argument grounded in theory and lived experience that speaks to how self-analysis is the initial step of a transfer-friendly pedagogical praxis.

In our final section, Peter Khost undertakes of the first empirical studies of the habits of mind the context of the FYC classroom. Specifically, Khost focuses on metacognition, expressed through students' self-perceptions of their habits of mind. Grounding his research design in theory on self-efficacy, Khost's data show that focusing students' metacognition on the habits of mind is likely to increase their self-efficacy as academic writers. E. Shelley Reid contributes to important work on the cognitive/affective balance by representing student voices about disposition problems, which hinder writing. Reid labels these dispositions problems as "soft skills," charts them in the writing of over 70 students, and concludes by offering how writing instructors can link soft skills to more concrete and commonly addressed writing challenges. Kathleen Blake Yancey offers our final chapter in this collection. She continues her award-winning work with Liane Robertson and Kara Taczak by again drawing from *How People*

Learn and returning to an emphasis on prior knowledge, an emphasis which formed a large portion of Yancey, Robertson, and Taczak's *Writing Across Contexts*. Yancey reports on case studies data of students drawing on prior knowledge when composing, particularly reporting on the role of the prior in digitally multimodal composing processes. These case studies are student-focused and led by student voice.

We then offer an afterword by Linda Flower. This afterword is only fitting in that John R. Hayes, Flower's long-running research partner, opens our collection and Flower closes it. As composition studies critiqued and then moved away from their cognitive processes model, Flower productively absorbed the critiques and continued her research into writing as a social-cognitive process. Through social inquiry driven by empirical research, Flower offered thoughtful prose and findings that spoke to the social mind in context and the perennial contingent knowing versus certainty debate—a debate driving much of this collection. Here we think specifically of three of her single-authored or co-authored books: *Reading-to-Write: Exploring Cognitive and Social Process* (1990), *The Construction of Negotiated Meaning: A Social Cognitive Theory of Writing* (1994), and *Learning to Rival: A Literate Practice for Intercultural Inquiry* (2000).

We situate Flower's contribution to this collection as an afterword and select this noun intentionally. Flower does not offer a conclusion or final utterance because our collective work on cognition and writing is ever ongoing. What we offer in this collection is a historical marker of where we were and where we might go. We also offer a classroom map for navigating the multifaceted challenges with teaching writing and what our current research and best practices tell us about how to work with writers. The scholars in this collection reach across disciplines and form interdisciplinary bonds—not borders—to help us envision better ways to work with writers and writing. In this collection, we join with the 26 scholars representing the 19 contributions to this collection. We join with these voices—and the many others represented in the words on the page—in seeking out the promise and possibility of contemporary perspectives on cognition and writing.

REFERENCES

Adler-Kassner, L. & Wardle, E. (Eds.). (2015). *Naming what we know: Threshold concepts of writing studies.* Logan, UT: Utah State University Press.

Bandura, A. (1985). *Social foundations of thought and action: A social cognitive theory.* Upper Saddle River, NJ: Prentice Hall.

Behm, N. N., Rankins-Robertson, S. & Roen, D. (2017). Introduction. In N. N. Behm, S. Rankins-Robertson, and D. Roen (Eds.), *The framework for success in postsecondary writing: Scholarship and applications* (pp. xxi–xxxii). Anderson, SC: Parlor Press.

Berkenkotter, C. (1991). Paradigm debates, turf wars, and the conduct of sociocognitive inquiry in composition. *College Composition and Communication, 42*(2), 151–169.

Berkenkotter, C. & Huckin, T. N. (1996). *Genre knowledge in disciplinary communication: Cognition/culture/power.* Hillsdale, NJ: Lawrence Erlbaum.

Claparede, E. (1974). Preface. J. Piaget, *The language and thought of the child* (pp. 11–18). New York: New American Library.

Clark, A. & Chalmers, D. J. (1998). The extended mind. *Analysis, 58*(1), 7–19.

Cognition. (n.d.). In *Oxford English Dictionary.* Retrieved from http://www.oxford dictionaries. com/definition/english/cognition.

Council of Writing Program Administrators, National Council of Teachers of English & National Writing Project. (2011). *Framework for success in postsecondary writing.* Retrieved from http://wpacouncil.org/files/framework-for-success-postsecondary-writing.pdf.

Fleckenstein, K. (1999). Writing bodies: Somatic mind in composition studies. *College English, 61*(3), 281–306.

Flower, L. (1994). *The construction of negotiated meaning: A social cognitive theory of writing.* Carbondale, IL: Southern Illinois University Press.

Flower, L. S. & Hayes, J. R. (1981). A cognitive process theory of writing. *College Composition and Communication, 32*(4), 365–387.

Flower, L., Long, E. & Higgins, L. (2000). *Learning to rival: A literate practice for intercultural inquiry.* Mahwah, NJ: Lawrence Erlbaum.

Flower, L., Stein, V., Ackerman, J., Kantz, M. J., McCormick, K. & Peck, W. C. (1990). *Reading-to-Write: Exploring a cognitive and social process.* Oxford: Oxford University Press.

Franchi, S. & Bianchini, F. (2011). On the historical dynamics of cognitive science: A view from the periphery. In S. Franchi & F. Bianchini (Eds.), *The search for a theory of cognition: Early mechanisms and new ideas* (pp. xi–xxvi). New York: Rodopi.

Goodwin, J. (2012). Graph illustration composing writers' processes. *Citational Network Graph of Literary Theory Journals.* Retrieved from http://jgoodwin.net/rhet-browser/topic48.html.

Hawhee, D. (2004). *Bodily arts: Rhetoric and athletics in ancient Greece.* Austin, TX: University of Texas Press.

Hutchins, E. (1995). *Cognition in the wild.* Cambridge, MA: MIT Press.

Isocrates. (1929). *Antidosis.* (G. Norlin, Trans.) Vol. 2., Loeb Classical Library, pp. 179–367. Cambridge, MA: Harvard University Press.

Kirshner, D. & Whitson, J. A. (1997). Editors introduction. In D. Kirshner & J. A. Whitson (Eds.), *Situated cognition: Social, semiotic, and psychological perspectives* (pp. 1–16). Mahwah, NJ: Lawrence Erlbaum.

Knoblauch, A. A. (2012). Bodies of knowledge: Definitions, delineations, and implications of embodied writing in the academy. *Composition Studies, 40*(2), 50–65.

Lave, J. & Wenger, E. (1991). *Situated learning: Legitimate peripheral participation.* New York: Cambridge University Press.

Lotier, K. M. (2016). Around 1986: The externalization of cognition and the emergence of postprocess invention. *College Composition and Communication, 67*(3), 360–384.

Marrou, H. I. (1982). *History of education in antiquity* (G. Lamb, Trans.). Madison, WI: University of Wisconsin Press.

Miller, S. (Ed.). (2009). *The Norton book of composition studies.* New York: Norton.

O'Neill, P., Adler-Kassner, L., Fleischer, C. & Hall, A. (2012). Creating the *Framework for Success in Postsecondary Writing. College English,* 74(6), 520–524.

Piaget, J. (1974). *The language and thought of the child.* New York: New American Library.

Prior, P. (1998). *Writing/Disciplinarity: A sociohistoric account of literate activity in the academy.* Mahwah, NJ: Lawrence Erlbaum.

Prior, P. (2006). A sociocultural theory of writing. In C. A. MacArthur, S. Graham & J. Fitzgerald (Eds.), *Handbook of writing research* (pp. 54–66). New York: The Guilford Press.

Roen, D. (2015, March). *Using the framework for success in postsecondary writing.* Presentation at Cognition and Writing SIG at annual meeting of the Conference on College Composition and Communication, Tampa, FL.

Rogoff, B. (1990). *Apprenticeship in thinking: Cognitive development in social context.* New York: Oxford University Press.

Rogoff, B. (1995). Observing sociocultural activity on three planes: Participatory appropriation, guided participation, and apprenticeship. In J. Wertsch, P. Del Rio & A. Alvarez (Eds.), *Sociocultural studies of the mind* (pp. 139–164). Cambridge, UK: Cambridge University Press.

Rose, M. (2004). *The mind at work: Valuing the intelligence of the American worker.* New York: Viking.

Syverson, M. (1999). *The wealth of reality: An ecology of composition.* Carbondale, IL: Southern Illinois University Press.

Villanueva, V. & Arola, K. (Eds.). (2011). *Cross-talk in comp theory: A reader* (3rd ed.). Urbana, IL: National Council of Teachers of English.

Vygotsky, L. (1986). *Thought and language* (Ed. A. Kozulin). Cambridge, MA: MIT Press.

Yancey, K. B., Robertson, L. & Taczak, K. (2014). *Writing across contexts: Transfer, composition, and sites of writing.* Logan, UT: Utah State University Press.

SECTION I: HISTORICAL CONTEXT

CHAPTER 1

THE PSYCHOLOGY OF WRITING SITUATED WITHIN SOCIAL ACTION: AN EMPIRICAL AND THEORETICAL PROGRAM

Charles Bazerman
University of California, Santa Barbara

The chapters in this volume demonstrate the renewed interest in psychological issues in writing studies, exploring fresh dimensions of cognition, affect, attention, disposition, social orientation, neurological processing, and neurodiversity that extend beyond previous information-processing models of writing to shed light on processes we have may sensed only hazily through experience. These chapters point to richer psychological accounts that respect and reveal the complexity, difficulty, and remarkable accomplishment of writing. But before looking forward to these new visions of knowledge, it would be useful to consider a question that has been around for a while: How are psychological processes of writing conditioned by the fact that every act of writing is situated and purposeful within the social and historical events the writer participates in, using the available tools and social arrangements that have emerged within shorter and longer histories (Bazerman, 2015). Sociohistoric research about writing has often been seen as opposed to psychological studies, which seem to characterize psychological processes as attributes of individuals. However, over the years I have struggled in my own research and theory building to see how psychological processes work out within situated individuals engaged in social processes. In some recent studies, which I will share in the latter half of this essay, I have identified ethnographically grounded cognitive markers and associated situated writing practices with locally valued cognitive change. These studies suggest how cognition and affect can be studied as responses to motivated, socially located writing situations and tasks. As I walk through the studies that have led me to my current research, I will articulate a way to understand the complexity of the psychological activity mobilized by writing. I hope the viewpoint pulled together from these studies may help us consider, as we move forward to new lines of psychological investigation, how to reconcile psychological and social processes in every act of writing.

Writers always think—and feel. Readers too. Writing can powerfully overtake the mind of each. As writers and readers focus on meanings invested in and evoked by words, they block out the immediate world around them. The more difficult the meanings they are inscribing and reconstructing, the more they must concentrate and the more other stimuli distract or irritate them. Sometimes their bodies tense, sometimes they laugh, sometimes they shudder with frisson. Sometimes they feel emotional attachment, sometimes reward, and sometimes disappointment. All this happens as they engage in a social interaction mediated by the text.

Any of us in the business of teaching of writing has some taste of the divine madness Keats talks about in the introduction to the "Fall of Hyperion":

> For Poesy alone can tell her dreams,
>
> With the fine spell of words alone can save
>
> Imagination from the sable charm
>
> And dumb enchantment. Who alive can say,
>
> "Thou art no Poet may'st not tell thy dreams?"
>
> Since every man whose soul is not a clod
>
> Hath visions, and would speak, if he had loved
>
> And been well nurtured in his mother tongue. (ll. 8–15)

This realization of imagination in the written word is what makes writing such a calling, and the nurturing of the imagination of others calls us to teach to tell their dreams. Yet with experience we also may learn that this madness of the imagination comes not from the universal, timeless place of the gods, but from the earthly time and space of humans—with whom we share, connect, coordinate, contend with through our writing, even if only to bring into being a future meeting with our friend by an email.

Yet for all our powerful internal experiences with writing, it is another thing to understand this madness through publically shareable evidence and coherent theory—that is, to imagine this knowledge as a science, to bring it beyond the private enchantment of our dreams of writing to confirmable communal knowledge. Unfortunately, the search for a science can be clumsy, making us more doltish than we are, as we try to simplify and pick apart complex phenomena and experiences to look at one aspect at a time. Confirmable knowledge requires us to design inquiries in order to locate strong evidence of one identifiable thing. If we know with confidence one thing, we can then add another to it, and start to reconstruct a richer, multidimensional picture. To confirm with evidence phenomena that we think are already self-evident means we may have to go backward, and we may even have to correct some ideas or redirect intuitive leaps. At the end we will know more, more comprehensively, with greater certainty and greater clarity.

Such a history of clumsy early steps has been, I believe, the history of composition research, which has required us to be narrow and simple in our first inquiries, but eventually will bring us to more complex and satisfying knowledge that begins to carry the richness of our experience, and gives us the reflexive means to understand and direct our choices better. This is particularly true for the aspects of writing that are less visible, lost in the recesses of minds and feeling, for our introspective felt sense may lead us to create idiosyncratic explanations, and to overgeneralize our particular private experiences. While our felt sense may be well grounded, our explanations may produce theoretical castles in the air.

A STARTING POINT

Because the purpose of this essay is to explain my own particular path of understanding psychological issues of writing within my larger empirical and theoretical projects, I will start this story where I entered the field, motivated to help basic writing students in their struggle with academic tasks. Teaching my first writing class in 1971, I soon became aware of the speculative theory of James Moffett (1968) and Anne Berthoff (1972) which grew out of their experiences as teachers and Janet Emig's (1971) sensitive observations of students' writing processes. These texts resonated with my experience of the complexity of writing, and the richness of internal processes. I was also excited, as many were, by Peter Elbow's (1973) *Writing Without Teachers*, which directed us to grab ahold of our own processes to discover the meanings within us, freed from constraining anxieties of propriety and instruction. This too felt rich.

Shortly thereafter, as I was discovering my own teaching imperatives, two other empirical research programs emerged attempting to understand writing processes. Mina Shaughnessy (1977) adopted error analysis from applied linguistics, working from texts and student commentaries to understand how writers worked hard to make decisions that resulted in sentences that were perceived as faulted. Linda Flower and John R. Hayes (1981) adopted think-aloud methods from cognitive psychology. Although later researchers would refine or reject their proposed first models, they made us more aware of the cognitive complexity of problem solving in writing. Yet there was a cost. To make those advances, each method limited awareness of the social situation and purposes of the emergent text, the social forces and experiences that provided writing resources and practices and that conditioned the moments of production, and the histories that brought the moments of writing into being. They treated each writer largely as a separate individual, making choices in isolation, out of time, place, or interaction and collaboration.

These missing social components, nonetheless, could not be avoided in my own quest to understand writing, as I wanted to discover what my students needed to learn to be able to succeed at the university. As I began to inquire into academic writing, the contexts, social organization of the university, disciplines and intertexts loomed ever larger as the contexts of thought. James Britton, Tony Burgess, Nancy Martin, Alex McLeod, and Harold Rosen's (1975) work about the effect of school tasks and writing relationships within secondary school illuminated how tightly writing development was tied to the enacted curriculum. Yet, as I developed a more sociocultural view of writing, looking into genres, their histories, and activity systems, I always kept ahold of how students developed their thinking in these contexts, and ultimately expressed new thoughts and meanings.

So my independent line of inquiries started with the idea of providing a sociology and history of what writing was, what resources were available and what conditions, activities, and tasks established each writing event, but my intent was this sociology and history was to be integrated with the psychology. Accordingly, I never rejected the early psychology inquiries, even though I was aware of their limitations and reinterpreted their findings through different theoretical lenses. As I studied forms of writing within social activities, I remained haunted that every text required many acts of thinking of an individual writer and prompted acts of thinking in the readers. I repeatedly returned to the individual and what happened within, but engaged as part of specific socio-historic situations, mediated by social forms, and using the communicative experiences as a resource and a framework for understanding. To guide me in bringing together the social, textual and psychological I repeatedly looked to Lev Vygotsky (1986) and his collaborators A. R. Luria (1978) and Alexsei Leont'ev (1978) and later elaborators (such as Cole [1996] and Bruner [1990]) to understand the relation of thought to expression and social interaction, but I also fund inspiration in the pragmatists John Dewey (1910), G. H. Mead (1962), and Harry Stack Sullivan (1953), who articulated how emotions and thought formed within context. In recent years I found my orientation reinforced by brain research showing the flexibility of the brain as an organ that was sensitive to context, developing and reorganizing itself and its resources in response to situations, ultimately designed to help us respond flexibly and creatively and purposefully within situations (see both Talbot and Clark in this volume),

THINKING WITHIN GENRES AND ACTIVITY SYSTEMS

My initial textual study comparing prominent articles in biochemistry, sociology and literary studies (Bazerman, 1981) suggested that the differences in textual forms (which I was later to associate with genres) in various disciplines displayed different forms of reasoning, different authorial positions and relationships to disciplinary colleagues, different ways of characterizing different phenomena, and different positioning with the disciplinary literatures. Thus the texts displayed and directed the readers towards different forms of cognition with social textual, epistemic, and intertextual components. But to get beyond the cognition *displayed* in the textualized reasoning of the article, to get at the reasoning the writer used to *produce* the article, I felt I needed some process data. I searched archives of the papers of prominent scientists to locate a series of drafts that would reveal the processes and choices made by the writer. This culminated in the study of the drafts of a paper by Arthur Holly Compton that contributed to his establishing empirical evidence of quantum theory (Bazerman, 1984). But to understand the purpose of the article and the decisions made by Compton in producing and revising the drafts, I had to recover the historical situation at his time, the debates over quantum theory, his own research program and intellectual progress, and the series of articles he had already produced on this theme. The article and the decisions involved in it were rhetorically situated within specific social and historical circumstances which needed to be revealed to reconstruct the logic of the choices. Those choices were shaped and carried out by the canons of good scientific practice of the time (revealed in the analysis), but activated and directed by particular puzzles presented by the situation of the article. This study then pointed out to how processes were disciplinary and task specific, making them embedded in circumstances and more flexible, complex, and variable than previous writing process studies that sought universal architectures of information processing were indicating.

This study of Compton initiated a series of studies on the experimental articles in science, focused on the changing textual form and its displayed textualized cognition, but also with the recognition that these textual forms also implied differing forms of productive reasoning. Much of the volume *Shaping Written Knowledge* (Bazerman, 1988) was focused on the changing social and textual forms in emergent science, but at a few points psychological issues came to the fore. One of these was in considering the epistemic puzzle of how changing textual forms also embodied changing relations to the material. The argument in Chapter 11, "How language carries out the work of science," pointed out that for the individual scientist, learning textual practices was coincident with learning material practices and carrying out concrete activities in the laboratory or field, according to the training and practices of the discipline. The developing symbolic representations were tied to changing orientations towards and perceptions of the material world, and the active, sensing feeling, reasoning human being stood between the material and the text. The study of the formation of the APA manual (earlier published in 1987) showed how the regulation of textual form was intertwined with regulating forms of material experience, reasoning, and even interpreting and evaluating other disciplinary texts.

INNOVATIVE THINKERS AND COMMUNAL COGNITIVE PRACTICES

Shaping Written Knowledge also included a case study of an innovative thinker, Isaac Newton, who created new forms of textual representation, pushed by the rhetorical exigencies of persuading the contemporaries of his novel theories based on original inquiries. These new textual forms then became models of shared public reasoning, which disciplined readers into ways of looking at and thinking about nature. In studies after *Shaping Written Knowledge* I continued considering the role of creative thinkers who through the textual innovations developed new modes of thinking about nature, new relations to peers and other audiences, and greater connections with the texts of others. These cases revealed ever more intensively the way idiosyncratic individual writers influenced how communities participated in science and the formation of communal knowledge. These studies revealed deeper modes of perception, reasoning and rhetorical thought that lay behind the textual innovations they proposed, a kind of psychological baggage smuggled in with the newly attractive textual forms.

I was led to the study of Joseph Priestley's (1777) scientific rhetoric because I was trying to track down the development of modern intertextual practices that position each new work within an intertextual field (Bazerman, 1991). What I found was that Priestley's innovations in reviewing prior literature came out of a communitarian ideology that saw human millenarian advancement possible, but only through mutual respect for each other's experience and cooperative collaboration in developing common wisdom. This ideology formed a view of human society, relations with others, and the social organization of natural inquiry, as well as the relation of individual cognition to group experience and reasoning. Priestley's recommendations and modeling of intertextual practices were only part of a complex set of recommendations on how scientific practice should proceed communally and how individual cognition should be attentive to and learn from communal practices. Priestley's rhetorical innovations could go so deeply in part because he had an integrated multidimensional view of life which included rhetoric. Early in his career he gave a series of lectures on rhetoric (Priestley, 1777). Throughout his career gave further thought to the best forms for human communication as his own views of life and activity deepened. Rather than unthinkingly relying on existing forms, he innovated to be able to accomplish new things socially within growing social visions.

Adam Smith similarly was another eighteenth-century multidimensional thinker who early on delivered a series of lectures on a rhetoric (notes from which were only recently discovered and published, Smith, 1983) and then continued to think about human cooperation, the basis of social order, and his rhetorical role as a philosopher to advance human happiness. My study of his life corpus led me to conclude that what is considered a kind of distinct invention of modern capitalist economics in *The Wealth of Nations* was really a rhetorical invention growing out of his changing perception of how people could cooperate and communicate effectively. Beyond the specifics of his case and innovation I see this study identifying how writing is an outgrowth and extension of one's growing understanding of the world one lives in, and is a response to one's perception of the rhetorical situation. For deeply reflective writers who are also reflective about the social world and their role in it, this means that writing innovation is part of a creative remaking of communicative resources. The writer's engagement with others in the rhetorical innovation, enlists others into the writer's view of the world. For less reflective writers with less reflective social understandings this means they are drawn into the psychological world shaped by the successful innovators. In both cases writing development is deeply tied to many dimensions of psychological development, and each new act of writing is positioned within and grows out of that psychological development, which has formed perceptions of the rhetorical world the writer addresses.

SOCIAL UNDERSTANDINGS AND INDIVIDUAL MEANINGS

Actually, to be understood by others and engage with them, writers must do both, understanding the world as others see it, within their typified worlds of genres and activities and also reformulating those worlds to their own ends and visions as much as they can do effectively.

My book-length study of Edison's rhetorical actions (Bazerman, 1999) displays how a major social and technological innovator had to fill multiple dimensions of existing discourses with his own intentions to carry out his ambitious intentions of creating a central system of light and power, using incandescent lighting as an intelligible and persuasive technology to gain the symbolic and material commitments needed to realize his plan. In some of these discourses he and his colleagues stayed close to the standard forms and actions, such as dealing with the corruption-filled urban governments during an age of economic expansion and civic construction in order to gain permissions to build his systems, but in others he used standard forms to make novel claims reflecting his innovative ideas—such as in the patent system, where his surrogate patent agents used current tools of patent application and litigation, but based on the emergent designs for his technology. His laboratory notebooks reflected even greater rhetorical invention in transforming the free-lance inventor's notebook from a personal and legal record to a means of coordinating the knowledge and thought of a collaborative industrial laboratory. The notebooks left on a central laboratory table became the locus of a collective mind—orienting, directing, and informing the individual minds of the team members.

An even more fundamental rhetorical creativity grew out of Edison's early experiences with the interaction of changing patterns of newspapers, urbanization, and telegraphic and rail technology. Starting with his early experiences selling newspapers on an early railroad and continuing with his experiences as a telegraphic inventor, he understood how he could play the new environment of newspaper celebrity to advance his projects. He learned how to plant stories and give interviews that fulfilled the needs of journalists and newspapers to sell copies. He learned how to project himself as the wizard of Menlo Park, enlisting public support and creating symbolic capital to convert to monetary capital from financiers. On the other hand, his largest communicative failure was in his not being able to develop an appropriate role within new large corporations. In the early days of developing light and power with small companies (which he proliferated as separate entities), Edison fostered a charismatic form of communication where he remained the center of all communications; but when the power companies grew and were consolidated into Edison General Electric Company, he could not manage the distributed organizational communications and lost control. He was displaced by corporate leaders who imposed more organizational bureaucratic communications.

Although this story seems most obviously historical and social, it indicates his mode of thinking, communicating, and strategic planning, developed over a history of experiences, and reflecting individual dispositions, qualities, and character and forming a personal and social identity. He was a communicative thinking actor who had a perception of both the social world and his material goals, influencing the thinking of those around him through available communicative forms within organized activities (such as the patent system and journalism), but also in which he asserted innovations of forms and strategies. At the same time, his experience and perceptions that made him see his role as charismatic center rather than corporate manager made him less successful in building organizational communications.

FROM INNOVATIVE INDIVIDUALS TO DISCIPLINARY ENCULTURATION

These studies of rhetorical innovators expose the developmental phenomenology of writers, but the insights can be applied to more practical educational issues of students' disciplinary enculturation and can be corroborated with other forms of systematic data. I pursued the practical implications through two lines of research. The first looked at the displayed thoughts of students learning to produce the forms of expressed thought associated with disciplinary thinking within an introductory oceanography course at the university. The second looked at indicators of student thinking in an MA-level teacher education program as they learned to write the genres and intertextual practices fostered by their academic program.

The set of studies in oceanography began with a collaboration between a geology professor and a science education researcher to examine student scientific thinking in an introductory course. A major goal of the course was that students should begin to understand science as a process of argument over theories using evidence, and that students needed to learn evidence-based forms of scientific argument. Early on I began consulting with the team and eventually I became co-author of two of the papers emanating from this project. In one of the earlier studies (Takao, Prothero & Kelly, 2002), a set of the student papers which had been already assigned grades by the instructor and teaching assistants were coded, with each claim assigned an epistemic level. These epistemic levels followed the particular logic of the discipline and the assignment, with the most concrete referring to the specific data given in the data base provided for the assignment, with higher levels assigned for observing relational connections among the data, identifying geologic features and processes, and ultimately making claims from plate tectonic theory. Those papers that were scored higher by the professor and graduate teaching assistants had more claims at more levels with more semantic relations among claims of different levels, so as to create denser webs of connections between data to theory with all the intermediary stages. Lower-graded papers jumped between levels, often skipping intermediary levels, and having few sematic connections among claims at all levels; for example the paper might have some specific data from the data base and some general theoretical claims from the textbook, but with little reasoning or evidentiary connection between the two, with little identification of geologic features or processes. Thus, the evaluation of student disciplinary reasoning could be tied to the presence, structure and relation of claims made in the paper.

To investigate more fully the displayed structure of reasoning in these papers, we analyzed papers from the following year (Kelly & Bazerman, 2003). Based on changes made in the instruction to include identification of epistemic level of claims and the importance of making connections among them, the full set of papers from the class improved in this respect. In a detailed examination of a subset of four of the papers we examined how well the statements were located within the reasoning structure of the paper (a locally modified version of a standard scientific report, to fit the particulars of the discipline and assignment). The better the claims were placed in the paper structure, the better was the score they received from the professor and teaching assistants. In addition, we found a structure of lexical and semantic cohesion that corresponded in their abstraction to the reasoning structure of the paper, such that the more theoretical terms appeared in the abstract and introduction and conclusion, while concrete data terms appeared most strongly in the methods and findings. Relational, feature, and process identification terms appeared more in the latter half—in the discussion and conclusions. Thus the entire paper formed an organized reasoning structure of terms and claims. We were able to confirm these observations in a full set of papers from the following year ($N=21$) (Kelly, Bazerman, Skukauskaite & Prothero, 2010).

Although these studies showed student reasoning expressed in texts corresponded to disciplinary thought evaluated by instructors, this does not necessarily mean the student internal thinking has changed, except in that they are learning how to produce acceptable texts. They have gained knowledge of the form and are able to follow rules of form, but that may not mean that they are able to think better in terms of the subject or can perceive events through the concepts and categories of the field. To provide evidence of this more fundamental psychological claim about psychological processes being changed through learning disciplinary writing practices, my research team looked at student writing, speech, and thought over a year-long master's level teacher education program. Because the students in the program were selected for their academic excellence, they were already highly skilled learners and successful writers in their undergraduate program; however, the concepts and activities of the program were new to them, so we could distinguish discipline and genre-specific cognitive change which might come from overall writing development. Further, the program was coherent in its goals, curricula, and activities, and available for ethnographic observation and study, so we could understand the particular forms of cognition valued in the program and the practices directed toward the expected growth, as well as the contexts within which students produced writing and carried on discussions. Further, we had access to student scripts and discussions for both formal and informal assignments, so we could analyze displayed cognition both in the assignments aimed to elicit that thought as well as in activities where forms of thought would be displayed incidentally, spontaneously, and independently of formal evaluation. Finally, the program was also long enough (12 months) for developmental change to become evident. The combination of ethnographic, textual, longitudinal, and quantitative methods allowed us to situate cognitive development within precise, calibrated scales of local values, to locate indicators of development within the texts and discussions, and to provide statistical warrant for claims about cognitive behavior.

Based on an earlier article (Bazerman, 2008), we hypothesized that writing in particular genres would identify distinct problem spaces but also offer particular tools for the solution of those problems. The structured problem solving would elicit particular forms of thought, information gathering, synthesizing, and organized reasoning, which would provide pathways for cognitive development. With the teacher education students we indeed found that thoughts expressed corresponded to the expectations of the assignment, and even within the separate sections of a single text, the requirements of each section elicited distinct patterns of thought. Further we found that kinds of thinking required in formal evaluated assignments carried over into more spontaneous, informal activities such as electronic forums and class discussions. We also found indications that over time students working in these focused genres grew cognitively in the expected directions. Yet each student followed an individualized line of cognitive development that reflected individual sets of interests, concerns, and questions. Overall, we were able to establish that practice in certain genres led to internalization of the disciplinary concepts appropriate to the genres, affecting perception, evaluation and reasoning. That is, the students came to be more skilled in the forms of perception, thought, and action valued in the program (Bazerman, Simon, Ewing & Pieng, 2013).

As a by-product of the coding and analysis of student texts, we found that citation behavior also correlated with the nature of the assignment that elicited different kinds of discussion of the literature. More importantly we found that the citation behavior also correlated with cognitive sophistication in terms of the program's goals and values. Specifically, in all assignments we found sentences that contained references showed greater cognitive sophistication than other sentences in the same assignment. Further, for these assignments and this program (although not necessarily for other contexts), students used the literature for conceptual content rather than methods (see also Bazerman, 2012b for the internalization and externalization of concepts), examples, data, findings or other purposes. Thus, in the earlier assignments students took from the readings ideas that helped them explain their experiences, but in later assignments they were able to discuss and compare ideas more flexibly, thus moving into more equal intellectual positions with the authors of the cited texts. We found that over the year the representations of the cited texts became more compact (that is, moving from extensive quotations to more focused, purposeful summary). At the same time the discussion of each text become much longer, moving from under 2.4 sentences in the initial paper for each intertextual event (that is, discussion of the literature) to over 6.4 sentences for each intertextual event in the M.Ed. thesis at the end of the program. These unanticipated results confirmed that attention to readings facilitated development of expressed thought and engagement in the intellectual world of the discipline (Bazerman, Simon & Pieng, 2014).

AFFECTIVE PROCESSES MOBILIZED IN SOCIAL MEANING MAKING

The findings from the studies of the innovative writers and the educational contexts together reveal how enculturation into the writing practices of a discipline, profession, or any organized social field, provides the orientations and tools to participate within that social field. The social field may be highly typified through long historical processes that identify preferred genres with text organization, styles, vocabulary, and contents that recognizably carry out the work of the social field, as in disciplines, or it may be freshly reconceived by an innovative social thinker and actor, who desires to reshape social arrangements and thinking, creating new roles and positions for the writer who adopts fresh communicative strategies, identifies atypical opportunities and occasions, and refigures forms and expectations. Whether at the more conventional or unconventional ends to the spectrum, individual thought is directed toward forming meanings and bringing them into social intelligibility that will achieve the desired effect. In this process of bringing communicative impulses into shared expression, many psychological processes will be mobilized and directed, responsive to the writer's perception of the activity context.

But other psychological processes are as well mobilized. Any participation in a social field raises the possibility of anxieties as one's behavior will be potentially observed and o to by other participants. In fact, communicative behavior anticipates and seeks that response by the other at least to understand one's meaning and act in recognition and acceptance of that meaning. Even being ignored can raise anxiety. Thus writing puts one at high risk, evoking great potential for anxiety. As George Herbert Mead (1962) and other social thinkers have noticed, the response of the other is central to our processes of identity formation and perception of ourselves as social actors. The psychiatrist Harry Stack Sullivan (1953) articulated the potential for this reflection on social presence for raising anxiety that interferes with our clear thinking and problem solving in situations. In fact, Sullivan sees the anxiety system as core to our sense of selves and pervasive in all our relations. Thus even as we put ourselves at risk, anxiety can impair our ability to respond creatively and precisely to the risk.

In writing the stakes can be even higher, for a number of reasons. For one, our writing can stay around and not just vanish into the air, so that people can judge us long after the moment has passed. Further as texts persist they can be inspected more closely for deviance or error than transient speech. Even more, so much of writing and learning to write is associated with highly evaluative contexts of schooling; people may make from our writing evaluations of our education, cultivation, intellect and even intelligence. Then because no matter how much we write in a collaborative context, parts of writing are carried out in semi-privacy where we may reflect on the words we are producing, evaluate them and worry about the effect; there is more time and space for anxieties to grow. Thus putting ourselves "on the line" with writing creates psychological resistances, opportunities for failures of courage, backing away from our statements, insecurities and uncertainties, and general lack of clarity of thought, as Sullivan elaborated in his theory of anxiety. While I have not carried out empirical studies of these anxiety phenomena and the relation of writing to identity formation, I have recognized them introspectively and in pedagogic dialog with my students. I have also written some theoretical articles on them (Bazerman 2001a, 2001b, 2005).

TOWARD A SYNTHESIS OF PSYCHOLOGICAL AND SOCIOCULTURAL UNDERSTANDINGS OF WRITING

The issues I have investigated do not exhaust the ways in which psychological processes are organized and directed to meet social exigencies and contexts, nor how social situations and meanings are the consequence of psychological processes carried out by the participants in specific situations. In an attempt to create a broader vision I have synthesized how sociocultural studies can inform psychological studies of writing (Bazerman, 2015) and how psychological studies might proceed in a way that recognizes the sociocultural nature of writing (Bazerman, 2012a). Most comprehensively in my book *A Theory of Literate Action* (Bazerman, 2013) I bring together sociocultural, historical, textual and psychological views in order to form a more complete theory of writing.

Overall, these syntheses argue that writing is a complex social participatory performance, in which the writer asserts meaning, goals, actions, affiliations, and identities within a constantly changing, contingently organized social world, relying on shared texts and knowledge. The projection of meaning and shared orientations at a distance requires making assumptions and predictions about who will be reading the texts, what their interest and knowledge are likely to be, and how they may be using the information. Understanding of genres and activity systems helps in making those judgments and identifying how to write effective texts in those situations that meet the criteria and expectations of the readers. Because writing involves so many problem-solving judgments, it is best learned through a long sequence of varied problem solving experiences in varied situations. The teaching of general skills and practices provides only some elements necessary for the complex situated problem solving of writing specific texts, both within the structured and limited worlds of schooling and in the more varied worlds beyond schooling. Research, assessment, and curricular goals would benefit from being attentive to this more complex view of writing for instruction and preparation, as well as for motivation and engagement of students.

Written symbols were added to the human social and communicative repertoire recently, around 5,000 years ago, and it has become an important survival skill for individuals only in the last century; consequently biological adaptation for writing is unlikely, and writing relies on the repurposing of prior adaptations and neurological capacities. Writing further extended the possibilities and complexity of social relations, supporting higher degrees of coordination and sharing of attention, subtlety of stance, extended reports of information, refinement of social relations and hierarchies, and individualization of interaction. But writing also created new cognitive and affective challenges, which required post-partum psychological development of individuals. Further, different forms of apprenticeship and schooling have developed in different societies. Thus, it is reasonable to assume that people manipulate and contemplate these symbols in different ways and then use them differently to facilitate the development and sharing of their thoughts.

These differences are likely to occur not only among the major different systems of literacy but even among languages using the same systems of written symbols—as evidenced by the differences in learning between alphabetic languages with substantially different phonologies, such as English and Spanish.

Cognition and affect are best studied as responses to real writing situations and tasks—personal, educational, and professional. Writing accomplishes social actions within socially shaped forms and provides occasions and tools for cognition and affect. With writing, cognitive and affective orientations and resources develop over histories of social communicative engagements. Through literacy we have learned to think about different things in different ways, but these too are associated with extensive cognitive apprenticeship in the skills, practices, and knowledge associated with any particular literate domain.

Rather than considering writing as an isolated modularized psychological function, we might look it as a complex accomplishment, enlisting varying assemblies of human psychological and material capacities which we learn how to redirect and coordinate for these special purposes, and that over time might create more enduring or automatized assemblies that take shape in individuals, perhaps influenced by available social practices and organized instruction. We might think about how psychological resources and processes are brought together in contingent and variable functional systems, though there may be enduring aspects of organization, processes, or components.

In the past few pages I have offered a particular program and vision for integrating sociocultural and psychological approaches to writing that point to a way to consider psychological studies as we move forward, pursuing the various research agendas proposed in this volume. Other paths to bringing sociocultural and psychological approaches to writing are also possible and may turn out to be preferable. The one thing that would be a mistake, I believe, is to separate the investigation of the psychological functions of writing apart from the sociocultural contexts and purposes that make writing a meaningful and important human activity and that provide the motives for its creation and elaboration, even as we move into new digital media for text creation and dissemination.

REFERENCES

Bazerman, C. (1981). What written knowledge does: Three examples of academic discourse. *Philosophy of the Social Sciences, 11*(3), 361–388.

Bazerman, C. (1984). The writing of scientific non-fiction: Contexts, choices and constraints. *Pre/Text, 5*(1), 39–74.

Bazerman, C. (1987). Codifying the social scientific style: The *APA Publication Manual* as a behaviorist rhetoric. In J. S. Nelson, A. Megill & D. McCloskey (Eds.), *The rhetoric of the human sciences* (pp. 125–144). Madison, WI: University of Wisconsin Press.

Bazerman, C. (1988). *Shaping written knowledge: The genre and activity of the experimental article in science.* Madison, WI: University of Wisconsin Press.

Bazerman, C. (1991). How natural philosophers can cooperate: The rhetorical technology of coordinated research in Joseph Priestley's *History and present state of electricity*. In C. Bazerman & J. Paradis (Eds.), *Textual dynamics of the professions* (pp. 13–44). Madison, WI: University of Wisconsin Press.

Bazerman, C. (1993). Money talks: The rhetorical project of Adam Smith's *Wealth of nations*. In W. Henderson, T. Duley-Evans & R. Blackhouse (Eds.), *Economics and language* (pp. 173–199). New York: Routledge.

Bazerman, C. (1999). *The languages of Edison's light.* Cambridge, MA: MIT Press.

Bazerman, C. (2001a). Anxiety in action: Sullivan's interpersonal psychiatry as a supplement to Vygotskian psychology. *Mind, Culture and Activity, 8*(2), 174–186.

Bazerman, C. (2001b). Writing as a development in interpersonal relations. *Journal for the Psychoanalysis of Culture and Society, 6*(2), 298–302.

Bazerman, C. (2005). Practically human: The pragmatist project of the interdisciplinary journal. *Psychiatry. Linguistics and the Human Sciences, 1*(1), 15–38.

Bazerman, C. (2008). Genre and cognitive development. In C. Bazerman, A. Bonini & D. Figueiredo (Eds.), *Genre in a changing world* (pp. 283–298). Fort Collins, CO: The WAC Clearinghouse and Parlor Press. Retrieved from https://wac.colostate.edu/books/genre/.

Bazerman, C. (2012a). Writing, cognition, and affect from the perspective of sociohistorical studies. In V. Berninger, (Ed.), *Past, present, and future contributions cognitive writing research to cognitive psychology* (pp. 89–104). New York: Psychology Press.

Bazerman, C. (2012b). Writing with concepts: Communal, internalized, and externalized. *Mind, Culture and Activity, 19*(3), 259–272.

Bazerman, C. (2013). *A theory of literate action.* Fort Collins, CO: The WAC Clearinghouse and Parlor Press. Retrieved from https://wac.colostate.edu/books/literateaction/v1/.

Bazerman, C. (2015). What do sociocultural studies of writing tell us about learning to write? In C. MacArthur, S. Graham & J. Fitzgerald (Eds.) *Handbook of writing research* (pp. 1–2). New York: Guilford.

Bazerman, C., Simon, K., Ewing, P. & Pieng, P. (2013). Domain-specific cognitive development through writing tasks in a teacher education program. *Pragmatics & Cognition, 21*(3), 530–551.

Bazerman, C., Simon, K. & Pieng, P. (2014). Writing about reading to advance thinking: A study in situated cognitive development. In P. Boscolo & P. Klein (Eds.), *Writing as a learning activity* (pp. 249–276). Boston: Brill.

Berthoff, A. E. (1972). From problem-solving to a theory of the imagination. *College English, 33*(6), 636–649.

Britton, J., Burgess, T., Martin, N., McLeod, A. & Rosen, H. (1975). *The development of writing abilities.* London: Macmillan.

Bruner, J. (1990). *Acts of meaning.* Cambridge, MA: Harvard University Press.

Cole, M. (1996). *Cultural psychology.* Cambridge, MA: Harvard University. Press.

Dewey, J. (1910). *How we think.* Boston: D. C. Heath.

Elbow, P. (1973). *Writing without teachers.* New York: Oxford University Press.

Emig, J. (1971). *The composing processes of twelfth graders.* Urbana, IL: National Council of Teachers of English.

Flower, L. & Hayes, J. (1981). A cognitive process theory of writing. *College Composition and Communication, 32*(4), 365–387.

Kelly, G. & Bazerman, C. (2003). How students argue scientific claims: A rhetorical-semantic analysis. *Applied Linguistics, 24*(1), 28–55.

Kelly, G. J., Bazerman, C., Skukauskaite, A. & Prothero, W. (2010). Rhetorical features of student science writing in introductory university oceanography. In C. Bazerman, B. Krut, K. Lunsford, S. McLeod, S. Null, P. Rogers, A. Stansell (Eds.), *Traditions of Writing Research* (pp. 265–282). New York: Routledge.

Leont'ev, A. N. (1978). *Activity, consciousness, and personality.* Englewood Cliffs, NJ: Prentice-Hall.

Luria, A. (1979). *The making of mind.* Cambridge, UK: Cambridge University Press.

Mead, G. H. (1962). *Mind, self, and society.* Chicago: University of Chicago Press.
Moffett, J. (1968). *Teaching the universe of discourse.* Boston: Houghton Mifflin
Priestley, J. (1777). *A course of lectures on oratory and criticism.* London: J. Johnson.
Shaughnessy, M. P. (1977). *Errors and expectations: A guide for the teacher of basic writing.* New York: Oxford University Press.
Smith, A. (1983). *Lectures on rhetoric and belles lettres* (J. C. Bryce, Ed.). Oxford, UK: Clarendon Press.
Sullivan, H. S. (1953). *The interpersonal theory of psychiatry.* New York: Norton.
Takao, A. Y., Prothero, W. A. & Kelly, G. J. (2002). Applying argumentation analysis to assess the quality of university oceanography students' scientific writing. *Journal of Geoscience Education, 50*(1), 40–48.
Vygotsky, L. (1986). *Thought and language.* Cambridge, MA: MIT Press.

CHAPTER 2

THE EVOLVING RELATIONSHIP BETWEEN COMPOSITION AND COGNITIVE STUDIES: GAINING SOME HISTORICAL PERSPECTIVE ON OUR CONTEMPORARY MOMENT

Ellen C. Carillo
University of Connecticut

In *Naming What We Know: Threshold Concepts of Writing Studies*, Howard Tinberg (2015) makes an important distinction between cognition and metacognition, especially significant in light of composition's recent focus on the transfer of learning, which scholars largely agree, depends upon metacognition. He explains:

> cognition refers to the acquisition and application of knowledge through complex mental processes . . . but the effective accomplishment of writing tasks over time requires even more. It calls upon metacognition, or the ability to perceive the very steps by which success occurs and to articulate the various qualities and components that contribute in significant ways to the production of successful writing. (2015, p. 76)

If we parse the tasks Tinberg names here, he describes cognition in terms of the acquisition and application of knowledge while metacognition, which is also defined by acquisition and application, additionally involves perception and articulation. Although composition's focus on metacognition is fairly new, since its inception, composition has been interested in cognition. Looking closely at the discipline's history, we can better understand the role that cognitive studies has played in the field and how an initial interest in cognition ultimately developed into a focus on metacognition. Taken together, the disciplinary-defining moments explored in this chapter represent important historical antecedents to the field's contemporary research on transfer and metacognition, as well as its most recent turn back toward questions surrounding individual cognition. After decades of privileging sociocultural approaches to understanding and teaching writing, the last few years have seen an increase in the number of studies that explore how individuals' dispositions affect the transfer of writing knowledge. This chapter ultimately argues that this reintroduction of studies of individual cognition is an important way of enriching discussions of transfer, but must not overshadow or forestall the work that still needs to be accomplished through more socially inflected studies of transfer. As such, after exploring composition's historical relationship to cognition, this chapter recommends the adoption of David N. Perkins and Gavriel Salomon's (2012) detect-elect-connect model of transfer because it highlights where dispositions are most important in the complex process of transfer, and it does so while also considering the importance of context.

THE 1960S: COMPOSITION CALLS FOR THE STUDY OF THE "PSYCHOLOGICAL DIMENSION OF WRITING"

The field of composition is often traced to 1963 (Bridwell-Bowles, 1989; Crowley, 1998; North, 1987), a watershed year wherein the Conference on College Composition and Communication's annual meeting shifted its focus to the relationship between composition and rhetoric, accounting for what some called the revival of rhetoric. That same year saw the publication of far-reaching and influential studies such as Albert Kitzhaber's (1963) *Themes, Theories, and Therapy* (1963) and Richard Braddock, Richard Lloyd-Jones, and Lowell Schoer's *Research in Written Composition* (1963/2009). The latter, more commonly called The Braddock Report, provided an overview of 485 research studies on writing and laid the groundwork for the founding of *Research in the Teaching of English* (*RTE*), which remains the flagship research journal of the National Council of Teachers of English.

Research in Written Composition was arguably the most influential publication within the field in the 1960s and, thus, offers an early artifact that allows us to begin to understand composition's longstanding relationship to cognitive studies. As is well-known, the committee, led by Braddock, was charged in 1961 to investigate "the state of knowledge in composition." One of the studies the committee examined was John Andrew Van Bruggen's (1943) "Factors Affecting Regularity of the Flow of Words During Written Composition." Braddock et al. explain that it "probes into the psychological realm underlying or accompanying the act of composition" (1963/2009, p. 31) and that this study, among others, suggests "that the psychological dimension of writing needs to be investigated" (p. 31). These are descriptions that offer important insights into composition at the time, a point to which I will return after describing the study in more depth. In this study, Van Bruggen measured the flow of junior high school students' writing using a kymograph in order to determine "how the composing structure—that is the number, length, and location of pauses between words—differs in compositions of superior and inferior quality and in compositions written with rapid and slow flow of words" (as cited in Braddock et al., 1963/2009, p. 31). Although the Braddock Report does not use the term "cognition," its description of the study's psychological underpinnings, as well as the report's call for more work in this vein, indicate the field's initial interest in the relationship between writing and mental processes. However, a closer look at this early conceptualization of this relationship reveals that understandings of the relationship between writing and the mind are rather undeveloped. As indicated above, the "psychological realm" is said to "underlie" or "accompany" the act of composition. I would argue that the "or" here is indicative of the committee's uncertainty about this relationship in that the psychological elements may reside somewhere below the surface of the writing process or alongside it. In fact, amidst all of the factors that Van Bruggen studies as affecting the rate of flow—including compositional, academic, personal and environmental factors—it is not readily clear which factor Braddock and his committee are deeming psychological in nature. An educated guess is that the "psychological realm" refers to the "personal" factors affecting the rate of flow since the other factors are largely external. In his conclusion, Van Bruggen describes the effect of personality on writing and, by extension, on teaching:

> The problem of personality development cannot be divorced from teaching. The dominating, extrovertive, and emotionally stable pupils wrote with a rapid flow of words while those with introvertive tendencies and lack of emotional balance paused often and long during composition writing. It is evident that something must be done for the latter group to give them more confidence and place them more at ease if they are to use their abilities to the best advantage and show improvement in composing rate. (1943, p. 154)

Although this is arguably an early iteration of the importance of studying the effect of (what are now called) dispositions on the learning and transfer of writing knowledge, Braddock et al.'s description of the study as psychological in nature and the trouble the committee has describing the relationship between writing and the mind suggests that composition needed to refine its understanding of writing's relationship to individual cognitive processes. Moreover, it would also need to clarify how those cognitive processes are affected by a range of both internal and external factors. In fact, Braddock et al. go on to call for the use of case studies and longitudinal studies to showcase the effect of "individual differences" on writing (1963/2009, p. 32). But, as Braddock's committee notes, before composition teachers can conduct these kinds of studies, "they must learn how to do so" (1963/2009, p. 23). As described in the next section of this chapter, Janet Emig (1971), among others, would undertake this work. These scholars borrowed concepts from psychology that would allow them to address the individual differences—cognitive and otherwise—that their students exhibited.

THE 1970S AND 1980S: THE ROLE OF COGNITIVE STUDIES IN PROCESS THEORIES OF WRITING

Although in the 1960s the Braddock Report anticipated the benefits of exploring what it called the psychological dimensions of writing—seemingly defined by how students' personalities affected their compositions—in the 1970s and 1980s, composition moved toward explorations of cognitive psychology. Cognitive psychology had methodologies that seemed conducive to studying something as complex as writing. Moreover, methodologies such as think-aloud protocols, protocol analysis, problem-solving models, case studies, as well as longitudinal studies—all methods used in that field—seemed far more legitimate than those employed in the studies described in the Braddock Report. These approaches were also more conducive to studying processes rather than products, which, of course, the field was moving toward, as well.

Composition's focus on the writing process—and later and more accurately—on writing processes, was initially encouraged by Janet Emig's groundbreaking decision to concentrate her research not on students' compositions, which had been the focus of the Van Bruggen and other studies— but on the process of writing. Rather than defining writing as a method of transcribing one's ideas, Emig's (1971) study, *The Composing Processes of Twelfth Graders*, described writing as integral to those ideas. Emig suggested, in other words, that writing allowed one to discover, to develop, and to shape ideas. Emig (1977) would go on to publish "Writing As a Mode of Learning," which was heavily influenced by Carl Bruner's work in educational and cognitive psychology, as well as the process movement in composition. This shift in focus away from product and toward process offered a critique—if not rejection of—"traditional, product-driven, rules-based, correctness-obsessed writing instruction" (Tobin & Newkirk, 1994, p. 5). Because of early process theorists such as Emig, students' writing processes supplanted attention to their written products as "students themselves, rather than the texts they produced, became the locus of instruction" (Crowley, 1998, p. 202). The field of composition, in other words, began studying the "individual differences" (Crowley, 1998, p. 32) among student-writers that the Braddock Report anticipated would be so crucial to explore.

This new focus on students' processes meant that if compositionists were going to study the cognitive aspects of writing they needed to reimagine their object of study. No longer were students' final compositions thought to provide the insights they once had. Studying students' writing processes, instead, allowed compositionists to better understand and target students' difficulties, particularly important as America saw unprecedented numbers of students attending postsecondary institutions in light of changing admissions policies. In 1970, for example, the City University of New York (CUNY) adopted an open admissions policy and saw enrollments "jump from 174,000 in 1969 to 266,000 in 1975" (Shaughnessy, 1977/2009, p. 387). As Shaughnessy explains, in addition to the newly adopted open-enrollment policies, "many four-year colleges began admitting students who were not by traditional standards ready for college. . . . In some the numbers were token; in others . . . the number threatened to 'tip' freshman classes in favor of the less prepared students" (1977/2009, p. 387). This change in the student population would necessarily have a profound effect on writing instruction as "academic winners and losers from the best and worst high schools in the country, the children of the lettered and the illiterate, the blue-collared, the white-collared, and the unemployed, some who could barely afford the subway fare to school" (Shaughnessy, 1977/2009, p. 387) all sat side by side—or more accurately—were immediately given placement exams and separated into different classes since their preparations were so uneven.

These uneven preparations resulted in the development of basic writing programs across the country, and the changing face of the college student suggested the need to study and compare the composing processes of inexperienced and experienced writers, which Linda Flower and John R. Hayes, among others, did by drawing on cognitive psychology. In fact, their own model of writing as a problem-solving activity was borrowed, in Hayes' words, "quite directly" (1992, p. 11) from cognitive psychologists (and colleagues at Carnegie Mellon) Allen Newell and Herbert Simons' "general problem solver (GPS)" concept(as cited in Vipond, 1993, p. 128). Researchers like Flower and Hayes believed that rather than prescribing the writing process, they could study the mental moves that experienced and successful writers made throughout their writing to develop cognitive models of successful writing processes. They could then translate those models into pedagogies to assist the poorer, less experienced writers. Flower and Hayes' conceptualization of writing as a form of problem-solving laid the groundwork for the field's current discussion of the effect of "problem-exploring" and "answer-getting dispositions" on students' transfer of learning, discussed below.

Flower and Hayes' scientific approach, which studied the act of writing as a problem-solving enterprise led others to do the same. This work, however, incited debates within the field. Although the Braddock Report called for more scientific approaches, the field's borrowing of concepts and methodologies from cognitive psychology was publicly rejected by Ann E. Berthoff (1971), for example, whose exchanges with Janice Lauer were published in *College Composition and Communication*. Favoring hermeneutically oriented approaches to understand the writing process rather than empirically oriented ones, Berthoff warned the field, "When we make problem-solving central to a philosophy of education we effectively separate learning from knowing: the results are philosophically disastrous and politically dangerous" (1971, p. 240). Lauer (1970), on the other hand, contended that "unless both the testmakers and the teachers of composition investigate beyond the field of English, beyond even the area of rhetorical studies for the solution to the composition problem, they will find themselves wandering in an endless maze" (p. 396). Robert Connors (1983), like Berthoff, was vocal about what he saw as a mismatch between composition and science: "We are not a science and will not be one in the foreseeable future, and we must beware lest our understandable desire to share in the cachet of science lead us to a barren enactment of imitation science" (p. 19). Through the 1980s, compositionists like William F. Irmscher (1987) remained unconvinced of the uses of science to composition: "We need to reassert the humanistic nature of our own discipline, which in this context means its concern for the individual as a human being, not as a quantity or specimen" (p. 85).

Others within composition had different criticisms of this scientific turn. Although the initial Flower-Hayes model (1977) was a "breakthrough in describing how the three key recursive cognitive processes involved in writing (planning, translating, and reviewing) interact within the constraints of memory and the task environment" (Berninger, 2012, p. 221), Patricia Bizzell (1982/2009) and others would go on to critique its incomplete approach to studying writing because it ignored "the social context afforded by recognition of the dialectical relationship between thought and language" (p. 486). With the major shift in the student population, differences beyond degree of experience, including class, race, and gender were becoming obvious, and generalizations based on case studies of experienced and inexperienced writers—with no acknowledgement of other differences—were becoming suspect. By the beginning of the next decade, studies on individual cognition were met with criticism in favor of studies that took into account writing's social dimensions. This new paradigm, later called the "social turn," removed the writer (and her individual cognition) from isolation, situating her, instead, as a social being affected by cultural, political, and social forces.

John Trimbur (1994) describes this turn as characterized by a representation of "composing as a cultural activity by which writers position and reposition themselves in relation to their own and others' subjectivities, discourse practices, and institutions" (p. 109). Cognitive approaches that focused on individual students' thinking and writing processes were no longer sufficient now that other differences among students had been exposed so dramatically. Lillian Bridwell-Bowles (1989) explains this shift:

> We needed a theoretical foundation for our data, one that drew from philosophy, critical theory, sociology, and politics to account for the writer at work within a larger socio-political-philosophical matrix. The whole field of composition studies ha[d] shifted its interest. . . . methodologies shifted from experiments or clinical observations, cloaked in the respectability of "objectivity," to narratives and complex ethnographies. (para. 10)

The shifts in focus and methods Bridwell-Bowles describes just above would potentially allow compositionists access to the range of factors and elements that shaped students' consciousness and subjectivities, and, therefore, access to their writing and thinking despite the differences among students and contexts.

Although the field remained somewhat polarized between those who thought that empiricism and methodologies from cognitive psychology had a lot to offer composition and those who wanted to define composition on its own terms, this was a moment in which composition sought to integrate cognitive and social theories of composing. Compositionists such as Flower began employing what they called sociocognitive approaches that valued individual cognition, but also considered the social (and other) contexts that condition individual cognition. In 1989, recognizing the importance of the social nature of knowledge, Flower described this new integrated theory as a means to "explain[ing] how context cues cognition, which in its turn mediates and interprets the particular world that context provides" (p. 282). Before attention to individual cognitive aspects of writing would largely disappear as the social turn gained momentum and the field moved toward cultural studies, many scholars (Bloom, 1986; Brand, 1987; Brandt, 1986; Larson, 1985; Schoenfeld, 1983) developed studies that sought to synthesize cognitive and social constructivist methodologies.

Social constructivist approaches to studying and teaching writing would ultimately dominate before giving way to other more politically inflected theories of writing and teaching writing. During this period, psychology, and particularly cognitive psychology, was not as germane to the work of composition. It would not be until a decade or so into the twenty-first century that composition would again begin to see a proliferation of scholarship drawing on cognitive studies, and specifically cognitive psychology, as composition turned its attention to the transfer of learning.

FROM COGNITION TO METACOGNITION: TEACHING FOR TRANSFER IN THE TWENTY-FIRST CENTURY

Transfer is a concept that has been studied for years by educational and cognitive psychologists, only recently becoming an interest of those in composition. Compositionists most often rely on educational psychologists Perkins and Salomon's (1992) conception of transfer, which they describe as "instances in which learning in one context or with one set of materials impacts on performance in another context or with other related materials" (para. 1). Although as early as 1908 educational psychologist Charles Judd's experiments showed that transfer was, in fact, possible, it would take until very recently for those in composition to ask: "If transfer is possible are there ways we can teach writing to promote transfer?" One of the answers to this question is that teaching writing with an emphasis on metacognition can help facilitate transfer.

As the opening to this chapter reminds us, though, metacognition and cognition are not the same. The contemporary emphasis on metacognition, as opposed to cognition, underscores the influence of social constructivism as the field's interests now lie in how contexts—disciplinary, generic, cultural, among others—don't just cue individual cognition but challenge the very concept of individual cognition as something separable from its surrounding contexts.

With the field's emphasis on context came the rise of WAC and WID programs, which depend on a conceptualization of writing not as a general skill, but one that is context-specific. These programs highlight the role that disciplinary conventions, context, genre, and audience play in effective writing. Still, as WPAs and others began assessing these programs they found that students were not transferring what they were learning in lower-level writing courses to other courses. Anne Beaufort (2007) and Elizabeth Wardle (2009) both found in their research that even when students described their first-year writing courses as valuable, they were largely unable to imagine how that writing connected to other courses. For example, Wardle (2009) explains that students "did not appear to make even near connections of those skills, much less transfer those skills to very different contexts . . . no students suggested they were being asked to write a persuasive paper in order to be able to write persuasively in other courses" (p. 777). While Wardle followed students during the course of their first two years in college, Beaufort followed a single student throughout his entire college career, ultimately concluding that his early writing courses did not prepare him to succeed in later writing courses he took within his majors. Gerald Nelms and Ronda Leathers Dively (2007) at Southern University of Illinois at Carbondale studied the extent to which students transferred writing skills and knowledge from their general, first-year writing courses to their writing-intensive courses in their majors. Ultimately, they found that a great deal of what was covered in the introductory courses was not transferring to the upper-level courses, thereby creating a significant "disconnect" between the lower-level courses and the upper-level courses.

Here again, cognitive (and educational) psychology proved useful in describing precisely what was prohibiting this transfer. It was not that the students lacked certain cognitive abilities. Instead, students lacked the metacognitive abilities that allowed them to abstract and generalize concepts from one course (i.e., context) to use them in another course (i.e., context). As the definitions that open this chapter suggest, metacognition is more complex than mere cognition. One way to imagine this complexity is in terms of how the various facets of memory work. Metacognition depends upon "external cues to trigger retrieval processes in long-term memory, so information about a thinking skill can move into working memory, where it can be consciously considered" (Halpern, 1998, p. 453). This chain of events, though, is complicated by the fact that there are no "obvious cues in the novel contexts that can trigger the recall of the thinking skills" (Halpern, 1998, p. 453) that would allow the transfer of knowledge into that new context. In a classroom setting, students, themselves, become responsible for creating "retrieval cues from the structural aspects of a problem or argument, so when these structural aspects are present in the novel context, they can serve as cues for retrieval" (Halpern, 1998, p. 453). Creating these retrieval cues is not an easy task, and in his chapter in this volume, Marcus Meade points out some of the problems posed by a way of learning that depends on cognitive dissonance.

Despite the challenges that Meade describes, compositionists continue to recommend pedagogies that emphasize metacognition in order to help students anticipate future uses of what they are learning so that they can make the sort of connections that Wardle, Beaufort, and Nelms and Dively found were absent. These pedagogies also cue students to draw on prior knowledge that might be useful in the current context. Wardle and Downs' "writing about writing" pedagogy depends upon students using their metacognitive abilities to generalize what they are learning about writing while Rebecca Nowacek (2011) recommends the use of what she calls the interdisciplinary learning community model of first-year composition, "which immerses students into disciplinary contexts" (p. 133) and replaces the more general first-year writing course. Most recently, Kathleen Blake Yancey and her colleagues (2014) tested the benefits of deliberately teaching for transfer. They found that students in courses with instructors who taught for transfer actually did transfer their writing skills and knowledge more regularly than students who were in other types of writing courses. No matter their approach, all of the scholars mentioned above call for the importance of deliberately teaching for transfer by incorporating metacognitive exercises into writing courses so that students can succeed across courses and contexts both within and beyond academia.

A (RE)TURN TO INDIVIDUAL COGNITION

In the last few years, as compositionists have studied courses, curricula, and even writing centers that put transfer front-and-center, they have begun to realize that while it is important for students to engage in metacognitive exercises so they can apply, adapt, and transform knowledge across contexts, metacognition alone cannot account for successful instances of transfer or, in some cases, for the lack of transfer. Such findings led researchers in composition to turn their attention to dispositions or "individual, internal qualities" (Driscoll & Wells, 2012) that seemed to have affected the transfer of learning. There is, of course, nothing new about focusing on dispositions. As discussed above, as early as Van Bruggen's 1943 study, described in the Braddock Report, researchers were exploring the impact of students' individual dispositions (e.g., extrovertiveness and emotional stability). Although the individual (student) has never been totally absent from theories of writing and of teaching writing, it has recently been overshadowed by the privileging of social and cultural contexts.

Dana L. Driscoll has described this belated treatment of the individual learner as a pattern within the field: "As composition has sought to understand fundamentals like rhetorical situations, literacy development, and genre theory, it has done so by, first, gravitating toward context. Only later does it self-correct to include the impact of the individual learner." Still, as the field turns its attention once again to individual cognition by focusing on dispositions, as well as the "habits of mind" described in Council of Writing Program Administrators, National Council of Teachers of English, and National Writing Project's (2011) *Framework for Success in Postsecondary Writing*, composition runs the risk of leaving important work on the transfer of learning unfinished. Moving too quickly and too narrowly toward (re)privileging individual cognition by focusing on dispositions could potentially be detrimental to the advancement of research in the field. Although Driscoll and others who study transfer through the lens of dispositions acknowledge that attention to dispositions should not foreclose other perspectives on transfer, Paul Kei Matsuda (2003) has aptly described what often happens as new approaches seek to replace older ones. He points out how "new 'paradigms' criticiz[e] previously dominant theories and pedagogies for certain features while appropriating or ignoring other features" (2003, p. 74). As composition shifts its attention toward the individual learner's dispositions, it is crucial that the field work against caricaturizing earlier approaches to studying transfer. These socially inflected and context-driven theories of transfer are necessary for a comprehensive understanding of transfer, as well as comprehensive understandings of dispositions. After all, as Meade notes in his chapter in this volume, dispositions, too, are contextual.

So how does composition (re)introduce individual cognition (through a study of dispositions) back into the conversation while simultaneously acknowledging the embeddedness of dispositions in contexts? Perkins and Salomon's (2012) detect-elect-connect model of transfer is especially helpful here because it highlights specifically where dispositions are most important in the complex process of transfer, and it does so without bracketing context. I conclude this piece with a description of this model and an exploration of how it holds promise for further explorations of the role of individual dispositions in the transfer of learning.

THE DETECT-ELECT-CONNECT MODEL OF TRANSFER

In David N. Perkins and Gavriel Salomon's detect-elect-connect model, the learner is understood as "detecting a potential relationship with prior learning, electing to pursue it, and working out a fruitful connection" (2012, p. 248). Rather than focusing on that final step—as do most outcomes-based models of transfer—this model posits that the acts of detecting and electing are particularly useful in considering how a range of dispositions come into play because it is precisely dispositions and habits of mind like curiosity, motivation, and self-efficacy, for example, that impact whether a learner will detect a potential relationship and then elect to pursue it. Perkins and Salomon refer to each step as a mental bridge. These bridges may occur serially or simultaneously, and any one of those bridges may be "too far" and lead to failure of transfer (Perkins & Salomon, 2012, p. 250). The point is that by breaking up the process of transfer into these three bridges and focusing on the first two, researchers can study the conditions—such as learners' dispositions—that inform that final bridge of connection, the bridge most often privileged in studies of transfer. Moreover, such a model does not assume that the *ability* to detect a potential relationship with prior learning will automatically result in a connection between that prior learning and the current context. Instead, parsing transfer into these three mental bridges foregrounds the distinction between ability and action, a distinction particularly germane to the study of dispositions, which are not the same as the abilities or skills that are being transferred. Ultimately, Salomon and Perkins' integrated model allows researchers to consider how contexts contribute to individual dispositions which, in turn, affect transfer.

The fact that contexts contribute to the development of dispositions (Driscoll & Wells, 2012; Meade, this volume; Perkins & Salomon, 2012) is promising since this gives teachers the opportunity to create academic contexts that don't just seek to promote the transfer of learning, but also encourage the cultivation of the dispositions that will make that transfer more likely. To this end, Salomon and Perkins call for the development of a "learning culture of opportunity" rather than a "learning culture of demand." The latter, which they argue describes the current state of education in America, expects and rewards students for showing knowledge on demand while a learning culture of opportunity engages students in more open-ended experiences that have far-reaching effects beyond that immediate academic context (2012, p. 257). Within composition, Wardle (2012) has explored the importance of contexts and the characteristics they can share with individuals. Drawing on Bourdieu, Wardle has considered how fields, in addition to individuals, inhabit dispositions. Each system or habitus, Bourdieu explains, is characterized by a set of dispositions that affect how actors within it behave (Wardle, 2009). Wardle's specific interest lies in what she calls problem-exploring vs. answer-getting dispositions that characterize both individuals and academic fields. Like Perkins and Salomon's (1992) "learning culture of opportunity," problem-exploring dispositions "incline a person toward curiosity, reflection, consideration of multiple possibilities, a willingness to engage in a recursive process of trial and error, and toward a recognition that more than one solution can 'work'" (Wardle, 2012, para. 13). The characteristics that make up problem-exploring dispositions are very much aligned with the habits of mind described in the *Framework*. On the other hand, Wardle's answer-getting dispositions echo Perkins and Salomon's "learning culture of demand" in that these dispositions "seek right answers quickly and are avers to open consideration of multiple possibilities (Wardle, 2012, para. 13). Although Bourdieu maintains that the dispositions of both individuals and fields are not easily changeable, Wardle (and Perkins and Salomon) argues that it is still necessary to work toward the goal of constructing educational fields characterized by problem-exploring dispositions so that these fields can support students' cultivation of problem-exploring dispositions. Similarly, education scholar Erik De Corte argues for the development of "powerful learning environments for thinking and problem solving" that prepare students for future learning (De Corte & Masui, 2012, p. 365). To test the efficacy of such environments, De Corte and his colleague Chris Masui created a learning environment that privileged the dispositions of "orienting" and "self-judging," as well as other "self-regulation skills" (2012, p. 375). Ultimately, the students in this learning environment were better prepared for and more successful in the new context—another course—than the students in the control group.

Intentionally creating a specific type of environment that inhabits certain dispositions need not be something that goes on wholly behind-the-scenes. In this volume, E. Shelley Reid makes a compelling case for openly talking to students about the environmental factors and dispositions that impact the transfer of learning. In her own study, she found that students recognize that "dispositions are connected to their work as writers." As such, class discussions about how their "dispositional approaches interact[t] with their school writing endeavors" can go a long way toward empowering students to engage in transfer as they become more aware of their learning dispositions. Taking into consideration Reid's encouraging findings, it seems as though a related productive route to follow would be one that engages students in discussions about the effects of the dispositions inherent in the *range* of institutions—beyond academia—that surround them and how those dispositions affect their own dispositions. Students' religions and cultures have a habitus, as do their individual families; discussions about this would only enrich the types of conversations Reid describes. By way of conclusion, I will now turn to the implications of Reid's approach, as well as the arguments put forth by De Corte and Massui, Wardle, and Perkins and Salomon.

WHERE TO GO FROM HERE

The discussion above is intended to point toward the need to keep context in discussions of individual cognition. The integrative approach of the detect-elect-connect model allows for—and seems to even invite—research on aspects of transfer that still remain understudied, including, Which dispositions in particular tend to lead to transfer most regularly? Moreover, this model's distinct approach to studying transfer that focuses on much more than outcomes opens up a range of questions about what (external elements) inform transfer and dispositions, how those dispositions are formed, and how they may change (or not) over time. These questions could not be pursued if the pendulum swings too far toward a focus on dispositions and individual cognition, and would be in particular danger if scholars studying individual cognition begin to caricaturize previous, socioculturally inflected theories.

Keeping integrative approaches to studying transfer in play, so to speak, will encourage other studies that address how context affects individual cognition. As Dylan Dryer and David Russell point out in this volume, there is important work emerging from cognitive-science investigations that allow researchers to actually see what happens while people compose. Studies that use applications that capture keystrokes and eye movement, for example, have demonstrated that cognitive processes are affected by "environmental conditions." Unlike when Bizzell and others challenged the Flower-Hayes model, new technologies are allowing researchers to actually see how this happens during the composing process. To shift the field's focus too much toward the individual cognitive realm would forestall the important work that can be done by observing these cognitive activities and understanding how they are affected by environmental conditions.

Rather than closely controlling or bracketing the context in which we study individual learners, the detect-elect-connect model can help researchers foreground the environmental conditions and the individual learner's place within social (and other) context(s). We can, thus, begin imagining different ways of intervening in students' learning. These approaches would go beyond creating curricula and pedagogies that foster the transfer of skills and abilities toward those that also create environments that facilitate the dispositions that are determined to be most germane to transfer.

Discovering precisely which dispositions are most important to transfer and how they might be measured are perhaps the next steps. As discussed throughout this chapter, compositionists are already developing lists of dispositions that seem relevant to writing, including self-efficacy, curiosity, confidence, and motivation, all of which are more precise than the dispositions Van Bruggen sought to study in 1943. Although the Braddock Report criticized Van Bruggen's study on many counts, this early study—and others like it—cannot be discounted as important historical antecedents to the work on dispositions that compositionists are beginning to pursue. Van Bruggen's concepts of introvertive and extrovertive personalities, as well as his interest in studying the effect of what he calls "emotional stability" on the writing process are certainly not as precise as they might be, but his study still gets at the crux of one of the field's current questions: What other aspects of one's cognition affect writing? Developing ways to explore this and other questions—perhaps with our students alongside us (as Reid, in this volume, might urge)—is a step toward a more comprehensive understanding of transfer. The detect-elect-connect model of transfer, which itself offers a more comprehensive approach to the transfer question by valuing what happens before a learner makes a connection between two contexts, is a promising integrated approach to studying transfer that depends upon both individual learners' dispositions and the contexts that inform those dispositions.

REFERENCES

Adler-Kassner, L. & Wardle, E. (2015). *Naming what we know: Threshold concepts of writing studies.* Logan, UT: Utah State University Press.

Applebee, A. N. (1974). *Tradition and reform in the teaching of English.* Urbana, IL: National Council of Teachers of English.

Beaufort, A. (2007). *College writing and beyond.* Logan, UT: Utah State University Press.

Berninger, V. W. (2012). *Past, present, and future contributions of cognitive writing research to cognitive psychology.* New York: Psychology Press.

Berthoff, A. E. (1971). The problem of problem solving. *College Composition and Communication, 22*(3), 237–242.

Bizzell, P. (2009). Cognition, convention, and certainty: What we need to know about writing. In S. Miller (Ed.), *The Norton book of composition studies* (pp. 479–499). New York: Norton. (Reprinted from *PRE/TEXT*, 1982.)

Bloom, L. (1986). Anxious writers in context: Graduate school and beyond. In M. Rose (Ed.), *When a writer can't write* (pp. 119–133). New York: Guilford.

Braddock, R., Lloyd-Jones, R. & Schoer, L. (2009). From research in written composition. In S. Miller (Ed.), *The Norton book of composition studies* (pp. 193–213). New York: Norton. (Reprinted from *Research in written composition*, by R. Braddock et al., 1963, Champaign, IL: National Council of Teachers of English.)

Brand, A. (1987). The why of cognition: Emotion and the writing process. *College Composition and Communication, 38*(4), 436–443.

Brandt, D. (1985). Review: Versions of literacy. *College English, 47*(2), 128–138.

Brandt, D. (1986). Text and context: How writers come to mean. In B. Couture (Ed.), *Functional approaches to writing* (pp. 93–107). London: Francis Pinter.

Bridwell-Bowles, L. (1989). Designing research on computer assisted writing. *Computers and Composition, 70*(1). Retrieved from http://computersandcomposition.candcblog.org/archives/v7/7_1_html/7_1_6_Bridwell.html.

Connors, R. J. (1983). Composition studies and science. *College English, 45*(1), 1–20. doi: 10.2307/376913.

Council of Writing Program Administrators, National Council of Teachers of English & National Writing Project (2011). *Framework for success in postsecondary writing.* Retrieved from http://wpacouncil.org/files/framework-for-success-postsecondary-writing.pdf.

Crowely, S. (1998). *Composition in the university.* Pittsburgh, PA: University of Pittsburgh Press.

DeCorte, E. & Masui, C. (2004). The CLIA-model: A framework for designing powerful learning environments for thinking and problem solving. *European Journal of Psychology of Education, XtX*(4), 365–384. Retrieved from http://www.lamolina.edu.pe/innovacioneducativa/images/files/libros/de%20Corte%20&%20Masui%20The%20CLIA%20model.pdf.

Driscoll, D. L. & Wells, J. (2012). Beyond knowledge and skills: writing transfer and the role of student dispositions. *Composition Forum, 26*. Retrieved from http://compositionforum.com/issue/26/beyond-knowledge-skills.php.

Emig, J. (1971). *The writing processes of twelfth graders*. Urbana, IL: National Council of Teachers of English.

Flower, L. & Hayes, J. R. (1977). Problem-solving strategies and the writing process. *College English, 39*(4), 449–461.

Irmscher, W. F. (1987). Finding a comfortable identity. *College Composition and Communication, 38*(1), 81–87.

Judd, C. H. (1908). The relation of special training to intelligence. *Educational Review, 36*, 28–42.

Kitzhaber, A. R. (1963). *Themes, theories, and therapy: The teaching of writing in college*. New York: McGraw-Hill.

Larson, R. (1985). Emotional scenarios in the writing process: An examination of young writers' affective experiences. In M. Rose (Ed.), *When a writer can't write* (pp. 19–42). New York: Guilford.

Lauer, J. (1970). Heuristics and composition. *College Composition and Communication, 21*(5), 396–404.

Matsuda, P. K. (2003). Process and post-process: A discursive history. *Journal of Second Language Writing*, 12, 65–83.

Nelms, G. & Dively, R. L. (2007). Perceived roadblocks to transferring knowledge from first-year composition to writing-intensive major courses: A pilot study. *WPA, 31*(1–2), 214–240.

North, S. (1987). *The making of knowledge in composition*. Upper Montclair, NJ: Boynton.

Nowacek, R. (2011.) *Agents of integration: Understanding transfer as a rhetorical act*. Carbondale, IL: Southern Illinois University Press.

Perkins, D. N. & Solomon, G. (1992). Transfer of learning. International Encyclopedia of Education (2nd ed.). Boston: Pergamon Press. Retrieved from https://jaymctighe.com/wordpress/wp-content/uploads/2011/04/Transfer-of-Learning-Perkins-and-Salomon.pdf.

Perkins, D. N. & Solomon, G. (2012). Knowledge to go: A motivational and dispositional view of transfer. *Educational Psychologist 47*(3), 248–258. Retrieved from http://dx.doi.org/10.1080/00461520.2012.693354.

Schoenfeld, A. H. (1983). Beyond the purely cognitive: Belief systems, social cognition, and metacognition as driving forces in intellectual performance. *Cognitive Science, 7*(4), 329–363.

Tinberg, H. (2015). Metacognition is not cognition. In L. Adler-Kassner & E. Wardle (Eds.), *Naming what we know: Threshold concepts of writing studies* (pp. 75–76). Logan, UT: Utah State University Press.

Tobin, L. & Newkirk, T. (Eds.). (1994). *Taking stock: The writing process movement in the 90s*. New York: Heinemann.

Trimbur, J. (1994). Taking the social turn: teaching writing post-process. *College Composition and Communication, 45*(1), 108–118.

Vipond, D. (1993). *Understanding writing and its teaching from the perspective of composition studies*. Westport, CT: Praeger.

Wardle, E. (2009). "Mutt genres" and the goal of FYC: Can we help students write the genres of the university? *College Composition and Communication, 60*(4), 765–789.

Wardle, E. & Downs, D. (2014). *Writing about writing: A college reader.* New York: Bedford/St. Martins.

Yancey, K. B., Robertson, L. & Taczak, K. (2014). *Writing across contexts: Transfer, composition, and sites of writing.* Logan, UT: Utah State University Press.

CHAPTER 3
ATTENDING TO PHENOMENOLOGY: RETHINKING COGNITION AND REFLECTION IN NORTH AMERICAN WRITING STUDIES

Dylan B. Dryer
University of Maine

David R. Russell
Iowa State University

As detailed elsewhere in this collection (esp. Bazerman; Carillo; Talbot), when North American Writing Studies of higher education and workplaces (henceforth, NAWS) turned to European continental philosophies, it turned away from information-processing (IP) cognitive theories. Those theories were early casualties of this "social-turn" (e.g., Bartholomae, 1985; Bizzell, 1982; Brand, 1987); today, NAWS seems somewhat squeamish about the fact that the brain is an organ with a broadly generalizable structure, predictable development, capacity constraints, operating costs, and so on. Yet cognitive research is a dynamic and thriving field that does not much resemble the after-image that persists in NAWS. Some of these changes in cognitive research have been driven by high-profile advances in laboratory methods, such as functional Magnetic Resonance Imaging (which monitors intensities of blood-flow as a proxy measure for specific areas of the brain that are engaged by a task), but other changes have been conceptual and thus largely invisible to NAWS.

To make these changes more visible, we first emphasize that NAWS and cognitive research on writing have both suffered from their estrangement. Second, we describe one of the most significant of these conceptual shifts: namely, research in phenomenology and neuro-phenomenology, which challenges IP cognitive constructs by positing embodied and enactive theories of neural functioning that are based on biological rather than cybernetic machine models. As will be seen, this research also challenges notions of "reflection" as currently valorized in NAWS. Third, we indicate how reconceiving reflection phenomenologically could help both NAWS and cognitive research on writing. Finally, we describe the pedagogical and curricular implications of phenomenological reflection for faculty seeking to responsibly operationalize national consensus documents like the WPA Outcomes Statement for First-Year Composition.

THE STATE OF THE FIELDS

Dueling caricatures hamper effective collaboration between NAWS and cognitive research. To transcend these caricatures, two points must be acknowledged: first, John R. Hayes was fair in saying that English departments (the institutional homes of most NAWS scholars) have an "unfortunate tendency to faddishness" (1996, p. 12). Yet these departments' discomfort was not just *au courant* mistrust of empiricism (Berkenkotter, 1989; Charney, 1996); NAWS was wary that a scientifically or pseudo-scientifically grounded determinism would explain away (or even attempt to erase) the socially produced differences among writers from different backgrounds that the field was learning to understand as *motivated*. At this point, NAWS has used poststructuralist critiques of linguistic transparency, substitutability, presence, and innocuity to investigate nearly every conceivable configuration of writer-identity, writer-task, writer-context, and writer-history. NAWS' sensitivity to the interpersonal, intertextual, intergeneric, and inter-situational complexities of writing events are at an extraordinary pitch. For instance, it is not typical in mainstream NAWS research (as it still is in cognitive research in the Hayes tradition) to speak of "writing ability," "writing quality," "the writing process" or "the writer" in any general sense. That is, decades of solid work uncovering the influences of genre and technological affordance on composing processes, the complications of language identity and inheritance in school (Berkenkotter, Huckin & Ackerman, 1988; Brodkey, 1994; Casanave, 1992) and workplace (Paré, 2002) composing tasks, and the complexities involved in any attempt to transfer writing practices among different contexts, have made such generalizations unsustainable.

However, having determined that writing is not simply an "in-head phenomenon" (Rowe, 2008, p. 410) NAWS hypercorrected by equating the sociality of writing with complete context-dependency (Blythe, 2016). For all its sensitivity to the contextual, NAWS seldom acknowledges the materiality and structure of the brain, closing itself off from developments in the cognitive sciences that might have usefully informed its deepening commitment to the cultivation of "reflective" writers. Anthologies or handbooks designed to introduce graduate students (e.g., Matsuda & Ritter, 2010; Vandenberg et al., 2006; Villanueva & Arola, 2011) or undergraduates (e.g., Downs & Wardle, 2014; Kinkead 2016) to NAWS seldom acknowledge cognitive research after the 1980s (but see Miller, 2009, pp. 1032–1048); in fact, we observe that even in this collection, references to Flower and Hayes (1981) and earlier abound, but no mention of Hayes' work since. NAWS has allowed itself to stop paying attention once "our" colleague left the partnership.

But cognitive science has continued to find writing an interestingly complex activity to study. Hayes, for one, is still at work refining construct-models of writing. In two substantial revisions (1996; 2012) to the model he and Flower advanced in 1980, Hayes integrated feedback loops to show that motivation, affect, and dispositions influence working and long-term memory and cognitive processes (1996, p. 4, Figure 1.3). Later he incorporated more prominent and specific roles for "task environment," including "transcribing technology" and "task materials" (2011, p. 371, Figure 2). These developments are entirely consistent with and could yet enrich the social-turn developments described above. For example, the construct of a limited "working memory" as a structural constraint for writers at early age or diminished experience levels retains considerable explanatory power for phenomena like the predictable lower-level skill-regression writers experience when encountering a new kind of composing task or composing technology.

Some traditions of inquiry not concerned with process modeling (i.e., those that test theories by manipulating variables like task-sequence, composing tool, or environmental condition) are oriented toward diagnostic and therapeutic agendas—isolating particular subroutines or brain functions, differentiating among types of learners and/or their abilities, impairments, difficulties, language affiliations or developmental stage. But others parallel recent interest in NAWS on motivation, intention, self-efficacy, and self-regulation—capacities that potentially bear on reflection. Barry J. Zimmerman and Rafael Risemberg (1997), whose names are usually associated with this tradition of research in cognition, appear to have arrived independently at the much greater weight Hayes assigned to "physical environment" and "social environment" a year earlier (1996, p. 4, Figure 1.3). As they find, "[m]otivational processes such as perceptions of self-efficacy and positive self-reactions during learning are as essential to setting effective writing goals and sustained achievement as cognitive measures of writing competence" (1997, p. 76). In a recent metastudy, Tanya Santangelo, Karen Harris, and Steve Graham (2016) confirm that explicit teaching of at least five of the ten self-regulation strategies that Zimmerman and Risemberg hypothesized—including approaches already widely endorsed in NAWS, such as prewriting to brainstorm and organize ideas—consistently produce positive measurable effects on the quality of student writing. Yet NAWS has been slow to take up empirical research in social and affective dimensions of cognition that might have helped it perceive and address development of writing abilities among its client populations (or even to help it better understand the causality behind certain practices it has long endorsed).

The second point that must be acknowledged is that much cognitive research on writing operates with impoverished constructs for text products. For instance, it is still common to find a measure of "text quality" designed as the dependent variable of interest, but no description of the specific traits that judges (also rarely identified) evaluated, or with what kind of scale. We know of only two studies that attempt to account for the effect of genre on any measure of text quality (Beauvais, Favart, Passerault & Beauvais, 2014; Olive, Favart, Beauvais & Beauvais, 2009). Revision remains predominantly locked in the stage-process paradigm (e.g., generation-production-review) that Flower and Hayes problematized 35 years ago, and editing remains conflated with "mistake detection" (e.g., Kellogg, 1996). Moreover, extrapolations from clinical/laboratory composing contexts are vulnerable to empirical challenge from NAWS' critical-cultural tradition. It seems unlikely, for instance, that the self-regulation strategies of a young woman of color whose schooling has trained her to distrust and demean the sound of her own "voice" will much resemble those of "Lynn" (Emig, 1971) or Flower and Hayes' "*Seventeen* magazine writer." Learning-disabled writers have been a consistent focus, but contemporary cognitive models have no way yet to account for influences like cultural trauma (Cushman, 2011), postcolonial composing contexts (Giltrow, 2003), or identity conflicts like stereotype threat (Schmader & Johns, 2003) and anxieties about assimilation (Ivanič, 1998). We share enthusiasm for the newly unobtrusive and affordable software applications that pair keystroke-logging, screen-capture data and even eye-movement, since such applications have begun to show us real-time enactment of the self-monitoring and resource-management strategies hypothesized in the late twentieth century. However, the conclusion of Huub van den Bergh, Gert Rijlaarsdam, and Elke van Steendam (2016) that at "different points in the writing process, different cognitive activities dominate the configuration" (p. 58) should remind us that the cognitive processes we can capture with these applications are responsive to environmental conditions such as genre, timing, history with task, and so on (Yancey, this volume, might call these effects the existence of "the prior" in the lab; Taczak and Robertson, "historical baggage").

Thus we find contradictions: while it continues to be an article of faith in the cognitive sciences that "efficiency" and "automaticity" of mental processes are universally desired ends (Flower & Hayes, 1980, p. 25; Kellogg & Whiteford, 2009, p. 251; Kellogg et al., 2013, pp. 162–163), NAWS seems determined to slow down and disrupt these processes (Cooper, 2011, p. 441; Mays & Jung, 2012, p. 55; Reiff & Bawarshi, 2011, pp. 331–332) to trigger metacognition and critical engagement. Meanwhile, its obliviousness to contemporary cognitive approaches to writing notwithstanding, mainstream NAWS remains ironically cognitivist in its current priorities, investing considerable pedagogical and curricular energies in "critical thinking," "genre awareness," "metacognition," and "reflection." In other words, NAWS wants to change the way we think about writing and help people understand how writing makes us think, but is not much interested in the specific mechanisms by which that thinking gets done. The unfortunate effects of this "crypto-cognitivism" are 1) that NAWS seldom informs these aims of critical thinking or reflection with what's known about motivation or self-regulation and 2) even now finds itself having to remind those attempting to incorporate reflection in their writing classrooms that reflective writing *itself* must be taught, practiced, and developed over time (Sommers, 2011; Ihara, 2014; Yancey, Roberston & Taczak, 2014, p. 4).

PHENOMENOLOGY AND REFLECTION

It is ironic that when composition "left" cognitive theories to IP cognitive psychology in the late 1980s, it left them for continental philosophy firmly in the tradition we emphasize here: the phenomenological tradition most closely associated with Maurice Merleau-Ponty (2014). Known as "the philosopher of the body," Merleau-Ponty's work has been a consistent, if largely unremarked, influence on NAWS. Unlike many of his students (Foucault and Bourdieu among them), he emphasized the positive aspects of agency—the existential human freedom of the subject. It is this version of continental theory that is gaining influence in cognitive science (Gallagher, 2012), providing an alternative to IP models in a way that is strikingly consistent with the expansive cultural-historical and embodied approaches to theorizing writing now in favor in NAWS itself. (For another alternative to the IP tradition, see Kristie Fleckenstein's provocative formulation of an "eco-cognitive" methodological orientation for NAWS (2012, pp. 86–97).)

In this section, we sketch a model of reflection that is on the one hand consistent with what we have learned from the last 35 years of social inquiry into composing processes and on the other hand, could contribute to a more robust construct of "writing" for cognitive research. NAWS currently sees reflection as a means to many ends: to help facilitate transfer, to help students avoid unknowing entrapment in dominant discourses; to preserve and respect linguistic difference; and, perhaps most frequently, as a means of assessing growth as a writer. To be sure, reflective writing as an institutional phenomenon—and in particular as an assessment phenomenon—has come under ideological critique from the perspective of ethics (Conway, 1994); genre (Bower, 2003;

Emmons, 2003) and subjectivity (Jung, 2011; Scott, 2005). We raise a different question here: less ideology than feasibility. Barbara Tomlinson (1984) raised still-unsettled questions about the limitations of what she called "retrospective accounts" of composing, and phenomenological cognitive research since then suggests that reflection is more of a post-hoc by-product of unconscious decision-making than a deliberative prelude to it (Freeman 2000; Kahneman, 2003). As such, we need to attend to work in cognition that suggests significant operational constraints on our ability to reflect, especially in contexts like compulsory writing classes. Put another way, we need a way to describe the cognition in reflection, and the phenomenological tradition can help us do this.

Marilyn Cooper (2011) redefines agency as "the process through which organisms create meanings through acting into the world and changing their structure in response to the perceived consequences of their actions," whether conscious or nonconscious (p. 426). Drawing on neurological research on what is termed "prereflective awareness," she explains that "we do not experience our intentions as causing our bodily movements," but we nevertheless can attribute the actions to our "own" agency (2011, p. 434). This reframing, we suggest, can be extended to reflection. The first principle is that there is a first-order pre- (or non-) reflective self-awareness, "primordial feelings," in Antonio Damasio's (2012) account, which result from nothing but the living body and precede any interaction between the machinery of life regulation and any object. Primordial feelings are based on the operation of upper-brain-stem nuclei, which are part and parcel of the life-regulation machinery. Primordial feelings are the primitives for all other feelings. (Damasio, 2012, p. 108)

A second-order, "reflective self" as Damasio calls it, is the narrative or autobiographical self, the self that takes into consideration past and future, planning and imagining, or in Damasio's words again, "the kind of consciousness illustrated by novels, films, and music and celebrated by philosophical reflection" (2012, p. 168). This "self" is what brain research has largely studied, in part because it is the most fully human self (we share primordial feelings with all animals), but also because the areas of the brain implicated in these activities are closest to the skull, where electrodes can monitor them most easily. But mounting research shows that the reflective self is not a separate add-on feature, but grows out of and is fully integrated with first-order self-awareness. The second is built on the first and cannot function without it. Each affects the other dynamically. As Sean Gallagher (2012) points out, this pre-reflective self-awareness "also includes a sense of agency—a sense that I am in control of my actions." We never ask, "someone is thinking this, who is it?" (Gallagher, 2012, p. 132).

Although the conscious reflective self sometimes overrides the non-conscious processing of meanings (Cooper's term) or images (Damasio's term), conscious reflection is seldom required for decisions nor is it typically the end-result of a sequence of conscious reasoning (though people can and do justify unconscious choices with retrospective reasoning [Kahneman, 2003; Lehrer, 2010]). Similarly, people are capable of a great deal of learning without conscious reflection on it. We need only engage in skillful coping, where "acting is experienced as a steady flow of skillful activity in response to one's sense of the situation" (Dreyfus, 2005, p. 378). In skillful coping, we focus on the intentional object (the chessboard, the road ahead, achieving the goal of the writing task), not our bodily movements or our process of reasoning or our cognitive states—unless there is an interruption, a breakdown, a need to consciously reflect. This "feedback loop between the learner and the perceived world" (Dreyfus, 2005 p. 132) is what Merleau-Ponty calls "the intentional arc," and one monitors—always unconsciously but sometimes also consciously—one's movement along this arc. This is what Merleau-Ponty (in Dreyfus' 2005 formulation) describes as "next step" monitoring of progress. In order to act, we do not need to have a final goal "in mind" or a mental representation of the action. We only need to move, in a way motivated by our sense of direction, and monitor whether that movement seems to feel as if we're going in the right direction, in coordination with others (though not in lockstep imitation or even agreement). It is not a matter of matching behavior to a goal, but weighing whether and how much one's behavior moves one along one's "intentional arc." It is only novices or those with cognitive impairments who must reflect on their process in order to accomplish it—who "need to think about" engaging the clutch in driving, or forming letters and words.

This "ideomotor" theory rejects the separation of perception and action. Humans, like animals, have what William James theorized as "common coding" (Prinz, 1990). We perceive and respond integrally as we engage with the world (Downey, 2010), or as Merleau-Ponty puts it, we are "geared" to the world. Recent research on imitation shows that much of our action and learning (development of habits of engagement with the world) is based not on stepwise or algorithmic processes, on the model of a computer, but rather on imitation, mimesis. Neurobiology has provided much support for this view with the discovery in the 1990s of "mirror neurons," which are engaged both when we perform an action and when we see it being performed (see Remley; Talbot, this volume). IP cognitive theory's postulation (Fodor, 1975) of "a language of thought" that intervenes between perception and action through a separate level of mental representations proves unnecessary. In the phenomenological view, what the IP tradition would consider "task definition" would be called "perception"—a more foundational construct than language or thought. We perceive the world in order to respond to it, in writing as in any other way. But, crucially, we respond to the world in order to perceive it. Perception, such as our perception of situations that might require writing (exigence or genre perception), has an intentional arc set against a background of motivated action. And those motives, that direction, are always already social. Any definition of task includes the cultural frames of reference by which we come to understand certain things (and not others) as tasks to be defined (this was Bartholomae's influential critique (1985)), as well as our own near and distant histories with the language, relevant genres, and seemingly similar contexts laminated into our responses.

This conflation of perception and action does *not* mean that conscious reflection has no role in mimetic learning. As Greg Downey (2010) points out, even in forms of physical education (e.g., sports, dance) teachers/coaches "scaffold" students' imitation with sophisticated techniques that draw students' conscious attention to mimesis, and the same might be said of musical performance, touch typing, or writing (as in the complex mimesis that is paraphrase). What it *does* mean is that learning to perform some action—including writing—is always a combination of conscious and nonconscious learning, and that the substantial roles played by proximity to others, shared tools and physical contexts, affective states, etc., in this learning are largely unavailable for detached scrutiny—at least not without years of training in such detachment. We need not decompose analytically and reflect on each component of performance to learn to perform, even at the initial stages of learning. We only have to have a sense of the next step, within the horizon of attention both before and behind us.

As Alfred North Whitehead (1920) posited nearly a century ago, "what we perceive as present is the vivid fringe of memory tinged with anticipation" (p. 73). In this light, when van den Bergh et al. (2016) concede that the precise nature, location and function of what has been variously called the "monitor," the "central executive," and the "control level" (p. 68)—that is, the "master" cognitive function that apportions attentional resources to specific subroutines—have been quite difficult to pin down, we could respond in two ways. We could conclude that this difficulty indicates gaps in existing models that need filling, or we could conclude that what's needed is a more expansive operating construct of "consciousness."

REFLECTION, COGNITION AND COMPOSITION: A NEUROPHENOMENOLOGICAL CONVERGENCE

Having sketched a phenomenological account of reflection to complement Cooper's (2011) account of agency, we disaggregate several different understandings of reflection (though often used interchangeably) from two that emerge from phenomenology. We can start with dictionary definitions: reflection as serious thought, consideration, or deliberation—serious in the sense of an atypically systematic or analytic approach to a problem. This remains the definition that obtains in machine modeling, as suggested by the formal "cogitation" or "cognition" on problem-solving (Flower & Hayes, 1977). It is also worth noting the literature on embodied decision-making from studies of neural responses to economic choices (Kahneman, 2003; Lehrer, 2010), and a budding field of neurorhetoric. Both fields point strongly to the pre-conscious and emotive bases of decision-making, and the retrospective dimensions of conscious deliberation.

These understandings we distinguish from "critical reflection," which has a long history in educational theory and research, especially in teacher education, and which originates from John Dewey's (1993) view of teachers (and students) as agents of progressive change in schools and society. To do so they must be, Dewey wrote, open-minded, responsible, and wholehearted (that is, courageous and persistent in the face of adversity). A long tradition of theorizing various stages or levels or kinds of reflection is summarized by Deborah Yost, Sally M. Sentner, and Anna Forlenza-Bailey (2000). Much of composition's view of critical reflection lies in this tradition, whether explicitly acknowledged or not, in terms of its value for transfer, for social consciousness and critique, and so on. But it is important to note that *composing* reflections has been especially important here as a key pedagogical technique in teacher education. This technique is also frequently applied in professional education; in business and technical communication, for instance, students in internships are assumed to develop professional skill and identity through reflective writing. This assumption was theorized in a very influential way by Donald Schön in the 1980s, and his formulation of the "reflective practitioner" (1987) has guided theory and research not only in professional education but also in management and organizational communication, where it has been expanded beyond the individual to a plural "reflective organization" (Gray, 2007).

A fourth understanding, metacognition or "thinking about thinking," has been substantially investigated in psychology departments, some of which comes from IP cognitive psychology, some from different traditions. Closely related to this is a two-decade-old tradition of research on "social metacognition," which is pursued in social psychology, especially branches influenced by cognitive psychology. This research examines people's "complex determinations about the reliability of our own thoughts, feelings, and beliefs as well as attributions about the thoughts, feelings, and beliefs of others around us" (Jost, Kruglanski & Nelson, 1998, p. 137). Several lines of inquiry here speak to issues that have become recently visible in composition research: people's thoughts about their past and future in personal development; people's formation of cultural attitudes; the formation and reformation of stereotypes, prejudice, and bias; as well as issues important to professional communication and cultural theory, such as metacognition in teams and organizations, and in consumer choice (Briñol & DeMarree, 2012).

Those four ways of conceptualizing "reflection" are instructive to compare with two distinctly different understandings of reflection that emerge from phenomenological traditions: mindfulness and *neuro*phenomenology. The first, cultivation of contemplation, meditation, or mindfulness in writing, dates back almost to the founding of the field. Sondra Perl published "Understanding Composing," an alternative theory of the writing process based on the work of Eugene Gendlin (1982), a humanist psychologist and philosopher who was an important U.S. exponent of Merleau-Ponty's phenomenology of the body. Perl (1980) adapted Gendlin's therapeutic techniques of body awareness to analyzing what we would call today the socio-cognitive processes of writing. In that same decade, James Moffett explored yoga as a pedagogy (1982), and Peter Elbow (1989) investigated the phenomenology of freewriting. Perl took up this work again in 2004 with *Felt Sense*, writing exercises based on the principle of phenomenological bracketing, of becoming aware of one's intentional arc and monitoring one's feelings to know—or rather feel—what the next step is. Again, reflection is not something that is set apart in time or space from the writing processes. It is integrated, moment by moment, into the process (e.g., van Manen, 1990). Contemplative practices such as mindfulness and yoga have begun to be developed and studied empirically (both qualitatively and quantitatively) in a number of fields, most notably Mathematics and Physical Education and a pedagogical literature has begun developing in NAWS (Rifenburg, 2014; Walker, 2015; Wenger, 2015).

Neurophenomenology, however, comes from the legacy of Alexander Luria, the greatest of Vygotsky's collaborators. As he and his colleagues put it, "to understand the brain foundations for psychological activity, one must be prepared to study both the brain and the system of activity" (Luria et al., 1979, p. 173). Psychologists pursuing this legacy have used introspective methods, including phenomenology, to understand the structure of the neural system. They have used phenomenological description—the description of one's own mental phenomena "bracketed off" from immediate action—in conjunction with neural imaging to produce "neuro-phenomenology," a term coined in the mid-1990s by the Chilean cognitive neuroscientist Francisco Varela (1996). The goal of neurophenomenology is to use first-person phenomenological description to expand and enrich third person accounts drawn from the experimental methods of neuroscience and vice versa (Gallagher, 2012, pp. 36–37, 107–108). The classic study is of Nepalese monks who reported that their meditation practice increased their "clarity" (see Thompson, 2007). Neuroscientists intrigued by the monks' first-person reports attached electrodes and measured their brain activity (third-person scientific description), while at the same time asking them to rank their feelings of clarity on a Likert scale before, during, and after the episodes of meditation where they reported "clarity" (first-person phenomenological description). Novice monks formed a control group. Experienced monks' ratings of "clarity" corresponded with increases in high amplitude gamma synchrony as compared with the novices. Thompson points out that not only do the self-reports show these things are "really going on," but without the phenomenological self-report data, the changes in gamma synchrony would just be "noise" in the data to the neuroscientists. Further, the bridging of first and third person perspectives shows that cultural differences in the ways people live their lives (in this case highly trained mental states) involve specific neural/somatic differences. Similar neurophenomenological studies have been undertaken in a range of areas, most notably pain management.

In this view, the brain is not best understood, in Marvin Minsky's words, as a "computer made out of meat," manipulating internal symbols in order to solve exterior problems out in the world (as cited in Hall, 2013, p. 22). Where machine/computer models understand writing as the transcription of inner speech or thought into external inscription, emerging models of cognition are biological, understanding cognition as an attribute of all animals—only developed in humans to the point that they are capable of that kind of tool-use known as writing. As Rafael Núñez, Laurie Edwards, and João Filipe Matos (1999) describe this paradigm in their seminal discussion of embodied cognition in mathematics education: "cognition is about enacting or bringing forth *adaptive* and effective behavior, not about acquiring information or representing objects in an external world" (p. 49, emphasis added). The concept of "adaptation" is also crucial to Cooper's reframing of rhetorical agency, discussed above, which—not coincidentally—also draws on neurophenomenological research (2011, pp. 426–427).

Neurophenomenology may provide a new way of looking at reflection in writing and on writing, both as a method of research investigation and, perhaps, as a method of improving writing processes (although it should be acknowledged that as of this writing, most of these studies examine effects at the level of word-choice or sentence-revision tasks on very specific populations, which limits their usefulness for broad theorizing (e.g., dysgraphics or dyslexics v. "normal" writers or readers; writers of alphabets v. ideograms, and so on). This limitation reflects the need for feasibly controllable study-design, although it also reflects assumptions in the cognitive sciences about what "writing" is. We await studies over a longer timespan with the same group of writers, which might help us monitor developing genre knowledge as evidenced by increasingly efficient orchestration routines in the brain. We also imagine that traditional methods such as document-based interviews, screencasting, probes during writing, etc. might be combined with clinical methods of brain imaging to address questions of how structures of attention (viz., short-term memory) are managed with and without conscious reflection, how anxiety is managed, with implications for writer's block, how multi-modal genre features are perceived and managed, among a range of other presssing topics.

This quick survey of approaches to "reflection" in NAWS is intended to show the wide range of understandings of reflection in the field, to point up the need for greater clarity in discussions of reflection in writing, and to suggest that (neuro)phenomenology may offer an account of it that is compatible with but goes beyond IP accounts. Moreover, neurophenomenology and embodied cognition can be seen as picking up phenomenological strands of writing processes theory and pedagogy that have been part of NAWS just as long as IP cognitive writing process theory has, though far less developed as an empirical research program. What is clear is that the complex cognitive activities that NAWS calls "reflection" involve socially and historically distributed mental processes, are necessarily diffuse and ill-defined, and even when these processes are most deliberate and purposeful, they are applied to a (re)construction of equally diffuse and ill-defined moments in a writer's past. NAWS is beginning to acknowledge that "reflection" is not usefully understood as a final step in "the" writing process. The elaborate scaffolding for thinking-about-thinking or thinking-about-feeling some contributors describe elsewhere in this collection (e.g., Khost; Reid; Winslow & Shaw) are one way to glimpse the significant *obstacles* to reflection in the short-term physical and social environment of a compulsory class on "writing"—relative, to make a pointed comparison, to the physical and social contexts in which the Nepalese monk-adepts achieved their states of "clarity" (see also Mays & Jung, 2012, p. 55).

IMPLICATIONS

If the mind is a function of the body's (including the brain) material engagement with the rest of the material world—a world that includes other human bodies and minds—cognition, like language itself, is intersubjective. Writing is always already intersubjectively engaged with others even when physically or temporally separated (a separation which writing crucially affords). While it is certainly true that writing allows us to engage with (cope with and shape) the non-human material world through cultural artifacts, it is also true that we write with our bodies, literally engaging with physical tools, writing instruments and surfaces, cobbling together writing routines and abilities we need from available materials and neural substrates for motor control, depth perception, and language processing systems (Bazerman, 2013, p. 60). Such tools and surfaces, as activity theorists have long pointed out, "distribute" our cognition beyond the skull and among the instruments that help us expand our capacities. Yet our cognition appears to be shared among other bodies as well: in a womb, the mother-child heartbeats synchronize; in a room, interlocutors perceive each other's bodies (motion, sound, smell, and sometimes touch or taste—e.g., in a kiss). When writing with others physically present (i.e., the phenomenon of "coworking" Pigg, 2014; Spinuzzi, 2011), this is literally true, but even when a writer is alone, others' physical/sensory dimensions are present, and a writer's body responds emotionally and physiologically (for example, with writing anxiety or avoidance—see Reid, this volume). Thus, a full account of writing would acknowledge that we think *with* our bodies: the nervous system is tied to the endocrine system, both in our heads and throughout our bodies, fusing the electrical and chemical. These electrochemical processes are tied in complex feedback loops to other systems: circulatory, muscular/skeletal, and so on. It would also extend beyond subpersonal processes to suprapersonal processes: the social and material participation of writers in the world, well beyond the skin barrier and backward and forward in time.

Summing up a substantial tradition of research on genre in NAWS, which is largely—though seldom acknowledged as such—underpinned by Alfred Schutz's concept of typification (Schutz & Luckmann, 1989), Bazerman (2009) hypothesized that the language affordances of established textual forms position readers and writers in "defined problem spaces" that at once define the task as well as suggest tools for its completion (p. 136). Structured encounters with problem spaces defined by fields and professions refigure cognition. The neural legacies of these encounters are what we experience as "learning": how to define problems or tasks as "problems" or "tasks" in the first place and how we acquire the ability to accept and reject potential solutions and means of working toward them. What "cognitive reconfiguration" in the Vygotskian tradition brings is a focus on development over time, but not simply development of writing abilities (which has been the emphasis of IP cognitive psychology), but also the development of productive engagement—agentive participation—in a course, discipline, profession, or any social practice. What we emphasize here is that cognitive reconfiguration links brain and body and society—the biological and the cultural.

Negretti (2012) and Bazerman et al. (2013; 2014) have found evidence suggesting that cognitive development can be scaffolded and traced in this way. It is important to note that these studies used students' writing as a way to both harness and to measure metacognitive growth and that all three are longitudinal studies that take time as a salient independent variable and examine lexical and intertextual formations in students' writing as data in its own right, not as a source of students' claims about what they learned. That is, NAWS has historically looked at reflective writing as evidence that the student has become reflective, but these studies use writing as evidence of the development toward a future state—linguistic evidence of growth of which the student may not (or not yet) be fully aware in any explicit sense. By putting the onus on careful curricular creation of problem spaces (see also Yancey, Robertson & Taczak's "critical incident" model, 2014, pp. 120–128), cognitive refiguration sees reflectiveness as less a pedagogical intention and more an experiential effect.

Teachers, administrators and researchers who would benefit from external support for such curricular reenvisioning can find it in national consensus documents like the *Framework for Success in Postsecondary Writing* (2011) and the Council of Writing Program Administrators' Outcomes Statement for First-Year Composition (2014) both of which invite teaching and research faculty to conceptualize writing as much more than an "in-head" phenomenon. The original Statement, first published in 1999, uses a distinctly command-and-control set of verbs to describe the optimal experience of composition students: "focus," "use," "respond," "learn to," "adopt," "understand," "control" (2001, pp. 323–325). The revision distinctly recharacterizes first-year composition as an opportunity-space in which students can "develop facility," "gain experience," "develop flexible strategies," "explore . . . concepts," "practice applying" and "developing knowledge . . . through practice" (for an account of these revisions, see Dryer et al., 2014, pp. 136–143).

Faculty across the disciplines benefit from workshops in which they can compare the original and revised versions of the Statement (starting with the first line, which pointedly replaces "skills" with "practices" (Dryer et al., 2014, p. 142). While engaging these changes leads to better, more informed conversations about issues of curriculum design, we also observe that—likely because the new language frames writing in college as a matter of *experiences with new practices* and not as a set of skills to be learned—many faculty begin to recover a sense of the difficulties and pleasures involved in those experiences. Although "reflection" does not appear in the original Statement (an artifact of a moment in time before Yancey's pioneering efforts (1998) began to be fully felt) we find it situated in the discussion of "Processes" in the 2014 version, where it is proposed that students should "reflect on the development of composing practices and how those practices influence their work" (Dryer et al., p. 145). This is conscious—mindful—reflection on their experiences and practices, including changes in those routines, and the effects of these changes *on* a task and *in a context*. We see these changes as invitations to position the documents—and our teaching practices and traditions—in the phenomenological and neurophenomenological tradition, where brain and body and society all write and are written.

In this light, dueling caricatures begin to dissolve: "critical awareness" versus "automaticity" (or "individual development" versus "social change") is revealed to be a false dilemma. When we ask students to attend to problem spaces and the tools that seem available to bring to bear on them, we are working with their cognition and their sociality in a way that is construct-compatible with the understanding of "the present" that emerges from re-reading the phenomenological tradition. If consciousness is distributed, both laterally among artifacts, our entire bodies, and other humans as well as longitudinally across the extended timeframe we perceive as "the now," then the object or focus of any particular act of reflection becomes accordingly much more complex. Materiality, language affiliation, geography, race, class, embodiment, all become more available for consideration by NAWS and cognitive science alike. We look forward to the work ahead.

REFERENCES

Bartholomae, D. (1985). Inventing the university. In M. Rose (Ed.), *When a writer can't write: Studies in writer's block and other composing-process problems* (pp. 134–165), New York: Guilford Press.

Bazerman, C. (2009). Genre and cognitive development: Beyond writing to learn. In C. Bazerman, A. Bonini & D. Figueiredo (Eds.), *Genre in a changing world* (pp. 279–294). Fort Collins, CO: The WAC Clearinghouse and Parlor Press. Retrieved from https://wac.colostate.edu/books/genre/.

Bazerman, C. (2013). Meaning, consciousness, and activity: Luria. *A theory of literate action, Vol. II.* (pp. 56–62). Fort Collins, CO: The WAC Clearinghouse and Parlor Press. https://wac.colostate.edu/books/literateaction/v2.

Bazerman, C., Simon, K., Ewing, P. & Pieng, P. (2013). Domain-specific cognitive development through written genres in a teacher education program. *Pragmatics & Cognition, 21*(3), 530–551.

Bazerman, C., Simon, K. & Pieng, P. (2014). Writing about reading to advance thinking: A study in situated cognitive development. In G. Rijlaarsdam (Series Ed.) & P. D. Klein, P. Boscolo, L. C. Kirkpatrick & C. Gelati (Vol. Eds.), *Studies in writing: Vol. 28, Writing as a learning activity* (pp. 249–276). Leiden: Brill. (Retrieved from ProQuest ebrary.)

Beauvais, L., Favart M., Passerault J-M. & Beauvais C. (2014). Temporal management of the writing process: Effects of genre and organizing constraints in grades 5, 7, and 9. *Written Communication, 31*(3), 251–279.

Berkenkotter, C. (1989). The legacy of positivism in empirical composition research. *Journal of Advanced Composition, 9*(1), 269–282.

Berkenkotter, C., Huckin, T. & Ackerman, J. (1988). Conventions, conversations, and the writer: Case study of a student in a rhetoric Ph.D. program. *Research in the Teaching of English, 22*(1), 9–44.

Bizzell, P. (1982). Cognition, convention, and certainty: What we need to know about writing. *Pre/Text 3*(3), 213–243.

Blythe, S. (2016). Attending to the subject in writing transfer and adaptation. In C. M. Anson & J. L. Moore (Eds.), *Critical transitions: Writing and the question of transfer* (pp. 49–68). Fort Collins, CO: The WAC Clearinghouse and University Press of Colorado. Retrieved from https://wac.colostate.edu/books/ansonmoore/.

Bower, L. L. (2003). Student reflection and critical thinking: A rhetorical analysis of 88 portfolio cover letters. *Journal of Basic Writing, 22*(2), 47–66.

Brand, A. G. (1987). The why of cognition: Emotion and the writing process. *College Composition and Communication, 38*(4), 436–443.

Briñol, P. & DeMarree, K. G. (2012). *Social metacognition*. New York: Psychology Press.

Brodkey, L. (1994). Writing on the bias. *College English, 56*(5), 527–547.

Casanave, C. P. (1992). Cultural diversity and socialization: A case study of a Hispanic woman in a doctoral program in sociology. In D. E. Murray (Ed.), *Diversity as resource: Redefining cultural literacy* (pp. 148–182). Alexandria, VA: TESOL.

Charney, D. (1996). Empiricism is not a four-letter word. *College Composition and Communication, 47*(4), 567–593.

Conway, G. (1994). Portfolio cover letters, students' self-presentation, and teachers' ethics. In L. Black, D. A. Daiker, J. Sommers & G. Stygall (Eds.), *New directions in portfolio assessment: Reflective practice, critical theory, and large-scale scoring* (pp. 83–92). Portsmouth, NH: Boynton/Cook.

Cooper, M. M. (2011). Rhetorical agency as emergent and enacted. *College Composition and Communication, 62*(3), 420–449.

Cushman. E. (2011). The Cherokee syllabary: A writing system in its own right. *Written Communication, 28*(3), 255–281.

Damasio, A. (2012). *Self comes to mind: Constructing the conscious brain*. New York: Vintage.

Dewey, J. (1933). *How we think: A restatement of the relation of reflective thinking to the educative process*. New York: D. C. Heath and Company.

Downey, G. (2010). "Practice without theory": A neuroanthropological perspective on embodied learning. *Journal of the Royal Anthropological Institute, 16*(s1), S22-S40.

Dreyfus, H. (2005). Merleau-Ponty and recent cognitive science. In T. Carman & M. B. N. Hansen (Eds.), *The Cambridge Companion to Merleau-Ponty* (pp. 129–150). Cambridge University Press.

Dryer, D. B., Bowden, D., Brunk-Chavez, B., Harrington, S., Halbritter, B. & Yancey, K. B. (2014). Revising FYC outcomes for a multimodal, digitally composed world: The WPA outcomes statement for first-year composition (version 3.0) *WPA: Writing Program Administration, 38*(1), 32–51.

Elbow, P. (1989). Toward a phenomenology of freewriting. *Journal of Basic Writing, 8*(2), 42–71.

Emig, J. (1971). *The composing processes of twelfth graders.* Urbana, IL: National Council of Teachers of English Research Report #13.

Emmons, K. (2003). Rethinking genres of reflection: Student portfolio cover letters and the narrative of progress. *Composition Studies, 31*(1), 43–62.

Fleckenstein, K. (2012). Reclaiming the mind: Eco-cognitive research in writing studies. In L. Nickoson & M. P. Sheridan (Eds.), *Writing studies research in practice: Methods and methodologies* (pp. 86–97). Carbondale, IL: Southern Illinois University Press.

Flower, L. & Hayes, J. R. (1977). Problem-solving strategies and the writing process. *College English, 39*(4), 449–461.

Flower, L. & Hayes, J. R. (1980). The cognition of discovery: Defining a rhetorical problem. *College Composition and Communication, 31*(1), 21–32.

Flower, L. & Hayes, J. R. (1981). A cognitive process theory of writing. *College Composition and Communication, 32*(4), 365–387.

Fodor, J. A. (1975). *The language of thought.* (Vol. 5). Cambridge, MA: Harvard University Press.

Freeman, W. J. (2000). *How brains make up their minds.* New York: Columbia Press.

Gallagher, S. (2012). *Phenomenology.* New York: Palgrave Macmillan.

Gallagher, S. & Schmicking, D. (2010). *Handbook of phenomenology and cognitive science.* New York: Springer.

Gendlin, E. T. (1982). *Focusing.* New York: Bantam.

Giltrow, J. (2003). Legends of the center: System, self, and linguistic consciousness. In C. Bazerman & D. R. Russell (Eds.), *Writing selves/writing societies* (pp. 363–392). Fort Collins, CO: The WAC Clearinghouse. Retrieved from https://wac.colostate.edu/books/selves_societies/.

Gray, D. E. (2007). Facilitating management learning developing critical reflection through reflective tools. *Management Learning, 38*(5), 495–517.

Hall, G. M. (2013). *The ingenious mind of nature: Deciphering the patterns of man, society, and the universe.* New York: Springer.

Hayes, J. R. (1996). A new framework for understanding cognition and affect in writing. In C. M. Levy & S. Ransdell (Eds.), *The science of writing: Theories, methods, individual differences, and applications* (pp. 1–28). Mahwah, NJ: Lawrence Erlbaum.

Hayes, J. R. (2012). Modeling and remodeling writing. *Written Communication, 29*(3), 369–388.

Hayes, J. & Flower, L. (1980). The dynamics of composing: Making plans and juggling constraints. In L. Gregg & E. R. Steinberg (Eds.), *Cognitive processes in writing* (pp. 31–50). Mahwah, NJ: Lawrence Erlbaum.

Ihara, R. (2014). Student perspectives on self-assessment: Insights and implications. *Teaching English in the Two-Year College, 40*(3), 223–258.

Ivanič, R. (1998). *Writing and identity: The discoursal construction of identity in academic writing.* Amsterdam: John Benjamins Publishing Co.

Jost, J. T., Kruglanski, A. W. & Nelson, T. O. (1998). Social metacognition: an expansionist review. *Personality and Social Psychology Review, 2*(2), 137–154.

Jung, J. (2011). Reflective writing's synecdochic imperative: Process descriptions redescribed. *College English, 73*(6), 628–647.

Kahneman, D. (2003). Maps of bounded rationality: Psychology for behavioral economics. *The American Economic Review, 93*(5), 1449–1475.

Kinkead, J. (2016). *Researching writing: An introduction to research methods.* Logan, UT: Utah State University Press.

Kellogg, R. T. (1996). A model of working memory in writing. In C. M. Levy & S. Ransdell (Eds.), *The science of writing: Theories, methods, individual differences, and applications* (pp. 75–71). Mahwah, NJ: Lawrence Erlbaum.

Kellogg, R. T. & Whiteford, A. P. (2009). Teaching advanced writing skills: The case for deliberate practice. *Educational Psychologist, 44*(1), 250–266.

Kellogg, R. T., Whiteford, A. P., Turner, C. E., Cahill, M. & Mertens, A. (2013). Working memory in written composition: An evaluation of the 1996 model. *Journal of Writing Research, 5*(2), 159–190.

Lehrer, J. (2010). *How we decide.* Boston: Houghton Mifflin Harcourt.

Luria, A. R., Cole, S. & Cole, M. (1979). *The making of mind: A personal account of Soviet psychology.* Cambridge, MA: Harvard University Press.

Mays, C. & Jung, J. (2012). Priming terministic inquiry: Toward a methodology of neurorhetoric. *Rhetoric Review, 31*(1), 41–59.

Merleau-Ponty, M. (2014). *Phenomenology of perception* (D. A. Landes, Trans.). London/New York: Routledge.

Miller, S. (2009). *The Norton book of composition studies.* New York: Norton.

Moffett, J. (1982). Writing, inner speech, and meditation. *College English, 44*(3), 231–246.

Negretti, R. (2012). Metacognition in student academic writing: A longitudinal study of metacognitive awareness and its relation to task perception, self-regulation, and evaluation of performance. *Written Communication, 29*(2), 142–179.

Núñez, R. E., Edwards, L. D. & Matos, J. F. (1999). Embodied cognition as grounding for situatedness and context in mathematics education. *Educational Studies in Mathematics, 39*(1–3), 45–65.

Olive, T., Favart, M., Beauvais, C. & Beauvais, L. (2009). Children's cognitive effort and fluency in writing: Effects of genre and of handwriting automatization. *Learning and Instruction, 19*(4), 299–308.

Paré, A. (2002). Genre and identity: Individuals, institutions, and ideology. In R. Coe, L. Lindgard & T. Teslenko (Eds.), *The rhetoric and ideology of genre* (pp. 57–71). Cresskill, NJ: Hampton.

Perl, S. (1980). Understanding composing. *College Composition and Communication, 31*(4), 363–370.

Perl, S. (2004). *Felt sense: Writing with the body.* Portsmouth: Boynton/Cook.

Pigg, S. (2014). Emplacing mobile composing habits: A study of academic writing in networked social spaces. *College Composition and Communication, 66*(2), 250–275.

Prinz, W. (1990). *A common coding approach to perception and action.* New York: Springer.

Reiff, M. J. & Bawarshi, A. (2011). Tracing discursive resources: How students use prior genre knowledge to negotiate new writing contexts in first-year composition. *Written Communication, 28*(3), 312–337.

Rifenburg, J. M. (2014). Writing as embodied, college football plays as embodied: Extracurricular multimodal composing. *Composition Forum 29*. Retrieved from http://compositionforum.com/issue/29/writing-as-embodied.php.

Ritter, K. & Matsuda, P. K. (2010). *Exploring composition studies: Sites, issues, perspectives*. Logan, UT: Utah State University Press.

Rowe, D. W. (2008). Development of writing abilities in childhood. In C. Bazerman (Ed.), *Handbook of research on writing* (pp. 401–419). Mahwah, NJ: Lawrence Erlbaum.

Santangelo, T., Harris, K. R. & Graham, S. (2016). Self-regulation and writing: Meta-analysis of the self-regulation processes in Zimmerman and Risemberg's model. In C. A. MacArthur, S. Graham & J. Fitzgerald (Eds.), *Handbook of writing research* (2nd ed.) (pp. 174–193). New York: Guilford Press.

Schmader, T. & Johns, M. (2003). Converging evidence that stereotype threat reduces working memory capacity. *Journal of Personality and Social Psychology, 85*(3), 440–452.

Schön, D. (1987). *Educating the Reflective Practitioner*. San Francisco: JoseyBass.

Schutz, A. & Luckmann, T. (1989). Structures of the life-world (Vol. I). (R. M. Zaner & H. T. Engelhardt Jr., Trans.). Evanston, IL: Northwestern University Press. [1983].

Scott, T. (2005). Creating the subject of portfolios: Reflective writing and the conveyance of institutional prerogatives. *Written Communication, 22*(1), 3–35.

Sommers, J. (2011). Reflection revisited: The class collage. *Journal of Basic Writing 30*(1), 99–129.

Spinuzzi, C. (2011). Working alone together: Coworking as emergent collaborative activity. *Journal of Business and Technical Communication, 26*(4), 399–441.

Thompson, E. (2007). Mind in life: Biology, phenomenology, and the sciences of mind. Cambridge, MA: Harvard University Press.

Tomlinson, B. (1984). Talking about the composing process: The limitations of retrospective accounts. *Written Communication, 1*(4), 429–445.

Vandenberg, P., Hum, S. & Clary-Lemon, J. (2006). *Relations, locations, positions: Composition theory for writing teachers*. Urbana, IL: National Council of Teachers of English.

Van den Bergh, H., Rijlaarsdam, G. & van Steendam, E. (2016). Writing process theory: A functional dynamic approach. In C. A. MacArthur, S. Graham & J. Fitzgerald (Eds.), *Handbook of writing research* (2nd ed.) (pp. 57–71). New York: Guilford Press.

Van Manen, M. (1990). *Researching lived experience: Human science for an action sensitive pedagogy*. New York: State University of New York Press.

Varela, F. J. (1996). Neurophenomenology: A methodological remedy for the hard problem. *Journal of Consciousness Studies, 3*, 330–350.

Villanueva, V. & Arola K. (2011). *Cross-talk in comp theory: A Reader* (3rd ed.). Urbana, IL: National Council of Teachers of English.

Walker, C. (2015). Composing agency: Theorizing the readiness potentials of literacy practices. *Literacy in Composition Studies, 3*(2), 1–21.

Wardle, E. & Downs, D. (2014). *Writing about writing: A college reader.* New York: Bedford/St. Martin's.

Wenger, C. I. (2015). *Yoga minds, writing bodies: Contemplative writing pedagogy.* Perspectives on Writing. Fort Collins, CO: The WAC Clearinghouse and Parlor Press. Retrieved from https://wac.colostate.edu/books/wenger/.

Whitehead, A. N. (1920). *The concept of nature.* Cambridge, UK: Cambridge University Press.

Writing Program Administrators. WPA outcomes statement for first-year composition. (Revisions adopted July 17, 2014). *WPA: Journal of the Council of Writing Program Administrators, 38*(1), 142–146.

Yancey, K. B. (1998). *Reflection in the writing classroom.* Logan, UT: Utah State University Press.

Yancey, K. B., Robertson, L. & Taczak, K. (2014). *Writing across contexts: Transfer, composition, and sites of writing.* Logan, UT: Utah State University Press.

Yost, D. S., Sentner, S. M. & Forlenza-Bailey, A. (2000). An examination of the construct of critical reflection: Implications for teacher education programming in the 21st century. *Journal of Teacher Education, 51*(1), 39–49.

Zimmerman, B. J. & Risemberg, R. (1997). Becoming a self-regulated writer: A social cognitive perspective. *Contemporary Educational Psychology, 22,* 73–101.

SECTION II: RECONSIDERING APPROACHES TO TEACHING AND LEARNING

CHAPTER 4
NEUROSCIENCE OF READING: DEVELOPING EXPERTISE IN READING AND WRITING

Alice S. Horning
Oakland University

In the opening of *The Shallows: What the Internet Is Doing to Our Brains*, author Nicholas Carr (2011) invokes the film *2001: A Space Odyssey*, describing astronaut Dave's dismantling of Hal's brain, and Hal's complaint that his mind is going. Carr says he himself feels this way, feels that his mind is going as a by-product of the time he spends online. In the discussion that follows, Carr specifically talks about what is happening to his reading and his ability to pay attention to text for an extended period of time. A similar description arises in a more recent book, *A Deadly Wandering* (Richtel, 2014), reporting on a fatal traffic accident in Utah that happened while a young man was texting while driving. The point of these publications is that we are increasingly distracted, increasingly unable to pay attention to anything for an extended period of time. This research explores the impact of online behavior on attention and distraction when we interact with texts; understanding these and other findings with respect to reading from a cognitive perspective has useful implications for the teaching and learning of writing.

This chapter will first discuss the relevance of reading research for writing; Ellen Carillo's (2015) work shows that the two have been separated far too long even though most scholars and writing teachers agree that they are related processes. Both processes suffer when we are distracted, particularly as we try to learn new skills. According to a Pew study done in 2012 surveying high school advanced placement teachers and those who participated in the National Writing Project, almost 90% of teachers see students' distraction by technology as a problem in terms of their reading, research and writing (Purcell et al., 2012). Then, the chapter will discuss key studies on reading which reveal the cognitive and psycholinguistic features of the process. This material includes, among others, Stanislas Dehaene's (2009) report showing how the brain works during reading along with studies using MRI and fMRI to reveal the kinds of cognitive processing people engage in during reading. Work by Yellowlees Douglas (2015) and Naomi Baron (2015), supports Dehaene's findings. Additional research comes from the use of eye-tracking technology to see what readers actually do with text. Particularly revealing studies show how students read in the course of peer review. Work by Chris Anson and Robert Schwegler (2012) shows what students do when they read for peer review. The findings of eye tracking show that a good deal of reading goes on in writing and responding to others, but it is not very good reading. Daniel Keller's (2014) recent book explores the relevance of this kind of cognitively based research for reading, writing, and overall literacy development.

Finally, the implications for writing will be considered; a definition of academic critical literacy and a model of expert reading that addresses the problems revealed by brain research together lead to useful insights about the teaching and learning of writing. My own case studies suggest that expert readers have particular kinds of awareness of text structure, context and language as well as skills in analysis, synthesis, evaluation and application that they bring to bear on their reading and by extension on their writing. Only when novice writers think and respond like these expert readers can they move toward becoming critically literate, expert writers.

RECONNECTING READING AND WRITING

I have been banging a drum for the last decade or so about the relevance of reading for the teaching and learning of writing. In a number of presentations and publications (including a co-edited book with the same title as this section; see Horning & Kraemer, 2013), I have been arguing that we cannot improve students' performance in writing without paying attention to their reading. A steadily growing pile of reports (ACT, 2015, among others) makes clear that students coming to college have problems with the kind of careful reading of extended nonfiction prose that most college courses require These problems are not improving, nor are they being addressed as directly as it seems to me they should be. The implications of these problems are abundantly clear from the highly regarded Citation Project study of students' use of sources in their writing (Jamieson & Howard, 2012). Other scholars see the same problems and needs; American University linguist Naomi Baron (2015), for example, points out that if college faculty and society more generally want students to be voting intelligently and participating fully in our society, they will need to be able to focus on reading, especially extended nonfiction prose (p. 168). Recently, it appears that writing teachers are starting to pay attention to my drumbeat: Keller (2014) and Carillo (2015) offer detailed discussions of the role of reading in composition theory and pedagogy. These scholars' insights are relevant because they make clear why and how reading is relevant for a more cognitively based approach to the teaching and learning of writing.

The work that is of interest here comes from a number of different fields. Besides work in composition studies mentioned previously, there is research in cognitive psychology and in neuroscience that is helpful. The two fields overlap to some degree, but Baron provides a particularly clear explanation of the difference between them:

> The mental workings of the brain are now studied in two allied fields: cognitive psychology and neuroscience. What is the difference? Simplistically, cognitive psychology studies the mental functioning of people (say, when you ask them to remember a list of words). Neuroscience looks either at what the brain is physically doing during those cognitive tasks or . . . how the brain changes as a result of practice. It is the same brain at work in cognitive and neuroimaging studies, regardless of how we measure its activity. (2015, p. 159)

The following discussion begins with the work in composition studies and then integrates findings of these other fields.

Keller's (2014) recent book, *Chasing Literacy,* is the earlier of two works from composition studies that connect reading and writing from a cognitive perspective. His study included case studies of nine high school students, with a follow-up focus on four in first-year college courses, and interviews with a teacher, a librarian and family members. He notes the need for more focus on reading but disputes the distraction problems. Using the concepts of acceleration and accumulation, Keller suggests that we can understand the online environment where so much reading and writing takes place as an entirely different venue (2014, pp. 166–167). Readers of all kinds (not just students) work with texts in distinct ways online, making use of what he calls "foraging." Foraging is a kind of reading to find sources and material of interest; he draws on the work of Duke University technology scholar and literary critic Katherine Hayles on deep and surface reading as the basis for this idea. One of the processes that takes place in the course of foraging is accumulation—the pile up of different kinds of materials as a by-product of the use of literacies from different kinds of sources, including traditional print, screens, sound, among others, and different forms of access—laptops, phones, tablets, and so forth. This concept is related to and draws on Brandt's work with vertical and horizontal literacy accumulation—vertical is different forms, formats, media; horizontal is different types of literacy that have developed over time, such as, traditional, digital, media, and the like.

A key difference in types of literacy, according to Keller, has to do with the speed at which text is processed, his concept of acceleration. Here, Keller says the increasing numbers of materials require faster reading through skimming, scanning, and willingness and ability to switch between reader and writer roles through social media and other forms like blogs. But teachers need to watch out for "digital literacies tourism" (2014, p. 160). Students, especially if they don't read well, are too likely to engage in shallow review of too many resources in too many different forms. Deep reading is still essential. Therefore, slow and fast rhetorics need to be considered in teaching. Slower speeds can be useful for some things, and faster speeds can be useful for others. If the goal is deep exploration of a topic, common in academic material, then slower is a better choice. If the goal is attracting wide attention, then faster is better. Students can be made aware of these options (Carillo has specific recommendations for doing so, discussed below) and a theory of reading should include how the meaning of a text might be constructed under these different conditions.

Thus, in connecting reading and writing, Keller suggests that there might be what he calls "oscillating" in the course of foraging, varying reading "between different levels of depth and rates of speed" (2014, p. 166). Students engaged in research, according to his study, engage in both foraging and oscillating, as well as multi-tasking. In the latter, Keller makes a distinction between intentional and unintentional multitasking (2014, p. 167). Intentional multi-tasking is done by choice and with awareness of limits and choices being made. By contrast, unintentional multi-tasking is casual and when one is not really aware of the activity; this kind of multi-tasking is commonly unproductive as it entails much distraction. In his research, Keller observed all of these phenomena among the high school and first-year college students he followed. These findings show that reading, writing, technology and cognitive processing are related, so careful understanding of the relationships among them is essential.

Carillo (2015) agrees with Keller's findings, making the case for connecting reading and writing more explicitly in teaching composition. Her book reports a study done under the auspices of a Conference on College Composition and Communication (CCCC) Research Initiative grant in 2012 in which she did an online national survey of college faculty on reading in first-year writing. She had 100 self-selected participants gathered through the WPA listserv; of these participants, almost half also did a follow-up interview. The participants who were willing to do so also shared a link with students and through this process 93 students responded to a set of questions about their reading experiences in first-year writing and seven did a follow-up interview. The book warrants careful reading for its findings and for its discussion of the ways in which composition studies as a field has had what might fairly be described as a love-hate relationship with reading over many years.

For the purposes of this discussion, though, what is useful from Carillo's study is her claim that students need to learn more about reading from a metacognitive perspective in first-year writing in order to take their knowledge of reading with them to the rest of their courses and into their professional lives. Carillo argues for a cognitively based approach to reading to achieve the goal of academic critical literacy I will set later in this discussion. Reviewing research in cognitive psychology, Carillo explains that transfer of learning occurs when students "recognize and generalize" information or practices from a course or experience to other contexts (2015, p. 105). Moreover, students must be made aware of their recognition and generalization to make transfer happen (Carillo, 2015, p. 107). If one of the goals of first-year writing is to connect reading and writing in ways that support and encourage transfer, this work relies on the metacognitive features that connect these processes.

Carillo ultimately proposes "mindful reading," She defines this phrase in a way that makes its metacognitive connection clear:

> I use the term "mindful" to underscore the metacognitive basis of this frame wherein students become *knowledgeable, deliberate,* and *reflective* about *how* they read and the demands that contexts place on their reading. . . . The term "mindful," when modifying reading, describes a particular stance on the part of the reader, one that is characterized by intentional awareness of and attention to the present moment, its context and one's perspective. (2015, pp. 117–118)

This approach could fairly be described as a "reading about reading" approach, particularly because Carillo invokes Doug Downs and Elizabeth Wardle's "writing about writing" approach. She steps carefully away from recommending a particular reading strategy or advocating rhetorical, close or any other angle on reading. Instead, she is in favor of any approach that makes students think about their reading and make conscious choices in their own strategies; in this view, she supports the needs for awareness advocated by Keller. It should also be clear that like Keller, Carillo has built on studies of cognitive processes to propose "mindful reading." "Mindful reading" is moreover entirely consistent with my observations of expert readers to be discussed below.

UNDERSTANDING READING

While both Keller and Carillo draw on cognitive and metacognitive work to advocate for the connection of reading to writing, a more direct argument is offered by University of Florida hypertext scholar and professor of management communication, Yellowlees Douglas in *The Reader's Brain: How Neuroscience Can Make You a Better Writer* (2015). Much of the research she cites is also discussed in a *New York Times* best-selling book, *Reading in the Brain* by French cognitive scientist Stanislas Dehaene (2009); Douglas herself also refers to this book. Dehaene's work is commonly referenced in almost all recent publications on reading because he synthesizes the insights gained from neuroscience, cognitive psychology, education, linguistics, and various other fields to explain the reading process. While he does talk about writing, Dehaene's focus is chiefly on reading, so his work provides a research-based backdrop to the more recent work of Douglas and others focused on reading-writing connections. References to Dehaene's work appear here only as relevant for this reason.

Turning to Douglas (2015), then, she quickly reviews the main features of research on the reading process to offer five key principles for good writing that are based in the findings of neuroscience: Clarity, Continuity, Coherence, Concision, and Cadence (p. 9). Douglas explains reading's key features, its speed (word recognition takes place in tiny fractions of seconds), its use of prediction (by relying on schemas or sets of expectations derived largely from prior knowledge), and its complexity (reflected in readers' use of inference), all features revealed by neurological research using MRIs, PET scans and the like. Dehaene's book covers much of the same ground but goes a bit further by claiming, based on fMRI studies, that there is one area in the brain devoted to reading, which he calls the brain's "letterbox" (2009, pp. 74–78). Drawing on Dehaene's and others' research findings, Douglas (2015) advises concrete word choice, standard sentence patterns and connections and predictable overall structure to create effective writing (p. 28). Citing neuroscientific research on the lexical, syntactic and inferential processing that happens in reading (2015, p. 34), Douglas makes these specific suggestions to support Clarity in writing: using active voice, action verbs, and concrete subjects and objects, and structuring sentences so that subjects and verbs appear together and at the start of sentences.

Drawing on research on cognitive load, or the amount of information being presented in a text, Douglas points out the potential for cognitive overload if the writer does not help readers through the use of principles of continuity (2015, pp. 63–64). Writers who build continuity into their writing help readers make the predictions on which comprehension is built (Douglas, 2015, p. 66). The principle of cognitive overload was established unequivocally, as she points out, in a study of information processing by George Miller (1956), "The Magical Number Seven, Plus or Minus Two." Miller's work, frequently cited and replicated a number of times, shows that we can manage and recall somewhere between five and nine unrelated pieces of information in short-term memory. So, Douglas concludes, writers need to help readers avoid cognitive overload and make appropriate predictions through techniques including placing important information at the ends of sentences, paragraphs or articles, using transitional words and phrases, making use of consistent grammatical subjects, and presenting unfamiliar information after known material (2015, p. 84).

To make the case for coherence as an essential feature of good writing, Douglas gives a quick overview of competing theories of how readers make sense of text: a top-down view that suggests readers rely on schemas (i.e., prior knowledge and expectations), a bottom-up view that readers use the visual array of the text itself as their primary resource for getting meaning, or an interactive view that is a complex combination of the two. Regardless of the preferred view, writers need to help readers see how the parts of a text fit together (Douglas, 2015, pp. 85–91). To do so, writers should provide strong introductions to the whole text and also within the paragraphs of the text to guide readers through their ideas. A thesis at the end of the opening helps readers set up their expectations (consciously or not) for the rest of the text, while benefitting from the "recency effect" that the most recent information stays with readers most effectively (Douglas, 2015, p. 112). Similarly, conclusions help readers to review key ideas, and research says that readers remember best information they encounter more than once (Douglas, 2015, pp. 115–116).

Continuity and Coherence are important for another reason that has to do with cognitive processing in reading. In discussing attention issues, computer scientist and author Cal Newport argues for the focused attention needed to do what he calls "deep work" (2016, p. 3), work done with full attention that is free of distractions, electronic or otherwise. Studies Newport cites point to the problem of "attention residue" (2016, p. 41; cf. Leroy, 2009), which shows up as a by-product of multi-tasking and is one of the many reasons multi-tasking is a poor work strategy. When switching from one task to another, attention tends to stay behind, so a person is thinking about task A even after switching to task B. When writers provide a text that has the features of Continuity and Coherence, these characteristics make it easier for readers to stay focused on the developing ideas and argument without getting distracted.

Douglas offers a number of suggestions for her fourth C, Concision, without spending much time on the psycholinguistics of reading, other than to say that short common words are easier to understand and remember than longer less-common ones according to research (2015, p. 140). Otherwise, Concision requires avoiding repetitive phrasing and hemming and hawing in the text. Turning back to the work of Dehaene, it is clear that much repetition is unnecessary because in normal reading relatively little information is taken from the printed page. Readers generally only see a small sampling of what is in the visual display, as the eyes move from fixation point to fixation point in jumping movements called saccades (Dehaene, 2009, pp. 13–18). In terms of physical processing, readers can only see what is at the fixation point as the periphery is blurry even if vision is fine. Moreover, the eyes are moving so quickly between fixations that readers are effectively blind. Given that there is so little sampling from the visual array going on anyway, repetition is clearly not needed if writers want to help readers get meaning from their text.

But with the discussion of his last C, Cadence, Douglas returns to research on the mental processing required in reading and the resulting advice for writers that arises from it. With respect to Cadence, then, Douglas discusses research showing that when reading, the brain makes use of areas involved in speaking and listening as well as those involved in seeing (2015, pp. 150–151). Other work discussed by Dehaene in the context of dyslexia supports these findings; Dehaene shows that people with dyslexia have problems with phonological processing (2009, pp. 235–261). Strategies for treating dyslexia that improve letter-sound relationships or the processing of sounds help children learn to read and improve their reading (Dehaene, 2009, pp. 258–261). In addition, the findings of recent PET scan research (Douglas, 2015, p. 150) confirm much earlier claims made in a famous article entitled "Reading is Not Strictly Visual" by Paul Kolers (1968). The oral and aural areas turn out to be neurologically connected and to have been wired to work together by the demands of reading and writing through the brain's ability to learn and change, its neuroplasticity (Douglas, 2015, pp. 148–155). It's the latter ability that helps to account for why when people lose one ability, such as vision, their hearing improves as the brain learns to compensate for lost input. Recommendations for writers to vary sentence structure and length and to begin a list with the shortest items and end with the longest arise from these findings (Douglas, 2015, pp. 155–160). And finally, Douglas advocates reading well-written material when writing because, though limited, some research shows that what writers read affects their ability to write with all five of the C characteristics, but especially Cadence (2015, pp. 161–162).

The unification of reading and writing advocated by all of these scholars draws on other research in cognitive psychology that supports this approach. Going back to Newport's *Deep Work* (2016) discussion, he cites the work of psychologist K. Anders Ericsson on the importance of practice of a certain kind. Ericsson's research is one of the sources used by Malcolm Gladwell (2008) and others in advocating 10,000 hours of practice to develop expertise in any area. To achieve expertise, and use it in deep work requires deliberate practice, that is, practice of the skill that is done with full, focused attention. Such practice benefits from coaching where the coach provides specific feedback on how to focus attention. Newport summarizes these characteristics of deliberate practice as follows:

> Its core components are usually identified as follows: (1) your attention is focused tightly on a specific skill you're trying to improve or an idea you're trying to master; (2) you receive feedback so you can correct your approach to keep your attention exactly where it's most productive.... The first component ... emphasizes that deliberate practice cannot exist alongside distraction, and that it instead requires uninterrupted concentration. (2016, p. 35)

Brain research, Newport (2016) goes on to point out, shows that deliberate practice and focused attention produce physical changes in the brain such that the connections between brain cells are supported and effectively glued together by a substance called myelin (p. 36). When reading and writing are done together with good feedback from a teacher, and when there is focused attention of the kind described here, students are on their way to developing expertise.

THE ROLE OF THE EYES IN READING

Although the psycholinguistic and cognitive research on reading demonstrates clearly that the eyes do relatively little in the reading process, there are nevertheless important insights about reading to be gained from how the eyes work while readers look at a text. This research makes use of devices that track eye movements during reading of texts of various kinds, on paper or on a screen. Eye tracking allows researchers to see where readers look and for how long in these activities. Some of the work that has been done relates to how readers use information from a website, but the work that is of particular interest here explores students' peer reviews.

A quick look at the research on websites shows that eye movements follow clear patterns. Jakob Nielsen (2006), for example, focuses on the design of websites for commercial use. He has looked at Web usability, finding that readers typically follow an F-shaped pattern that has led to a fairly standard design for most websites. Joyce Locke Carter (2012), a former chair of CCCC, has analyzed the eye movements of readers of letter of application to a graduate program. Her findings show that expert readers are distracted by errors, but also pay close attention when writers use key words reflecting their identification with the program to which they are applying. Eye tracking, then, appears to shed some light on the cognitive processes of readers.

This technology has allowed those interested in the teaching and learning of writing to see what happens in peer review. Two reports provide useful insights into students' reading of one another's work. The first by Eric Paulson, Jonathan Alexander, and Sonya Armstrong (2007) used eye tracking to see how 15 students reviewed an essay written by another student. The readers looked at errors initially and much more closely than they looked at organization, rhetorical features, and other global matters; their comments and feedback to the writer reflected their eye-tracking results. Paulson and his colleagues concluded that peer review might be more effective if readers are told to attend to errors first and then to move to more global issues, a very different strategy than most teachers use. It's also worth noting that Carter found a similar pattern among expert readers of application letters as discussed above.

Building on these results, Anson and Schwegler (2012) also used eye tracking to observe students' work in peer review. In their report, they thoroughly explain how eye tracking works to reveal where readers look in a text and how the eyes move around on a page or screen; as they say, the current technology is "extremely accurate" in recording eye movements and processing (2012, p. 153). Eye tracking supports most of the points discussed above about the relatively small role of the visual display in the reading process according to Anson and Schwegler (2012, pp. 153–157). They also found, like Paulson et al. that different types of errors have different impacts on readers' understanding and attention, so that a hierarchy of errors might be created and discussed with students (2012, pp. 158–159). Anson and Schwegler suggest that there is great potential in this kind of work for understanding what is happening when students use sources in their writing, as studied by the Citation Project (Jamieson & Howard, 2012, p. 166) and other kinds of research on the intersection of reading and writing. The work on eye tracking, then, confirms a number of the features of cognitive processing discussed earlier in this chapter; it suggests that the teaching and learning of writing can benefit from a better understanding of reading.

INSIGHTS FROM EXPERT READERS

As noted at the outset, I have been making this case for the relevance of reading for writing for a number of years in various venues. My work with expert readers and writers provides some further support for my case. Although my research has involved a relatively small number of novice and expert writers, I believe that the data from my study provides good support. In my IRB-exempt project, I gathered data from eight novice readers and five experts, all reading both on paper and on screens, and all writing summary notes. The novices were all students at my university; the experts were people with graduate degrees who are academics or work with texts in closely related fields like editing or publishing. In the course of their reading, the participants provided a think-aloud protocol about what they were paying attention to and why in response to instructions to read and summarize with the intention of using the material for a paper or other school assignment. For a baseline, I obtained all the participants' scores on the reading portion of the ACT; the novices had all taken it for college admission while the experts completed the reading section from a sample test I obtained from ACT.

Results from the experts show that they have three kinds of awareness and four skills for dealing with texts, whether on paper or on a screen. The first kind of awareness is meta-textual: experts see the overall organizational structure of a text, can separate main ideas from details and easily note when a writer is providing examples, description or comparison/contrast to expand an idea. The second awareness is meta-contextual, an awareness of the context of the text within its field, within its discipline or in the world at large: here, experts can relate the ideas presented to other ideas they know about in the field or subject area, or to historical events or other aspects of the larger domain of the text's topic. The third awareness is meta-linguistic, including attention to or knowledge of the language of the text such as definitions or specialized uses of particular words or phrases; genre-related linguistic features such as strategies for reporting research results might be included here. A key finding is that my novice readers showed almost no awareness of any kind in the reading I asked them to do.

Beyond these awarenesses, experts have four key skills that they bring to bear on all kinds of reading: analysis, synthesis, evaluation and application. These are easily defined, and found, albeit to a much more limited degree, among the novices as well. Analysis reflects the ability to take a text apart and see its sections as well as how the parts fit together. Synthesis is the ability to relate a text to other texts, observing similarities and differences, points of agreement between two or more texts and so forth. Evaluation focuses on these points: authority, accuracy, currency, relevancy, appropriateness and bias, a heuristic developed by faculty librarians at my institution (Lombardo, 2016). Many experts are able to evaluate materials almost unconsciously as it is such a regular part of their reading process while the novices need instruction and reinforcement for this skill. Finally, the application of information gained from reading to one's own purposes is again almost unconscious among experts, as so much of what they do entails using material they have read in their own work. In contrast to the experts who have all of these skills, the novices show some analysis, a bit of synthesis, but little ability to evaluate or apply.

This project (Horning, 2012) led me to propose the following definition of academic critical literacy:

> Academic critical literacy is best defined as the psycholinguistic processes of getting meaning from or putting meaning into print and/or sound, images, and movement, on a page or screen, used for the purposes of analysis, synthesis, evaluation and application; these processes develop through formal schooling and beyond it, at home and at work, in childhood and across the lifespan and are essential to human functioning in a democratic society. (p. 41)

This definition reflects the skills noted among experts on which I believe they have built their awarenesses. That is, if readers have these skills, they will develop their awarenesses of text and become expert readers as well as writers. Setting a clear goal, it seems to me, can help teachers reconnect reading and writing so that novice students can move toward expertise in both.

MONDAY MORNING APPROACHES

All of this research points clearly to the kinds of work faculty members can and should do to help students improve their reading and thereby improve their writing. The work is needed not only in writing classes but also in every course and every discipline. Faculty should see that they can achieve their own goals or learning outcomes by helping students read better so that they can succeed in every course and in their professional lives. There are a variety of intensive and extensive strategies that build on the cognitive research discussed above that can be integrated in all kinds of courses to move students toward academic critical literacy. It's useful to distinguish between intensive strategies, which are about reading per se and extensive strategies that give students opportunities to practice and develop the skills cognitive science research suggests are essential to academic critical literacy.

Some intensive strategies that can be helpful include talking to students about the reading process itself in the ways presented above. When readers understand how reading takes place, they can work on key features, such as building prior knowledge. If faculty members teach critical reading strategies, they send two messages: first, that critical reading is a key feature of success in courses, and second, that such reading is a learnable and transferable skill. One way to do this teaching is to read a portion of an assignment aloud to students and explain the thought process involved while moving through the text. Students are often surprised at the ways expert readers interact with a text. Two other techniques can move students toward more cognitively aware and critical reading: 25-word summaries (Bazerman, 1995), a tool for deeper analysis of any text, and reading guides (Herber, 1978) that can help students get not only key ideas and details, but move on to synthesis, evaluation and application. These approaches support the development of academic critical literacy, building on what we know about the cognitive processing that takes place during reading. When students can read in these ways, they can help each other and themselves with their writing.

In addition to intensive strategies that focus on reading itself, students also need the kind of focused practice described in the research reviewed above. Like any skill, reading requires as much or more practice than shooting free throws or playing an instrument as we know from the work of Ericsson as discussed by Newport earlier in this chapter. Fostering opportunities for practice and focused feedback that supports the cognitive processes in reading includes having students read extended nonfiction prose. They might do so as part of a campus-wide reading program or common book but can also practice with discipline-specific materials faculty are likely to be assigning as part of regular course work. Faculty need to provide the guidance and feedback required to read these texts successfully. And faculty behavior can make a real difference, according to Linda Nilson, founding director of the Office of Teaching Effectiveness and Innovation (OTEI) at Clemson University. Nilson (2010) writes in the 3rd edition of *Teaching at Its Best* that faculty should resist the temptation to lecture on the content of assigned reading. It is much more effective to have students do something with what they have read, like write about it (!) on a discussion board, prepare a book review, or fill in some type of graphic organizer, and to make that work count 20% in the course grade (2010, pp. 211–222). A final approach entails connection to faculty librarians. The professional organization for college and university librarians has recently released a new *Framework for Information Literacy* (http://www.ala.org/acrl/sites/ala.org.acrl/files/content/issues/infolit/Framework_ILHE.pdf) that includes specific support for academic critical literacy in work with traditional and online texts. This valuable resource and the librarians who work with it can support reading development in every classroom drawing on the cognitive processing mechanisms discussed here. There are, it should be clear, quite a large number of cognitively based strategies any faculty member can use to improve students' reading, their critical literacy and their writing.

ONLY CONNECT OR RECONNECT

In drawing this chapter to a close, it is interesting to reflect backward from the definition of academic critical literacy as a goal to see how much of the research in cognitive psychology and neuroscience discussed here supports various elements of the definition. For example, the recent work of Keller and Carillo shows that reading and writing can and should be reconnected. Keller's work drawing on case studies with novices reveals the ways in which students' access to texts and ways of interacting with them has changed in electronic venues; the need for these novice readers to understand how they are reading and why they might read differently for different purposes and situations makes clear some places where reading and writing go hand-in-hand. Carillo's goal of transfer through "mindful reading" offers a specific path to achieve both Keller's goal and my own in academic critical literacy. The work of Douglas, supported by neuroscientists and cognitive psychologists provides further backing for reconnecting reading and writing in ways that can help writers build Douglas' five C characteristics in their writing: Clarity, Continuity, Coherence, Concision and Cadence. My case studies with novices and experts show that expert readers build on their textual, contextual, and linguistic awareness through application of their skills in analysis, synthesis, evaluation, and application to demonstrate their expertise in reading and in those five Cs proposed by Douglas for writing. Classroom strategies can help move students toward the critical reading essential to effective writing. Cognitive and neuroscientific research has offered much not only to our understanding of expert reading and writing but also to a clear goal of academic critical literacy and some ways to achieve it.

REFERENCES

ACT. (2015). The condition of college and career readiness—Michigan. Retrieved from https://www.act.org/content/dam/act/unsecured/documents/CCCR15-NationalReadinessRpt.pdf.

Anson, C. M. & Schwegler, R. A. (2012). Tracking the mind's eye: A new technology for researching twenty-first-century writing and reading processes. *College Composition and Communication, 64*(1), 151–171.

Baron, N. (2015). *Words onscreen: The face of reading in a digital world.* Oxford, UK: Oxford University Press.

Bazerman, C. (1995). *The informed writer.* Reissued by WAC Clearinghouse, 2011. Retrieved from https://wac.colostate.edu/books/informedwriter/.

Carillo, E. C. (2015). *Securing a place for reading in composition: The importance of teaching for transfer.* Logan, UT: Utah State University Press.

Carr, N. (2011). *The shallows: What the Internet is doing to our brains.* New York: Norton.

Carter, J. L. (2012). How do experts read application letters?: A multi-modal study. In *SIGDOC '12 Proceedings of the 30th ACM International Conference on Design of Communication* (pp. 357–358). New York: ACM. doi: 10.1145/2379057.2379125

Dehaene, S. (2009). *Reading in the brain: The science and evolution of a human invention.* New York: Viking Penguin.

Douglas, Y. (2015). *The reader's brain: How neuroscience can make you a better writer.* Cambridge, UK: Cambridge University Press.

Ericsson, K. A. (2014). Why expert performance is special and cannot be extrapolated from studies of performance in the general population: A response to criticisms. *Intelligence, 45*, 81–103. doi: 10.1016/j.intell.2013.12.001.

Gladwell, M. (2008). *Outliers: The story of success.* New York: Little, Brown and Co.

Hayles, N. K. (2010). How we read: Close, hyper, machine. *ADE Bulletin, 150,* 62–79. doi: 10.1632/ade.150.62.

Herber, H. L. (1978). *Teaching reading in content areas* (2nd ed.). Englewood Cliffs, NJ: Prentice-Hall.

Horning, A. S. (2012). Reading, writing, and digitizing: Understanding literacy in the *electronic age.* Newcastle-Upon-Tyne, UK: Cambridge Scholars Publishing.

Horning, A. S. & Kraemer, E. W. (Eds.). (2013). *Reconnecting reading and writing.* Anderson, SC: Parlor Press and The WAC Clearinghouse. Retrieved from https://wac.colostate.edu/books/reconnecting.

Jamieson, S. (2013). What students' use of sources reveals about advanced writing skills. *Across the Disciplines, 10*(4). Retrieved from https://wac.colostate.edu/atd/reading/jamieson.cfm.

Jamieson, S. & Howard, R. M. (2012). The citation project. Retrieved from http://site.citationproject.net/.

Keller, D. (2014). *Chasing literacy: Reading and writing in an age of acceleration.* Logan, UT: Utah State University Press.

Kolers, P. A. (1968). Reading is only incidentally visual. In K. S. Goodman & J. T. Fleming (Eds.), *Psycholinguistics and the teaching of reading* (pp. 8–16). Newark, DE: International Reading Association.

Leroy, S. (2009). Why is it so hard to do my work? The challenge of attention residue when switching between work tasks. *Organizational Behavior and Human Decision Processes, 109*(2), 168–181.

Lombardo, S. (2016). *Evaluating sources.* Handout available at Kresge Library, Oakland University, Rochester, MI.

Miller, G. A. (1956). The magical number seven, plus or minus two: Some limits on our capacity for processing information. *Psychological Review, 63*(2), 81–97. doi:10.1037/h0043158.

Newport, C. (2016). *Deep work: Rules for focused success in a distracted world.* New York: Grand Central Publishing.

Nielsen, J. (2006). F-shaped pattern for reading Web content. Retrieved from http://www.nngroup.com/articles/f-shaped-pattern-reading-web-content/.

Nilson, L. B. (2010). *Teaching at its best: A research-based resource for college instructors* (3rd ed.). San Francisco: Jossey-Bass.

Paulson, E. J., Alexander, J. & Armstrong, S. (2007). Peer review re-viewed: Investigating the juxtaposition of composition students' eye movements and peer-review processes. *Research in the Teaching of English, 41*(3), 304–335.

Purcell, K., Rainie, L., Heaps, A., Buchanan, J., Friedrich, L., Jacklin, A., . . . Zickuhr, K. (2012, Nov. 1). How teens do research in the digital world: A survey of Advanced Placement and National Writing Project teachers finds that teens' research habits are changing in the digital age. Washington DC: Pew Research Center's Internet &

American Life Project. Retrieved from http://www.pewinternet.org/files/old-media/Files/Reports/2012/PIP_TeacherSurveyReportWithMethodology110112.pdf.

Richtel, M. (2014). *A deadly wandering: A mystery, a landmark investigation, and the astonishing science of attention in the digital age.* New York: HarperCollins.

CHAPTER 5

LANGUAGE ATTACHMENT THEORY: THE POSSIBILITIES OF CROSS-LANGUAGE RELATIONSHIPS

Bonnie Vidrine-Isbell
University of Washington

Globalization in higher education has brought with it growing numbers of students whose home language is not English. Many of these students come to higher education believing that their English skills are sufficient to participate in the academic community, but on arrival, are disillusioned by the fact that their English test scores can be high while their ability to interact within the composition course is severely limited. Bakhtinian theory and findings from social neuroscience shed light on this phenomenon. For Mikhail Bakhtin (1987), every word is already embedded in a history of expressions by others in a chain of ongoing cultural and political movements, so that

> when we select words in the process of constructing an utterance, we by no means always take them from the system of language in their neutral, *dictionary* form. We usually take them from *other utterances,* and mainly from utterances that are kindred to ours in genre, that is, in theme, composition, or style. (p. 87)

Bakhtin is ascribing a social nature to language, which he calls "interindividual," one in which the writer mirrors others with whom he or she feels a "kindredness" or relational bond. Dirk Remley's discussion of mirror neurons also comes into play here, as he explains the dynamic nature of speaker and audience response. "As a speaker positions him or herself closer to that reality and shared experiences of the audience he or she mirrors that audience and the audience understands that mirroring, eliciting empathy and favor from the audience" (Remley, this volume). Adding the understanding of mirror neurons to Bakhtin's theory generates a more interactive component to language, one in which the writer seeks to align with the audience and the audience with the writer. A word becomes more than the concept or the symbol it represents. A word becomes imbued with a neural network of words, meanings, emotions, and contexts, which this chapter argues are best constructed in human relationships. The human element engages the brain, as the language of the writer is shaped through the social world and the kindred voices that world offers.

But, what if, a language or even a word, is learned devoid of this social "interindividual" context in which audience and speaker interact, such as in the case of many of the L2 writers in our composition courses? As part of an IRB-approved mixed-method study titled *Language Attachment: The Impact of Social Bonding in Adult Language Learning,* I read and analyzed 77 language autobiographies written by international students in my composition courses. From these narratives, a common theme emerged: English as a Second Language had been mainly studied for test achievement, with methods such as textbook memorization and cram schools that emphasize grammar over communication. In agreement with Peter Khost (this volume), high stakes testing and test prep worked to suppress creativity, engagement, and curiosity in these students and in many of their EFL contexts, there was a lack of opportunities to interact in English in cross-cultural communication (Chen & Yang, 2014). In light of these findings, it is not surprising that second language studies have found that research participants often report less emotional connectivity in the L2 (Chamcharatsri, 2012; Dewaele, 2008; Pavlenko, 2005) as well as difficulty understanding the social and cultural context of language (Rintell, 1990). Findings from social neuroscience offer a framework for analysis of this phenomenon. Research on memory formation now integrate what Bakhtin theorized, mainly, that the emotions, social context, and human interactions that occur during the encoding of memory will become part of the fabric of that memory, which can be stored in multiple areas of the brain (Cozolino, 2002; Schumann, 1997). When someone whose L1 is English hears a single utterance, for example, "San Francisco," both implicit (unconscious) and explicit (conscious) memories and emotions associated with that utterance could be present because of past exposure to the word in social contexts. The song "If you're going to San Francisco" by Scott McKenzie, the American TV series *Full House* (Franklin, 1987), support for the LGBT community, or a past trip taken there could all impact recall of this utterance for an American L1 English speaker. There is a complex neural network connected to this concept, which causes resilience in learning. Because the frames of reference are robust, the term is deeply embedded in memory. However, many L2 writers lack this type of heteroglossia due to lack of emotional experiences and social engagements in their L2. Moreover, students in my study who considered their early English learning environments to be "stressful," "pressured," or even "traumatizing" often re-experienced negative emotions when producing English. Those whose language acquisition was primarily a process in which words are taken from "the system of language in their neutral, *dictionary* form" (text memorization) rather than from "other utterances" (Bakhtin, 1987, p. 86) often lack certain types of L2 language fluency, ones that are socio-emotional and socio-cultural (Rintell, 1990). Moreover, many associate English with feelings of anxiety, stress, and low self-worth.

Department leaders, composition instructors, and L2 writers in expository writing programs search for avenues to mitigate these types of issues, but have found traditional ESL pedagogies insufficient to bring students to this next level of language use. It is in this problematic area that my contribution, the theory of "language attachment," offers insight. Language attachment theory holds that human bonding is central to language acquisition in both infants and adults, and it seeks to reframe and extend existing pedagogical practices in composition accordingly. These relationships, *language attachments*, are in no way meant to bring L2 writers closer to a native speaker model, but to benefit both L1 and L2 English writers through development of cross-cultural repertoires able to rhetorically respond in a globalized world. Language attachment theory emerged from my interdisciplinary work with the University of Washington's Language and Rhetoric program and the Institute for Learning Brain Sciences (ILABS). Relying on support from both departments, I developed language attachment theory and am currently testing its application in the composition classroom.

This chapter argues that language attachments are both the practical means by which composition instructors can offer L2 writers more embodied rhetorical repertoires as well as a helpful approach through which L1 English writers can develop cross-cultural repertoires for addressing various types of cultural audiences who use World Englishes (Schaub, 2003). Beginning with a review of neurological language development studies and behavioral psychology's well-known "attachment theory," the chapter will interweave understandings of how human engagement has been found as the catalyst for both changes in neural activity leading to language acquisition— "the social gating hypothesis" and the formation of behavioral patterns, *attachment styles,* in human relationships. Following the review, the chapter will describe language attachment theory in detail, showing how the social attachments created in a language impact the brain, emotions, and expressions of the bilingual writer. Support for this theory comes from a range of studies on the bilingual brain (Pallier et al., 2003), behavioral and relational psychology (Cozolino, 2013), and cross-linguistic differences in emotion (Pavlenko, 2005). The chapter ends by situating language attachment theory within the field of composition as a clearer frame with which to pursue a set of pedagogical practices aiming to accomplish the following goals:

1. Encourage intercultural understandings that reduce isolating behaviors,
2. Support socio-cultural and emotional fluency in L2 writers, and
3. Promote bilingualism and global e-connection as a norm in the classroom.

This theory could be beneficial for both aiding department leaders and composition instructors as they deal with overall issues of diversity that emerge in the classroom (Horner, Lu & Matsuda, 2010) and as they work to internationalize the field of composition (Schaub, 2003). The chapter concludes with a call for researchers to investigate this new avenue of thought, particularly in its application to composition classroom. The term *cognition/cognitive* is used broadly in this chapter, to encompass its use across both the fields of cognitive psychology and social neuroscience.

LITERATURE REVIEW

Patricia Kuhl, co-director of the University of Washington's Institute for Learning and Brain Sciences (ILABS), posed the "social gating" hypothesis in 2007, as the result of her work on language acquisition in the infant brain. I will briefly recount some of the history of her hypothesis to offer a clearer understanding of its context. In 1992, Kuhl, Karen Williams, Francisco Lacerda, Kenneth Stevens, and Björn Lindblom were trying to understand why and how an infant's brain could acquire any global language from birth to nine months. Their study was built on the understanding that the infant brain had a sensitive period for language, in which the phonemes of any language could be discriminated and potentially acquired (Kuhl et al., 1992). According to these cognitive psychologists, the infants were conducting "statistical analysis" on the phonemes of their first languages by paying attention to and retaining the ability to distinguish the phonemes they heard most frequently. With age, infants lost their ability to distinguish between less frequent sounds. Understood linguistically, between six and nine months, a shift occurs in the learners to begin to normalize the input of a target language's phonetic identity due to the regularity of those specific sounds, and with this shift, the brain optimizes toward the language being heard and used, saving energy by no longer retaining that "global" ability to acquire any language in the world.

Curious if an environment could be created where infants did not lose this ability, Kuhl, Feng-Ming Tsao, and Huei-Mei Liu (2003) designed two experiments. The first tested nine-month-old American infants, who had only been exposed to English. They separated the American infants into two groups—a control group that only heard more English and a test group which was exposed to a live L2 Mandarin tutor as the source of L2 input. Findings showed that infants in the test group did retain the ability to distinguish the phonemes in both English and Mandarin, even showing performance levels equal to Taiwanese infants that had grown up hearing Mandarin only. In addition, the window of time for having this phonetic distinguishing ability, normally six to nine months, was extended in this "bilingual" group. The other group, the control group only exposed to more English, as expected, did not acquire the ability to distinguish Mandarin phonemes. However, the social element—the live Mandarin tutor—was yet to be understood. Did the medium of language exposure impact language acquisition? Would infant brains respond similarly to videos or audios of Mandarin?

Therefore, the second experiment evaluated when an infant brain would be triggered to perform statistical analysis on the phonemes in a new language. American infants only exposed to English were recruited and grouped into three separate groups. Each was exposed to Mandarin twelve times over a four-week period. Group 1 listened to audio of the Mandarin tutors. Group 2 watched videos of the Mandarin tutors. And Group 3, she explains in her 2010 TED talk, had what we might think of as "Mandarin relatives visiting for a month" (Kuhl, 2010). As shown previously in this same study (Kuhl et al., 2003), the live L2 tutor, who played, read stories, and interacted with the infants caused those infant brains to respond to the new language. Groups without this social engagement showed absolutely no acquisition of Mandarin phonemes; whereas both English and Mandarin phonetics were maintained in those participants who had exposure to a live Mandarin tutor, creating the possibility for a future English-Mandarin bilingual.

From this study, among many others, Kuhl (2007) posed the "social gating hypothesis," which holds that social interaction opens the brain to perform the internal work of phonetic analysis of a new language. In this article, she claims that language is gated by the motivating properties (such as attention and arousal) inherent in social interactions (2007, p. 114), and her hypothesis, if correct, would hold that the degree of social interaction and engagement with the tutor would correlate with language learning. Barbara Conboy and Kuhl (2011) confirmed this correlation by expanding their tests to include both phonetic learning and word learning as well as added measures for specific interactions, and found that, indeed, increased social engagement, (i.e., shown through shifting eye gaze from the tutor's eyes to the newly introduced toys) showed greater learning as interpreted by ERP brain measures of phonetic and word learning.

What is groundbreaking about this study is that infants exposed to Mandarin via video or audio-only showed no evidence of learning in their ERP measures. Also, their behavioral test scores from the head-turn analysis did not differ from the infants in the control group who heard no Mandarin whatsoever. On the other hand, those with human engagement not only had the period for global language learning extended but also performed equivalently on the recognition of Mandarin phonemes as same aged infants in Taiwan who had listened to Mandarin for 10 months. This leads us to question what this means for our L2 composition students that have studied English in contexts that use memorization and textbook recordings over L2 human interaction to teach the English language. It also requires composition instructors to revisit human attachment in more detail, as few would argue against its significance.

While the social gating hypothesis powerfully argues the centrality of social interaction for language learning, it does not deeply investigate the nature and impact of the human relationship on socio-emotionality. However, a complementary theory to Kuhl's exists from behavioral psychology, one that has revolutionized psychotherapy and has contributed to studies on metacognition and mindfulness. Attachment theory, first formulated by psychologist John Bowlby and extended by Mary Ainsworth and her colleagues, poses that relationships are the basis of human survival (Bowlby, 1988), and that our initial bond with our caregiver (usually mother) impacts our behavioral patterns of relating and emotionality (Ainsworth, Blehar, Waters & Wall, 1978). More recently, as attachment theory has been integrated with neuroscience, affect regulation and emotional attunement have become increasingly more important as factors that shape the overall socio-emotional development of a person (Schore, 2003). Although attachment theory is not a theory of language in itself, our understandings of the simultaneity of language encoding with memory and emotion render it helpful in our conceptualization of affect and social bonding in language acquisition.

Here, I will briefly synopsize the historical research leading to the two main concepts from attachment theory referenced here. First, attachment theory connects human survival to the ability to secure an attachment to another human. Beginning post-WWII, London hospitals were witnessing high infant mortality rates. The hospitals used strict sterilization practices meant to safeguard infants against infection, but Bowlby, who was working there at the time, began to develop theories of maternal deprivation and attachment, theorizing a correlation between touch and infant survival. His work began to impact hospital protocol. Nurses, who were previously instructed to touch the infant as little as possible to avoid exposure to germs, were now instructed to hold, talk to, and engage with the infants. These new protocols increased infant survival rates dramatically and lead to the practices used today. In 1969, Bowlby published his seminal work, *Attachment and Loss*, which argues that attachment to a mother is a determinant of survival and overall normal health in an infant.

After Bowlby's initial theory connecting infant-mother bonding to survival, attachment studies proliferated, showing a second main contribution—mainly, that repeated sets of patterned behaviors in children and adults could be linked to a person's initial bond with their primary caregiver (Ainsworth et al., 1978; Holmes, 2014; Riley, 2011). One famous experiment called the "strange situation" tested the nature of the bond and linked certain behaviors to it (Ainsworth et al., 1978). Though there are different variations of the experiment, the main purpose is for a caregiver to leave their child briefly, allowing the child to experience a brief period of distress, and then return to comfort the child. The child's response to the caregiver's departure and return is categorized into an attachment style. These behavioral, emotional responses offer insight into how the caregiver attaches to the child on a daily basis, with later studies emphasizing self-awareness and emotional regulation as correspondent to socio-emotional health (Holmes, 2014). To synopsize, the attachment styles for children are divided into two types: secure and insecure. Within the category of insecure, there are three subdivisions: insecure, avoidant, insecure-ambivalent, and insecure-disorganized. The first category, secure attachment, was attributed to caregiver-child affectional bonds in which the caregiver responded to the child's needs, made eye contact, and offered affection or space accordingly. Secure attachment was characteristic of children who were comforted easily, returned to play and displayed signs of exploration and curiosity. The second category, insecure-avoidant attachment showed caregivers who were emotionally distant or rejecting and children whose coping strategies included avoiding their own needs for attachment (e.g., ignoring caregiver's departure/return, avoiding eye contact). The next category of insecure, insecure-ambivalent, was characteristic of caregivers that were emotionally enmeshed or inconsistent with the child. These children often demonstrated ambivalent behaviors such as clinging to the caregiver but not accepting or responding to their comfort. The final category, insecure-disorganized attachment, is rare and was added to classify erratic caregiver-child bonds, in which the caregiver is frightened or frightening and the child responds with self-soothing strategies such as disassociation or self-harm (e.g., rocking in fetal position). These initial attachment categories have been extended and applied to adult relationships (George & West, 2012) as well as teacher-student relationships (Riley, 2011). According to Bowlby, the initial affectional bond with the caregiver produces internal working models of attachment, "relatively fixed representational models," that are used to predict and relate to the world (Holmes, 2014, p. 63), and though Bowlby (1969) wrote about attachment as lasting from the "cradle to the grave," even he questioned its malleability (p. 208).

As attachment research continued, results showed that pedagogical and therapeutic strategies that used healthy human bonding could heal insecure attachments in both children and adults, students and teachers. In fact, the evidence showed the ability for bidirectional changes in attachment (Cozolino, 2013, 2014). In other words, healthy, securely attached infants might experience abuse or neglect as teenagers and revert to an insecure attachment style, just as insecurely attached infants could experience a healthy attachment in adulthood that reprograms their attachment style to be secure. This evidence corroborates with that found in Gwen Gorzelsky, Carol Hayes, Joseph Paszek, Ed Jones, and Dana Lynn Driscoll (this volume) and Irene Clark (this volume), where neuroplasticity is being documented in adults who have acquired a skill (e.g., jugglers, stroke victims, taxicab drivers). In addition, mindfulness or metacognitive practices have been thought to impact attachment, as pausing to think about thought processes fosters a space to reflect on the emotions, bodily reactions, and memories that enter a present moment/activity. Metacognitive practices which promote a compassionate, curious, and non-judgmental stance towards the self, have been said to heal insecure attachments, as individuals learn to develop a secure attachment with themselves (Snyder, Shapiro & Treleaven, 2012). In each of these movements toward social bonding, whether in relationship with the self or another person, the language used during these interactions encodes into memory, imprinting into linguistic socio-emotional development of the individual. And even though this resonates with infant language studies (Kuhl, 2007) and primary language acquisition studies (Lee, Mikesell, Joaquin, Mates & Schumann, 2009) in their argument for the power of human interaction, these conclusions have not been readily extended to secondary language acquisition in adults.

In regard to second language acquisition, adult neuroplasticity has been problematic, with researchers more often restricting their analysis to infants, offering explanations about why infant brains are much more "plastic" than adult brains. For one, the infant brain's sensitivity to phonemic discrimination ends around twelve months, as plasticity is traded for speed, optimization, and specialization (Kuhl, 2007). Second, the neuropeptides or hormones that orchestrate human affiliation and bonding, are at incredibly high levels in infancy, but decrease with age. More specifically, adult language learners have one hundred times less levels of opiates in their brains than at the time of birth (Lee et al., 2009). Although both Kuhl and Lee et al. offer thorough evidence for the vast differences neurologically and linguistically between infant/adult and primary/secondary language acquisition, their important contributions, the interactional instinct (Lee et al., 2009) and the social gating hypothesis (Kuhl, 2007), correspond with research from the social sciences and neuropsychology that suggests that regardless of age, the human relationship—social bonding and attachment—contains transformational qualities that may have the power to shift what was thought to be set behaviors (Cozolino, 2013, 2014; Riley, 2011). This overlap merits further investigation into extending their work for the adult language classroom. In fact, much of the research from neuropsychology also acknowledges that individuals who gain awareness of their cognitive processes can have agency over their future behaviors and personal development. This concept is echoed in Clark's chapter in this collection as she discusses the ever-changing connectomes within an individual and the potential that person has to gain consciousness and agency in shaping and performing their own various identities. Discussions such as these regarding neuroplasticity led me to question whether human relationships could increase the brain's propensity for second language acquisition in adults while addressing issues of emotional and socio-cultural fluency in L2 writers.

LANGUAGE ATTACHMENT THEORY

Language attachment theory posits that L2 acquisition in adulthood and the resulting changes in neural plasticity this requires could be fundamentally built upon the brain's optimization towards attachment as a survival mechanism, and that even though adults no longer depend on attachment for survival, human bonding may hold residual power with respect to language acquisition and use. Studies of international adoptees adopted post-critical period offer an interesting perspective on whether or not social bonding has the power to impact brain plasticity for language. Pallier et al. (2003) gathered fMRI data on a group of Korean-born adults who were adopted between the ages of 5 to 8, post-critical period, into French families. Though these Korean participants had lived in orphanages in Korea before their arrival, so that exposure to Korean should have been extensive (infancy to five years of age), they reported no memory of Korean (L1). They had become native-like in French (L2), the language of their adopted families. When tested with control groups (monolingual French speakers), they performed equally. When shown Korean symbols or played Korean audio against other foreign languages, their brains showed no distinction. fMRI data imaging showed no Korean ability. It appeared that the second language had completely replaced the first language. Though this study focused on language attrition not the impact of attachment on language, it is likely that the majority of these adoptees had experienced one or more social separations with their native language attachments, creating insecure attachments. However, as they developed social bonds with their L2 French families, these relationships were likely powerful enough to trigger their brains to accept French at this dramatic level of fluency. Reasons their brains chose to delete its first language, Korean, can only be hypothesized, but emotion and painful memory recall has been documented in similar cases of trauma (Pavlenko, 2005). At its extreme, language attachment would help explain deletion of a first language, but could also help explain structural reorganization in the adult bilingual brain in terms of shared conceptual mapping as well as other features of bilingualism found in behavioral and cognitive studies such as the bilingual brain's propensity to acquire theory of mind (i.e., predict the mind of another), flexibility of thought (i.e., implement a new rule quickly after performing a habitual task), and enhanced cognitive control, which was shown to protect against the onset of dementia later in life (Bialystok, 2009; Bialystok, Craik & Luk, 2012; Buchweitz & Prat, 2013). These features of a bilingual brain would, according to language attachment theory, be evidenced in bilinguals who had experienced social bonding in the L1 and L2.

In addition, language attachment theory also integrates concepts on how relationships and the brain interact to influence learning ability and identity formation. In his text, *The Social Neuroscience of Education*, Louis Cozolino (2013) describes how human relationships have been found to build and rebuild brains by reviewing neuroscientific studies showing how healthy human bonding can reshape behaviors that were once thought to be set. Specifically, Cozolino addresses some of the anxiety studies that Charles Bazerman (this volume) discusses. He describes studies in which insecure attachments, stress, and high levels of anxiety negatively impact the brain to impede learning and compares these studies to those showing how emotional attunement, play, and story-telling build human bonds that stimulate the brain for learning. He offers educators the concept of the "tribal classroom," one that is salient for a composition setting in which students have various language resources that can be explored in writing. His notion of the tribal classroom resides on the basic premise that "the more the environment of a classroom parallels the interpersonal, emotional, and motivational components of our tribal past, the more our primitive instincts will activate the biochemistry of learning" (2013, p. 239). The tribal society showed characteristics of small groups, equality and fairness, shared responsibilities, and democratic decision making as opposed to industrialized society's large groups, individualism, competition, and dominance hierarchy. Also, these small communities, in which human connection is central, the learner is put into a fabric of social, emotional, cultural, political experiences that offers a multiplicity of classroom voices from which to shape L2 learners' experiences of their second language. Likewise, valuing the multiple perspectives inherent in linguistically diverse students enriches the composition setting and stimulates learning and cultural competence. Language attachment theory uses these frameworks within the context of composition and applies them to L2 writers in hopes to ameliorate some of the cultural, emotional, and social isolation commonly reported on in L2 literature (Motha, 2014; Ortmeier-Hooper, 2008; Toohey, 2000).

Language attachment theory also maintains that memory, emotion, and the body are interconnected and engaged with others even when physically or temporally separated. Studies on memory and the body, such as those cited in the text, *Emotions in Multilingualism* point to what Steven Corbett (this volume) refers to as embodied cognition, the understanding that cognition is intrinsically social, shared among other bodies and just as much biological and physical as it is mental. In connection to second language acquisition, language attachment asserts that the language used (L1 or L2) during the encoding of the memory becomes part of the network of neural synapses associated with its recall. Studies on cross-linguistic differences in L2 writers support this, showing swear words, terms of endearment, shame, anger, and frustration to be experienced differently (and often more intensely) according to the language used most for encoding that emotion (Dewaele, 2010; Pavlenko, 2005). It is not surprising that these researchers most often found that the language used between caregiver-infant (L1) reportedly was the writer's preference for emotional expression in writing, though exceptions have been noted. Some of these exceptions include when expression of a particular emotion is not socially acceptable in the L1 (e.g., fear in Thai, Chamcharatsri, 2013), cases where the emotion expressed was emotionally disturbing in the L1 (Pavlenko, 2005), cases in which one did not wish to assert an identity they associated with their L1 (Koven, 2007), and cases where the L1 would not address the writer's desired audience (Pavlenko, 2005). Many of these studies aided Pavlenko (2005) in developing the theory of language embodiment, which is specific to multilinguals. Similar to embodied cognition, language embodiment corroborates with the view that the words of a language can invoke both sensory images and physiological reactions. Integrating arguments from Michel Paradis (1994), Pavlenko explains that because primary language acquisition greatly involves the limbic system and other brain structures such as the amygdala, language acquisition generates emotions, drives, and motivation that become part of a process of affective linguistic processing. The result is this language embodiment, in which sensory representations, desire to produce a message, and autobiographical memory become integrated into the language itself. This language embodiment, she argues, normally does not occur in second language acquisition, in which a decontextualized classroom develops word meanings through "definition, translation, and memorization" rather than through a "consolidation of personal experiences channeled through multiple sensory modalities." Another reason Pavlenko offers for language embodiment not occurring in the L2 is that the limbic system can only be involved in language production when a speaker has a need or desire to produce a certain message (Paradis, 1994), and in many L2 language classrooms, "utterances are elicited from learners who, on top of being unwilling interlocutors, focus on the structure rather than the meaning of the messages," a process that only creates language learning anxiety and connects that anxiety to the L2 (Pavlenko, 2005, p. 155). This exactly describes both my experiences with international students in composition courses over the past ten years, as well as, what my most recent research study, a mixed methods study, has found.

Over the last two years, I have engaged in an IRB-approved mixed-method study of international students in composition courses. The study surveyed one hundred and three students (my former students included) on their language attachments in English, their perceptions of the English language, their comfort level in emotional expression in English, and their L2 language learning histories. The study also collected and analyzed classroom assignments from international students who took the survey. These participants were former students from my own composition courses from the past five years, and the documents I collected from them included translingual poetic writing (fifty-two participants) and in-depth language autobiographies recounting language learning histories (seventy-seven participants). After using grounded theory to analyze themes in these collected documents, five writers (all former students) were recruited to be interviewed as case studies. These case studies furthered understanding of findings from the survey and document analysis, by providing a more detailed description of L1/L2 rhetorical choices, the impact of language attachments on emotional expression in L1/L2, and autobiographical memory and emotional experiences in the composition course. Though a complete review of the findings is beyond the scope of this chapter, Pavlenko's theory of language embodiment was confirmed. Specifically, survey results showed that English and negative emotions were most often paired, with explanations of the English education as "stressful" or "pressured" given as descriptors of its acquisition. Also, nearly all preferred the L1 for emotional expressive writing, and a surprising thirty-seven percent listed that they had no close friends with whom they used English. The theme of language attachment was explored in more depth during the interview and document analysis with case studies. Autobiographical data was divided into two main categories, depending on whether the student's primary, early connections to the English language were described with more positive or negative descriptors. The majority of these language autobiographies described their early English learning experiences more negatively, a finding that corroborated the survey results showing English to most often be paired with negative emotions. These autobiographies portrayed "dutiful" students, those who often described learning English in cram schools, boarding schools, and schools that focused on exam preparation. The anomalies were four autobiographies whose narratives described their early English learning experience more positively and discussed L2 socio-emotional connections made before studying abroad. Two of these were via human connection using the common L2-English (a Filipino nanny and a Norwegian online gaming friend). The other two were socio-emotional connections made with TV series characters with whom the students felt bonded due to watching numerous hours of the series and memorizing portions of the script. These four "subversive" students report trying to find a "better" way to learn English than the methods used in their classrooms. It is important to note that the other writers (termed *dutiful*) may have had bonds not discussed in their autobiographies as well as stories that began positively but turned to have more negative descriptors than positive. It is also important to reiterate that this data reflects early connections to the English language, rather than post-study abroad connections (though the survey seems to report on "lasting" negative attachments to the English language even after moving outside the home country). In addition, these results only represent a small set of international participants in university composition courses. If the study were duplicated in another region and university, the results might differ. However, the insights gained from this participant group asks us as instructors and researchers to consider the language attachment history of an L2 learner, especially when we notice anxiety associated with the English language.

Though some may argue that having embodied cognition in language learning is not important for L2 writing development in academic settings, my findings show that L2 writing and rhetoric benefit from an embodied approach. Moreover, survey results showed that nearly all L2 learners who reported no close friends in the L2, desired to have one. From this evidence and the theories offered above, language attachment theory asserts that when bilingual brains have had L2 exposure through human connection and bonding, that L2 writing increases in complexity, emotionality, the use of translingual rhetoric, and overall embodied cognition in writing. The goal, then, in addressing the L2 writers in our composition courses who lack socio-emotional and socio-cultural types of L2 language fluency, is to offer language attachment figures—caring, playful, L2 speakers that are willing to bond with the learner. Moreover, for mainstream students whose L1 is English and whose L2 is not particularly developed, language attachment pedagogies could function as a kind of empathy training, which may solve diversity issues that stem from negative, stigmatized views of the ESL student and encourage more cross-cultural awareness and sensitivity. In addition, translingual writing approaches become more important rhetorical moves as language attachments require composition students to develop their repertoires for addressing various types of cultural audiences, a much needed skill as writers participate in today's globalized social medias (e.g., the 2011 "Twitter revolution" in Egypt).

Language attachment theory is not in itself a new theory. It is a hybridized theory specific to reviving language pedagogies that rest upon human bonding and relationship. It is grounded in interdisciplinary work among the fields of neuroscience, psychology, and composition studies and is a response to globalization in higher education, which has caused an increasing number of linguistically diverse students and created the need for researchers and practitioners to better understand the bilingual brain in a composition setting. What is new about language attachment is 1. The position that adult language learning be situated inside of human attachment, and 2. A reframing of composition pedagogies for this framework. It is important to note that unlike Kuhl's Mandarin tutor, language attachment figures need not be a native speaker, but could be anyone with whom the L2 was the primary language used for interaction.

PEDAGOGICAL IMPLEMENTATION

What could a writing teacher do to encourage language attachments and social bonding in their composition classrooms? This question has fueled most of my pilot studies, which I offer here not as vetted pedagogies, but as potential directions for investigation. In what follows, I will offer pedagogical practices that evolved as a response to the theory of language attachment, all of which support human to human interaction as the most effective form of instruction. For the scope of this chapter, I have chosen to detail implementation of only one, which I consider most valuable to the composition classroom.

As a composition instructor, the most effective implementation of language attachment theory is to intentionally design long term pairs or groups in the course. These pilots were administered in a 10-week course first year "multilingual" composition course, where student self-select enrollment as they identify themselves as "someone who can read, write, and think in more than one language." The composition course met twice weekly for two hours. For the first two weeks of class, I (the composition instructor) observed student interactions, looking for signs that two or three students could be long-term friends. Signs include those Cozolino (2013) designates as stimulating for learning: laughter, play, and/or emotional attunement during story-telling or conversation. During these first two weeks, I also required autobiographical writing and classroom introductions that I used to pair students based on similar interests. During the quarter, students are required to spend a lot of time with their language attachment. They interview one another outside of class for a primary research skills assignment. They peer-review one another's papers. They also watch and analyze films from their home cultures as part of a cross-cultural assignment, and as Meade (this volume) mentions, grades are deemphasized in favor of engagement. As a result, some students who were interviewed six months after the course, reported continued bonding outside of class which resulted in positive emotional experiences with English. For example, one of my case studies, Shun (pseudonym), a Chinese-English speaker reported severe anxiety when using English, explaining short "freezes" or "blanks" during conversations in English due to stress. In discussing memory and emotion, he attributed the strict, pressured educational methods used to teach English in China as reason for his anxiety when using English. Shun's stress prevented him from feeling curiosity and creativity when using English. During my course, I paired Shun with Min (pseudonym), a Korean-English speaker. Their friendship lasted beyond my course to a weekly meeting at a pub, where they discussed their families, romantic relationships, future plans, and school. In our interview, Shun explained that talking to Min in English (their common L2) allowed him to practice his English in a non-academic, non-pressured environment, which he believed was therapeutic in reducing his anxiety. This long-term bond significantly impacted his cognition and experience of writing in the L2. As a result, Shun was a more relaxed writer, which added to his sense of self-confidence and enhanced his emotional connectivity to the English language. Shun also reported feeling more capable, a theme that echoes Khost (this volume) in his discussion of self-efficacy. In Shun's case, the language attachment figure Min becomes the pedagogical means by which the English language becomes slowly more embodied for Shun. As his anxiety decreases, he finds himself laughing, feeling sadness, and connecting emotionally as he expresses himself through writing poetically and autobiographically. He explains that he has never experienced English or writing this way, and laughs, as he tells me that he may not want to be a math major anymore.

Language attachments are the practical means by which composition instructors can offer L2 writers more embodied rhetorical repertoires, but it is also the means by which L1 English writers develop cross-cultural repertoires for addressing various types of cultural audiences who use World Englishes (Schaub, 2003). For a composition instructor in a mainstream composition course, where the majority of students speak English as their first language (but have often had some foreign language courses in high school), pairing students with language partners outside of the classroom is effective. If the institution has a language exchange program, the instructor can require that students sign up for a language partner. In this case, a language exchange program coordinator sends an introduction email giving participants each other's contact information. The language partners then meet casually outside of class to develop a relationship on their own, ideally speaking part of the time in each language or depending on participant's ability, simply gaining familiarity and practice with World Englishes. Also, social networking sites like ePals function to connect instructors or students globally to create language partners similar to the one described above in the language exchange program. In both scenarios, the ePal takes place of the old "pen-pal," offering connections beyond writing letters. Studies on ePals and other technology enhanced multimedia instruction networks like it connect language learners via video chat, email, and discussion boards to truly become involved in each other's lives (Chen & Yang, 2014). These language exchanges are the most fertile ground for addressing language diversity issues because they rely on the power of human relationships to challenge hegemonic perspectives. No longer is an "expert" English speaker helping the non-expert. Both parties assume an expert position (their L1) and a language learner position (the desired L2), fostering empathy, cross-cultural understanding, and possibly, life-long global friendships that could unite the United States and the globe.

Even monolinguals in our composition courses who "took high school foreign language but can't speak it" would be pushed to create language exchange partners. These partners could be used to complete assignments in our composition courses as well as requirements from other language courses. If successful, the implications for language attachment practice could extend to reform language policy in K-12. In the future, students could come to a composition course with already established language attachments from early years of foreign language study. Though this seems challenging, it is actually quite likely, as younger generations who live abroad are using technology such as ePals, videogaming, Facebook, and Twitter to build relationships cross-culturally in their second languages. Policy makers may need to catch up with these tech-savvy methods to language learning. Instead of the high school foreign language requirement emphasizing test achievement, the passing criteria would be to establish a social bond and communicative ability in a second language through a global technology enhanced multimedia instruction network. Foreign language teachers would design courses with other teachers globally, creating assignments that situate the relationship as central. If multilingualism became pervasive, the impact could be substantial—languages that had been isolated from the public sphere would be valued and Americans who may have been previously "monolingual" when leaving the K-12 system, may experience the benefits of having communicative ability and cross-language relations in two languages.

Other pedagogical moves that implement language attachment theory include requiring composition students to find one or two writing center tutors with similar disciplinary interests, with whom they consistently visit and bond with throughout their years at the institution. Another, which applies Nel Noddings' influential work on the ethics of care, is for teachers to be intentional in student-teacher bonding when conducting small group or one on one writing conferences. Next, as Chen and Yang (2014) report, instructors can promote exposure to World Englishes by co-developing courses internationally. Finally, including a service component to a composition course can also position human bonding between students and community members as students write about their experiences helping, listening, and connecting with others.

FUTURE AREAS OF RESEARCH

This theoretical framework is in its early stages of investigation, and the pilots discussed above would all need more research to produce a more stable theory from which to base pedagogical implementations. Therefore, future research could continue to investigate language attachment through pedagogical implementations. Additionally, it could seek to explore the following questions: What is the nature of human relationships in L2 socio-emotional learning? What are the existing emotional connections made to the L2 via the L1 attachment figures and their impact? How do we navigate the problem of neuroplasticity in adult language learning and the question of attachment and socio-emotionality in adult language learners? How could metacognitive practices play a part in addressing language attachment? Future studies could examine these questions by researching human bonding and language acquisition late in life. In addition, interdisciplinary researchers of cognition and writing might look at the role mirror neurons in infant-mother bonding and use this evidence to further instate imitation pedagogies (Clark, this volume). In referencing transfer, compositionists might explore social bonding between their students and the attachment figures of their future disciplines, to examine how professionals can serve to facilitate transfer from writing within the institution to writing within the workplace. Finally, in composition studies of metacognition, aspects of attachment and mindfulness may be helpful avenues of inquiry in connection to pedagogical practices.

CONCLUSION

I argue that some understandings from primary language acquisition and infant brain studies can aid our conceptualization of secondary language acquisition, particularly in positioning human bonding as a foundational element to adult language learning. Next, premised on these arguments, I offer language attachment theory as an example framework with which to explore new pedagogical investigations in the composition classroom. This framework works to provide a more Bakhtinian experience of language for the L2 writer, where embodied cognition and writing intersect, moving them closer to socio-emotional and socio-cultural fluency in the L2. Language attachment theory functions not to assimilate L2 learners into moving closer toward the inner circle of native speakers (Kachru, 1990), but to encourage all students to question the internalized ideology of the native speaker, its assumptions, and the impact these have on the learner. Language attachment also grounds itself in findings that report that healthy human bonding can rebuild and reprogram the brain, especially in instances where students display insecure attachments or bilinguals have negative emotions encoded with the English language due to past English education practices. In addition, through the cognitively transformative avenues of bilingualism and human relationships, this contribution has the potential to help both L2 and monolingual English writers by promoting social bonding as a means to globalizing the composition classroom. These integrated perspectives are particularly important, as globalization in higher education is increasingly demanding that the teaching of English composition and rhetoric appeal to more global audiences, in which multilingualism, new media, and World Englishes have become part of our everyday interactions.

REFERENCES

Ainsworth, M. D. S., Blehar, M. C., Waters, E. & Wall, S. (1978). *Patterns of attachment: A psychological study of the strange situation*. Hillsdale, NJ: Lawrence Erlbaum Associates; distributed by Halsted Press Division of Wiley.

Bakhtin, M. M. (1987). *Speech genres and other late essays* (V.W. McGee, Trans). Austin, TX: University of Texas Press.

Bialystok, E. (2009). Bilingualism: The good, the bad, and the indifferent. *Bilingualism: Language and cognition, 12*(01), 3–11.

Bialystok, E., Craik, F. I. & Luk, G. (2012). Bilingualism: Consequences for mind and brain. *Trends in cognitive sciences, 16*(4), 240–250.

Bowlby, J. (1969). *Attachment and loss*. New York: Basic Books.

Bowlby, J. (1988). *A secure base: Parent-child attachment and healthy human development*. New York: Basic Books.

Buchweitz, A. & Prat, C. (2013). The bilingual brain: Flexibility and control in the human cortex. *Physics of life reviews, 10*(4), 428–443.

Chamcharatsri, P. B. (2012). *Emotionality and composition in Thai and English* (Doctoral dissertation). Retrieved from ProQuest Dissertations and Theses. Paper 575.

Chamcharatsri, P. B. (2013). Emotionality and second language writers: Expressing fear through narrative in Thai and in English. *L2 Journal, 5*(1), 59–75.

Chen, J. J. & Yang, S. C. (2014). Fostering foreign language learning through technology-enhanced intercultural projects. *Language, Learning & Technology, 18*(1), 57–75.

Conboy, B. T. & Kuhl, P. K. (2011). Impact of second-language experience in infancy: Brain measures of first- and second-language speech perception. *Developmental Science, 14*(2), 242–248.

Cozolino, L. (2002). *The neuroscience of psychotherapy: Building and rebuilding the human brain.* New York: Norton.

Cozolino, L. (2013). *The social neuroscience of education: Optimizing attachment and learning in the classroom.* New York: Norton.

Cozolino, L. (2014). *The neuroscience of human relationships: Attachment and the developing social brain.* New York: Norton.

Dewaele, J. (2008). The emotional weight of "I love you" in multilinguals' languages. *Journal of Pragmatics, 40*(10), 1753–1780.

Dewaele, J. (2010). *Emotions in multiple languages.* Basingstoke, UK New York: Palgrave Macmillan.

Franklin, J. (Writer) & Zwick, J. (Director). (1987). Our very first show. [Television series episode]. In J. Franklin, T. L. Miller & R. L. Boyett (Executive producers), *Full House.* San Francisco, CA: ABC.

George, C. & West, M. L. (2012). *The adult attachment projective picture system: Attachment theory and assessment in adults.* New York: Guilford Press.

Holmes, J. (2014). *John Bowlby and attachment theory.* New York: Routledge, Taylor & Francis Group.

Horner, B., Lu, M. & Matsuda, P. K. (Eds.). (2010). *Cross-language relations in composition.* Carbondale, IL: Southern Illinois University Press.

Kachru, B. B. (1990). World Englishes and Applied Linguistics. *World Englishes, 9*(1), 3–20.

Koven, Michèle. (2007). *Selves in two languages: Bilinguals' verbal enactments of identity in French and Portuguese.* (Studies in Bilingualism). Amsterdam: Benjamins.

Kuhl, P. K. (2007). Is speech learning "gated" by the social brain? *Developmental Science, 10*(1), 110–120.

Kuhl, P. K. (2010, October). *The linguistic genius of babies* [Video file]. Retrieved from https://www.ted.com/talks/patricia_kuhl_the_linguistic_genius_of_babies.

Kuhl, P. K., Tsao, F. M. & Liu, H. (2003). Foreign-language experience in infancy: Effects of short-term exposure and social interaction on phonetic learning. *Proceedings of the National Academy of Sciences of the United States of America, 100*(15), 9096–9101.

Kuhl, P. K., Williams, K. A., Lacerda, F., Stevens, K. N & Lindblom, B. (1992). Linguistic experience alters phonetic perception in infants by 6 months of age. *Science, 255*(5044), 606–608.

Lee, N., Mikesell, L., Joaquin, A. D. L., Mates, A. W. & Schumann, J. H. (2009). *The interactional instinct: The evolution and acquisition of language.* New York: Oxford University Press.

Motha, S. (2014). *Race, empire, and English language teaching: Creating responsible and ethical anti-racist practice.* New York: Teachers College Press.

Ortmeier-Hooper, C. (2008). "'English may be my second language, but I'm not 'ESL.'" *College Composition and Communication, 59*(3), 389–419.

Pallier, C., Dehaene, S., Poline, J., LeBihan, D., Argenti, A., Dupoux, E. & Mehler, J. (2003). Brain imaging of language plasticity in adopted adults: Can a second language replace the first? *Cerebral Cortex, 13*(2), 155–161.

Paradis, M. (1994). Neurolinguistic aspects of implicit and explicit memory: Implications for bilingualism and SLA. In N. Ellis (Ed.), *Implicit and explicit learning of languages* (pp. 393–419). San Diego, CA: Academic Press.

Pavlenko, A. (2005). *Emotions and multilingualism.* Cambridge, UK: Cambridge University Press.

Riley, P. (2011). *Attachment theory and the teacher-student relationship: A practical guide for teachers, teacher educators and school leaders.* London/New York: Routledge.

Rintell, E. M. (1990). That's incredible: Stories of emotion told by second language learners and native speakers. In R. C. Scarcella, E. S. Anderson & S. D. Krashen (Eds.), *Developing communicative competence in a second language* (pp. 75–94). Boston: Heinle & Heinle.

Schaub, M. (2003). Beyond these shores: An argument for internationalizing composition. *Pedagogy, 3*(1), 85–98.

Schore, A. (2003). *Affect regulation and the repair of the self.* New York: Norton.

Schumann, J. (1997). *The neurobiology of affect in language.* Malden, MA: Blackwell.

Snyder, R., Shapiro, S. & Treleaven, D. (2012). Attachment theory and mindfulness. *Journal of Child and Family Studies, 21*(5), 709–717.

Toohey, K. (2000). *Learning English at school: Identity, social relations, and classroom practice.* Clevedon, UK: Multilingual Matters.

CHAPTER 6

MEANINGFUL PRACTICE: ADAPTIVE LEARNING, WRITING INSTRUCTION, AND WRITING RESEARCH

Gwen Gorzelsky
Colorado State University

Carol Hayes
George Washington University

Joseph Paszek
University of Detroit Mercy

Edmund Jones
Seton Hall University

Dana Lynn Driscoll
Indiana University of Pennsylvania

Robert Connors' influential 2000 essay, "The Erasure of the Sentence" documented decisive events in the field's history to explain how sentence rhetorics disappeared from writing studies conversations—despite empirical evidence of their effectiveness. Demonstrating the intersections between scholars' anxieties about repeated practice, the imitation of models, the risk of imposing a universal construct of cognition on diverse students, and suspicions about the value of empirical research, Connors showed that these concerns led us to abandon cognitive research studies investigating how writers develop a strong prose style at the sentence level. To do so, he reviewed not only the substantial body of empirical research demonstrating the effectiveness of sentence rhetorics in improving the sophistication, complexity, and nuance of students' prose but also the theoretical arguments that eventually shifted the field's focus away from this research. While he noted that "the reasons for the erasure of the sentence are multiple and complex," Connors argued that three themes underlay the field's abandonment of sentence rhetorics, themes that have importantly influenced writing studies in the decades since (2000, p. 110).

The first of these themes involved the shift in writing instruction and research from form to content. It arose from anxieties that emphasizing style, or form, suppressed creativity and adequate attention to content (Moffett, 1968; Rouse, 1979). The second theme entailed a suspicion of approaches to learning seen as emerging from behaviorist psychology, suspicions Connors characterized as "anti-automatism or anti-behaviorism" (2000, p. 113). Noting the intense distrust of behaviorist psychology among most humanists of the 1960s and 1970s, when sentence rhetorics had attained prominence, Connors explained that critiques of sentence rhetorics pedagogies viewed them as "inherently demeaning to students" because these exercises were intended "to build 'skills' in a way that was not meant to be completely conscious" (2000, p. 113). Critics argued that this approach undermined creativity and conscious choice making. Finally, Connors discussed 1980s critiques of empirical research as focused problematically on individual cognition, to the seeming exclusion of the extensive social influences on writing and humanist perspectives. Indeed, as Marcus Meade (this volume) notes, "individual cognition, as a focus of inquiry within composition, took a back seat to considerations of social factors."

Although Connors emphasized the field's decreased interest in writers' development of sentence-level stylistic expertise—a loss that we agree has serious negative implications—we view the field's turn away from *practice* as equally significant, and equally negative. We appreciate the concerns about creativity and content raised by critics of sentence rhetorics and certainly agree that sociocultural factors crucially shape thinking and writing, but we contend that the suspicion of writing practice "meant to tap into non-conscious behavioral structures" (Connors, 2000, p. 113) is misplaced. Specifically, we hold that, taken together, recent research findings on adult neuroplasticity, theories of situated cognition, and research on the role of practice in writing development suggest two salient points. First, both conscious choice and practice honing non-conscious capacities play crucial roles in writing development. Second, this practice must be integrated thoughtfully into learning situated in socially meaningful settings.

Although we believe that many curricula and pedagogical approaches can support effective writing practice, here we explore the potential benefits—and challenges—of integrating research-based adaptive learning platforms for writing into dynamic, well-designed writing courses to facilitate such practice. We show how such integration may better support writers' growth and extend existing research methods for investigating how writers develop proficiency. To do so, we summarize research on adult neuroplasticity, theories of situated cognition, and the role of practice in writing development, considering their implications for writing development and instruction. We then discuss how our focus on practice relates directly to three of the eight habits of mind outlined in the *Framework for Success in Postsecondary Writing* (developed by the leading professional organizations within the field of writing studies—The Council of Writing Program Administrators [CWPA], the National Council of Teachers of English [NCTE], and the National Writing Project [NWP]; see CWPA 2011, in reference list) as key to students' growing capacity to write effectively across contexts. To consider the conceptual and procedural writing knowledge that adaptive platforms might usefully help students to develop, we summarize findings from our prior multi-institutional research study of post-secondary writers' growth in and beyond general education writing courses, highlighting three specific knowledge areas, and link them to the three habits of mind that we believe can also be fostered by integrating adaptive platforms. Based on this work and a review of studies of adaptive platforms designed by researchers (not commercial vendors), we argue that writing studies researchers and teachers should seek to join the cross-disciplinary research teams now developing adaptive platforms for writing instruction and investigating their outcomes.

A LENS FOR RECONSIDERING PRACTICE: ADULT NEUROPLASTICITY

The value of practice highlighted in Connors' reprise of work on sentence rhetorics is reinforced by research in the last decade demonstrating the heretofore unsuspected neuroplasticity of the adult brain. Neuroscientists' accounts for lay readers (e.g., Doidge, 2007; Schwartz & Begley, 2002) emphasize the role of practice in eliciting changes in perceptual, affective, and behavioral habits, as well as in dispositions, which are typically seen as quite resistant to change. These accounts each summarized studies showing how stroke victims with motor loss previously thought irrecoverable regained motor skills through sustained practice that rerouted neural pathways to brain segments not typically linked to motor control of affected regions. They also highlighted studies showing how students with dyslexia benefit from practicing with recordings of slowed speech to learn to identify sound units they cannot ordinarily hear, then practicing with increasingly quicker speech until they can eventually hear these units when articulated at a normal rate of speech, with changes in neural structures (as shown through brain scans) paralleling changes in perceptual ability. Norman Doidge (2007) described research demonstrating marked differences in the balance between focused vs. holistic views between Easterners' and Westerners' perceptual habits and in their related neurological structures. Not only consistent practice but even consistently *visualizing* specific practice (e.g., of piano scales) produced substantial changes in ability as well as in neural pathways in relevant brain regions (Doidge, 2007; Schwartz & Begley, 2006). Both accounts recounted the results of a study of experienced London taxicab drivers, whose hippocampi (which store spatial memories) were substantially larger than those of other males in the same age cohort.

Strikingly, these and other accounts of research on neuroplasticity have shown the capacity of practice to revise deeply engrained cognitive, affective, and behavioral tendencies typically quite resistant to change. For instance, Alberto Chiesa, Paolo Brambilla, and Alessandro Serretti (2010) showed that pharmacotherapy, mindfulness-based behavioral treatments for depression, psychotherapy, and the placebo effect all substantively impacted activity in the amygdala, a brain region that processes negative emotions. However, unlike pharmacotherapy, which affected the amygdala directly, the latter three treatments moderated amygdala activity indirectly, by activating brain regions associated with intention and logic, specifically, areas such as the prefrontal cortex and orbitofrontal cortex, which in turn inhibited amygdala activity. Jeffrey Schwartz and Sharon Begley (2002) summarized comparable results for behavioral treatments of serious obsessive-compulsive disorder (OCD), while both they and Doidge (2007) reprised similar results from research on another behavioral treatment for clinical depression. In this collection, Jen Talbot notes in her discussion of the situated writer, that neuroplasticity "is at work in any form of learning." Dirk Remley (this volume) describes neuroplasticity similarly. James Austin (2009) explained that Yi-Yuan Tang and colleagues' study (Tang et al., 2007) compared outcomes for participants who practiced both relaxation techniques and awareness cultivation with outcomes for controls who practiced only relaxation techniques. Tests conducted after five days of training showed that, in comparison with controls, participants experienced stronger positive moods and decreased negative moods, better executive direction of attention, and decreased evidence of stress (in the form of decreased cortisol levels and higher immunoglobulin A levels) after performing mental arithmetic. Austin attributed these changes to quick increases in skills for focusing voluntary attention, that is, the top-down attention mechanisms controlled by intention, as opposed to the bottom-up mechanisms triggered by responses to stimuli. Meade's (this volume) description of mindfulness as an awareness that promotes agency in writers' self-reconstruction aligns with the findings from these studies, while Irene Clark (this volume) discussed the changes in identity that can result from such reconstructions. Taken together, these accounts of findings on adult neuroplasticity emphasize that individuals' initial learning and revisions of engrained habits and dispositions result from practice that intervenes at the intersection among physiological, behavioral, cultural, cognitive, and affective factors.

SITUATED COGNITION

The importance of this intersection appears in recent work on situated cognition, a theoretical framework positing that cognition is fundamentally shaped by both bodily experience (as distinct from strictly mental experience) and by emotional, socio-cultural, physical, and other environmental factors (Clancey, 2009; Robbins & Aydede, 2009). More traditional theories of cognition understand it from a Cartesian perspective (Mills, 1998), viewing it as a set of mental operations distinct from, and unaffected by, the body; as an individual phenomenon unaffected by socio-cultural context; and as an internal process unaffected by physical and other environmental factors. In contrast, theorists of situated cognition view it as emerging from a complex interplay among the brain, the body, and the environment (physical, socio-cultural, economic, etc.) These foundational components function in mutually constitutive ways, a view highlighted in Talbot's (in press) argument that social and material circumstances shape the writer's cognition and composing process. Although traditional theories of cognition tend to view influence as hierarchical and linear, with the mind influencing the body and then the environment, situated theories posit a more iterative process in which each component shapes the others, with no one taking primacy. As William J. Clancey explained, "the systems comprising cognition are in principle complexly related. Physiological, conceptual, and organizational systems are mutually constraining—not causally nested" (2009, p. 19) and "cognitive processes are causally both social and neural" (p. 12).

Further, situated cognition theorists have defined knowledge as dynamically constructed, remembered, and reinterpreted in social contexts. Through interactions among brain, body, and environment, individuals actively build knowledge, rather than passively receiving it. For example, situated cognition theorists argue that objects can play a role in cognition, as in the use of writing to record, revisit, and later use information not recalled directly. Because knowledge is actively constructed in this way, knowledge provides not objective understanding but rather a means of organizing and adapting to the world. That is, individuals interact with the world to achieve particular goals and construct knowledge in the process. Even supposedly pure knowledge emerges from such interactions and therefore offers a specific perspective, rather than an objective view. Because such interactions ground learning, learning occurs not only through after-the-fact reflection but also through action (Clancey, 2009). Thus knowledge is transformed as people learn, because learning inherently involves adaptation and interpretation based on the learner's perspective. Rather than knowledge moving statically from one context to another as individuals traverse environments, as traditional theories posit, knowledge is "improved in action, not simply transferred and applied" (Clancy, 2009, pp. 16–17). Read in light of findings from research on adult neuroplasticity, situated cognition theory implies that while practice is crucial to learning and the development of expertise, participation in rich social contexts—where knowledge is adapted to pursue particular socially defined goals—is equally crucial. Next we discuss the role of practice, particularly deliberate practice (defined below), to foster writing growth.

SCHOLARSHIP ON PRACTICE

Writing is a complex activity that requires intense cognitive effort; Ronald T. Kellogg (2006) compared the cognitive demands experienced by writers while composing to those experienced by expert chess players while evaluating multiple possible moves in the middle stages of a chess game (pp. 392–393). For novice writers, the cognitive demands are severe. Cognitive psychologists who study the stages of skill acquisition note that the cognitive effort required for any newly learned skill is highest for novices. Research on skill acquisition identifies three stages for learning: First, the beginner must not only learn the basics of the new domain, s/he must also apply concentrated effort to generating the required actions and avoiding egregious errors (Ericsson, 2006, p. 684). Second, learners perform at an acceptable level through much less effort; third, the learners' "performance skills become automated, and they are able to execute these skills smoothly and with minimal effort" (Ericsson, 2006, p. 684). Practice helps learners move through these stages.

Cognitive psychology research has suggested that repeated practice can help reduce demands on both executive attention (the "mindful and conscious attention that we bring to a task" [Cassity, 2013, p. 21]) and working memory, by helping writers to partially automate certain writing processes—albeit within limits (Kellogg & Whiteford, 2009). Kellogg and Alison P. Whiteford noted that in writing, practice can "reduce, not eliminate, the demands of component processes . . . to free attention for their coordination and control . . . practice allows one to be mindful of the whole task, rather than its components, and to be free to respond flexibly and adaptively to the unpredictable needs of the moment" (2009, p. 252). Expert writers adapt successfully to varying rhetorical situations across contexts because they have both content knowledge and some internalized writing knowledge. Thus they need not devote working memory to either. By helping novice writers to internalize knowledge of some writing components, like planning or syntactic constructions, sustained practice can reduce their cognitive load so they can respond with flexible adaptation to unexpected needs as they learn to write in new contexts.

In particular, Kellogg and Whiteford (2009) advocated "deliberate practice," in which the learner targets individual components of the desired skill for improvement through practice. Importantly, they note that the learner must be motivated to engage in the practice—rote drilling won't produce the desired gains. This research is based on K. Anders Ericsson's (2006) discussion of the "deliberate practice" that experts employ to gain their expertise. Ericsson argues that there's a skill acquisition phase that can *follow* the achievement of automatization—or relative automatization—of a learner's performance. For Ericsson, "deliberate practice" involves breaking down an already-learned skill into components and then deliberately focusing on those components in order to *de-automatize* them, so that they can be relearned in better ways. For teachers of writing who are interested in helping students achieve partial automaticity of at least some of the components involved in writing, this turn to "deliberate practice" might seem counter-intuitive. However, Barry J. Zimmerman (2006) showed the role of this practice in promoting effective self-regulation, explaining that experts' practice entails a "high level of concentration and the structuring of specific training tasks to facilitate setting appropriate personal goals, monitoring informative feedback, and providing opportunities for repetition and error correction (p. 705). In this approach, deliberate, strategic attention helps learners to "overcome prior habits, to self-monitor accurately, and to determine necessary adjustments" (Zimmerman, 2006, p. 705).

Novices learning a new skill can borrow some strategies from "deliberate practice" as Zimmerman's (2006) description of a study by Cleary, Zimmerman, and Tedd Keating (2006) showed. In this study, college students learned basketball free throws in physical education courses by combining "deliberate practice's" mindful focus on specific components of a skill with metacognitive self-regulation's attention to planning, monitoring, and evaluation. Some participants were asked to set goals not focused on higher shooting outcomes but on executing component skills of free-throws process (i.e., grip, elbow position, knee bend, and follow through). These participants learned to monitor performance on each component using a self-recording form after each shot. They performed significantly better than did two other groups: participants who had practiced free throws without instruction and participants who had set goals to execute component skills but not learned to monitor their performance. Participants who learned to reflect by connecting free-throw attempt outcomes with specific component skills performed best of all groups. Therefore, deliberate practice—or what we might rename "meaningful practice" to acknowledge that we're discussing skill acquisition for novices—can help to develop proficiency in new component skills through improved self-regulation of learning.

THE ROLE OF THE *FRAMEWORK:* HABITS OF MIND

The *Framework* (CWPA et al., 2011) discusses eight habits of mind: active, positive approaches to learning that help students adapt their writing knowledge in new contexts. Of those eight habits of mind, adaptive learning programs are particularly well designed to cultivate three: flexibility, persistence, and metacognition. *Flexibility* entails recognizing different rhetorical situations and adapting to their audiences, purposes, and contexts. Adaptive learning platforms can encourage flexibility by helping students explore different problem types within writing. For instance, an adaptive learning system for teaching genre awareness in GEW courses could present various genres from across disciplines to help students learn to recognize, analyze, and adapt to different rhetorical situations. *Persistence* involves sustained attention to a task over time. Adaptive learning systems use immediate feedback on student attempts to practice a particular component skill to help students recognize when they need additional practice. Finally, *metacognition* entails using reflection on one's writing choices to "improve writing on subsequent projects" (CWPA, 2011). Adaptive platforms could teach metacognitive reflection, scaffolding students' engagement in increasingly complex metacognitive thinking about writing tasks and their self-regulatory strategies (e.g., monitoring writing processes and outcomes, choosing alternate processes as needed, and evaluating their texts). By structuring students' practice in ways that promote persistence, flexibility, and metacognitive self-regulation, adaptive platforms could promote these three habits of mind in ways that support writers' growth. We turn next to specific component writing skills that adaptive platforms could foster through scaffolded instruction and practice.

FACTORS IN KNOWLEDGE TRANSFER/ADAPTATION

We focus on three component skills that our prior research has suggested promote writing transfer: genre awareness, use of sources, and metacognition. Specifically, we draw on findings from the first phase of The Writing Transfer Project, a two-year, cross-institutional, multi-modal study of writing transfer factors in postsecondary education. We found that students from all four diverse participating universities gained writing proficiency while taking general education writing (GEW) courses during the study's first semester. However, most students at all four universities lost writing proficiency while taking disciplinary writing courses during the study's second year, although some students did gain proficiency. We measured writing gains/losses through blind ratings of pre- and post-GEW writing samples and disciplinary course writing samples.

One factor—genre awareness, defined as a sophisticated understanding of genre as a social action, one directed toward a specific audience for a specific purpose—predicted gains from pre- to post-semester GEW writing samples. Three factors—measured by coding students' reflective texts—predicted changes in writing proficiency from post-GEW to disciplinary writing samples. Prior knowledge, or students' references to using high school writing knowledge in post-secondary settings, correlated *negatively* with gains in writing proficiency from GEW to disciplinary writing. In contrast, two other factors correlated positively with writing proficiency gains from GEW to disciplinary writing. The first we call "sources applied," as it involves the ability to apply a scholarly source as a conceptual tool to analyze, evaluate, or interpret a separate object of study. The second entails the ability to describe writing processes used for a specific writing task (as opposed to a general writing process).

We interpret the negative correlation between use of prior knowledge and writing proficiency gains from GEW to disciplinary writing as possibly indicating students' return to important but often formulaic writing conventions learned in high school (Kiuhara, Graham & Hawkin, 2009). As Mary Jo Reiff and Anis Bawarshi's (2011) work shows, college freshmen who apply high school writing strategies wholesale tend to be less successful in college writing courses than students who adapt such high school strategies to meet the demands of a new context. Thus we suggest that high reliance on unmodified prior knowledge may indicate that students don't recognize the need for such adaptation or don't know how to undertake it. To interpret the positive impact of sources applied, which Joseph Bizup (2008) describes as "methods source" use, we draw on Michael Carter's (2007) work with metagenres, or genre types (like the lab report or analysis paper) shared by several disciplines. Because applying a source as a conceptual lens for analyzing other texts or objects of study is a component writing skill used across many academic disciplines—academic metagenres—we're not surprised that facility in it predicted writing proficiency gains for students moving into disciplinary courses. Finally, we suggest that the ability to describe writing processes used in a specific composing task may predict writing proficiency gains (as opposed to awareness of a generalized writing process, which did not predict such gains) because this component skill helped students to reflect metacognitively on how well their strategies were helping them to effectively address the particular rhetorical situation, audience, purpose, and context of a given writing task.

The three component skills in writing development that predicted growth in writing proficiency—genre awareness, sources applied, and metacognitive reflection on a specific writing task—link directly to the three habits of mind discussed above—flexibility, persistence, and metacognition. Flexibility supports the development of genre awareness, as defined above (and vice versa). Persistence is required to learn challenging conceptual and procedural knowledge, including an understanding of genre as social action and how to use a source as a lens for analyzing another object of study. Metacognition that uses reflection to improve one's process in subsequent writing tasks both supports, and benefits from, metacognitive attention to the writing process used in a particular composing task.

As we argue below, because adaptive platforms can foster persistence, flexibility, and metacognitive development, they could encourage students' development of both the three component skills and the three linked habits of mind we've highlighted.

ADAPTIVE LEARNING OVERVIEW: PERILS AND PROMISE

To illustrate the potential value of integrating adaptive learning platforms into robust writing courses, we discuss computer-based writing instruction to date, including research findings on its limitations and efficacy. We wish to highlight a crucial point about these studies: researchers emphasize that computer-based writing instruction is not intended to replace instructors but rather to support well designed classroom instruction (Blumenstyk, 2016; A. Gibson, personal communication, April 26, 2016). We see adaptive platforms as potential vehicles for helping students to cultivate the analytical, synthetic, and metacognitive abilities that our prior research suggests predict successful transfer of writing knowledge into new contexts and, potentially, as vehicles for instructors' professional development.

We begin with Laura K. Allen, Matthew E. Jacovina, and Danielle S. McNamara's (2016) useful overview of research on computer-based writing instruction, which also introduces the authors' own adaptive learning platform, Writing Pal (W Pal). Like many other researchers in this domain, Allen et al. emphasize that developing effective adaptive platforms for writing entails substantially greater challenges than doing so for disciplines teaching well-defined problems, such as many science, technology, engineering, and math (STEM) fields, because writing is an ill-defined domain, or one in which problems do not have a single definitive answer. The authors address some of these challenges in summarizing research on three distinct but connected modes of computer-based writing instruction: Automated Essay Scoring, Automated Writing Evaluation, and adaptive learning platforms.

The first—and most criticized—mode of computer-based writing instruction, Automated Essay Scoring (AES), focuses strictly on summative assessment, often in high-stakes testing, without providing instruction or formative feedback. Although Allen et al. (2016) claim high levels of reliability and validity for AES systems generally, they do acknowledge critiques showing that students can subvert AES scoring through various approaches that exploit AES scoring features but do not produce high-quality texts, for instance, by repeating the same paragraph throughout an entire essay or by using syntactic sophistication and terms relevant to prompt content. Nonetheless, the authors contend that the AES system that functions within W Pal measures both superficial features (e.g., numbers of words in sentences and sentences in paragraphs) and more substantive features (e.g., semantic cohesion and use of rhetorical devices). However, the authors agree with critiques arguing that AES has significant validity concerns because such systems are, as yet, unable to measure meaningful aspects of writing such as creativity and development of specific ideas or whole arguments.

Unlike AES systems, Automated Writing Evaluation (AWE) systems provide both opportunities to practice and formative, as well as summative, holistic feedback on drafts. Allen et al. (2016) highlight prior research suggesting that AWE systems promote persistence and improved writing quality for students, despite challenges in providing specific feedback tied to particular aspects of students' drafts (Gikandi, Morrow & Davis, 2011; Grimes & Warschauer, 2010;), an important issue given that generalized feedback has proven less useful in prompting effective revisions. The W-Pal platform offers such holistic feedback.

Finally, in addition to the holistic practice and feedback that AWE systems offer students, Allen et al. (2016) emphasize that Intelligent Tutoring Systems (ITS), or adaptive platforms, provide writing content and strategy instruction, opportunities to practice component skills (e.g., drafting conclusions), and tailored performance feedback that also directs students to relevant instructional materials. In addition to providing holistic feedback, W Pal offers students tailored performance feedback on component skills. Writing samples scored by experts underlie platforms' feedback algorithms. Some adaptive systems, like W Pal, address boredom—reported by students participating in some adaptive platforms—by using a game-based approach, which has been shown by prior research to improve engagement. The authors highlight ongoing research investigating which types of feedback best promote writing development and more effective revision for particular students. For instance, because some research suggests that more effective writers use more flexible strategies for improving a text's cohesion across different writing tasks, adaptive platforms' feedback might be tailored to provide less flexible writers with prompts to experiment with more diverse approaches to establishing cohesion. While adaptive platforms generally do not address content and further research is needed to optimize feedback for individual students, research to date shows promise.

Further research on adaptive platforms bears out this promise. Using a robust model of revision, with an emphasis on global, substantive changes, rather than superficial editing, Jacovina et al. (2015) investigated how students using the W Pal adaptive platform transformed their drafts. Although holistic essay scores improved minimally across essays for the students participating in the 10-week summer program under study, use of the W Pal platform prompted students to make more global revisions and fewer superficial revisions in several areas, including elaboration (by adding details, examples, and other content); organization (clearer introduction-body-conclusion structures); cohesion; and semantic proficiency (as demonstrated by decreased word repetition). Pointing out that students undertook substantive revisions in all eight of the essays they drafted, the authors highlight as an example a student whose initial draft began with a strong introduction but moved into an under-developed body and conclusion. After receiving W Pal feedback suggesting that the body of the essay needed elaboration, the student requested and received additional optional feedback on a "Next Topic," in this case determined by the platform to be developing conclusions. In response, the student added a new body paragraph, example, sign-posting, and a concluding paragraph that more clearly restated the thesis. Suggesting that real-time feedback may more effectively motivate and help writers to revise, the authors argued that their findings suggest that W Pal successfully provided individualized feedback that prompted students to recognize and effectively use writing process strategies and related knowledge by focusing on substantive, rather than superficial, revisions.

While this research focused on the five-paragraph theme, which is not typically assigned in post-secondary writing courses, we contend that the improvements in students' writing and revision processes—including self-regulation strategies—*are* among the types we hope to promote for post-secondary writers. Allen and McNamara (2015) argued that the greatest potential benefit of adaptive platforms for writing instruction may be their capacity to promote students' capacities for effective self-regulation of their own learning. Erica L. Snow et al.'s (2015) study of an adaptive program's capacity to improve students' monitoring of their reading comprehension showed substantial gains in metacognitive monitoring and control, key components of self-regulated learning, as well as in students' explanations of texts read. Similarly, in their investigation of how an adaptive platform improved the accuracy of students' assessments of their drafts, Allen et al. (2015) showed that these gains resulted from a combination of writing strategy instruction, game-based practice, and holistic practice in drafting full essays. They compared writing gains for student study participants who took part in half the practice opportunities and received half the feedback offered to control group members. However, unlike controls, participants received instruction designed to improve their abilities to assess their drafts. Their results showed similar gains for participants and controls, with participants achieving the same gains controls did while completing only half the practice. The authors concluded that students were apparently learning to monitor their writing strategies more effectively based on instruction and feedback from the adaptive platform and that this improved monitoring explains participants' achievement of gains that equaled those of controls, despite participants' more limited practice time. In their report on development of a platform designed to provide formative feedback on students' reflective writing, Buckingham Shum et al. (2016) emphasized the goal of helping students to engage in metacognitive thinking focused on adapting and extending knowledge when moving from academic to pre-professional contexts. Andrew Gibson and Kirsty Kitto's (2015) discussion of their efforts to provide automated formative feedback intended to improve students' reflective writing focused on metacognitive strategies, particularly monitoring and control as means to promote more effective self-regulation of learning. Finally, a discourse analytics tool designed to provide instructors and researchers with data on students' discourse moves in online collaborative learning interactions also has the potential to provide individualized, context-sensitive formative feedback to students about the cognitive strategies enacted in their collaborative discourse moves (Rosé et al., 2008).

We agree with concerns raised about the perils of using AES for high-stakes summative writing assessment and the contention that all three modes of computer-based writing instruction require further development. Still, the promise of adaptive platforms for providing formative feedback designed to extend—not replace—effective in-class writing instruction suggests that writing studies scholars and researchers might fruitfully engage more deeply with the research on computer-based writing instruction described above. Below we argue for the potential value of seeking to join the group of cross-disciplinary researchers working to develop and investigate the effects of adaptive platforms for writing instruction.

MOBILIZING THE POTENTIAL OF ADAPTIVE LEARNING FOR WRITING STUDIES

Based on the potential of adaptive platforms, recent discoveries about how practice drives adult neuroplasticity, the principles of situated cognition, and the value of meaningful practice, we argue that, integrated thoughtfully, research-based adaptive platforms could provide the field with tools that offer rich potential for (1) improving writing instruction, (2) extending research on writing development, and (3) contributing to writing instructors' professional development.

We believe that weaving such platforms into dynamic writing classrooms can promote writers' growth. Adaptive systems can help to encourage deliberate practice and so help writers to more effectively self-regulate relevant cognitive and other learning-related behaviors. By mobilizing the potential of environmental resources (e.g., samples of various genres), physical and cognitive activity (e.g., highlighting and annotating genre samples), they can leverage practice's impact on neural networks in the processes of internalizing—and thus transforming—knowledge. For instance, by immersing students in extensive practice analyzing how sources are used or key features of new genres, adaptive platforms involve the body, given that reading and writing responses entail physical, as well as cognitive, activity. In the process, students engage extensively with external objects designed to scaffold their cognitive growth, namely sample texts illustrating types of source use and/or genre features. Such practice provides the required foundation for the physiological changes that neuroplasticity research shows coincide with developing new abilities or revising prior cognitive, perceptual, or behavioral habits.

Weaving such practice into robust writing curricula is crucial. Courses that engage students deeply in the social aspects of writing and writing development provide an essential context for the effective use of adaptive platforms. Such courses, particularly if designed to scaffold students' experiences of social contexts for their writing, are needed to help students see meaning and value in effective writing and therefore to motivate the extensive engagement required for successful use of adaptive platforms. Further, robust writing curricula provide students with the framework required to help them to use their growing knowledge of writing as a way to organize and adapt to the world, primarily by explicitly preparing students to write in concurrent or upcoming courses or in pre-professional, civic, or other venues. Instructors can facilitate students' connections between GEW courses and other writing contexts by explicitly linking assignments to students' use of the adaptive platform to foster proficiencies in analyzing source use, genre features, and their writing strategies. As students investigate how they can *learn to learn* to write in venues outside GEW courses, they can begin to develop the contextual understanding essential to assimilating writing knowledge in a way that adapts this knowledge to their particular perspectives and goals.

Similarly, we view the data on writing development that adaptive platforms can generate as useful means of complementing the array of textual, qualitative, and quantitative studies the field now collects to investigate writing growth. Such complementary data could extend the impact of our existing set of research methods in a number of ways. First, it will enable researchers to design and conduct multi-institutional studies of writing development with a reasonable degree of uniformity in data collection—a uniformity that has proven difficult to achieve to date, due to the wide variation in curricula and instructional practices shaped to meet the needs of diverse local writing program contexts. Second, adaptive platforms will provide keystroke data tracking students' uses of adaptive modules' materials and digital data on the levels at which they achieve each module's learning outcomes. These data could usefully be analyzed in conjunction with data on related phenomena: rating data assessing the quality of students' texts and revisions, survey data measuring their self-efficacy for writing and engagement with writing courses, and reflective data gauging their understanding and integration of key conceptual and procedural writing knowledge. Third, the keystroke data could also be used to measure difficult-to-study capacities such as self-regulation strategies and students' development of the key habits of mind discussed in this article. Finally, adaptive learning platforms offer opportunities to study the rich social contexts that well-designed writing courses establish. By collecting qualitative data on students' in-class engagement and comparing that data with evidence of students' uses of adaptive platforms to develop proficiency in key component skills, such as genre analysis, investigators can learn which features of such social contexts appear to motivate students to practice to develop greater proficiency in these component skills.

Finally, the use of well-designed adaptive modules has important implications for instructors' professional development, from both individual and programmatic perspectives. Using adaptive modules to teach conceptual and procedural writing knowledge can scaffold professional development for instructors with little expertise in the module's subject matter (e.g., teaching genre awareness). Because instructors can use the modules with minimal preparation and learn from the modules and their students' responses to module prompts, integrating a module on knowledge areas unfamiliar to the instructor offers an engaging, effective, and efficient means to develop teaching expertise in a new area. This approach substantially reduces the extensive revision of course materials typically involved in such an endeavor, a point suggested by our process of developing and testing paper prototypes of the adaptive modules we hope to construct.

Three co-authors piloted our paper prototypes of adaptive modules for Sources Applied, Genre, and Metacognition. Each module guided students' development in its knowledge area. Co-authors who piloted the prototypes found that their use enriched teaching—prompting one co-author to revise his course for future semesters and a second to integrate the metacognition module into an honors writing course. Co-authors found that adding the modules required little modification of their existing courses, although they did link course assignments to the modules' content. Each of the three courses was quite distinct, due to local contextual factors. While two co-authors were teaching revised writing about writing curricula (each different from the other and each adapted to fit its local context), a third took a theme-based approach. This curricular range, coupled with the successful use of the modules across these diverse courses in three distinctly different institutions with divergent writing programs, staffing, and student demographics, demonstrates the modules' capacity to support learning in various curricula and contexts.

This capacity, coupled with modules' potential to foster development of both key conceptual and procedural writing knowledge, on the one hand, and key habits of mind, on the other, means that data from adaptive modules might also usefully inform programmatic assessments and professional development efforts. The use of keystroke data showing students' engagement with adaptive modules and their level of mastery of each learning outcome in each module could complement existing textual, qualitative, and quantitative data used in programmatic assessments. Similarly, encouraging instructors to cultivate teaching expertise in new areas by incorporating well-designed adaptive modules into their courses could effectively supplement professional development workshops, instructor communities of practice, and the like. In sum, while the use of adaptive platforms raises legitimate concerns that must be carefully addressed, we see high potential value for writing studies researchers and teachers in seeking to join cross-disciplinary collaborations with other researchers working to design adaptive platforms for writing instruction. In addition to the substantial benefits to students' writing growth that may be gained by integrating such platforms thoughtfully into well-constructed writing courses, researchers may glean new and valuable types of data, while writing program administrators may obtain expanded approaches to assessment and professional development for instructors.

REFERENCES

Allen, L. K., Crossley, S. A., Snow, E. L., Jacovina, M. E., Perret, C. & McNamara, D. S. (2015). Am I wrong or am I right? Gains in monitoring accuracy in an intelligent tutoring system for writing. In C. Conati, N. Heffernan, A. Mitrovic & M. F. Verdejo (Eds.), *Artificial intelligence in Education: 17th international conference, AIED 2015 Madrid Spain, June 22–26, 2015, Proceedings* (pp. 533–536). New York: Springer.

Allen, L. K., Jacovina, M. E. & McNamara, D. S. (2016). Computer-based writing instruction. In C. J. MacArthur, S. Graham & J. Fitzgerald (Eds.), *Handbook of writing research* (2nd ed.) (pp. 316–330). New York: Guilford.

Allen, L. K. & McNamara, D. S. (2015). Promoting self-regulated learning in an intelligent tutoring system for writing. In C. Conati, N. Heffernan, A. Mitrovic & M.F. Verdejo (Eds.), *Artificial intelligence in Education: 17th international conference, AIED 2015 Madrid Spain, June 22–26, 2015, Proceedings* (pp. 827–830). New York: Springer.

Austin, J. H. (2009). *Selfless insight: Zen and the meditative transformation of consciousness*. Cambridge, MA: MIT Press.

Bizup, J. (2008). BEAM: A rhetorical vocabulary for teaching research-based writing. *Rhetoric Review, 27*(1), 72–86.

Blumenstyk, G. (2016). As big-data companies come to teaching, a pioneer issues a warning. *The Chronicle of Higher Education*. Retrieved from http://chronicle.com/article/As-Big-Data-Companies-Come-to/235400.

Buckingham Shum, S., Sandor, A, Goldsmith, R., Wang, X., Bass, R. & McWilliams, M. (2016). Reflecting on reflective writing analytics: Assessment challenges and iterative evaluation of a prototype tool. In *LAK 2016: Proceedings of the sixth international conference of learning analytics & knowledge* (pp. 213–222). New York: Association for Computing Machinery.

Carter, M. (2007). Ways of knowing, doing, and writing in the disciplines. *College Composition and Communication, 58*(3), 385–418.

Cassity, K. J. (2013). Practice, patience, and process in the age of accountability: What cognitive psychology suggests about the teaching and assessment of writing. *Journal of Teaching Writing, 28*(2), 19–40.

Chiesa, A., Brambilla, P. & Serretti, A. (2010). Functional neural correlates of mindfulness meditations in comparison with psychotherapy, pharmacotherapy, and placebo effect. Is there a link? *Acta Neuropsychiatrica, 22*, 104–117.

Clancey, W. J. (2009). Scientific antecedents of situated cognition. In P. Robbins & M. Aydede (Eds.), *The Cambridge handbook of situated cognition* (pp. 11–34). Cambridge, UK: Cambridge University Press.

Cleary, T. J., Zimmerman, B. & Keating, T. (2006). Training physical education students to self-regulate during basketball free throw practice. *Research Quarterly for Exercise and Sport, 77*(2), 251–262.

Connors, R.T. (2000). The erasure of the sentence. *College Composition and Communication, 52*(1), 96–128.

Council of Writing Program Administrators, National Council of Teachers of English & National Writing Project (2011). *Framework for success in postsecondary writing*. Retrieved from http://wpacouncil.org/files/framework-for-success-postsecondary-writing.pdf.

Doidge, N. (2007). *The brain that changes itself: Stories of personal triumph from the frontiers of brain science*. New York: Penguin.

Ericsson, K. A. (2006). The influence of experience and deliberate practice on the development of superior expert performance. In K. Anders Ericsson, N. Charness, P. J. Feltovich & R. R. Hoffman (Eds.), *The Cambridge handbook of expertise and expert performance* (pp. 683–703). Cambridge, UK: Cambridge University Press.

Gibson, A. & Kitto, K. (2015). Analysing reflective texts for learning analytics: An approach using anomaly recontextualisation. In *Proceedings of the fifth international conference on learning analytics and knowledge* (pp. 275–279). Poughkeepsie, NY: Association for Computing Machinery.

Gikandi, J. W., Morrow, D. & Davis, N. E. (2011). Online formative assessment in higher education: A review of the literature. *Computers & Education, 57*, 2333–2351.

Grimes, D. & Warshauer, M. (2010). Utility in a fallible tool: A multi-site case study of automated writing evaluation. *The Journal of Technology, Learning, and Assessment, 8,* 6. Retrieved from http://ejournals.bc.edu/ojs/index.php/jtla/article/view/1625/1469.

Jacovina, M. E., Snow, E. L., Dai, J. & McNamara, D. S. (2015). Authoring tools for ill-defined domains in intelligent tutoring systems: Flexibility and stealth assessment. In R. Sottilare, A. Graesser, X. Hu & K. Brawner (Eds.) *Design recommendations for intelligent tutoring systems: Authoring tools and expert modeling,* Vol. 3 (pp. 108–121). Orlando, FL: U.S. Army Research Laboratory.

Kellogg, R. T. (2006). Professional writing expertise. In A. Ericsson, N. Charness, P. J. Feltovich & R. R. Hoffman (Eds.), *The Cambridge handbook of expertise and expert performance* (pp. 389–402). Cambridge, UK: Cambridge University Press.

Kellogg, R. T. & Whiteford, A. P. (2006). Training advanced writing skills: The case for deliberate practice. *Educational Psychologist 44*(4), 250–266.

Kiuhara, S. A., Graham, S. & Hawkin, L. S. (2009). Teaching writing to high school students: A national survey. *Journal of Educational Psychology, 101,* 136–160.

Mills, F. B. (1998). The easy and hard problems of consciousness: A Cartesian perspective. *Journal of Mind and Behavior, 19*(2), 119–140.

Moffett, J. (1968). *Teaching the universe of discourse.* Boston: Houghton Mifflin.

Reiff, M. & Bawarshi, A. (2011). Tracing discursive resources: How students use prior genre knowledge to negotiate new writing contexts in first-year composition. *Written Communication, 28*(3), 312–337.

Robbins, P. & Aydede, M. (2009). A short primer on situated cognition. In P. Robbins & M. Aydede (Eds.), *The Cambridge handbook of situated cognition* (pp. 3–10). Cambridge, UK: Cambridge University Press.

Rosé, C., Wang, Y. C., Arguello, J., Stegmann, K., Weinberger & Fischer, F. (2008). Analyzing collaborative learning processes automatically: Exploiting the advances of computational linguistics in computer-supported collaborative learning. *Computer-Supported Collaborative Learning, 3,* 237–271.

Rouse, J. J. (1979). Knowledge, power, and the teaching of English. *College English, 40*(5), 473–491.

Schwartz, J. M. & Begley, S. (2002). *The mind and the brain: Neuroplasticity and the power of mental force.* New York: Harper Collins.

Snow, E. L., McNamara, D. S., Jacovina, M. E., Allen, L. K., Johnson, A. M., Perret, C. A, Weston, J. L. (2015). Promoting metacognitive awareness within a game-based intelligent tutoring system. In C. Conati, N. Heffernan, A. Mitrovic & M. F. Verdejo (Eds.), *Artificial intelligence in Education: 17th international conference, AIED 2015 Madrid Spain, June 22–26, 2015, Proceedings* (pp. 786–789). New York: Springer.

Tang, Y. Y., Ma, Y., Wang, J., Fang, Y., Feng, S., Lu, Q., . . . Posner, M. I. (2007). Short-term meditation training improves attention and self-regulation. *Proceedings of the National Academy of Sciences U.S.A., 104*(43), (pp. 17152–17156).

Zimmerman, B. J. (2006). Development and adaptation of expertise: The role of self-regulatory processes and beliefs. In K. A. Ericsson, N. Charness, P. J. Feltovich & R. R. Hoffman (Eds.), *The Cambridge handbook of expertise and expert performance,* (pp. 705–722). Cambridge, UK: Cambridge University Press.

SECTION III: NEUROSCIENTIFIC DISCOVERIES AND APPLICABILITY

CHAPTER 7

NEURAL IMPLICATIONS FOR NARRATIVE IN MULTIMODAL PERSUASIVE MESSAGES

Dirk Remley
Kent State University

Narrative is very much a part of persuasive rhetoric in both a traditional sense and a multimodal sense. Aristotle observes a relationship between narrative and persuasion, albeit very late in his work on *The Art of Rhetoric* (it is discussed only within the last five sections of the entire work), and Thomas Newkirk (2014) details links between narrative and persuasion. Also, scholarship in neuroscience related to persuasion articulates its value as well (Boudreau, Colson & McCubbins, 2011; Dooley, 2012; Nahai, 2012; Pillay, 2011). Narrative engages the audience with a way to assimilate with the speaker, and recent research in neuroscience has found that there are neural dynamics at work when an audience experiences any kind of rhetoric. I wrote previously about neural processes that occur with multimodal instructional messages (Remley, 2015) as well as persuasive messages (Remley, 2017), and my intent in this chapter is to encourage the integration of specific concepts of neuroscience into instruction and rhetorical analyses of persuasive messages, particularly those that include multiple modes of representation as characterized by The New London Group (1996) such as visual, print-linguistic, and aural. I show how teachers may connect neuroscience concepts to rhetorical principles, especially relative to persuasion and narrative, in instruction. This includes providing an example analysis that could facilitate demonstration of application and ideas for other related activities.

There are many attributes of a message that activate neural responses (Nahai, 2012; Pillay, 2011); for example, as a speaker compares him or herself with an audience, trying to make themselves seem like a member of the audience, mirror neurons are activated in the audience; the audience wants to be like that person represented in the narrative or feel some connection with him or her. Further, if an outcome of value to the audience is part of the narrative, reward neurons may be activated as well. For example, depending on who is providing the narrative or who is being used as the persona of the narrative, it may also elicit reward neurons if that person is esteemed in an audience's perception: "If I am like that person, I will have the same lifestyle and rewards he or she has;" or "That person has helped other people who are like me to gain something of value; so, he or she can help me, too."

Much has already been written on persuasive rhetoric within print-linguistic forms of composing; however, much less has been written about the neuroscience of persuasion in multimodal forms of composing. I acknowledge in this chapter that several concepts of neuroscience relate closely with those concepts of persuasion commonly understood by scholars of writing and rhetoric, and this link should be pursued more explicitly in instruction.

I do not expound on the full variety of stimuli that generate neural responses that affect an audience's perception of a message; such a text could overwhelm the reader with biological terminology requiring an extensive glossary. I limit this discussion to three relatively well-known attributes that have already been discussed to some degree in rhetoric and writing scholarship and are involved with persuasion: "mirror neurons," "reward neurons," and "plasticity."

Concepts from rhetoric such as logos, pathos, and ethos are closely connected to these concepts; and an evolving corpus of scholarship on multimodal rhetoric informs how to compose effective messages with different media and modes relative to various combinations. For example, researchers have found that certain colors elicit certain neural responses in viewers (Nahai, 2012). The goal of this chapter is to show why traditional principles of multimodal persuasive rhetoric may work, integrating a biological perspective and encouraging others to include such a perspective in discussion of such rhetoric. That is, the mirror neurons, reward neurons and elements of plasticity contribute biological concepts to an understanding of why a particular message is persuasive.

Pedagogy in rhetoric does not currently integrate this biological perspective. My suggestions at the end of the chapter encourage teachers to include this discussion in instruction and analytical practice to help explain why traditional concepts of persuasive rhetoric may work. I describe a specific commercial application to illustrate such integration; commercials can be used in composition coursework to illustrate points of persuasive rhetoric. I, also, encourage further research into these dynamics, how they can affect the design of persuasive messages and their efficacy in enhancing student learning of multimodal persuasive rhetoric.

BASICS OF MULTIMODAL RHETORIC

The New London Group (1996) identifies five different, unique modes of representation: print-linguistic, visual, audio, gestural, spatial; and they acknowledge that any two or more of these can be combined to form a multimodal representation. They acknowledge that, we argue that literacy pedagogy now must account for the burgeoning variety of text forms associated with information and multimedia technologies. This includes understanding and competent control of representational forms that are becoming increasingly significant in the overall communications environment, such as visual images and their relationship to the written word—for instance, visual design in desktop publishing or the interface of visual and linguistic meaning in multimedia. (New London Group, 1996, p. 60)

Subsequent to this call from the New London Group, researchers have been considering various combinations of modes of representation that can affect meaning-making. Further, scholars realize that pedagogy needs to integrate instruction in composing with these different modes of representation (see Selfe, 2007, for example). The importance of graphic images in these literate practices is noteworthy because of the different kind of literacy at work relative to each—print-linguistic text and image; though, both represent communication systems (Murray, 2009).

In the past fifteen years, another focus of study within literacy studies has emerged that focuses on effective combinations of multiple modes to communicate and related practices. Studies pertaining to this analysis seek to understand rhetorical attributes of mixed modes and when and under what conditions certain combinations are most productive (e.g., Lemke, 1998, 1999; Richards, 2003). Joddy Murray (2009), for example, indicates that a given combination may be meaningful for some people while the same combination will not be as productive for others because of differing personal backgrounds (p. 16).

RHETORIC AND NEUROSCIENCE OVERLAP

Rhetoric involves understanding one's audience toward presenting a message that will encourage the audience to act upon the information in the message relative to its purpose. An instructional message needs to engage the audience with the information in a way that enables the audience to understand it and be able to perform the task instructed. A purpose of persuasive messages is to move the audience from thinking about a given topic or issue to taking particular action on it.

Aristotle connects an audience's biological attributes to rhetoric. He acknowledges that a one must consider an audience's disposition when developing a message for it; this disposition may include social disposition and physical or biological disposition. He states that an audience may have "limited intellectual scope and limited capacity to follow an extended chain of reasoning (1991, p.

76). Even though, Aristotle makes this statement in *The Art of Rhetoric,* little of the scholarship in rhetoric and writing studies does much with that connection.

The Gestalt effect is involved in multimodal persuasion and considered in scholarship in both rhetoric and neuroscience. This is the idea that the whole is greater than the sum of its parts. One can understand an image when looking at the entire image rather than trying to piece together its different parts. The effect is identified in much of the scholarship on visual rhetoric, especially, (Arnheim, 1969); yet, it is also included as a term/concept in the neuroscience scholarship (Wallace, 2004). Mark T. Wallace (2004) states broadly that one of the roles of the brain "is to synthesize this mélange of sensory information into an adaptive and coherent perceptual Gestalt . . . this sensory synthesis is a constantly occurring phenomenon that is continually shaping our view of the world" (p. 625). A few studies find that as an optimal combination of senses is engaged the brain is able to process the information faster (Bremner & Spence, 2008; Keetels & Vroomen, 2012; Lewkowicz & Kraebel, 2004).

CROSSING TERMINOLOGY

As I mentioned above, there are a few terms not found in writing and rhetoric studies that contribute immensely to understanding persuasive rhetoric relative to neural processes. These terms are used regularly in neuroscientific scholarship. I provide information about them and briefly indicate their connection to persuasion here.

Mirror Neurons

Vittorio Gallese, Morris Eagle, and Paolo Migone (2007) and Giacomo Rizzolatti, Luciano Fadiga, Leonardo Fogassi, and Gallese (1996) first reported on the existence of neurons that appear to facilitate cognition of movements and behaviors that one observes another perform while doing a given task. Even before the observer tries to perform the same task he or she observed, he or she has acquired a sense of how to perform the task through a mental visual mirror. Further, they observe a connection between these neurobiological phenomena and social science. Rizzolatti et al. state

> Suppose one sees someone else grasping a cup. Mirror neurons for grasping will most likely be activated in the observer's brain. The direct matching between the observed action and its motor representation in the observer's brain, however, can tell us only what the action is (it's a grasp) and not why the action occurred. (p. 135)

Mirror neurons facilitate much cognition associated with experiences. However, they also contribute to persuasion in that an audience wants to mirror some aspect of the speaker or the speaker may want to resemble some aspect of the audience as a way to assimilate with it more. This is a basic principle in Chaïm Perleman and Lucie Olbrechts-Tyteca's (1969) *The New Rhetoric*. The speaker must always adjust to the audience's values and beliefs among other attributes. An audience's common experiences contribute to defining its understanding of reality (Perleman & Olbrechts-Tyteca, 1969; Schiappa, 2003). As a speaker positions him or herself closer to that reality and shared experiences of the audience he or she mirrors that audience and the audience understands that mirroring, eliciting empathy and favor from the audience.

This is echoed in Irene Clark's chapter in this collection. She states that one's identity can be influenced by elements of which one is conscious. As a speaker identifies closely with an audience, mirror neurons are more actively stimulated such that the audience feels as if he or she is the same as the speaker.

Reward Neurons

Several studies related to dopamine, a neuro-transmitter, recognize that the stimulated neurons are associated with perception of rewards and motivation. Activation of these neurons helps to enhance attention by conveying some kind of motivation to behave a certain way to the audience affected. Reward neurons play into persuasive messages when a speaker acknowledges some benefit the audience may experience.

There are many ways a reward may be experienced. For example, I may receive some financial benefit—a bonus; or I may feel that I am even more a part of a certain social group; or I may feel good about helping someone else. All of these act to motivate me to act a certain way because I perceive I will be rewarded somehow.

Neural Plasticity

In cognitive neuroscience, plasticity pertains to the ability of neurons to change their composition and behaviors relative to the information they process and experiences. Giovani Berlucchi and Henry Buchtel (2009) define neural plasticity as

> changes in neural organization which may account for various forms of behavioral modifiability, either short-lasting or enduring, including maturation, adaptation to a mutable environment, specific and unspecific kinds of learning, and compensatory adjustments in response to functional losses from aging or brain damage. (p. 307)

Plasticity can be affected by learning of one's culture as well as one's own experiences and social interactions generally. As such, plasticity is a biological aspect of one's social disposition. Neurobiologists recognize, much as humanities scholars such as James Paul Gee, Glynda Hull, and Colin Lankshear (1996), Steven Pinker (1997), and Richard A. Mayer (2001), that experience plays a role in learning and cognition. What one understands of a given bit of information and how they tend to best learn information affect how they learn new information. As a function of social interaction, this learning and cognitive development, also, affect what people value, impacting dynamics associated with reward neurons.

Studies related to plasticity tend to examine how one responds to a series of subsequent experiences of certain modal combinations after first exposure, especially related to cognitive development. Generally, the brain is able to process information more quickly as it learns more about that information and rewards associated with certain actions and values are re-enforced.

Because plasticity is affected by social interaction over time, culture also impacts persuasive rhetoric; a particular message may have a better persuasive effect in one culture but not another merely because of social expectations and perceptions of rewards or attributes of the product itself. A member of a particular culture may value something that a member of a different culture does not. This can affect how persuasive an audience perceives a given message. Considering that different audiences may have different social dispositions, two different audiences may not respond the same way to the same message.

THE RHETORIC OF NARRATIVE

In writing courses students learn a variety of modes of communication, including narrative. Narrative can be used in such coursework to help students learn various elements of writing and rhetoric because of narrative's versatility. Several years ago, Nancy Blyler and Jane Perkins (1999a) devoted an entire issue of the *Journal of Business and Technical Communication* to detailing the value of narrative in professional and scientific practice. Blyler and Perkins (1999b) also presented a compilation of works regarding how professionals in business and technical fields use narrative. Stephen Denning (2005) advances their work, calling attention to the use of narrative to move people to action, share values, and build trust. According to Blyler and Perkins (1999a), narratives help "align and consolidate activities" (p. 246) and "are vital to scientific invention and discovery" (p. 248). Blyler (1995), also, asserts that professional narratives can acculturate students to professional writing. Consequently, in addition to serving multiple purposes in practice, it can serve several purposes in business writing and technical writing pedagogies as well.

Professionals recognize narrative as a powerful rhetorical tool in business writing and technical writing settings. Ranging from its use in proposals to persuade readers to action to its use in resumes to move the reader to have interest in an applicant and use in other kinds of documents, narrative provides descriptive accounts of events while offering critical reflection to move an audience to action.

Narrative includes precise details of an event that occurred in the past which are reported in the same order in which they occurred, as well as an observation or evaluation of the information by the narrator (Rentz, 1992). This evaluation facilitates action based on the relationship between the events reported and that analysis. Narrative, generally, is distinguished from argument in its concern with the particular instead of with generalizations.

Much scholarship argues the rhetorical value of narrative in professional writing settings (Blyler, 1995, 1996; Blyler & Perkins, 1999; Denning, 2005; Jameson, 2004; Popken, 1999; Rentz, 1992; Rodgers, 1989).

NARRATIVE AS A MIRROR

Professional narratives integrate many of the attributes of personal narrative. While there is less focus on the individual who is writing the piece, the writer must be able to articulate a sequence of events and offer critical reflection about the relationship of those events to some particular issue or concern. Although such passages are shorter than those found in academic essays, they perform similar rhetorical functions.

Further, professional narratives offer insight into professional discourses. Students exposed to such narratives can learn the discourse of professionals within a given field toward mirroring that discourse (Blyler, 1995, 1996). Blyler (1996) acknowledges that narratives are valuable because they are related to the communities in which we live; as such narrative has ethnographic qualities about it, and social organization is maintained through stories (p. 295).

Indeed, the more one can establish himself or herself as a member of the audience's community the better one can persuade the audience to act on a message. Such a message activates mirror neurons. This may be through sharing an experience the speaker had that the audience is likely to have had or by posing as a member of that community by wearing clothes members of that community frequently wear. Consider the politician on a campaign trail who visits a local restaurant. He or she is more likely to be wearing informal shirt and pants than a suit more appropriate for the office to which he or she is vying for election. Herbert Simons and Jean Jones (2011) note that this is an effort to affect the audience's mirror neurons. The speaker/candidate is mirroring the target audience's appearance (Simmons & Jones, 2011, p. 166). A narrative can, also, establish mirroring of values, re-enforcing cultural disposition between speaker and audience.

Another attribute important to persuasion is establishing agreement between the speaker and audience to facilitate understanding and action. Srinivasan Pillay (2011) calls this "facilitated consensus." He states that, "an important part of the mirror neuron system (shared emotion) is implicated in the art of persuasion" (2011, p. 79). Pillay and others (Boudreau, Coulson & McCubbins, 2011; Dooley, 2012; Simons & Jones, 2011) note that the ethos of the narrator can also affect neural processes associated with persuasion. Specifically, trust and expertise are very important attributes of ethos that affect the audience's perception of the message, including narration. Pillay, in particular, notes that expertise may affect reward neurons (2011, p. 79).

Nathalie Nahai (2012), also, notes how narrative can be used to elicit empathy. The more one knows another's "story" the more they are to sympathize with that person's plight. Legal scholarship has found that "juries often empathize with plaintiffs" (Pfaff & Sherman, 2011, p. 420). Again, the mirror neurons are at work in such instances; the audience comes to understand why the plaintiff did something and consider a similar situation when they were affected similarly though may not have acted upon that feeling. Consequently, narratives elicit intersections of neural dynamics associated with mirroring, rewards and plasticity. In the next section, I describe a practical application of this intersection relative to principles common to persuasive rhetoric.

PRACTICAL APPLICATION

As indicated above, a "multimodal" composition includes any combination of print-linguistic, visual, aural, and spatial modes of representation. An automobile advertisement showing an image of the specific vehicle, someone driving it, and print linguistic text describing its features combines visual and print linguistic modes of representation. A commercial can integrate those as well as sound.

Companies can use multimodal persuasive messages in a variety of media and for various audiences—internal and external. Gordon Shaw, Robert Brown, and Philip Bromiley (1998) acknowledge 3M's use of narrative in business planning, using it to present "strategic stories" behind items in bullet-point listings. David Fleming (2001) acknowledges the importance of organizational leaders being able to assimilate with employees and encourage reform through narratives. He explains sense-making and sense-giving, two important functions of leadership, as "providing the insights and raw materials necessary to reform mindsets and practices essential to the newly emerging opportunities" (Fleming, 2001, para.

5). He goes on to explain that, "few tools are as powerful and readily available to the leader as the use of personal and organizational narrative. Learning to listen to, tell and interpret stories within the organization helps leaders to maximize their sensemaking/sensegiving role" (2001, para. 7). Such narratives trying to persuade employees toward organizational change can be delivered in writing or video or through live presentations.

One needs only to look at commercials and advertisements on television and the Web to find examples of multimodal persuasive rhetoric for external audiences. Consideration of rhetorical principles applied within advertising and commercials is often used within writing coursework instruction and practice—from composition-level courses to professional writing courses. One that I will use to illustrate the neuroscience associated with persuasion comes from the marketing materials of the law firm of Friedman, Domiano & Smith Co., LPA (2015). The law firm addresses several kinds of legal cases, including personal injury. One of the main purposes of advertisements, of course, is to persuade the viewer/reader to buy or use the advertiser's product or service. However, there is a unique dynamic within the advertisements of this law firm that is very uncommon among such advertising. These attributes and the neuroscience behind them bring about a certain perception of the law firm's ability to represent clients in personal injury cases especially.

Jeffrey Friedman is the face of the law firm in almost all of its advertisements and commercials, and he is paralyzed from the waist down (https://www.fdslaw.com/). In the commercials and advertisements, he sits in a wheelchair; and this is clearly visible to the viewer. In several commercials, in a gentle, sympathetic tone, he talks about his own experience in a car accident that caused the injuries that have put him in the wheelchair and how he can represent injured clients better than other attorneys could because of that experience. Several attributes of the multimodal forms in this narrative come together to make for a persuasive message: these include the speaker himself—physical appearance and ethos; the narrative he provides, and the tone of voice he uses (audio).

The visual appearance of this man in a wheelchair immediately elicits empathy and understanding from the viewer, who may be so injured. This activates mirror neurons, consequently; and the viewer identifies closely with the attorney. Even if one is not injured, one feels a connection to the speaker because he has some degree of expertise with the situation they may be experiencing—as an attorney specializing in personal injury and as one who actually experienced it. As an attorney trained in personal injury law, of course, he is considered an expert in personal injury law and litigation. We are conditioned to have a certain respect for professionals trained in a specific field. That conditioning affects, and is affected by, the elasticity of neurons that have been conditioned toward respecting such authority figures. Each time we learn more information about the kind of training one needs to earn a certain professional license and learn about one's professional successes, it causes more neurons related to that respect to develop. We, subsequently, learn to recognize that person as an expert who can be considered a credible source of information. Consequently, one knows that he is a credible source for legal knowledge and practice. However, he is also "expert" in the experiences one who has been severely physically injured one may have. Through neural plasticity, one who experiences certain injuries can not only sympathize with but can empathize with others who have experienced similar injuries. This empathy is socially constructed. As someone who has experienced such suffering, the viewer immediately understands that he can empathize with potential clients who have been so injured. The effect of this enhances the mirroring dynamic; he has actually experienced the pain and suffering a potential client is experiencing; as such, he is like the injured person.

The narrative further places him on the same level as anyone who has been injured in any kind of car accident. Depending on how long the commercial is he provides a certain amount of detail about the accident. The gist is that he suffered permanent injuries because of a driver's negligence. There is a detailed video and text on a particular page of the firm's website that more fully explain the accident.

The narrative provided on the webpage featuring his story includes introductory text describing his character: "When you meet Jeff in person, you experience first-hand his kind, hardworking, and genuine character. However, not everyone knows about his lifelong physical battles and how one car accident changed his life and enriched his spirit to become the successful human being and lawyer he is today" (Friedman, Domiano & Smith, 2015, para. 1). It goes on to describe details of the night on which the crash occurred. He was a passenger in a car. "The driver lost control of the vehicle and veered off the road. He crashed the car into one tree and then another" (Friedman et al., 2015, para. 2). It also includes information about his undergraduate education, professional training and academic and professional successes. The last paragraph of the narrative about the law firm and his story includes the statement, "When Jeff says to his clients, 'I know, I've been there,' it's the truth. He is the real deal." (Friedman et al., 2015, para. 10).

Finally, in commercials and the video on the webpage about his story he uses a calm, sympathetic voice as he talks about his story and the firm. Imagine the difference between being yelled at because you were in a car accident and someone comforting you with a gentle, sympathetic, even empathetic, voice. One is naturally drawn to the sympathetic voice. Consider how we are conditioned from birth to respond favorably to sympathy; our mothers, likely, used such a voice to calm us throughout our infancy, childhood, and adolescent year. Through our cultural experiences and plasticity, neurons developed to re-enforce the perceived connection between a sympathetic voice and a calming response and feeling reassured. That connection is a social construct. This makes using his firm more appealing an option, too. The perception from the commercial is that he understands his clients' needs and feelings more than a typical personal injury attorney can.

Another attorney in Northeast Ohio uses the statement "I'll make them pay" in his advertising (Misny, 2016). Consider the different reactions we have to Message A: "I understand your pain and needs," and Message B: "I'll make the other person pay" in persuading us to use their legal services. Message A is more about reassuring our own comfort and supporting us emotionally and financially; Message B is more about attacking the person who harmed us, penalizing them. It isn't as reassuring to us or comforting. It actually emphasizes the financial gain, shared by both the injured client and the attorney. Although Friedman et al. (2015) includes some aspects of financial gain in his message, that part of the message is minimized by the narrative of his injury experience that he emphasizes in commercials and advertisements.

The goal of personal injury litigation is some form of financial compensation to assist with life expenses, health care, and "pain and suffering" directly associated with the injury. The Friedman narrative includes information about the firm's successful litigation and specific awards for clients. The webpage, also, includes video testimonials from satisfied clients. These could activate reward neurons, because the viewer would begin to understand how much compensation he or she could receive by using the law firm to represent them. This is also part of the neural plasticity dynamics of the audience the message targets; the general American public is very interested in financial rewards, especially the potential of winning hundreds of thousands, if not millions, of dollars from litigation. When we read in the newspaper or on television or the Internet of such awards given to those who were injured, it becomes part of our culture. As mentioned above, neural plasticity facilitates learning of one's culture and how one understands the world. It shapes their understanding of reality.

If the firm is as successful representing the prospective client as it has been with others, they stand to gain a large amount of compensation. Recall that reward neurons are stimulated by the prospect of a reward, not by actually receiving the award; and they are part of the system that motivates one toward action. So, between appearing as a member of the same community as one who is injured, thereby understanding their needs better than other attorneys, and demonstrated successful litigation, based on previous successes, the advertisement is very persuasive. A viewer would perceive that they could be represented by one who, not only has their interests in mind, but empathizes with them; and the viewer may understand the likelihood of receiving a large financial reward given the firm's previous success.

This description of a particular multimodal persuasive message (one that integrates print-linguistic text, visual and aural modes of representation) and neural dynamics associated with it (mirror neurons, reward neurons and plasticity) provides an illustration of the kinds of practical applications students and practitioners alike can review to improve their understanding of persuasive narratives. In the next section I discuss how to facilitate such instruction and practice.

SUGGESTIONS FOR EXPLICIT INSTRUCTION OF THE NEUROSCIENCE OF NARRATIVE

Students need the opportunity to hone skills associated with developing effective narratives in coursework (Doyle, 1999). Alice Horning, in this collection, notes that students need to read metacognitively to learn how to compose well and transfer that learning to other contexts. She states that students should learn more about metacognitive attributes of reading in first year writing courses Ellen Carillo, also, notes in this collection the connection between metacognition and transfer. Including explicit instruction in narrative, including neural contents associated with it, in technical writing and business writing pedagogy will help students refine those skills and understand how to use them in the workplace.

Greg Columb (2010) acknowledges that in writing courses explicit teaching is "intended to bring about identifiable effects on qualities, features or other aspects of writing" (slide 6). He summarizes arguments against explicit teaching in writing courses as indicating that writing does not involve conscious processes and, therefore, writing is learned through subconscious processes (2010, slide 6). However, he challenges this by explaining that parts of writing are consciously understood, including planning, drafting and revising (2010, slide 7). He also acknowledges that "nonconscious processes can be influenced by consciously created dispositions;" that is, if one is aware that a particular rhetorical strategy can work in a given situation, he or she will consciously apply it (2010, slide 8).

Several studies find differences between explicit instruction, implicit instruction, and learning (see, for example, Leblanc & Lally, 1998; Morrison, Bachman & McDonald-Conner, 2005; Ziemer Andrews, 2007). While none is directly linked to instruction in narrative, they find that students learn complex topics better when they receive explicit instruction in that topic, while there seems to be little statistically significant difference in learning simple topics relative to either approach. Consequently, teachers should make explicit reference to neural dynamics in their instruction of narrative as a means of persuasion, and I have tried to facilitate an understanding of these dynamics so that teachers can discuss them explicitly in their instruction.

Teachers of writing courses can accomplish this explicit inclusion by:

1. Integrating explicit references to narrative and neural responses in examples of persuasive writing, and
2. Showing examples of narrative-style persuasive writing and discussing rhetorical and neural attributes.

Teachers can encourage students to think about rhetorical and neural attributes of their own persuasive messages within grading rubrics and reflection. A grading rubric for a multimodal persuasive assignment might include a category specifically listing possible neural responses associated with mirror neurons and reward neurons, for example. I provide such a rubric (2017).

Also, many instructors encourage students to reflect on their writing process, especially within multimodal assignments; and such reflections can include description of how the student perceives their message stimulates certain neurons in addition to the other rhetorical attributes influencing its perceived effectiveness. How does a certain attribute of a message elicit mirror neurons or reward neurons? How might an audience's experiences affected plasticity toward learning how to react to a certain persuasive effort?

RESEARCH IMPLICATIONS

This chapter considers pedagogical elements associated with including explicit instruction of neuroscience concepts in writing. Research in pedagogy includes examination of the effectiveness of explicit instruction versus implicit instruction (e.g., Colomb, 2010; Ziemer Andrews, 2007). Research related to such instruction can examine how integrating explicit instruction in these neuroscience concepts affects the efficacy of student learning of multimodal persuasive rhetoric. Such a study may not have to be interdisciplinary in nature; one could design a study that uses different pedagogies—one with explicit instruction, the other without, and review student products to ascertain which seem more effective, the ones from those who had explicit instruction or neither.

CONCLUSION

Composition instructors use narrative in writing classes to help students practice writing skills by engaging them in writing about something they know and understand most—their own experiences. Blyler and Perkins (1999a, 1999b) as well as Kathryn Rentz (1992) assert that narrative acts as a rhetorical tool for use in professional writing settings, and Blyler (1996) and Daphne Jameson (2004) acknowledge the value of narrative as a tool to help students understand discourse in professional settings and as a tool for ethnographic study. Professionals use narrative in their communications, and this use can vary from print-linguistic to multimodal.

An understanding of the neural processes at work in such messages can enhance learning of application of narrative in them. So, instruction in persuasive rhetoric should include explicit discussion of neural dynamics of multimodal messages. I have attempted to show how three particular concepts of neuroscience can be integrated into instruction of narrative in multimodal persuasive messages along with principles more familiar to writing faculty and scholars.

Further, interdisciplinary research can integrate scholarship from different disciplinary, not just theoretical, perspectives toward enhancing scholarship in rhetoric. As the concepts of logos, ethos, and pathos help to understand ways to present persuasive messages, an understanding of the neuroscience experienced by the audience helps to explain *why* specific details included in a narrative associated with a given approach may work well for a particular audience.

REFERENCES

Aristotle. (1991). *The art of rhetoric* (H. C. Lawson-Tancred, Trans.). London: Penguin.

Arnheim, R. (1969). *Visual thinking*. Berkeley, CA: University of California Press.

Beemer, C, Bowles, S. & Shaver, L. (2005). At your service: Teaching rhetoric in a business school writing center. *Praxis: A Writing Center Journal, 3*(1). Retrieved from https://repositories.lib.utexas.edu/handle/2152/31487.

Berlucchi, G. & Buchtel, H. A. (2009). Neuronal plasticity: Historical roots and evolution of meaning. *Experimental Brain Research, 192*(3), 307–319. doi: 10.1007/s00221-008-1611-6.

Blyler, N. R. (1995). Pedagogy and social action: A role for narrative in professional communication. *Journal of Business and Technical Communication, 9*, 289–320.

Blyler, N. R. (1996). Narrative and research in professional communication. *Journal of Business and Technical Communication, 10*, 330–351.

Blyler, N. R. & Perkins, J. (1999a). Guest editors' introduction: Culture and the power of narrative. *Journal of Business and Technical Communication, 13*, 245–248.

Blyler, N. R. & Perkins, J. (Eds.) (1999b). *Narrative and professional communication*. New York: Ablex.

Boudreau, C., Coulson, S. & McCubbins, M. D. (2011). Pathways to persuasion: How neuroscience can inform the study and practice of law. In Freeman, M. (Ed.), *Law and neuroscience: Current legal issues 2010* (Volume 13) (pp. 395–406). New York: Oxford University Press.

Bremner, A. J. & Spence, C. (2008). Unimodal experience constrains while multisensory experiences enrich cognitive construction. *Behavioral and Brain Sciences, 31*, 335–336.

Colomb, G. (2010, March). *Framework for a theory of explicit teaching*. Paper presented at Conference on College Composition and Communication, Louisville, KY. Retrieved from http://www.faculty.virginia.edu/schoolhouse/CCCC2010/Colomb ExplicitTeaching.pdf.

Denning, S. (2005). *The leader's guide to story-telling: Mastering the art of business narrative*. New York: John Wiley and Sons.

Dooley, R. (2012). *Brainfluence:100 ways to persuade and convince consumers within neuromarketing*. Hoboken, NJ: John Wiley and Sons.

Doyle, A. E. (1999). Dishing the personal narrative: Its present classroom ignominy, its classroom potential. *Bridgewater Review, 18*(1). Retrieved from http://vc.bridgew.edu/cgi/viewcontent.cgi?article = 1377&context = br_rev.

Fleming, D. (2001). Narrative leadership: using the power of stories. Originally appeared in *Strategy & Leadership, 29,* 4. Retrieved from http://www.emeraldinsight.com/doi/abs/10.1108/sl.2001.26129dab.002.

Forbes, C. (1999). Getting the story, telling the story: The science of narrative, the narrative of science. In N. R. Blyler & J. Perkins (Eds.), *Narrative and professional communication* (pp. 79–92). New York: Ablex.

Friedman, Domiano & Smith Co. LPA. (2015). Jeff Friedman's Story. Retrieved from https://www.fdslaw.com/about-us/jeffs-story.php.

Gallese, V., Eagle, M. N. & Migone, P. (2007). Intentional attunement: Mirror neurons and the neural underpinnings of interpersonal relations. *Journal of the American Psychoanalytic Association, 55,* 131–176.

Gee, J. P., Hull, G. & Lankshear, C. (1996). *The new work order: Behind the language of the new capitalism*. Boulder, CO: Westview Press.

Jameson, D. A. (2004). Conceptualizing the writer-reader relationship in business prose. *Journal of Business Communication, 41,* 227–264.

Journet, D. (1999). The limits of narrative in the construction of scientific knowledge: George Gaylord Simpson's The Dechronization of Sam Magruder. In N. R. Blyler & J. Perkins (Eds.), *Narrative and professional communication* (pp. 93–106). New York: Ablex.

Keetels, M. & Vroomen, J. (2012). Perception of synchrony between the senses. In M. Murray & M. Wallace (Eds.), *The neural bases of multisensory processes* (pp. 147–177). Boca Raton, FL: CRC Press.

Leblanc, L. B. & Lally, C. G. (1998). A comparison of instructor-mediated versus student-mediated explicit language instruction in the communicative classroom. *The French Review, 5,* 734–746.

Lemke, J. L. (1998). Multiplying meaning: Visual and verbal semiotics in scientific text. In J. R. Martin & R. Veel (Eds.), *Reading science: Critical and functional perspective on discourses of science* (pp. 87–114). London: Routledge.

Lemke, J. L. (1999). Discourse and organizational dynamics: Website communication and institutional change. *Discourse and Society, 10,* 21–47.

Lewkowicz, D. J. & Kraebel, K. S. (2004). The value of multisensory redundancy in the development of intersensory perception. In G. Calvert, C. Spence & B. E. Stein

(Eds.), *The handbook of multisensory processes* (pp. 655–678). Cambridge, MA: MIT Press.

Mayer, R. E. (2001). *Multi-media Learning.* Cambridge, UK: Cambridge University Press

Miller, J. S. (2008). *Resources for teaching acting out culture: Reading and writing.* Boston: Bedford St. Martin's.

Misny, T. (2016). Website. Retrieved from http://misnylaw.com/?ibp-adgroup = MLP PC&gclid = CLOF1r3z5csCFQsDaQodJVcClA.

Morrison, F. J., Bachman, H. J. & Connor, C. M. (2005). *Improving literacy in America: Guidelines from research.* New Haven, CT: Yale University Press.

Murray, J. (2009). *Non-discursive rhetoric: Image and affect in multimodal composition.* Albany, NY: SUNY Press.

Nahai, N. (2012). *Webs of Influence: The psychology of online persuasion.* Harlow, UK: Pearson.

Newkirk, T. (2014). *Minds made for stories: How we really read and write informational and persuasive texts.* Portsmouth, NH: Heinemann.

New London Group (1996). A pedagogy of multiliteracies: Designing social futures. *Harvard Educational Review, 66,* 60–92.

Perleman, C. H. & Olbrechts-Tyteca, L. (1969). *The new rhetoric: A treatise on argumentation* (J. Wilkinson & P. Weaver, Trans.). Notre Dame, IN: University of Notre Dame Press.

Pfaff, D. N. & Sherman, S. (2011). Possible legal implications of neural mechanisms underlying ethical behavior. In M. Freeman (Ed.), *Law and neuroscience: Current legal issues 2010* (Volume 13) (pp. 419–432). New York: Oxford University Press.

Pillay, S. S. (2011). *Your brain and business: The neuroscience of great leaders.* Upper Saddle River, NJ: Pearson/Financial Press.

Pinker, S. (1997). *How the mind works.* New York: Norton.

Popken, R. (1999). The pedagogical dissemination of a genre: The resume in American business discourse textbooks, 1914–1939. *JAC: Rhetoric, Writing, Culture, Politics, 19,* 91–116.

Remley, D. (2015). *How the brain processes multimodal technical instructions.* Amityville, NY: Baywood.

Remley, D. (2017). *The neuroscience of multimodal persuasive messages; Persuading the brain.* New York: Routledge.

Rentz, K. C. (1992). The value of narrative in business writing. *Journal of Business and Technical Communication, 6,* 293–315.

Richards, A. R. (2003). Argument and authority in visual representations of science. *Technical Communication Quarterly, 12,* 183–206.

Rizzolatti, G., Fadiga, L. Fogassi, L. & Gallese, V. (1996). Premotor cortex and the recognition of motor actions. *Cognitive Brain Research, 3,* 131–141.

Rodgers, P. (1989). Choice-based writing in managerial contexts: The case of the dealer contact report. *Journal of Business Communication, 23,* 197–216. Retrieved from http://deepblue.lib.umich.edu/bitstream/2027.42/36046/1/b1411779.0001.001.txt.

Schiappa, E. (2003). *Defining reality: Definitions and the politics of meaning*. Carbondale, IL: Southern Illinois University Press.

Selfe, C. (Ed.). (2007). *Multimodal composition: Resources for teachers*. New York: Hampton Press.

Shaw, G., Brown, R. & Bromiley, P. (1998). Strategic stories: How 3M is rewriting business planning. *Harvard Business Review, 76*, 42–44.

Simons, H. W. & Jones, J. G. (2011). *Persuasion and society*. New York: Routledge.

Wallace, M. T. (2004). The development of multisensory integration. In Calvert, G., Spence, C. & Stein, B. E. (Eds). *The handbook of multisensory processes* (pp. 625–642). Cambridge, MA: MIT Press.

Ziemer Andrews, K. L. (2007). The effects of implicit and explicit instruction on simple and complex grammatical structures for adult language learners. *Teaching English as a Second Language-EJ, 11*(2), 1–15.

CHAPTER 8

PEDAGOGY AND THE HERMENEUTIC DANCE: MIRRORING, PLASTICITY, AND THE SITUATED WRITING SUBJECT

Jen Talbot
University of Central Arkansas

The move away from Linda Flower and John R. Hayes' cognitive process model was driven in part by the writing studies' need to acknowledge the social contexts in which writers (including student writers) write. The cognitive process model is based upon four interrelated principles: that the writing process is best understood as "a set of distinctive thinking processes," which are used during the act of composing; that these processes have a "hierarchical, highly embedded organization;" that the act of composing is guided by the "writer's own growing network of goals;" and finally, that goals are created based on the writer's purpose and on new information gained through the act of writing itself (Flower & Hayes, 1981, p. 366). This conception of process, along with the protocols from which it was derived, did a great deal to advance composition as a discipline, and to expand the focus of writing instruction from the document produced to include the writer herself. This, in turn, brought the identity and constitution of the writing subject into the scope of inquiry. For example, in 1976, Susan Miller wrote that the writing process is "personal, private, and necessarily self-expressive" but ultimately the product was "public" and "judged by someone else" (1976, p. 94). Almost 25 years later, Thomas Kent (1999) wrote that writing was always "public, interpretive, and situated," ushering in the postprocess movement (p. 1). Although Miller's description evokes a consistent, though internal, process that is exported to be judged by a member of the public, Kent's description evokes a more fluid process by which external and social forces are internalized to shape the writing subject, who engages in a process of public expression.

Just as recent interest in neuroscience provides the opportunity to revisit cognitive process theory, so too does it serve as an opportunity to recontextualize Kent's 1993 paralogic rhetoric, from which the tenets of postprocess theory emerged. Kent's initial argument was that meaning is always negotiated through a "hermeneutic dance" (1993, p. 87), in which communicating parties "shift ground" through "guesswork" (p. 40) until they reach a moment of "triangulation" (p. 89) in which one's own mind, the mind of the other, and the shared world are all in accordance. This process is not a generalizable one, because each communicative interaction takes place during a specific, unrepeatable moment in time; it is not a rational one because triangulation may be based on such things as "skill, intuition, taste, and sympathy" (Kent, 1993, p. 40). Kent provides a useful starting point for several reasons: (1) his theory is an attempt to theorize the social mind; (2) it has been revisited, developed, and criticized at frequent intervals over the last fifteen to twenty years; and, most importantly, (3) its central metaphors of triangulation and hermeneutic dance intuitively map onto the concepts of affective neuroscience I will address in this chapter: mirror neurons and the plasticity of the brain.

The shift away from cognitive process, beginning with the social turn and extending through postprocess and beyond, has taken place against a backdrop of increased general philosophical and cultural attention to the affective, material, and contingent, a move which has, in many ways, ushered in a new wave of interest in brain science. In the 1990s, as the energy behind the cognitive process model was waning, interest in neuroscience, particularly in the areas of affect and plasticity, was gaining momentum. Taken together, these advances seem intuitively to support a move beyond a monolithic and decontextualized model of the cognitive process, and what we, as teachers, know about the role of affect in the writing classroom. While some critiques of process theory made from a postprocess perspective have been reductive, the hierarchical logic of cognitive process theory, while recursive, is not situated. Subsequent theoretical turns have deepened the consideration of context and situation as constitutive of the writing subject, first socially and discursively, and more recently, materially. Similarly, cognitive science has shifted its attention from abstract, "hardwired," and hierarchical cognitive processes to networked, plastic, neurological processes. In other words, thinking about the writing subject from a neurological rather than cognitive perspective is analogous to thinking about writing from a postprocess rather than process-oriented perspective.

Neurological inquiry into the writing process provides a mechanism by which to extend the composition theories roots in the cognition, while also incorporating a more complex and expansive notion of identity, in which the writing subject is also a historical and embodied subject whose past and current environmental conditions and experiences, both discursive and non-discursive, serve as ground for cognition. However, it is the temptation of hard science's aura of "epistemological certainty" that led Chris Mays and Julie Jung (2012) to warn against a wholesale incorporation of neuroscience. However, as Mays and Jung further point out, neurorhetorical inquiry differs from cognitive process theories in that it "presupposes the *un*finished nature of these [cognitive] processes for purposes of foregrounding the contested claims, competing epistemologies, and diverse disciplinary perspectives that circulate in the intersection of rhetoric-composition and social neuroscience" (2012, p. 43). Though I agree that a hasty application of neuroscience to pedagogy is to be avoided, I also argue that the implications of a shift from a presupposition of finishedness to one of unfinishedness provides ample theoretical ground in which to work out some of the complexities of that very intersection. I further argue that, rather than framing neurorhetorical inquiry as an appropriation, a productive first step looks at rhetoric-composition theory *alongside* developments in neuroscience, regarding each as an iteration of a broader cultural and philosophical shift from a humanist to a posthumanist perspective, or, more specifically, a shift from a situation model to an ecology or assemblage model.

Neuroscience and rhetorical theory converge around questions about the ability to know the minds of others. Kent's paralogic rhetoric is based on triangulation, in which there are three points of alignment necessary for successful communication: we must know our own minds, the minds of others, and the shared world (1993, p. 89). For Kent, "we cannot know our own minds—the concepts that form our thoughts—without knowing the minds of other language users; consequently, no split exists between our minds of others or between our minds and objects in a shared world" (1993, p. 92). Kent characterizes this move as "radically anti-Cartesian," which it is indeed, in terms of the division between the mind of one and the mind of another. However, the means of communication via triangulation is still based upon conceptual and linguistic models, in which the point of triangulation's triangle is abstract and disembodied; the shared ground that creates facilitates understanding is discursive. However, the cognitive load of consciously triangulating each communicative interaction would be insurmountable and endlessly proliferating; there is no mechanism for connecting the two minds to the world. If, however, we consider how the body might be a conduit for understanding others in the world, we ground the mechanism of triangulation in such a way that each interaction is uniquely situated, but operates within the parameters of the material situation, and with a level of automaticity that is more aligned with lived experiences of communication. Mirror neurons and plasticity are two embodied mechanism for knowing the minds of others.

TRIANGULATION AND MIRROR NEURONS

One neuroscientific concept of particular interest to rhetoric and writing is mirroring, because of traditional interest in mimesis, and the more contemporary role of modeling in learning and communication. In this volume, Dirk Remley points out that mirror neurons are central to persuasion, in that speakers will want to establish and maintain affinities with their audiences. Similarly, the neuroscience of mirroring behavior allows for a new reading on Kent's notion of communicative triangulation, in which the point of shared meaning is not abstract and conceptual, but rather an automated mechanism located in the very material of the brain. If we conceptualize mirroring as an automatic neurological function, it changes the way we think about how to foster the second of the habits of mind in the *Framework for Success in Postsecondary Writing*: openness. In particular, the third method of fostering openness is for students to "listen to and reflect on the ideas and responses of others." If, in fact, mirror neurons do what many cognitive neuroscientists claim they do, openness (and similarly, engagement, flexibility, and metacognition) is not based on consciously controlled intellectual intervention, but rather is a condition of embodied being, akin to Emmanuel Levinas' (1969) phenomenological account of the face-to-face encounter (a connection that Diane Davis [2010] makes in *Inessential Solidarity*).

Mirror neurons are associated with motor behaviors firing both in the performance of a particular action or expression, and when an action or expression is observed. The original experiment that led to the discovery of mirror neurons was conducted by a group of neuroscientists in 1992 in Parma, Italy, with the intention of examining the relationship between cells associated with perception and cells associated with movement. Through a serendipitous set of happenstances during these experiments, neurophysiologists Vittorio Gallese and Alvin Goldman (1998) noticed that clusters of cells in the F5 area of the brain lit up both when the macaque was performing an action, and also when they observed the action being performed. By 1996, they had coined the term "mirror neurons" to describe these cells (Gallese, Fadiga, Fogassi & Rizzolatti, 1996).

Mirror neurons are instrumental for establishing an affinity with another person, by syncing up neural (and therefore limbic and kinetic) activities, and also for delineating the boundaries between self and other. More specifically, mirror neurons are located in the parietal and frontal lobes in humans, areas that are associated with motor function. In monkeys, mirror neurons fire in response to viewing transitive acts, or action associated with a concrete object, such as grasping an item of food. In humans, however, mirror neurons fire in conjunction while viewing both transitive acts and intransitive acts, which are not associated with a concrete object (Rizzolati & Siniglia, 2008, p. 117). Additionally, mirror neurons fire differently for the same action according to the intention behind the action, such as reaching for a cup to drink from it vs. reaching for a cup to clear it from the table (Iacoboni, 2008; Rizzolati & Siniglia, 2008). The combination of these two factors allows for the possibility that the mirroring of gestures and bodily comportments are a means for the transmission of affects. This is a radical shift away from the traditional Cartesian relationship between mind and body in which the body is a ground and a conduit, rather than a container, for emotion and cognition.

Due to the radical implications for subjectivity, identity, relationships, and learning of all kinds, upon their discovery, mirror neurons become the focus of scholarly attention at an exponential rate. In 2000, four papers were published with mirror neurons mentioned in the title or abstract. In 2010, there were 135. By 2008, Marco Iacoboni was making such claims as:

> Building on and paralleling the research on monkeys, brain imaging and magnetic simulation data on humans have revealed a mirror neuron system that fulfills the same functions that it does in monkeys. In humans, however, its role in imitation is even more critical because imitation is so foundational for our exponentially greater capacity of learning and for the transmission of culture. Human mirror neuron areas also seem important for empathy, self-awareness, and language. (p. 260)

According to Iacoboni, we understand one another's emotional and affective states most quickly and effectively through mirroring and embodying the affect ourselves. Mirror neurons fire in response to the expressions and gestures; those responses extend into the limbic system, which governs the endocrine and autonomic nervous systems (and also includes the amygdala, which is central to primary emotion and affects social decision-making). According to some research, the neural foundation of mirroring behaviors provides the embodied basis by which "the sender and receiver [are] linked by a common understanding of what counts" (Rizzolati & Sinigaglia, 2008, p. 153). In other words, mechanisms of communicative triangulation are embodied, and the material mechanisms by which we understand contexts for utterances and gestures are inextricably linked to emotional centers in the brain. With time and repetition, connections and pathways are built into the brain itself; there is no clean delineation between the material and social because our bodies and brains are shaped by our movements through and within social forces and practices just as surely as the practices are shaped by material conditions.

Like Iacoboni, many neuroscientists argue that work on the role of mirror neurons in affectability suggests that a great deal of the openness necessary for "reading" people's intentions and emotions is shorthanded neurologically. One illustration of this is a study by David Neal and Tanya Chartrand (2011) conducted a study on people's ability to recognize and interpret the emotions of others based on the mirroring of facial expressions. The experiments in the study asked subjects to identify emotion portrayed in photographs that are cropped to reveal only the eyes and eyebrows. The first experiment of the study examined the emotional response of people who had received Botox injections, which hamper one's facial mobility. The second experiment used a restricting gel to increase skin resistance to muscular contractions, which in turn strengthens the neural signal associated with the facial expression. The subjects who had received Botox performed worse than the controls at recognizing emotion in facial expressions, while those who had been treated with the resistance gel performed better. It is important to note that Botox recipients were still able to recognize the emotions of others at approximately the same rate (70%) as control groups; however, they were significantly slower at doing so (Neal & Chartrand, 2011, p. 5). Neal and Chartrand concluded that mirroring behaviors, enabled by neural mechanisms, moderate the recognition of emotional states, suggesting that, in the absence of an inhibiting factor, the recognition of others' emotions is embodied and automatic. In the presence of inhibiting factors, expressions and comportments are "read" consciously and cognitively, through theory-building, rather than automatically and affectively. In addition to the emotional reading described by Neal and Chartrand, additional processes traditionally thought by neuroscientists to be "higher order and therefore attributed to cognitive systems; for example the perception and recognition of actions carried out by others, imitation, and gestural and vocal communication" may in be supported by the neural substrate that lies in the motor system (Gallese & Goldman, 1998; Rizzolati & Siniglia, 2008, p. 20).

The flurry of scientific interest in the potentially revolutionary implications of mirror neurons beginning in the 1990s also resulted in an increased incorporation of neuroscientific concepts in pop culture. In 2012, *Wired* magazine called mirror neurons "the most hyped concept in neuroscience," citing unsubstantiated claims made online and in social media, in which mirror neurons were touted as the cause for everything from people's enjoyment of romantic comedies to the benefits of hospital patients' having visitors (Jarrett, 2008, para. 4). Products and services were developed: Lumosity.com, for example, claims in its TV ads to offer "a workout for your brain" (Lumos Labs, 2012). Similarly, Neurodrinks claim to be "functional beverages based on science," containing ingredients designed to enhance energy, focus, sleep quality, or to reduce stress (Neuro, 2016, para. 2). In short, the rapidity with which neuroscience concepts, most often mirror neurons, were appropriated into popular culture made it difficult to sort out relevant discoveries, like those of Rizzolati and his team, from reductive misappropriations of the research.

Despite the rapid public interest in neuroscientific concepts in the 1990s and into the twenty-first century, some in the scientific community were more skeptical of the implications of mirror neurons than Iacoboni. For example, the connection to higher-order linguistic and cognitive function is not fully accepted. Robert Spunt and Matthew Lieberman (2012) claim that making judgments about emotion relies on the mentalizing systems, which are separate from the mirror systems; this reliance, they argue, "severely undermines the notion that the mirror system is the primary basis for emotion understanding" (p. 2). In 2008, Gregory Hickok published an article pointing out eight problems with mirror neuron theory, which was the basis for his 2014 book *The Myth of Mirror Neurons: The Real Neuroscience of Communication and Cognition,* which argues that there is not sufficient direct evidence that mirror neurons are the basis of action understanding in monkeys, and that in human cases the evidence actually makes a case against the theory.

Controversies like these serve as the basis for Jung and Mays' caution, cited above, against the wholesale adoption of neuroscience into writing studies, despite composition's historical association with cognitive science. The first wave of cognitive inquiry in composition—Flower and Hayes (1981), Janet Emig (1977), and others—did a great deal to lend disciplinary legitimacy to composition, similarly based on an aura of certainty. While the specific mechanisms of mirror neurons remain in question, which merits caution about certain types of appropriation, it is also the case that the phenomena related to mirror neurons are more relevant to writing studies than the neurons themselves. As Dylan Dryer and David Russell point out in this volume, "[North American Writing Studies] wants to change the way we think about writing and help people understand how writing makes us think, without much background or interest in the specific mechanisms of how 'thinking' and 'writing' gets done." While in many ways this is a critique of the field, it is also the case that the epiphenomena of connection, intersubjectivity, and mind-reading, because of their radical implications for identity and subjectivity, are relevant to writing studies whether mirror neurons are their mechanism or not. Developing and assessing teaching practices based on intersubjectivity is in line with a broader cultural and philosophical shift of which mirror neurons are just one part.

The complexities of social interactions are such that these habituated connections and responses are a way to offload a great deal of the cognitive and conceptual work necessary to establish a common communicative ground. Iacoboni (2008) describes this new understanding of how we understand one another as a radical departure from what he calls "theory theory" (p. 71). He explains that, prior to the discovery of mirror neurons, a small number of scholars proposed an alternate theory, known as "simulation theory." In the "moderate" version of simulation theory, people understand the minds of others by engaging in a "cognitive, deliberate, and effortful" process of envisioning themselves in the other's position. In the "radical" version of simulation theory, we envision ourselves in the other's position through some sort of automatic process. Iacoboni states: "On this question I am a radical, since this automatic, unconscious form of simulation maps well with what we know about mirror neurons" (2008, p. 73). Since the discovery of mirror neurons, and subsequent studies by Iacoboni and others, simulation theory is now the more accepted theory of how we know the minds of others, even though questions about the role of mirror neurons have been raised. Even the Parma groups' most stringent critics, such as Gregory Hickok, acknowledge that both of these channels exist. Hickok's primary critique is not about the channel itself, but about his skepticism that cognitive information flows that way. Most people who are neurotypical and in familiar situations rely on automated interpretation and understanding of people's affective states, depoying a cognitive and rational process in situations in which the simulation channel is not effective, as demonstrated by Neal and Chartrand.

Iacoboni, in particular, explicitly links his own findings about mirror neurons to Maurice Merleau-Ponty's (2002) philosophies of embodiment and subjectivities/intersubjectivities. Merleau-Ponty's concepts of embodiment are also significant to the philosophical lineage of the materialist and posthumanist turns in rhetoric (they are also cited by Dryer and Russell in this volume). For the purposes of rhetorical theory, this parallel is most useful as a way to consider material iterations of the social than as an unqualified description of the mechanisms at play; it is this permeable and plastic vision of the social body, I argue, that has fueled the recent fascination with neuroscientific inquiry across disciplines and cultural venues. The overarching ideas of intersubjectivity and automaticity that make the potentialities of mirror neurons so radical are also at play in the rhetorical theories of the last 15 years, which are based on ecological models (Edbauer, 2005), posthumanist philosophies (Hawk, 2011), and attunement to one's environment and those who share it (Rickert, 2013). All of these rhetorics share, along with Merleau-Ponty, an attention to the body as an instrument of affect, which is prior to and shapes cognition.

PLASTICITY AND THE HERMENEUTIC DANCE

Though brain structure and function govern behavior in the abstract—meaning that the brain in the processing center in which perceptions are connected to one another and responses are generated at the cognitive level—in the enworlded body, behaviors and brain structure develop in a reciprocally parallel fashion.

Just as the brain is useless without the senses, sensory organs, and nervous system as a means of input, the body is useless without a world to perceive and interact with. A brain without a world has no experiences. When experiences are repeated, neural activity in the relevant areas of the brain is reduced relative to the neural activity associated with a novel experience. This is a result of irrelevant neurons "dropping out," leaving the relevant neurons to be more tightly associated with one another (Wig, Grafton, Demos & Kelley, 2005, p. 1228). This is one reason why an expert performing a task shows less neural activity than a novice performing the same task; the brain has, through repetition, become more efficient with practice. This kind of brain reconfiguration is known as neuroplasticity. Though the most dramatic examples of and studies about neuroplasticity are among people who have sustained brain injuries or had strokes, which require that entire areas of the brain be remapped. However, the same basic phenomenon is at work in any form of learning.

Like mirror neurons, neuroplasticity is associated with motor function and emotional resonances more than with cognition as such; additionally, they are the mechanism by which embodied interactions with our environments and people in them sculpt the material of the brain, eliminating the boundaries between material and social. Very few characteristics are immutable. Some aspects of the genetic code are "hardwired," but most other aspects of subjectivity are plastic at various levels. Theories about brain structures that indicate that behaviors are hardwired were based in the now-obsolete idea that the brain did not produce new cells over the course of the lifetime, and further, that neural cells had specific roles that could not be changed (Draganski, et al., 2004). Though it is true that brain cells do not reproduce through mitosis, as do most cells, new brain cells can emerge from stem cells. Furthermore, existing brain cells can be reassigned to any role that becomes necessary based on interactions with the environment. The behaviors of the person, the tasks they perform, their interactions with the physical environment, are materially recorded in the structures of the brain, here pruning connections, there building them up with time and repetition, much like geological shifts from erosion and deposition. The brain is a relief map of enworlded experience, created through "a complex, multistep process that includes numerous time-dependent events occurring at the molecular, synaptic, electrophysical, and structural organization levels" (Sagi, et al., 2012, p. 1195).

Intimate and sustained interactions with people contribute to the maps of our brains. Our emotional experiences and routines are written on the brain and body, in ways that can be as fleeting as an adrenaline rush or as constant as embodied life itself. We can be conceptually primed to perform better in a singular and specific context, such as a test, or we can be primed and habituated throughout our lives with cultural expectations about our racial, ethnic, or gender identities. Because the brain is the point at which perception, sensation, habit, and thought converge, it makes a certain kind of sense to draw a boundary at the skull and say that our brains are us, my brain is me. But, as Alva Noë (2010) argues, without a body and without a world, the brain is no more definitive of who we are than the appendix. Noë states ". . . the world itself can be described as belonging to the very machinery of our own consciousness. This isn't poetry; this is a well-supported empirical hypothesis. Perceptual consciousness, at least, is a kind of skillful adjustment to objects (and the environment) (2010, p. 65). As long as we have living bodies, objects and the environment are always already priming us to adopt a specific comportment within the world. Or, as Dryer and Russell put it in this volume, contextual effects not only interact with, but co-produce "the complete organism, including the nervous system—and the brain."

For example, it is a commonplace in cognitive science that "neurons that fire together, wire together." In other words, the more frequently that a specific combination of neurons is activated through interaction with the environment, the more likely it is that sparking one of them will also involve the others, even in an instance which wouldn't if not for the history of connection, have elicited that response. In the short term, synaptic connections resulting from the release of neurotransmitters can be developed as quickly as two hours (Sagi et al., 2012). These quick connections are more likely to be associated with motor tasks, which are in turn, connected with emotional centers (Masterson, 2015; Sagi et al., 2012). Long-term changes associated with the acquisition of a cognitive skill over the course of weeks or months changes involve the development of new cellular structures (Sagi et al., 2012)

Because the changes to the material of the brain are incremental, multilayered, and contingent upon specific physical and emotional interactions, no two learning experiences are the same, even for a single person. Emotional resonances transmitted through the mirror systems can, in some cases, "enhance or inhibit" the formation of pathways in learning new skills (Immordino-Yang, 2008; Masterson, 2015, p. 1). The process of internalizing the goals of others "is critical for imitation or other social learning to take place, as well as for empathy, in essence the vicarious experience of another's emotional state" (Immordino-Yang, 2015, p. 69). Here we see the neurological parallel of Kent's initial critique of cognitive process: cognition and learning are not discrete, ahistorical functions that work the same way in different brains at different times; rather, all of the existing pathways in the brain created by prior knowledge, as well as relevant emotional and physical states in the moment create the conditions that determine whether and how well one will learn. The neuroscience of affect as a substrate of cognition tells us more about pedagogy than the cognitive process of writing itself.

THE SOCIAL BRAIN IN THE WRITING CLASSROOM

Reflecting on his attempts to enact a pedagogy rooted in postprocess theories (despite the theories' own critique of the pedagogical imperative) Matthew Heard (2008) points out that the practices in which he and his students engaged were not substantively different from process-oriented practices: ". . . I continued to deploy draft workshops, in-class writings, group work, and even lecturing. The subsurface difference, however, was in the epistemological stance underlying the selection and implementation of each assignment and activity" (p. 295). These epistemological differences emerged in the relationships cultivated in the classroom. Similarly, Gary Olson (1999), Lee Ann Kastman Breuch (2002), and Paul Lynch (2013) invoke the importance of, as teachers, adopting a comportment of receptivity and openness. As in Kent's metaphor of the dance, in the end Breuch's argument is that the major goal of a pedagogy is a conscientious attunement with students' needs: "It means becoming teachers who are more in tune to the pedagogical needs of students, more willing to listen, more willing to *be moved* by moments of mutual understanding (2002, p. 146, emphasis mine). Both Breuch and Kent resort to metaphors of movement in their descriptions of what postprocess theory is really about; this points to the implicit but central role of affect in postprocess theory. Like Davis (2010), Olson (1999) draws upon Donna Haraway and Jean-François Lyotard, for whom "what is needed . . . is to move away from a discourse of mastery and abstract cognition toward a way of being that recognizes affect, the body, and openness" (p. 13). In other words, theory and practice fall into sync as affective practices and the structures in which they take place are taken as seriously as formative elements as are the narratives surrounding them. The practices themselves are the same as those in process, but teacher/student interactions and institutional structures, which were always-already functioning alongside traditional pedagogical narratives, are acknowledged as an inherent part of rhetorical learning.

In many ways, the habits of mind outlined in the *Framework*—curiosity, openness, engagement, creativity, persistence, responsibility, flexibility, and metacognition—are a way of answering the "Monday morning question" posed by postprocess pedagogies. As described by Lynch (2013), the Monday morning question is when, in response to a new theory, one is compelled to say, "That's well and good, but what do I do when the students show up on Monday morning?" In other words, the habits of mind are a practical means to address the social brain. Cognitive processes are no longer self-contained and knowable, and so the habits provide a means for managing the affective and behavioral conditions in order to indirectly facilitate learning within the traditional composition classroom structure. However, while the habits do respond to some of the critiques posed by postprocess theories, specifically those about emotion and investment, they remain an attempt to create a systematic method of meeting institutionally determined goals. Such is the nature of the classroom. However, at its heart, postprocess theory is not only or even primarily a critique of process; rather, it is a critique of the rationalist institution that creates conditions that require cognitive process theory.

Though the habits of mind accommodate affect and behavior, they are not a means of incorporating automaticity into the structures and practices of writing instruction. As Sidney Dobrin (1999) pointed out, ". . . the knowledge that one is in a situation has no particular payoff for any situation you happen to be in, because the constraints of that situation will not be relaxed by that knowledge. . . . Being told you are in a situation will neither help you dwell in it more perfectly nor to *write* within it more successfully" (p. 351). In the context of the hermeneutic dance, then, an abstract understanding of the steps does not help you perform the steps more successfully or gracefully. The epistemic framework supporting a set of classroom practices will inform the instructor's performance of the steps and affective orientation toward the student(s), but an assertion of that framework does not offer more information to those within the situation than does simply working within it. Automaticity is best developed through one-on-one, problem-based interactions (Immordino-Yang, 2008, p. 71). From a postprocess perspective, Kent and Raúl Sánchez (2011) have both advocated for a one-on-one mentoring system, in order to provide the flexibility and deep situatedness that best replicates a "real" writing situation.

As Charles Bazerman points out in this volume, "cognition and affect are best studied as responses to real writing situations and tasks." The converse is also true: writing is best learned through the repetition of cognition and affect in response to real writing situations and tasks. In what ways can we, as teachers and scholars, be receptive to the greater unpredictability inherent in engineering rhetorical situations and allowing them to develop? Many programs have moved in this direction by incorporating writing across the curriculum, writing in the disciplines, service learning and other client-based projects, as well as a vertical integration of writing instruction. These types of instruction are not necessarily considered postprocess, despite the fact that they provide the institutional infrastructure to enact postprocess theories within the context of the university: spaces that allow for the affective and material constituents that exceed the composition classroom to be integrated into learning, but that also do not remove the writing subject from the equation altogether.

In conclusion, Kent's (1993) notions of triangulation and the hermeneutic dance serve as useful analogues to the neuroscientific concepts of mirroring and plasticity. These concepts are mechanisms that demonstrate that emotion and cognition is distributed among individual subjects, and that experiences shape the material of the brain. Kent's theory of paralogic rhetoric was an attempt to explain how people know the minds of others in order to communicate; it served as the basis for postprocess theories, which have been revisited periodically in writing studies since 1999. Each iteration of postprocess theory has more deeply integrated the role of affect and the body into the construction of the writing subject, and has more widely distributed the component elements of cognition. By 2011's edited collection *Beyond Postprocess,* many of the extensions of Kent's initial argument were influenced by posthumanist and new materialist philosophies. In these theories of mind and body, cognition is distributed among bodies, technologies, and environments, and the workings of the brain are conceptualized according to a networked logic rather than a computational logic. In this theoretical space, the cognitive and the social are not opposing influences, but rather are inextricably intertwined. As a result, while cognitive neuroscience dealing with the writing process itself remains in question, affective neuroscience has emerged as an influence on pedagogies and teaching practices.

REFERENCES

Breuch, L. (2002). Post-process "pedagogy:" A philosophical exercise. *JAC, 22*(1), 119–150.

Council of Writing Program Administrators, National Council of Teachers of English & National Writing Project (2011). *Framework for success in postsecondary writing.* Retrieved from http://wpacouncil.org/files/framework-for-success-postsecondary-writing.pdf.

Davis, D. (2010). *Inessential solidarity: Rhetoric and foreigner relations.* Pittsburgh. PA: University of Pittsburgh Press.

Dobrin, S. I. (1997). *Constructing knowledges: The politics of theory-building and pedagogy in composition.* Albany, NY: State University of New York Press.

Dobrin, S. I. (2011). *Postcomposition.* Carbondale, IL: Southern Illinois University Press.

Draganski, B., Gaser, C., Busch, V., Schurier, G., Boghdan, U. & May, A. (2004). Changes in grey matter induced by training. *Nature, 427,* 311–312.

Edbauer, J. (2005). Unframing models of public distribution: From rhetorical situation to rhetorical ecologies. *Rhetoric Society Quarterly, 35*(4), 5–24.

Emig, J. (1977) Writing as a mode of learning. *College Composition and Communication, 28*(2), 122–128.

Flower, L. & Hayes, J. (1981) A cognitive process theory of writing. *College Composition and Communication, 32*(4), 365–387.

Gallese, V., Fadiga, L., Fogassi, L. & Rizzolati, V. (1996). Action recognition in the premotor cortex. *Brain, 119,* 593–609.

Gallese, V. & Goldman, A. (1998). Mirror neurons and the simulation theory of mind-reading. *Trends in Cognitive Science, 2,* 493–501.

Greco, E. (2012, February 5). *Lumosity Commercial* [Video file]. Retrieved from https://www.youtube.com/watch?v=WfIbIsVRDcM.

Hawk, B. (2011) Reassembling postprocess: Toward a posthuman theory of public rhetoric. In S. I. Dobrin, J. A. Rice & M. Vastola (Eds.), *Beyond postprocess* (pp. 75–94). Logan, UT: Utah State University Press.

Heard, M. (2008). What should we do with postprocess theory? *Pedagogy, 8*(2), 283–304.

Hickok, G. (2008). Eight problems for the mirror neuron theory of action understanding in monkeys and humans. *Journal of Cognitive Neuroscience, 21*(7), 1229–1243.

Hickok, G. (2014). *The myth of mirror neurons: The real neuroscience of communication and cognition.* New York: Norton.

Iacoboni, M. (2008). *Mirroring people: The new science of how we connect with others.* New York: Farrar, Straus and Giroux.

Immordino-Yang, M. (2008). All smoke and mirror neurons: Goals as sociocultural and emotional organizers of perception and action in learning. *Mind, Brain, and Education, 2*(3), 67–73.

Jarrett, C. (2013, December 13). A calm look at the most hyped concept in neuroscience: Mirror neurons. *Wired.* Retrieved from https://www.wired.com/2013/12/a-calm-look-at-the-most-hyped-concept-in-neuroscience-mirror-neurons/.

Kent, T. (1993). *Paralogic Rhetoric: A theory of communicative interaction.* Lewisburg, PA: Bucknell University Press.

Kent, T. (1999). *Post-process theory: Beyond the writing process paradigm.* Carbondale, IL: Southern Illinois University Press.

Levinas, E. (1969). *Totality and infinity: An essay on exteriority.* Pittsburgh, PA: Duquesne University Press.

Lynch, P. (2013). *After pedagogy: The experience of teaching.* Urbana, IL: Conference on College Composition and Communication/National Council of Teachers of English.

Lyotard, J. F. (1984). *The postmodern condition: A report on knowledge* (G. Bennington & B. Massumi, Trans.). Minneapolis. MN: University of Minnesota Press.

Masterson, J. (2015). The role of emotion, vision, and touch in movement learning neuroplasticity and the mirror neuron system. *International Journal of Complementary & Alternative Medicine, 1*(2), 00008, doi: 10.15406/ijcam.2015.01.00008.

Mays, C. & Jung, J. (2012). Priming terministic inquiry: Toward a methodology of neurorhetoric. *Rhetoric Review, 31*(3), 41–59.

Merleau-Ponty, M. (2002). *Phenomenology of perception.* Routledge Classics (2nd ed.). London: Routledge.

Miller, S. (1976). *Writing: Process and product.* Cambridge, MA: Winthrop.

Neal, D. T. & Chartrand, T. L. (2011). Embodied emotion perception: Amplifying and dampening facial feedback modulates emotion perception accuracy. *Social Psychology and Personality Science, 2*(6), 673–678.

Neuro. (2016). *Why neuro?* Retrieved from http://www.drinkneuro.com/why-neuro/.

Noë, A. (2010). *Out of our heads: Why you are not your brain, and other lessons from the biology of consciousness.* New York: Hill & Wang.

Olson, G. (1999). Toward a post-process composition: Abandoning the rhetoric of assertion. In T. Kent (Ed), *Post-process theory: New directions for composition research* (pp. 7–15). Carbondale, IL: Southern Illinois University Press.

Rickert, T. (2013). *Ambient rhetoric: The attunements of rhetorical being.* Pittsburgh, PA: University of Pittsburgh Press.

Rizzolatti, G. & Siniglia, C. (2008). *Mirrors in the brain: How our minds share actions and emotions.* (F. Anderson, Trans.). Oxford, UK: Oxford University Press.

Sagi, Y., Tavor, I., Hofstetter, S., Tzur-Moryosef, S., Blumenfeld-Katzir, T. & Assaf, Y. (2012). Learning in the fast lane: New insights into neuroplasticity. *Neuron, 73,* 1195–1203.

Sánchez, R. (2011). First, a word. In Sidney I. Dobrin, J. A. Rice & M. Vastola (Eds.), *Beyond postprocess* (pp. 183–194). Logan, UT: Utah State University Press.

Spunt, R. P. & Lieberman, M. D. (2012). An integrative model of neural systems supporting the comprehension of observed emotional behavior. *NeuroImage, 59,* 3050–3059.

Wig, G. S., Grafton, S., Demos, K. E. & Kelley, W. M. (2005). Reductions in neural activity underlie behavioral components of repetition priming. *Nature Neuroscience, 8*(9) 1228–1233.

CHAPTER 9
NEUROPLASTICITY, GENRE, AND IDENTITY: POSSIBILITIES AND COMPLICATIONS[1]

Irene Clark
California State University, Northridge

> Helen: I thought there was no such thing as the self.
>
> Ralph: No such *thing*, no, if you mean a fixed discrete entity. But of course there are selves. We make them up all the time.
> —David Lodge (2001), *Thinks . . .*

In *Connectome: How the Brain's Wiring Makes Us How We Are*, Sebastian Seung (2011) maintains that what is usually considered "identity" is strongly linked to "the totality of connections between the neurons in a nervous system," (p. xiii), a phenomenon that he defines as a "connectome." Seung argues that "minds differ because connectomes differ" (2011, p. xiv), and that a person's "connectomes change throughout life" (p. xv), influenced by many factors, including skill acquisition, new knowledge, and life events. The concept of a connectome suggests that identity has a physical manifestation that can be discerned in neuronal activities, and that because these activities are perpetually in flux, the concept of identity should not be viewed as an essentialized, permanently etched static construct, but rather as a complex state of being that is subject to change. Moreover, it further suggests that because neuronal activity is activated by experiences, activities, and learning, "identity" can be influenced by performative elements, over which, at least potentially, the conscious performer can have agency.

What are the implications of this perspective on identity for Writing Studies scholarship? In this chapter, I will argue that current research in neuroplasticity—that is, changes in the brain that can occur through education and experience—problematizes the idea of an "authentic" identity and the extent to which

---

1   Some of the material in this chapter appears in Clark, I. L. (2016). "Genre, identity and the brain: Insights from neuropsychology." *Journal of General Education, 65,* 1–19.

it can be affected by awareness, conscious behavior, and performance. In the context of this research, I will suggest that the association of identity with neuronal activity raises questions about an issue that has received significant attention in Writing Studies/Genre scholarship—the ethical question concerning whether the privileging of academic genres, with their inherent ideologies and values, constitutes a colonizing impact on students' cultural identities. Finally, because current neuropsychological research implies that behavior and its attendant neuronal activity can significantly affect identity, I will recommend the use of several pedagogical approaches that can foster students' awareness of this issue and thereby contribute to their ability to make deliberate choices about their identity.

IDENTITY CHANGE AS AN ETHICAL ISSUE

The concept of identity change—the idea of being or behaving as someone other than who you *really* are—has long generated suspicion and mistrust, from Plato's contempt of the sophists as masters of deception, to the current view of politicians or used car salespeople, who are often disdained for their ability to alter their personas to suit different audiences, appearing to "be" anyone to achieve their own ends. Such people are often perceived as false and untrustworthy, schemers or "performers," ethically inferior to those who are true, sincere, and "authentic." Nevertheless, as educators who focus on communication as a means of achieving academic and professional success, we understand that it is necessary to play or "perform" different roles in different contexts and that everyone involved in social interactions does so, some with greater facility than others. Erving Goffman's (1959) book, *The Presentation of Self in Everyday Life*, using imagery associated with the theatre, discusses the importance of performance in our everyday life interactions as a necessary element in social interaction. In fact, as Dirk Remley notes in a chapter included in this collection, to maximize trust and credibility, a speaker may try to sound like a member of his or her intended audience, a performance that will then activate mirror neurons in that audience. Successful communicators are aware of the dialogic interrelationship between speakers/writers and audience and understand that absolute "authenticity," however the term may be defined, is both impossible and undesirable. In composition classes, we often discuss the importance of audience awareness, and the necessity of assuming an appropriate discoursal role, and we don't tend to view this advice as unethical or damaging to students' "real" selves, even though some of us may also encourage students to find their own "voice."

Most writing textbooks also include a section that discusses the relationship of audience to authorial identity, advice that is not usually tempered by warnings about being manipulative or sophistic. However, in terms of the "identity" issue addressed in rhetorical genre studies, the identity shift that some students may experience when they are immersed in academic genres is frequently viewed with concern. Such an identity shift may involve not only how one speaks, writes, and acts, but also how one thinks and views the world, and, as has been noted by a number of Writing Studies scholars (Bartholomae, 1985; Bazerman, 2002; Gee 2001; Hyland, 2002; Ivanič 1998; LeCourt, 2006; among others.), this identity change may have a particularly significant impact on educationally disadvantaged students, who initially experience the discomfort of being a cultural outsider in the academy and then, as they assimilate, may become alienated from their own cultures. As Bazerman (2002) observes in his discussion of how genres can impact identity, when people begin writing or speaking in a particular genre, they begin "thinking in actively productive ways that result in the utterances that belong in that form of life," taking on "all the feelings, hopes, uncertainties, and anxieties . . . associated with that identity" (p. 14). From this perspective, it is presumed that habitual involvement in a genre can have a substantial impact on the identity of the participant, because people may become permanently committed to the identity associated with that genre. In genre scholarship, this interconnection between genre and identity has raised the issue of whether students' engagement with new genres can be perceived as a type of identity threat, a phenomenon that presumably occurs when students encounter unfamiliar academic genres that normalize power inequities and are associated with ways of thinking, attitudes toward life, values, beliefs, ideologies, and behaviors that conflict with those in students' home cultures. The ethical question concerns whether students can become proficient in academic genres without permanently embracing the values inherent in these genres and whether we, as educators, should be troubled about that possibility.

THE ALIENATION NARRATIVE

Donna La Court (2006) referred to this idea as "the alienation narrative" because it suggests that academic discourse genres endorse power inequities by privileging middle class, elitist values and normalizing the superiority of one culture over another. Addressing the issue of whether students can become proficient "academic" writers without accepting the social hierarchies in which these genres participate and referring to "the classed nature of academic genres" (2006, p. 30), LeCourt noted that working-class and academic discourses exist in a dichotomous relationship where one discourse is depicted as in almost complete opposition to the other. Following this logic, working-class students succeed only if their class identity is stripped away in favor of a middle-class habitus. (LeCourt, 2006, pp. 30–31)

Roz Ivanič (1998) similarly addressed this issue, observing that when students from economically or culturally disadvantaged backgrounds "enter what is for them a new social context such as higher education, they are likely to find that its discourses and practices support identities which differ from those they bring with them" (p. 33). The problem arises not only because these students may experience an initial period of alienation but also because they may come to accept unquestioningly the hierarchical values inherent in academic discourse genres. As Anis Bawarshi (2000) similarly noted in his discussion of the "genre function," genres are not simply containers into which a writer inserts text. Rather, genres, themselves, exert an influence over writers, causing them to behave or "perform" in a particular way when they engage with a genre, influencing how they act and think—potentially generating change in who they become. This identity shift is similarly explored by Richard Coe (1994), Janet Giltrow (2002), and Anthony Paré (2002), among others, who stated that genres can influence how people think of themselves and who they want to be. As Ken Hyland (2010) has argued

> Identity is a person's relationship to his or her social world . . . *Who we are* and *who we might be* are built up through participation and linked to situations, to relationships, and to the rhetorical strategies and positions we adapt in engaging with others on a routine basis. (p. 160)

This view of how genres influence identity leaves educators in what Le Court referred to as a "paradoxically difficult pedagogical" position, because as Sharon O'Dair (2004) noted, as educators, we want to help economically and educationally disadvantaged students succeed in middle-class educational institutions, but we also want them to retain their personal and cultural sense of identity. Certainly a choice such as this constitutes an ethical dilemma.

THE DIALOGIC SELF

Nevertheless, although Writing Studies scholarship may view differences between a presumed "authentic" home identity and identities forged in school as an ethical issue, other disciplines, in particular Social Psychology and Philosophy, have long recognized the existence of a "distributed, multivoiced self" (Hermans, 2001, p. 245). The philosopher, William James (1890) in his discussion of the social aspect of the individual self, observed that "a man has as many social selves as there are individuals who recognize him" (p. 294), an idea supported by Mikhail Bakhtin's concept of the dialogical self, which is based on the "assumption that there are many I-positions that can be occupied by the same person."

(Hermans, 2001, p. 249). As Hubert H. J. Hermans explains, "The dialogical self is 'social,' not in the sense that a self-contained individual enters into social interactions with other outside people, but in the sense that other people occupy positions in a multivoiced self" (2001, p. 250).

Moreover, in their book, *Dialoguing across Cultures, Identities, and Learning*, Bob Fecho and Jennifer Clifton (2017) argue that "when a person acts and interacts in a particular context, that person is recognized by the self and by others—as acting and interacting as a certain 'kind of person'" (p. 26), that this type of recognition "is connected to identity" (p. 28), and that identity "can change from moment to moment with something as simple as an uttered word or a tossed gesture" (p. 31). They maintain that a person is always "in the throes of both being and becoming, and these ways of being and becoming are often contested and negotiated through ongoing dialogue with the self and with others, sometimes made visible through what a person is doing" (p. 93). This more nuanced perspective on identity is supported by the concept of neuroplasticity, which has become a popular topic in both academic and popular publications.

NEUROPLASTICITY[2] AND THE CONCEPT OF IDENTITY

Current research in neuroplasticity that demonstrates that the brain changes continuously as a result of new experiences, activities, and learning suggests that educators may not need to be concerned about *permanently* colonizing our students, because it demonstrates that the neuronal factors that constitute identity are perpetually in flux, reorganizing changing, and reassembling. This perspective suggests that identity is not a permanent entity, but rather is subject to frequent transformation, which means that who we *are*, in terms of how we view ourselves and present ourselves to others, is linked to what we *do*—how we act, speak, act and think. In addition, research concerning the relationship between the mind, the brain, and conscious behavior suggests that when we are *aware* of what we do—the activities we perform and the skills and knowledge we acquire—we can gain understanding of and increased agency over identity change. As Sharon Begley (2007) maintains,

> everything we do, our experiences and actions literally
> expand or contract different regions in the brain. . . . The
> brain devotes more cortical real estate to functions that its
> owner uses more frequently and shrinks the space devoted to
> activities rarely performed. . . . Merely thinking about playing

---

2   Many thanks to Dr. Spencer Wetter, Neuropsychologist, for helping me understand the concept of neuroplasticity.

the piano leads to measurable, physical change in the brain's motor cortex. (pp. 8–9)

Brains change according to what we do and think—how we perform in our lives—and as Seung (2011) maintained, neuronal movement makes us who we are. "Minds differ because connectomes differ" (p. xiv), and a person's "connectome changes throughout life" (p. xv). This is a profound concept for educators to understand.

IDENTITY, CONSCIOUSNESS, AND THE MIND

Seung uses the term *mind* to discuss the connection between activities and experiences that generate changes in the brain, a term that is also used by Susan Greenfield, Professor of Synaptic Pharmacology at Oxford and Director of the Institute for the Future of the Mind. In *You and Me: The Neuroscience of Identity*, Greenfield (2011) explains how our experiences are manifested in the brain, comparing them to a type of narrative or story. Whatever we do—that is, the stories we create and the roles we play in these stories—are registered directly in the brain, and what is particularly intriguing about Greenfield's scholarship is that she discusses studies in which different brain images can be detected when patients with a multiple personality disorder enact different identities. Differing identities, she notes, generate differences in "cerebral blood flow" (p. 35).

Greenfield's research on the concept of identity uses the term *mind*, whereas Stanislaus Dehaene (2014), Director of the Cognitive Neuroimaging Unit in Saclay, France and author of *Consciousness and the Brain: Deciphering How the Brain Codes Our Thoughts*, uses the term *consciousness*. Dehaene maintains that consciousness "is intimately related to the sense of self" (2014, p. 23), and he lists three ingredients of conscious thought—"focusing on conscious access, manipulating conscious perception, and carefully recording introspection" (p. 12), arguing that although complete understanding of the relationship of consciousness to the self is impossible, the habit of metacognition can foster the "capacity to think about one's own mind" (p. 24) enabling us to "reflect upon ourselves" (p. 25). Dehaene refers to the "signatures of consciousness"—patterns of brain activity that appear when a scanned person is having a conscious thought—noting that "several markers of brain activity change massively whenever a person becomes aware of a picture, a word, a digit, or a sound" (2014, p. 13).

Whatever term may be preferred—*mind* or *consciousness*—advanced brain imaging has brought the realization that what we do and think is manifested directly in the brain and that the brain can also influence the doing and thinking. In fact, scientists at University College, London have claimed that certain *beliefs*, as represented in political views, may actually be linked to brain structure. In their study, 90 students were asked about their political views and then underwent brain scans. The results indicated that there were differences in the brain according to whether the subjects had liberal or conservative views, those with liberal views tending to have one particular area in the brain larger than normal (the anterior cingulate cortex), while those with conservative views more likely to have the amygdala of larger size (Alford et al., 2005, as cited in Greenfield, 2011, p. 88). An explanation for this, according to Ryota Kanai and colleagues (2011), is that "individuals with a large amygdala are more sensitive to fear and therefore might be more inclined to integrate conservative views into their belief system" (as cited in Greenfield, 2011, p. 91). The relationship of the brain to one's political views constitutes an interesting research direction, although the issue of what constitutes liberal or conservative positions is extremely complicated and, as Greenfield cautions, one cannot assume a direct, measurable relationship between a political view and a direct manifestation in the brain.

STUDIES INDICATING THE IMPACT OF LEARNING ON THE BRAIN

Particular beliefs or political views may not be easy to pinpoint on a brain scan. But several recent studies demonstrate that the learning of a skill does have a discernible, corresponding manifestation in the brain and have a tangential connection to the genre/identity issue. Several of these studies are summarized below:[3]

THE JUGGLERS STUDY

Published in the journal *Nature* by Bogdan Dragonski and colleagues (2004), the Jugglers Study discusses an experiment in which young adults were taught to juggle until they were able to keep three balls in the air at once. fMRI images, taken before and after these adults learned to juggle, showed a density increase in a small part of the brain associated with vision and movement (as cited in Zull, 2004) when the jugglers were at the height of their skill and that the brain then decreased when they no longer could juggle. This study shows how practicing a skill is registered in neuronal activity.

---

[3] It is important to recognize, however, that although fMRI imaging has yielded thought provoking information about how skills are manifested in neuronal activity, the technique is still fairly new and is limited in the extent to which it can provide detailed information concerning brain function. See Sutton, B. S. et al. (2009). Current trends and challenges in MRI acquisitions to investigate brain function, *International Journal of Psychophysiology.* (73.1), 22–42.

THE TAXI DRIVERS STUDY

A study of London taxi drivers that indicated how the learning of a skill is manifested in the brain was conducted by scientists at University College London. The study involved taxi drivers who were given brain scans before and after they had memorized the names of London streets, the post scans showing change in the driver's gray matter, particularly the hippocampus, which is the part of the brain that is concerned with navigation.

BRAIN CHANGE IN CHILDREN WITH DYSLEXIA

Another study demonstrating how the learning of a skill is manifested in the brain concerns children diagnosed with dyslexia. Conducted by Elise Temple and colleagues (2003), the study involved 20 children with dyslexia, ages 8–12 who were tested before and after they engaged in in a remediation program that focused on auditory processing and aural language. The results indicated that the degree of students' improvement in both oral language and reading performance was manifested directly in brain activity in particular parts of the brain, such as the left temporo-parietal cortex, "bringing brain activation in these regions closer to that seen in normal reading children" (p. 2860).

MUSICAL TRAINING

Musical training, has also been associated with discernible changes in the brain as was reported in a study by Jason D. Warren (1999). Warren's study shows that with advanced fMRI techniques, differences between musicians and nonmusicians in terms of right and left hemisphere blood flow in the brain.

Of course, one may question whether the impact on the brain of learning a specific skill, such as juggling or street name memorization, corresponds to what may be manifested when students become familiar with academic genres or whether this sort of learning can have an impact on identity. Being proficient in any type of skill can certainly affect one's self-esteem and may, indeed, affect one's habitual behavior and sense of self. But in the context of the genre/identity issue, these studies are significant primarily because they demonstrate that learning has an effect on the brain, that the effect can be discerned in increased neuronal activity, that the brain can change, and that it does so often. These studies also indicate that if activities are no longer practiced, presumably, the brain will change again—no state of brain can thus be viewed as "permanent"—in essence, a the situation may be considered a "use it or lose it" relationship.

WRITING ABILITY AND THE BRAIN: THE NUN STUDY

The studies summarized above, concerned with juggling, map memorization, reading, and musical training, all focused on learning particular "skills" that generated corresponding neuronal activity. But a longitudinal study titled The Nun Study indicates that even writing ability, a much more abstract concept than learning a particular skill, may also have a physical equivalent in the brain. In 1930, a group of 678 nuns wrote short biographical sketches that included details of parenting, significant childhood events, schooling, and reasons for the nuns' decision to enter the convent. These texts were then examined in 1986 and assessed for a number of variables, the most significant being grammatical complexity and "idea density," which can be understood in terms of the number of idea units or propositional density in a text. As the nuns aged, some of them began to manifest symptoms of decreased cognitive function, and several studies (see Snowdon et al., 1996) revealed an inverse correlation between low cognitive performance in these essays written when the nuns were young and cognitive impairment in later life.

The findings from the Nun Study indicate that the ability to write texts that are "idea dense" may be manifested in the brain in some way and raise intriguing questions about the connection between literacy and cognitive function. They also complicate issues concerning the relationship between genre and identity. The genres that the nuns wrote in 1930 were short narratives or stories that addressed biographical content, and presumably, the nuns were familiar with the genres they were expected to produce. But some wrote stories with greater detail (idea density) than others, a finding that raises a number of interesting questions. Did the nuns whose texts were characterized by idea density differ in some way from those whose texts were less so? Did these nuns perhaps read more frequently than did the other nuns and were the "idea dense" texts perhaps influenced by engagement with literature? Was there greater neuronal activity in the brains of nuns who wrote idea-dense texts? And did that mean that perhaps their sense of self or "identity" may have been different from that of the other nuns? Another question concerns whether the connection between the ability to write idea-dense texts and Alzheimer's disease was causal or correlational. Did the ability to write idea-dense texts *prevent* dementia in some way? Or was the poor linguistic ability and dementia related to some other factor that affected both?

AGENCY AND AWARENESS

Although we do not have answers to the complicated issues raised by the Nun Study, current research in neuroplasticity strongly suggests that what we learn and what we do correlates with neuronal activity, which, presumably, has an impact on what we term "identity." This insight suggests the importance of helping our students learn to "perform" in ways that will enable them to succeed both academically and professionally and to develop awareness of that performance so that they can gain agency over what they *choose* to do and whom they *choose* to be. Helping students understand that all social situations involve role playing and gain insight into how their "identity" can change according to situation and audience can maximize their choices, as does encouraging students to reflect on these issues.

This relationship between context, content and writer identity has been addressed in some detail by Amy Burgess and Roz Ivanič (2010), who, while acknowledging that academic writing often poses a conflict of identity for students because the "self" that is required in academic discourse feels alien to them, argued that *all* writers assume and must assume different identities when they write in different contexts for different audiences. Although all writing involves the assumption of an identity, and although "asking a person to write a particular type of text" requires "that person to identify with other people who write in this way" (Burgess & Ivanič, 2010, p. 228), identity

> has multiple facets; is subject to tensions and contradictions; and is in a constant state of flux . . . It includes the "self" that a person brings to the act of writing, the "self" she constructs through the act of writing, and the way the writer is perceived by the reader(s) of the writing. (p. 228; see also Ivanič, 1998)

Referring to a study concerned with returning students, Burgess and Ivanič argue that "for most students, identities in educational contexts are transitory, mediating identities; hence, the practices in which they engage while attending courses may be for extrinsic purposes, not part of the identities to which they aspire for the rest of their lives" (2010, p. 230).

Actually, despite scholarship that expresses concern about the inadvertent colonization of our students, it is likely that many are already aware of how their engagement with unfamiliar academic genres can affect how they are perceived by and interact with others, both of which can contribute to alterations in identity. In *The Mind and the Brain: Neuroplasticity and the Power of Mental Force*, Jeffrey M. Schwarz and Sharon Begley (2002), discussing perspectives on free will and moral responsibility, use the term "volitional brain," referencing the work of Ben Libet, who they maintain, put "free will on the neurobiology radar screen" (p. 303). Inspired by work reported in 1964 by Hans Kronhuber and Luder Deecke, Libet used an electorencephalograph (EEG) to explore the chronological relationship between a voluntary movement and brain activity. Kronhuber and Deeke discovered that before subjects initiated a voluntary movement, there appeared to be a "slow, electronically negative brain wave termed the Bereitschaftpotential, or readiness potential" (Schwarz & Begley, 2002, p. 303), which they compared to the "whine of an idling jet engine shifting in pitch before the plane takes off (p. 303). Building on this idea, Libet and his colleagues focused on determining the moment when a person became aware of the conscious desire to act and whether a person had the ability *not to act*, even when preceded by a significant readiness movement. According to Libet (1999), conscious will can affect the outcome of an action, even when an action is initiated by unconscious cerebral processes, arguing that "everyone . . . has the ability to act or refuse to act, even when the readiness impulse is triggered in the brain" (pp. 51–52).

Libet's work, as applied to the genre/identity issue, suggests that with sufficient awareness, student writers have the capacity to make a decision about the identity they wish to portray in their writing and elsewhere. Whatever might be the requirements of a particular academic genre, student writers (and all writers) possess what Ivanič referred to as an "autobiographical self," which they bring to all literacy activities, and which continues to exert an influence over other "selves" that are developed through involvement in new discourse communities. Ivanič defined this autobiographical "self" as being continually influenced by experiences and social interactions of various kinds, maintaining that it retained a strong influence over other "discoursal" selves that students may perform in the context of academic genres. To examine this relationship between students' "identities" and academic writing, Ivanič conducted a study in which students were taught to analyze what is meant by an "academic" identity and to indicate the extent to which they wished to embrace it. Many indicated that they did wish to acquire such an identity—that is, to become academic thinkers and writers. But other students "felt that the conventions forced them to dismiss other aspects of their identity, for example, being committed, caring or funny" (Ivanič, 1998, p. 234). In fact, one student discussed "trying identities on for size" (Ivanič, 1998, p. 234). In the context of the genre/identity issue, then, this experiment suggests that if students have sufficient self-awareness and insight into other ways of being, they will not only be able to *choose* an identity, but also to explain the rationale for their choices. Recent work on consciousness, the mind, the self, and the brain supports this perspective and suggests pedagogical possibilities for enhancing students' choices.

IDENTITY AS PERFORMANCE

The complex interactions between the neuronal activity, overt behavior, and consciousness indicates that what we refer to as "identity" is extremely complex and that identity in the context of academic literacy can be viewed as a type of performance. These interactions also suggest that this performance will not result inevitably in a profound identity change over which students have no control. After all, stage and film actors perform on a regular basis, and even when they have performed the same role frequently—sometimes for many years—they don't usually *become* the characters they are playing, because they are aware that they are performing. Even if a particular acting role triggers a subconscious element in an actor's mind or consciousness, actors understand that they are playing a role and do not undergo a significant transformation from their everyday selves. An interesting example of the interconnections between one's everyday self and the habitual playing of a role as an actor can be noted in the two volumes of Leonard Nimoy's autobiography. Nimoy, who, for many years played the character of Mr. Spock on the TV series, *Star Trek*, titled Volume I of his autobiography *I Am Not Spock* (1975) and then retitled the second volume, published in 1995, *I Am Spock*. Referring to the change in title of the second volume, Nimoy explained that the character of Spock had always been a part of him and revealed that throughout his life, he often had internal conversations with the calm, logical element within himself that is associated with the character of Mr. Spock. However, despite the title of the second volume, it is significant to note that Nimoy considered the character of Mr. Spock as a "part" of himself, perhaps representative of particular character traits that Nimoy had himself or valued. However, the character of Spock was not identical to the person who was Leonard Nimoy, and the fact that Nimoy was analyzing his connection to this character indicates that as an actor, he was aware that he was performing a role and understood what that performance involved. Helping our students gain this type of self-awareness, I argue, should be a goal in our classes.

Actually, according to James Gee (2001), the assumption of an academic persona for most students, but particularly those from educationally disadvantaged backgrounds, always involves an element of performativity. Gee referred to the use of an academic voice as a type of "identity kit," complete with an appropriate costume and instructions about how to act, speak and think for the duration of the performance. Gee's perspective on the academic persona constructs identity as a type of disguise—a "self" used in a particular context—separate from the other "selves" that a person may have. The metaphor of an "identity kit" raises a visual image of how performance and identity correspond with one another. Assuming that students want to assume an academic persona, they are likely to begin with less than perfect mimicry. In fact, Gee maintained that the performance is always imperfect, a form of mushfake, never quite the real thing, which Gee (2001) defines as "making do with something less when the real thing is not available" (p. 533)—a phenomenon that many of us have noted when novice students use an unnecessarily large vocabulary in order to "sound" more like an established academic. But eventually, students become more comfortable in the role they wish to play and the performance will become more convincing, an outcome that perhaps can be viewed positively, as indicative of educational progress or sophistication. Although in the current culturally sensitive climate, we now interrogate and are suspicious of what that progress represents in terms of power dynamics, not too long ago, the idea of learning to play that role was considered unquestionably advantageous for our students. We may recall David Bartholomae's (1985) well-known statement, "the student has to learn our language, to speak as we do, to try on the peculiar ways of knowing, selecting, evaluating, reporting, concluding, and arguing that define the discourse of our community" (p. 134), or Patricia Bizzell's (1986) assertion that "students must master academic discourse if they are to participate in the academic community" (p. 53).

APPLYING INSIGHTS FROM NEUROSCIENCE TO THE CLASSROOM

Insights derived from current work in neuroscience reveal the complexity of identity and problematize the ethical issue of the interrelationship between genre and identity. They also suggest possible pedagogical approaches that can be used to enable students to gain agency over the identities they wish to assume. In the next section, then, I will argue for the importance of helping students develop metacognitive and genre awareness and discuss the use of imitation and modeling in the writing class as a means of enabling students to practice playing various roles and thereby gain agency whom they choose to be.

Fostering Metacognitive and Genre Awareness

In the classroom, it is useful for students to have the opportunity to reflect on the values inherent in academic genres and discuss the extent to which those values may differ from those of their home culture. Reflection has now become an approach that many of us in Writing Studies are using in our classrooms for a variety of reasons, and, indeed, the *Framework for Success in Postsecondary Writing*, prepared by the Council of Writing Program Administrators, the National Council of Teachers of English and the National Writing Project in February 2011, has endorsed the importance of cultivating "habits of mind" as critical for academic success. These habits include critical reflection and self-awareness, which are similar to Pierre Bourdieu's (1997) definition of the "academic habitus," associated with "a set of acquired patterns of thought, behavior, and taste" (p. 1). Helping students understand what is meant by an academic "habitus" and realize that a habitus can be acquired or performed can provide students with the agency that enables choice and self-determination.

As our classrooms become increasingly diverse, it is important for teachers to encourage students to reflect on their own identities, values, and cultures and explore how they may be different from those they are acquiring at the university. It would also be helpful for students to become aware of some of the ethical issues being discussed concerning genre and identity and, in fact, to discuss research in neuroscience that pertains to this topic. Two theoretical frameworks, genre analysis and metacognition theory, combined in the work of Raffaella Negretti and Maria Kuteeva (2011) endorsed the use of metacognition and genre awareness in L2 students' ability to complete academic reading and writing assignments and suggests that reflection can be empowering for our students as they engage with unfamiliar genres which promote particular cultural values. These values can help students make performative choices with greater insight since, as Hyland maintained

> Identity isn't what we say we are or think we are, it is what we do—how we represent ourselves in talk again and again and again. It is about belonging to a group and being an individual member of that group. It's always a balancing act between community and individuality. (Hyland, as cited in Rouault [2014, p. 16]).

This distinction between community and individuality and culture is necessary for students to understand to help them gain agency over the identity they wish to assume.

A particularly intriguing classroom activity that can help students gain this understanding is suggested in an essay by Nicholas Carr (2011) titled, "The Lovesong of J. Alfred Prufrock's Avatar." Discussing Prufrock's oft-quoted anxiety about preparing a "face to meet the faces that you meet," Carr analyzed people's tendency to create online "selves," on Facebook and elsewhere, and in the context of fostering students' awareness of the genre/identity issue, a useful and entertaining exercise might be to have students create an avatar with a name, gender, occupation, values, and other characteristics. Students might then explore the similarities and differences between the created avatar and their everyday selves—physical appearance, age, personality, values, interests, and concerns—and write in the "voice" of that avatar. Actually, when students play video games, they often create an avatar, and if used strategically in the writing class, this approach can help students gain a deeper understanding of the genre/identity issue.

In this context, Chris Thaiss and Terry Myers Zawacki's (2006) discussion of "open-mindedness" as an important value across academic disciplines is relevant here. When students understand that an important element of the academic persona is to be "open-minded," they can then realize new possibilities for assuming multiple selves. Involvement in academic genres thus can allow an *expansion* in identity—not a mindless substitution of one for another.

Providing Opportunities for Practice:
Reconsidering Imitation in the Writing Class

Another pedagogical insight that is suggested by current research in neuroplasticity is the importance of practice in enabling learning, certainly an idea that we all support. As James Zull (2004), author of *The Art of Changing the Brain*, explained,

> When we practice something, the neurons that control and drive that action fire repeatedly. If a neuron fires frequently, it grows and extends itself out toward other neurons, much like the branches of bushes. Moreover, when the neurons begin to touch one another, these places form signaling connections called synapses, which, in turn, form networks, the physical equivalent of knowledge. Changes in these networks is learning. (p. 69)

One way of thinking about these changes is to view them metaphorically as if we were forging a pathway across a field of long grass. The first time the path is forged—whatever the activity might be—juggling or learning to write using an academic genre—the grass is high and forging the path involves considerable effort. But then, after several times, the grass becomes beaten down, requiring less energy to forge the path. With this sort of practice, one can do it without difficulty, and according to Zull, this is the way that neural pathways are created.

In the classroom, practice can be achieved through a number of strategies, but one approach that has not recently received a great deal of attention in Writing Studies is to provide opportunities for students to imitate the genres with which they are expected to engage. Imitation, however, although greatly respected in ancient western rhetorics and curricula, has not only been neglected in Writing Studies—it has been strongly disdained. As Paul Butler (2001) pointed out, using imitation and modeling in the writing class has drawn criticism from "two sites of composition theory: the process movement and the expressivist idea of individual genius" (p. 108). Process oriented views have argued that offering students examples or models simply gives them a "product" to analyze, without enabling them to develop a writing "process" that they can apply to other writing tasks, and expressivist views privilege individual self-expression in order to help students find their own voice. The common objection seems to be that a pedagogy that includes imitation and modeling is inconsistent with rhetorical invention, squelches possibilities for creation and discovery, may result in formulaic writing, and, in fact, could encourage plagiarism. Nevertheless, in the context of providing students with opportunities to practice writing in unfamiliar genres, reflective, mindful imitation can help students develop a deeper, metacognitive understanding of genre and enable them to practice with greater insight.

To reintroduce imitation into the classroom, I suggest we eliminate the various negative adjectives that are often associated with the term, such as "slavish" or "mere" because imitation can be both creative and generative. Its purpose is to show what might be done, not what must be done on particular assignments, and to generate mindful reflection that can lead to deeper understanding of the interrelationship between text and authorial persona. Most writers imitate—ideas, approaches, structures, patterns, styles—and when we do so, we assume different authorial roles. Imitation can be used to foster understanding of those roles and need not be done mindlessly.

THE COMPLEXITY OF IDENTITY—OUTSIDERS AND INSIDERS

One of the most important implications of current research on neuroplasticity is that it demonstrates the complexity of identity and the understanding that identities are subject to frequent alteration. This changeability is useful to discuss with students, enabling them to acknowledge that they do sometimes feel like outsiders, both at the university and within their own families and cultures and that such feelings are not uncommon. At the university where I teach, many students are the first in their families to attend post-secondary education, and when we discuss the genre/identity issue, some do admit that they feel a bit on the outside when they attend family gatherings or "hang out" with friends who are not attending a college or university. For some students, however, being an outsider might yield a fresh perspective on previously unexamined cultural values, both within and outside of the academy. Perhaps the role of an outsider, while not always comfortable, might be desirable—possibly inevitable—as students mature and learn.

Current neuropsychological research suggests a new perspective on the complex interrelationship between genre and identity and the ethical concerns that have been addressed in rhetorical genre scholarship. Actually, Shakespeare addressed this issue many years ago in his well-known lines:

> All the world's a stage,
>
> And all the men and women merely players;
>
> They have their exits and their entrances,
>
> And one man in his time plays many parts.

For our students, insight into this issue can maximize possibilities for self-determination.

REFERENCES

Alford, J. R., Funk, C. L. & Hibbing, J. R. (2005). Are political orientations genetically transmitted? *American Political Science Review, 99*, 153–167.

Bartholomae, D. (1985). Inventing the university. In M. Rose (Ed.), *When a writer can't write* (pp. 134–65). New York: Gilford Press.

Bawarshi, A. (2000, January). The genre function. *College English, 62*, 335–360.

Bawarshi, A. (2003a). *Genre and the invention of the writer: Reconsidering the place of invention in composition*. Logan, UT: Utah State University Press.

Bawarshi, A. (2003b). Sites of invention: Genre and the enactment of first year writing. In P. Vandenberg, S. Hum & J. Clary-Lemon (Eds.), *Relations, locations, positions: Composition theory for writing teachers* (pp. 103–137). Urbana, IL: NCTE.

Bazerman, C. (2002). Genre and identity: Citizenship in the age of the Internet and the age of global capitalism. In R. Coe, L. Lingard & T. Teslenko (Eds.), *The rhetoric and ideology of genre: Strategies for stability and change* (pp. 13–38). Creskill, NJ: Hampton Press.

Begley, S. (2007). *Train your mind, change your brain. How a new science reveals our extraordinary potential to transform ourselves*. New York: Ballantine Books.

Berninger, V. W. (Ed.). (2012). *Past, present, and future contributions of cognitive writing research to cognitive psychology*. New York: Psychology Press.

Berninger, V. W. & Richards, R. L. (2002). *Brain literacy for educators and psychologists*. Amsterdam: Academic Press.

Bizzell, P. (1986). Foundationalism and anti-foundationalism in composition studies. *PrelText, 7*, 37–56.

Bourdieu, P. (1997). *Outline of a theory of practice*. (R. Nice, Trans.). London: Cambridge.

Burgess, A. & Ivanič, R. (2010). Writing and being written: Issues of identity across timescales. *Written Communication, 27*(2), 228–255.

Butler, P. (2001). Toward a pedagogy of immersion: Using imitation in the composition classroom. *Journal of College Writing, 4*(1), 107–114.

Carr, N. (2011). The love song of J. Alfred Prufrock's avatar. In S. Vie (Ed), *(E)dentity* (pp. 159–166). Southlake, TX: Fountainhead Press.

Coe, R. (1994). Teaching genre as process. In A. Freedman & P. Medway (Eds.), *Learning and teaching genre* (pp. 157–168). Portsmouth, NH: Boynton/Cook.

Coe, R., Lingard, L. & Teslenko, T. (Eds.). (2002). *The rhetoric and ideology of genre: Strategies for stability and change*. Creskill, NJ: Hampton Press.

Council of Writing Program Administrators, National Council of Teachers of English & National Writing Project. (2011). *Framework for success in postsecondary writing.* Retrieved from http://wpacouncil.org/files/framework-for-success-postsecondary-writing.pdf.

Dehaene, S. (2014). *Consciousness and the brain.* New York: Penguin Books.

Devitt, A. (2004). *Writing genres.* Carbondale, IL: Southern Illinois University Press.

Dragonski, B., Gase, C., Busch, V., Schierer, G., Bogdah, U. & May, A. (2004). Changes in grey matter induced by training. *Nature, 427*(6972), 311–312. Retrieved from http://dx.doi.org.libproxy.csun.edu/10.1038/427311a.

Fecho, B. & Clifton, J. (2017). *Dialoguing across cultures, identities, and learning: Crosscurrents and complexities in literacy classrooms.* New York: Routledge

Freedman, A. & Medway, P. (Eds.). (1994). *Learning and teaching genre.* Portsmouth, NH: Boynton/Cook.

Gee, J. P. (2001). Literacy, discourse, and linguistics: Introduction and what is literacy? In E. Cushman, E. R. Kintgen, B. M. Kroll & M. Rose (Eds.), *Literacy: A critical sourcebook* (pp. 525–544). Boston: Bedford St. Martins.

Giltrow, J. (2002). Meta-genre. In R. Coe, L. Lingard & T. Teslenko (Eds.), *The rhetoric and ideology of genre: Strategies for stability and change* (pp. 187–206). Creskill, NJ: Hampton Press.

Goffman, E. (1959). *The presentation of self in everyday life.* New York: Anchor Books.

Greenfield, S. (2011). *You and me: The neuroscience of identity.* London: Nottinghill.

Hermans, H. J. M. (2001). The dialogical self: Toward a theory of personal and cultural positioning. *Culture and Psychology, 7*(3), 243–281.

Herrington, A. & Curtis, M. (2000). *Persons in process: Four stories of writing and personal development in college.* Urbana, IL: National Council of Teachers of English.

Hyland, K. (2002). Authority and invisibility: Authorial identity in academic writing. *Journal of Pragmatics, 34,* 1091–1112.

Hyland, K. (2007). Genre pedagogy: Language, literacy, and L2 instruction. *Journal of Second Language Writing, 16,* 148–164.

Hyland, K. (2010). Community and individuality: Performing identity in applied linguistics. *Written Communication, 27*(2), 159–188.

Iacono, D. et. al. (2009). The Nun Study: Clinically silent AD, neuronal hypertrophy, and linguistic skills in early life. *Neurology, 73* (9), 665–673.

Ivanič, R. (1998). *Writing and identity: The discoursal construction of identity in academic writing.* Amsterdam: John Benjamins.

James, W. (1890). *The principles of psychology* (Vol. 1). New York: Henry Holt.

Kanai, R., Feilden, T., Firth, C. & Rees, G. (2011). Political orientations are correlated with brain structure in young adults. *Current Biology, 26,* 677–680.

LeCourt, D. (2006). Performing working-class identity in composition: Toward a pedagogy of textual practice. *College English, 69*(1), 30–51.

Leggett, H. (2009, July 8). Nun brains show language skills predict future Alzheimer's risk. *Wired.* Retrieved from http://www.wired.com/wiredscience/2009/07/nunstudy.

Libet, B. (1985). Unconscious cerebral initiative and the role of conscious will in voluntary action. *Behavioral & Brain Sciences, 8,* 529–566.

Lodge, D. (2001). *Thinks. . . .* New York: Penguin.

Negretti, R. & Kuteeva, M. (2011). Fostering metacognitive genre awareness in L2 academic reading and writing: A case study of pre-service English teachers. *Journal of Second Language Writing, 20*, 95–110.

O'Dair, S. (2003). Class work: Site of egalitarian activism or site of embourgeoisement? *College English, 65*, 593–606.

Paré A. (2002). Genre and identity: Individuals, institutions, and ideology. In R. Coe, L. Lingard & T. Teslenko (Eds.), *The rhetoric and ideology of genre: Strategies for stability and change* (pp. 57–71). Creskill, NJ: Hampton Press.

Rogers, M. F. & Hoover, K. M. (2010). Outsiders/within and in/outsiders: Varieties of multiculturalism. *Journal of Educational Controversy, 5*(2), Article 5.

Rose, M. (1989). *Lives on the boundary*. New York: Penguin Books.

Rouault, G. (2014, March/April). Second language writing, genre, and identity: An interview with Ken Hyland. *Language Teacher, 38*(2) 13–17. Retrieved from http://jalt-publications.org/tlt/articles/3655-second-language-writing-genre-and-identity-interview-ken-hyland.

Satel, S. & Lilienfeld, S. O. (2013). *Brainwashed: The seductive appeal of mindless neuroscience.* New York: Basic Books.

Schwartz, J. M. & Begley, S. (2002). *The mind and the brain*. New York: Harper Perennial.

Seung, S. (2012). *Connectome: How the brain's wiring makes us how we are.* Boston: Houghton Mifflin Hartcourt.

Snowdon, D. A., Kemper, S. J., Mortimer, J. A., Greiner, L. H., Wekstein, D. R. & Markesbery, W. R. (1996). Linguistic ability in early life and cognitive function and Alzheimer's disease in late life. *JAMA, 275*(7), 528–532.

Taxi drivers' brains "grow" on the job. (2000, March 14). *BBC News*, Science/Nature. Retrieved from http://news.bbc.co.uk/1/hi/677048.stm.

Temple, E., Deutsch, G. K., Poldrack, R. A., Miller, S. L., Tallal, P., Merzenich, M. M. & Gabrieli, J. D. (2003, March 4). Neural deficits in children with dyslexia ameliorated by behavioral remediation: Evidence from functional MRI. *Proceedings of the National Academy of Sciences of the United States of America, 100*(5), 2860–2865.

Thaiss, C. & Zawacki, T. M. (2006). *Engaged writers and dynamic disciplines.* Portsmouth, NH: Boynton/Cook Heinemann.

Warren, J. D. (1999). Variations on the musical brain. *Journal of the Royal Society of Medicine, 92*, 571–575.

Villanueva, V. (1993). *Bootstraps: From an American academic of color.* Urbana, IL: National Council of Teachers of English.

Zull, J. E. (2004). The art of changing the brain. *Educational Leadership, Stylus, 62*(1), 68–72.

SECTION IV: WRITING-RELATED TRANSFER AND IMPLEMENTING THE HABITS OF MIND

CHAPTER 10

TEACHING METACOGNITION TO REINFORCE AGENCY AND TRANSFER IN COURSE-LINKED FIRST-YEAR COURSES

Dianna Winslow and Phil Shaw
Rochester Institute of Technology

The Council for Writing Program Administrators, National Council of Teachers of English, and National Writing Project's (2011) *Framework for Success in Postsecondary Writing* presents eight "habits of mind," which are "both intellectual and practical" and "approach learning from an active stance" (p. 4). Of these, our interest in this study is related to the eighth habit, Metacognition, and how students transfer metacognitive strategies between courses in different disciplines, and then into future learning. In particular, we want to investigate the efficacy of linked courses—one first-year writing and one a course in STEM—to promote the possibility of transfer of metacognitive practices to the students' future learning and composing.

When course links and learning communities are talked about in higher education, it is most often in terms of the benefit these have on first- and second-year student retention. Faith Gabelnick, Jean MacGregor, Roberta S. Matthews, and Barbara Leigh Smith (1990) have documented the affordances of linked courses and learning communities to help build curricular cohesion, produce positive social connections, and involve students in shared, sustained inquiry. Terry Myers Zawacki and Ashley Taliaferro Williams (2001) cite linked courses as a way "to increase first-year student retention by creating a comfortable, less isolating learning environment" (p. 115). Course links have also been shown to play an important role in helping students to understand the connections among the knowledge built in their multiple courses. Vincent Tinto (2003) describes this "shared knowledge" and "coherent curricular experience" as an important commonality in linked courses which "seek[s] to promote higher levels of cognitive complexity that cannot easily be obtained through participation in unrelated courses" (p. 2). Other scholars describe what we consider to be a deficit model of linked course work, where courses are linked in terms of "content" courses and "service" courses that provide "a shared experience for students that focuses on a content-based course that is actively supported by a skills course" (Kellogg, 1999, pp. 2–3). It is important to note that the courses in this study operated independently, e.g., the first-year writing class we will describe was not set up as a "skills course" for writing in the genres and hybrid-genres of academic science courses.

In the spring of 2015, we had the opportunity to pilot a FYW curriculum, "A Science of Writing," thematically built on metacognition in writing tasks linked to a similarly themed first year science course. The science course, Metacognitive Approaches to Science, was specifically designed to support and track cohorts of first-generation students and Deaf and hard-of-hearing (D/hh) students in order to increase academic performance and retention for these two, often overlapping, populations. Through a multi-year NSF grant awarded to the College of Science (COS) at Rochester Institute of Technology (RIT), Scott Franklin and Elizabeth Hane established the Integrating Metacognitive Practices and Research to Ensure Student Success (IMPRESS) program. Representing the University Writing Program (UWP), we began meetings with Franklin and Hane to design curriculum that linked two first year writing (FYW) class sections with the grant-funded introductory science class. Our primary interest in participating with the IMPRESS program was to explore the ways these linked courses might facilitate transfer of writing knowledge when the curriculum in each was explicitly teaching metacognitive strategies of thinking and learning. In the writing courses, student positionality to the university and its discourse communities into which students were entering was also openly investigate.

Phil Shaw taught the two Science of Writing sections with IMPRESS students who had either taken the Metacognitive Approaches to Science course in fall 2014 or were enrolled in that class concurrently that spring. After enrollment of the IMPRESS students, remaining seats were filled by non-grant students. Although there were many variables, the pilot helped focus the curriculum, evaluate what metacognitive concepts were transferring, and begin to identify how often students were transferring these concepts from one course to another.

Although the IMPRESS grant was written with the specific intention of supporting academic performance and retention for the target populations of first-generation and D/hh students, the FYW courses were designed to serve a mixed population of hearing and D/hh students, some of whom were first generation students, and some who were not. Our FYW pilot study was not designed to look particularly at the teaching and learning of the IMPRESS target population. We designed these first courses to investigate the usefulness of using metacognition concepts to encourage the transfer of those practices from the writing class into students' other courses. The common metacognitive practices in both classes allowed all students, first generation, D/hh, hearing, or post-first year, to experience, in two different contexts, the application of metacognitive strategies, like concept mapping, task perception, and self-evaluation and reflection. This provided them with the opportunity to develop similar approaches to the writing tasks in each class. The two courses were disciplinarily distinct, but they shared the academic context of the classroom and some similar writing tasks (reflection, online discussion forums, etc.).

STUDY DESIGN/METHODS

The focus of this study is 23 IMPRESS students and 12 non-grant students enrolled in two sections of Shaw's fall 2015 FYW courses. All of the IMPRESS students in Shaw's FYW sections were enrolled in the COS course at the same time, and some had also participated in a four-week summer IMPRESS course focused on scientific inquiry and research.

Constructing this case study, we chose a mixed methods research approach, using qualitative research methods (Denzin & Lincoln, 2003; Stake, 2001; Tedlock, 2003), and teacher research (Cochran-Smith & Lytle, 1993; Ray, 1992, 1993). This project is a small case study—partially instrumental, partially intrinsic (Stake, pp. 3–4)—and is intended to be exploratory and descriptive, while possibly offering a forward look to potential future studies of more scope and scale from which larger generalizations might be made. As a small study, aspects of qualitative research were employed to understand the phenomenological aspects of the case, describing the conditions and multiple contexts of the material, institutional and pedagogical conditions that allowed Shaw to teach the course the way he did, as well as analyze students' participation as co-investigators of their own metacognitive practices.

The students were made aware by the COS faculty teaching the science class that they were part of a grant and study designed to understand the retention benefits of teaching metacognition as a practice of scientific research. Similarly, Shaw was transparent about his role as teacher-researcher and use of teacher research methods, sometimes modeling his reflections about the way the class was unfolding as a form of his own metacognitive practice. Additionally, we conducted personal and small group interviews, which were essential to the data gathering process. Because the participant pool in these communities was small, all informants were "key" ones (Schensul, Schensul & LeCompte, 1999, p. 128) with intimate knowledge of the course structure, whole-class discussions, and the writing and reflection tasks they were expected to complete. All participants were interviewed in a self-selecting process, in which in-depth, open-ended interviewing methods were used to investigate topics relevant to the research topic

(Schensul et al., 1999, pp. 121–161). The advantage of this type of interviewing was that it allowed us the flexibility to pursue, in the moment, topics that arose spontaneously from the conversations that occurred during the interview process.

The case study includes observations of Shaw's role as participant-observer, critically reflecting on his role as teacher and participant (Tedlock, 2003, p. 151). Although this was not a formal ethnographic study, we were influenced by ideas drawn from ethnography about negotiating the paradox of "distance, objectivity, and neutrality" in relation to "closeness, subjectivity, and engagement" (Tedlock, 2003, pp. 151–152). Working collaboratively to analyze course artifacts and interview transcripts and "emphasize relational . . . patterns, interconnectedness . . . and dialogue" (Tedlock, 2003, pp. 151–152), helped us to mediate the closeness of Shaw's classroom role. This framework assisted in parsing how the participation narratives students shared with us were both personally, socially and institutionally mediated.

By studying a particular classroom setting and a finite set of students, we participated in teacher research as it has evolved in Composition Studies and English Education. Teacher research is can be referred to as "studies of 'classroom ecology' . . . [which] presume that teaching is a highly complex, context specific, interactive activity in which differences across classrooms, schools and communities are critically important" (Cochran-Smith & Lytle, 1993, p. 6). Sometimes designed as collaborations between education researchers and particular classrooms and teachers, teacher research is often considered to be "studies conducted by teachers of their [own] school system, school, [and/or] class" (Ray, 1992, p. 173). It is a form of qualitative research specific to education, and draws legitimacy from its use of methods from anthropology, the social sciences and linguistics, and include "[field] journal keeping, participant observation, interviews, surveys, questionnaires and discourse analysis of student texts" (Ray, 1992, p. 172). Shaw used "methodical data gathering" and a "reflective stance towards teaching and learning" (Ray, 1992, p. 173) to inform and improve teaching and learning practices for this course, teacher research methods used to focus on local and particular contexts to solve local and particular problems (p. 175). We used their methods and reflective practices to assess where and to what extent the course carried out its major goals and objectives and also where it failed to do the work intended.

PEDAGOGICAL FRAMEWORK OF THE SCIENCE OF WRITING FYW COURSE

Shaw's Science of Writing course is designed using principles from Doug Downs and Elizabeth Wardle's (2007) writing about writing essay "Teaching about Writing, Righting Misconceptions": it focuses on building knowledge about writing, rather than attempting to only improve writing skills. Adding a metacognitive focus to writing about writing provides students with opportunities to reflect and take stock of their writing knowledge by building awareness and regulation of their overall learning, not just about writing. Shaw introduces metacognitive practices and concepts using Raffaella Negretti's (2012) key components of student metacognitive learning processes, as well as vocabulary for talking about those processes.

Most students developed metacognitive awareness of how their performance and learning either challenged or confirmed what they were reading in peer-reviewed journal articles that described different studies about students in FYW. Class discussion often led to course and learning outcome evaluation, offering valuable opportunities for students to evaluate their approaches to assignments and readings, and gave Shaw the opportunity to be more transparent about his role as teacher-researcher. Students signed participant consent forms and read articles that built on teacher research; they were aware from the beginning that this course was part of our research.

Course Unit One: Metacognition and Writing about Writing

This FYW course, the Science of Writing, is separated into three distinct units over the 16-week semester. The design of this course first builds explicit knowledge about writing and metacognition, then applies that knowledge toward developing student agency within institutional contexts, and ends with students formulating their own metacognitive approaches to their writing processes. Articles in the first five-week unit introduce students to metacognitive practices, writing about writing, and transfer (Downs & Wardle, 2007; Negretti, 2012; Pacello, 2014; Rounsaville, Goldberg & Bawarshi, 2008). Students respond to these readings through online discussion board posts due before the class meeting during which the article or reading will be discussed. Discussion posts are projected on the board and the student-writer presents what they have written. Other students participate in the presentation by asking questions, and when a student has replied before class to another student's post, that student is asked to explain and elaborate on what they have "added to the [Burkean] conversation" of the posting student's original thread (Harris, 2006).

The utility of discussion posts and digital technology toward creating learner-centered classroom is nothing new, but by virtue of the metacognitive focus of this course, when the students present their posts, they are talking about what they were thinking about when they wrote what they wrote. With regards to Deaf/hard of hearing (D/hh) students and the online discussion posts, presenting discussion by voicing, or using ASL, images, and nonverbal media offers greater opportunity for meaning-making. Allan Paivio and others' work has shown that technology aids D/hh student cognition by presenting verbal and non-verbal information (Paivio, 1991, 2006; Sadoski & Paivio, 2013), though the assumption that D/hh students are inherently audio-visual learners by virtue of hearing loss has been rightly questioned (Marschak, Morrison, Lukomski, Borgna & Covertino, 2013). In our experience, the student-centered approach of (re)presenting discussion posts composed before class allows students of any communication medium multiple modalities for understanding and responding to texts and the interpretations of others.

As a metacognitive practice, the students self-regulate their presentation by focusing not on what they wrote (i.e., reading it off the screen), but on what they consider the most "interesting" (Harris, 2006) claim they themselves have made in writing about the article. This gives students an opportunity to reflect on and prepare a short re-visioning of what they wrote for a new context: the asynchronous discussion board post becomes the beginning of a synchronous discussion, and the texts students create before class increasingly reflect this awareness as the context and genre become more comfortable. There are 15 total posts during the course of the semester, and the first few in the beginning of the course were mostly summaries and reactions. By midway through the course, students are employing links to videos, memes and other visuals; creating more complex "forwarding" or "countering" (Harris, 2006) arguments; offering questions for class discussion; reflecting on prior learning and educational experiences; and making connections between multiple articles, academic and non-academic discourse communities, and other contexts.

The first unit of the course brings together metacognition as "thinking about thinking" and a FYW writing about writing pedagogy. The effect of this combination of writing about writing and thinking about thinking is that students begin to approach the course as writing about the process they are going through to thinking about "thinking about writing."

Course Unit Two: Authority, Discourse, and the Institution

After students begin exploring and employing metacognitive practice—through task perception, reflection, self-regulation, and monitoring—the second unit of the course turns their attention toward student positionality and authority in the institutional contexts that both support and regulate their learning. Thinking about our own thinking, and regulating our own knowledge in an effort to gain new knowledge, is itself regulated by the thinking of others, and their thinking about our thinking. The question of unit two becomes, "What happens when we turn metacognition outward?"

This social approach to metacognition is supported by the *Framework* (CWPA et al., 2011). The eight "habits of mind" promote student learning both in and out of school and posit that students who take "an active stance" in their learning are better prepared "for the learning they will experience in college and beyond" (CWPA et al., 2011, p. 4). In order for students to take an active stance within and then beyond their classroom(s), this unit frames course readings as discussions about issues of identity, agency, and institutional power. As Charles Bazerman (2013) calls for in his chapter in this collection, and in *A Theory of Literate Action*, we are trying to find meaningful ways to bring both the sociocultural and psychological dimensions of writing in order to approach writing as "complex social participatory performance, in which the writer asserts meaning, goals, actions, affiliations, and identities within a constantly changing, contingently organized social world, relying on shared texts and knowledge" (p. 11). When students bridge the sociocultural and psychological, they develop a more active stance toward writing and learning in other disciplines.

Course Unit Three: Process, "Taking an Approach," and a Science of Writing

In *Rewriting*, the fourth chapter may be the most interesting and conceptually difficult for students. In "Taking an Approach," Joseph Harris (2006) reimagines the initial three moves of his book (Coming to Terms, Forwarding, and Countering). Those initial moves draw lines between an author's thinking and the student's use or analysis of it, especially in the "yes, and" and "yes, but" explanation of forwarding and countering. In taking an approach, the move is less clear: "When taking the approach of another writer both your thinking and theirs needs to change" (Harris, 2006, p. 74). The focus on metacognition in the FYW course eases this shift from responding to adapting, as one student claims:

> [T]aking an approach not only answers the question as to how we can be successful with diverging our ideas from other authors, but become self-aware about why these sources influence our work. This self-awareness ultimately leads to the direction a paper can head in, because the influence sources had. It really goes to show why, after this class, most of us look down on high school writing; it's almost like subconsciously we knew something was wrong, and wanted to express our millennial perspectives in a way in which others will listen. (Harris, 2006, p. 74)

With this metacognitive awareness of how sources influence their work, students begin their seven-week research project, which includes prewriting, database research, annotated bibliography, multiple drafts, an abstract, multimodal project presentation, final draft, and reflection letter. Some students in the course took a consciously auto-ethnographic approach and blended their research with reflection and analysis of their prior learning and experiences in educational and other contexts.

RESULTS AND ANALYSIS

Analyzing survey data, student artifacts and group discussions conducted during the following semester helped to support (and challenge) the following claims:

- Linked Coursework facilitates near and far transfer,
- Metacognitive practices support high-road and far transfer,
- Explicit discussions of transfer and metacognition support interdisciplinary thinking, and
- Interdisciplinary transfer of metacognitive practices increases student agency.

LINKED COURSEWORK FACILITATES NEAR AND FAR TRANSFER

The shared knowledge evoked by having both the Science course and the FYW course tied thematically by the teaching and learning of metacognitive strategies did more than support first year students' sense of security and belonging in their new academic context. The shared, yet disciplinary-specific use of metacognitive strategies between the two courses created the condition for David N. Perkins and Gavriel Salomon's (1992) conceptions of "near" and "far" transfer, with near being "largely reflexive," and far accomplished through "mindful abstraction." Although both near and far transfer can be what Perkins and Salomon call "low-road" and "high-road" transfer, low-road transfer occurs most often in conjunction with near transfer, when similarly configured conditions of the transfer context (i.e., the academic classroom and reading response assignment), "trigger[s in students] well-developed semi-automatic responses" (Perkins & Salomon, 1992). High-road transfer, on the other hand, requires students to look for connections between their immediate academic learning context and other contexts that may or may not be school-related, and see how the overarching theory of their learning can be adapted and applied.

These formed the basis for successful near transfer for some students, while the application of similar metacognitive strategies that asked them to engage mindfully and deliberately to discipline specific problem sets optimized the possibility of far transfer as well.

METACOGNITIVE PRACTICES SUPPORT HIGH-ROAD AND FAR TRANSFER

In an internal online survey, students in the course responded to a number of qualitative questions about metacognition and transfer. The first three questions asked about the frequency of using metacognitive writing strategies in UWRT150, in COS Metacognitive Approaches to Science, and in other STEM coursework. The next two questions asked about transfer between FYW/COS and then FYW /other STEM coursework. Our numbers for this pilot were small, $N=17$: 10 IMPRESS grant students, 7 non-grant students, and are not reliable enough to make wide generalization, but the results do suggest a common-sense pattern: students used metacognitive writing strategies most frequently in UWRT 150, somewhat less frequently in COS, and less frequently still in other STEM coursework. In the second set, students were more likely to transfer metacognitive writing strategies between the linked courses, and less likely to transfer them into other STEM coursework. Not surprisingly, linked coursework affords more frequent and likely opportunities for near transfer.

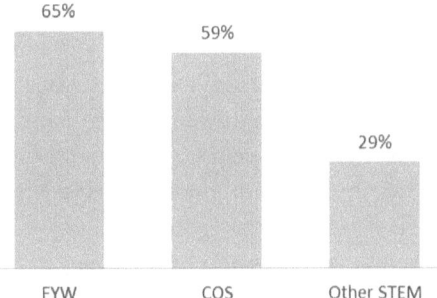

Figure 10.1. Percentage of students reporting use of metacognitive writing strategies as frequently/very frequently/all the time.

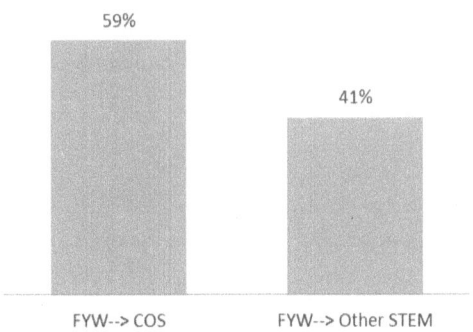

Figure 10.2. Percentage of students reporting transfer of metacognitive writing practices between courses as frequently/very frequently/all the time.

Students were able to elaborate their Likert scale answers by responding to the short answer question on the survey, "How do you use metacognitive strategies in your STEM coursework?" Some students reported that they were using metacognitive strategies in useful ways: to track their progress, approach tasks, overcome obstacles, find connections, gain process awareness, become more analytical of themselves and their instructors, and evaluate "why I'm being asked to do that stuff." Others said that they used metacognition to compare what they had done in other writing contexts (i.e., high school, work, community organizations, etc.) to what they were learning about their own behavior as writers in this course. They are engaging in what Kathleen Blake Yancey calls in her chapter of this volume and elsewhere "mapping the prior": "I look back to what I already know," "the various knowledge that I learned," etc. One student's discussion board post illustrates this:

> Negretti's paper related to how I wrote and how I learned to write all the way from my middle school to high school career. Because of my ability to write well in analytical formats, I was always considered a "good" writer . . . but I never really understood what *made* a good writer, and why other people in my class didn't have whatever that was. I never thought so much about how I wrote, or how I thought about thinking about how I wrote (I never even tried to contemplate changing the way I wrote, considering it seemed beneficial to a good grade). Reading Negretti's paper made me think about my shortcomings as a writer, and how I could change my writing style just by analyzing my own thought processes and writing processes to further my "rhetorical consciousness."

In addition to mapping prior knowledge, the student is having what Jan Meyer, Ray Land, and Caroline Baillie (2010) call an "encounter with troublesome knowledge" (p. xi), in which her prior knowledge ("I was always considered a 'good' writer") is now frustrated by a new kind of knowledge ("rhetorical consciousness").

This new knowledge, juxtaposed with the old knowledge, thrusts the student into what Meyer et al. term a "liminal state" (2010, p. xi), where the student now investigates what is now true about her writing. Operating in this liminal state, she begins to integrate new knowledge from both her COS and FYW courses to shift her conceptual frame about her own writing. In her Unit 1 paper, the student continues to question why she self-categorized herself as a "good" writer, connecting that perception to the Dunning-Kruger effect concept from a reading in her COS class—a concept which suggests that that the less knowledgeable or skilled a person is in a particular area, the more likely they are to overestimate the quality of their performance.

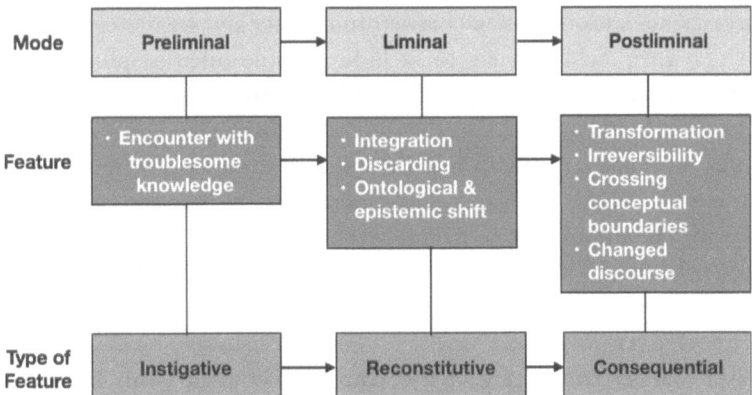

Figure 10.3. A relational view of the features of threshold concepts (Meyer et al., 2010, p. xii).

The Dunning-Kruger effect is referred to in passing in the Negretti reading from her FYW class, but it is a major concept in the linked COS course. The student brings the Dunning-Kruger concept to bear on the Negretti reading: "In reading Negretti's study, I constantly wondered . . . whether this 'Dunning-Kruger' effect applied to the students in [Negretti's] the study." This student-author is engaging in near transfer: the linked coursework on metacognition makes this connection and cross-conversation feel natural, especially as her conceptual framework about her writing shifts to include new knowledge. She also, however, is beginning a deeper exploration of her own agency in the writing process. Reading these authors, discussing these ideas in her linked classes, she feels empowered to alter her familiar approach to writing task to "change [her] writing style just by analyzing [her] own thought processes and writing processes."

EXPLICIT DISCUSSIONS OF TRANSFER AND METACOGNITION SUPPORT INTERDISCIPLINARY THINKING

Rochester Institute of Technology (RIT) is somewhat fondly referred to by students as "Brick City" where brick buildings represent different colleges: Engineering, College of Applied Science and Technology, College of Science, College of Imaging Arts and Sciences, etc. As an RIT student, it is natural to think of each building as the home for a particular discipline, a specific place for a particular kind of learning which has implications for their careers. In this context, FYW seems for many students to be not only unrelated, but an unnecessary use of time in a competitive educational environment where students are advised to delve quickly into their field-specific knowledge.

Most undergraduate students have not yet been "disciplined" to the degree that these specializations become barriers to transfer and are therefore more likely to widen their field of view to include possible interdisciplinary connects between their classes. This helps them to avoid the "monotonic" (Bazerman, 2011) kinds of research questions that stay safely in the field of Writing Studies. In relating his experience with interdisciplinary, Bazerman writes that the diverse "theory, findings, and data I encountered carried baggage, very interesting baggage, which tempted me to rummage about and even play costume games" (2011, p. 13). For FYW students, these costume games are liberating and, because they are participating in these outside of their home disciplines, these games are relatively low-risk.

These "Science of Writing" FYW courses encouraged this kind of interdisciplinary perception, first through the title of the course itself, and then supported by the research project assignments. The students' research topics maintained a focus on Writing Studies, but were encouraged to find innovative ways of blending writing topics and questions from their home disciplines, like "Photojournalism: Visual Storytelling in Media" and "Musings on the Triangular Homogeneity of Metacognition, Writing, and Chess." In "Writing in Math," one student investigated the current underutilization of writing tasks in mathematics education. Acknowledging that the majority of research focuses on teaching math through writing in K-8 contexts, she calls for complicating and expanding writing tasks in math education for college students; because many math teachers "make the learning areas so small and concrete." In her reflection, she discusses her interdisciplinary approach to this project and learning in other classes:

> In First Year Writing we focused on transfer and metacognition and how it would help us to relate our outside courses. In my experience, this helped me greatly. It allowed me to really get a feel for everything I was learning all at once as one giant web structure. It made me more aware as I was trying different concepts from one engineering class to the other or from First Year Writing to a paper in Metacognitive Approaches to Scientific Inquiry. I also took some of the concepts and writing strategies learned in this class and put them into my project for my Calculus class.

By moving knowledge from one context to another, she builds a "giant web structure" of learning that allows her to see connections and applications across her classes in different disciplines in spite of the brick-reinforced disciplinary compartmentalization at RIT. Students without this awareness may not see learning as interdisciplinary and struggle to make these connections. If we are serious about encouraging transfer between disciplines, having students experience the permeability of these disciplinary walls is important, especially at the beginning of their academic careers.

INTERDISCIPLINARY TRANSFER OF METACOGNITIVE PRACTICES INCREASES STUDENT AGENCY

King Beach (1999) identifies a number of "crevasses" in analyzing the transfer metaphor, one of which is that transfer has an "agency problem" (p. 108). He uses the analogy of a cyclist who learns that the faster she rides, the easier it is for her to balance and arrive at her destination in good time and without injuring herself. The agency problem is that the cyclist may not be aware of how her interactions with the bicycle lead to her arriving unscathed at the destination, and this lack of understanding of her role in bicycle physics means that she doesn't recognize her role in causing this outcome. Regardless of the prudence in picking at one metaphor (transfer) with another (bicycles), Beach's point is clear: Even if she is in control, she has no sense of control and therefore sense of agency because she is unaware of her role.

Metacognition helps to bridge this crevasse. By presenting transfer and metacognition in an interdisciplinary linked course model, students develop an awareness of how their learning in one context/discipline is brought into another. Once that awareness begins to develop, students see themselves doing the work that is described in the articles read in the courses. One student reflects on how his experience in this FYW/COS linked coursework connects to James Pacello's (2014) study of a metacognition-focused developmental reading and writing course:

> In terms of continuously reflecting on our work, I think RIT's IMPRESS program has so far stayed true to Pacello's studies, and the previous readings on metacognition. We already are going through the processes of writing, and re-writing, sending self-reflections, and even completing these discussion posts to receive feedback from our peers and professors. Along with this, Pacello thinks that if classes are connected with one another, a more cohesive educational bond is created to help students learn, which also occurs at RIT. Although I wish some of the science and math departments approached

education this way, I can still apply metacognitive skills to them in ways to help myself learn more successfully.

Like the students completing blog posts in Pacello's study, this student is examining the activities of the linked courses and assessing whether or not they fulfill the kinds of activities that "assist students in recognizing how the literacy skills developed in the course could be helpful to their success in college classes and in other contexts" (Pacello, 2014, p. 121). The student concludes that they do, citing a number of literate activities ("processes of writing, and re-writing, sending self-reflections, and even completing these discussion posts") that he and his classmates complete in the linked courses. But where he illustrates agency most clearly is in the last line, when after "wish[ing]" that the approach of his non-linked STEM coursework leveraged this approach, he concludes that it doesn't really matter because he can still apply the skills anyway, and thus get the benefits without the teacher specifically helping him to do so.

Not all students feel comfortable with the processes of metacognitive reflection, and do not necessarily feel empowered with agency. In responding to David Bartholomae's (1986) article, this student fumes:

> I mean sure I have my own essay voice, but it's super sarcastic and a little annoying, and when I write for my reader it sounds so much smarter, like I know the subject on an expert level. To put it in better words I was "trying on the discourse even though I lacked the knowledge to make the discourse a routine." Instead of writing as a student with a minor knowledge I pretended to be an expert on what I was saying, which according to Bartholomae is something every student does whenever they write. Maybe we can never escape [pretending] unless we write for ourselves and with the knowledge that we actually have. And I'll admit right now I have NO idea what I'm doing right now, I don't even know what I'm saying. I usually don't, but it's hard to not pretend that I do, because I was so used to doing it all my life in everything I wrote.

This student is expressing the difficulty of knowing what she is doing as she does it, and how this pretending toward authority unsuccessfully disguises this difficulty. She is developing an awareness of how her thinking and experience, as well as the expectations of others, complicates her writing process and that there is work to do to self-regulate her own writing process from the knowledge she herself feels she authentically possesses. Being aware, and having the authority to act on that awareness are not the same for her just yet. Not all cyclists know that they are in control of how well or poorly their bikes perform for them; when they do understand the mechanics of it, it may take time before they are ready to repair or adapt it to their needs' ends. Not all writers and learners know how their writing and learning works, or if they do, they may not be ready to trust their knowing. Thinking about the approach to an activity, whether riding or writing, increases the possibility for development and growth.

CHALLENGES AND CONCLUSIONS

Working with the students, watching their metacognitive awareness evolve, and enlisting them as co-investigators has helped us shift our own conceptual framework about the usefulness of teaching writing with a metacognitive. We have identified the following five challenges to teaching writing with an emphasis of thinking about "thinking about writing."

Metacognition is a hard habit. As the above relational mapping of metacognitive skills acquisition by Meyer et al. (2010) suggests, it takes exposure over time to fully incorporate a solid metacognitive awareness and practice. In post-course interviews the following semester, a few students brought a complaint: "I just need something to remind me to do metacognition." This desire to transfer metacognitive practice into new learning situations that do not explicitly present it is what Meyer et al. would characterize as an ontological, epistemic shift in the liminal mode: the students know that they would benefit from applying metacognition in their coursework. However, for these students, post-liminal irreversibility and transformation is not yet achieved because the feature is not habituated. While their discourse has changed in talking about the linked FYW course with us in the context of a post-course interview, it appears that the discourse has not yet changed in contexts/courses that do not explicitly call for it. Student interviews seemed to suggest that they wanted more explicit metacognitive practice in classes they took *after* FYW. At the very least, writing faculty and interdisciplinary writing-intensive faculty could work together to bridge FYW and W-I Gen Ed classes across the Arts and Sciences by using shared curricular practices of journaling about assignment elements and how to accomplish them (task perception), diagraming where their ideas might come from outside the class/discipline (concept mapping) and outlining a revision plan from peer review notes on a writing project (self-regulation and reflection).

Teaching metacognition requires a deep understanding of metacognition. Echoing Downs and Wardle's (2007) call for expert instructors in writing about writing courses, we agree that teachers presenting metacognition as a component of their course need to have conceptual and pedagogical understandings of metacognition and its impacts for student learning. Simply "adding in" strategies to build metacognitive awareness without first understanding it can lead to what Nance C. Wilson and Haiyan Bai (2010) observed in their assessment of MA Education graduate students, that even with a rich understanding of metacognition, contradictions between theory and practice can and do appear. They present a number of valuable explanations for this, including pressures to cover a lot of material and institutional pressures to teach set curricula (Wilson & Bai, 2010, p. 286). In assessing our own pedagogy moving from the spring 2015 pilot to the present fall 2015–2016 course, we can agree from experience that teacher education and professional development are imperative for successful implementation of metacognitive practices in FYW.

Linking FYW and metacognition puts metacognition in a writing box. The course is still called UWRT150, not META150, and as students transition from this course to other classes, knowledge learned in UWRT150 is likely to be labeled as "writing knowledge," "writing skills," or "English class." This can be an impediment to transfer, particularly in STEM contexts, because Liberal Arts courses are widely regarded as general or unrelated to coursework in STEM majors. Even with the College of Science course link, presenting metacognition in a writing context may have the unintended consequence of leading students to believe that it is a special part of Writing Studies, particularly if metacognition is not presented in future courses as part of that discourse community's concerns.

Metacognition is hard to recognize and assess. This is due, in large part, to the course not explicitly measuring or assessing levels of metacognition; unless there are explicit assessment measures built into the writing process, knowing exactly where and when these strategies were employed during the process is hard to pinpoint. While students did complete reflection letters and discussed their metacognitive strategies, self-response measures like Virginia Jimenez-Rodriguez, Maria Alexandra Ulate-Espinoza, Jesus Maria Alvarado-Inzquierdo, and Anibal Puente-Ferreras' (2015) EVAPROMES assessment scale or introducing more student self-assessment frameworks like those gathered by Kristen Nielsen (2014) may help to make metacognition a more visible part of students' writing process.

Metacognition enhances transfer. Low-road and near transfer may transfer unconsciously, but high-road and far transfer is less likely to happen without a student consciously evaluating how their prior learning can be applied to or influence new learning contexts. Kathleen Blake Yancey, Liane Robertson, and Kara Taczak's Teaching for Transfer (TFT) curriculum turns reflection into a "systematic activity keyed to transfer" (2014, p. 33) and goes a long way toward making student discussion of transfer an explicit goal of the course. In addition to this, wider metacognitive practices beyond reflection, such as self-regulation, self-evaluation, and task perception open more opportunities for what Perkins and Salomon (1988) call "deliberate mindful abstraction of skill or knowledge from one context or application to another" (p. 25).

For students to engage in mindful transfer, focusing on the habit of metacognition is a valuable addition to curriculum designed for transfer.

The purpose of metacognition. In assigning reflection, we are asking students to re-envision their prior thinking and doing; in task perception, we ask students to interpret new tasks based on their prior experience with similar (and dissimilar) tasks; in self-evaluation, we ask students to see their own work from an outside point of view in order to assess it; in self-regulating, we ask students to take responsibility for their own learning. The purpose of all this metacognitive activity is to regulate, change, or otherwise impact cognition. We want students to think differently, divergently, potentially disruptively, and we want them to continue this habit beyond these linked courses. When students become aware of how they gain, present, and organize knowledge, they are better equipped to transfer that knowledge as well as regulate new knowledge in the future.

REFERENCES

Bartholomae, D. (1986). Inventing the university. *Journal of Basic Writing, 5*(1), 4–23.

Bazerman, C. (2011). The disciplined interdisciplinarity of writing studies. *Research in the Teaching of English 46*(1), 8–21.

Bazerman, C. (2013). *A theory of literate action.* Fort Collins, CO: The WAC Clearinghouse and Parlor Press. Retrieved from https://wac.colostate.edu/books/literateaction/v1/.

Beach, K. (1999). Consequential transitions: A sociocultural expedition beyond transfer in education. *Review of Research in Education, 24*(1), 101–139.

Cochran-Smith, M. & Lytle, S. L. (1993). *Inside/outside: Teacher research and knowledge.* New York: Teachers College Press.

Council of Writing Program Administrators, National Council of Teachers of English & National Writing Project (2011). *Framework for success in postsecondary writing.* Retrieved from http://wpacouncil.org/files/ framework-for-success-postsecondary-writing.pdf.

Downs, D. & Wardle, E. (2007). Teaching about writing, righting misconceptions: (Re)envisioning first-year composition as introduction to writing studies. *College Composition and Communication, 58*(4), 552–584.

Denzin, N. K. & Lincoln, Y. S. (2003). *Strategies of qualitative inquiry* (2nd ed.). Thousand Oaks, CA: Sage.

Gabelnick, F., MacGregor, J., Matthews, R. S. & Smith, B. L. (1990). Learning communities: creating connections among students, faculty, and disciplines. New Directions for Teaching and Learning, 41. San Francisco: Jossey-Bass.

Harris, J. (2006). *Rewriting: How to do things with texts.* Logan, UT: Utah State University.

Jiménez-Rodríguez, V., Ulate-Espinoza, M. A., Alvarado-Inzquierdo, J. M. & Puente-Ferreras, A. (2015). EVAPROMES, an assessment scale for metacognitive processes in writing. *Electronic Journal of Research in Educational Psychology, 13*(3), 631–656.

Kellogg, K. (1999). Learning communities. *ERIC Digest,* ED430512 (pp. 1–6).

Marschark, M., Morrison, C., Lukomski, J., Borgna, G. & Covertino, C. (2013). Are deaf students visual learners? *Learning and Individual Differences, 25,* 156–162.

Matsuda, P. K. (2006). The myth of linguistic homogeneity in U.S. college composition. *College English, 68*(6), 637–651.

Meyer, J. H. F., Land, R. & Baillie, C. (2010). Editor's preface. In J. H. F. Meyer, R. Land & C. Baillie, (Eds.), *Threshold concepts and transformational learning* (pp. ix–xlii). Champaign, IL: Sense.

Negretti, R. (2012). Metacognition in student academic writing: A longitudinal study of metacognitive awareness and its relation to task perception, self-regulation, and evaluation of performance. *Written Communication, 29*(2), 142–179.

Nielsen, K. (2014). Self-assessment methods in writing instruction: A conceptual framework, successful practices and essential strategies. *Journal of Research in Reading, 37*(1), 1–16.

One, O. (2005). Punk power in the first-year writing classroom. *Teaching English in the Two-Year College, 32*(4), 358–369.

Pacello, J. (2014). Integrating metacognition into a developmental reading and writing course to promote skill transfer: An examination of student perceptions and experiences. *Journal of College Reading and Learning, 44*(2), 119–140.

Paivio, A. (1991). Dual coding theory: Retrospect and current status. *Canadian Journal of Psychology 45,* 255–287.

Paivio, A. (2006). *Mind and its evolution: A dualcoding theoretical interpretation.* Mahwah, NJ: Lawrence Erlbaum.

Penrose, A. M. & Geisler, C. (1994). Reading and writing without authority. *College Composition and Communication, 45*(4), 505–520.

Perkins, D. N. & Salomon, G. (1988). Teaching for transfer. *Education Leadership, 46*(1), 22–32.

Perkins, D. N. & Salomon, G. (1992). Transfer of learning. *International Encyclopedia of Education.* Oxford, England: Pergamon.

Ray, R. (1992) Composition for the teacher-research point of view. In G. Kirsch & P. A. Sullivan (Eds.) *Methods and methodology in composition research.* (pp. 172–189). Carbondale, IL: Southern Illinois University Press.

Ray, R.. (1993). *The practice of theory: Teacher research in composition studies.* Urbana, IL: National Council of Teachers of English.

Rounsaville, A., Goldberg, R. & Bawarshi, A. (2008). From incomes to outcomes: FYW students' prior genre knowledge, meta-cognition, and the question of transfer. *WPA: Writing Program Administration, 32*(1), 97–112.

Sadoski, M. & A. Paivio. (2013). *Imagery and text: A dual coding theory of reading and writing.* New York: Routledge Press.

Sanders-Reio, J., Alexander, P. A., Reio, Jr., T. G. & Newman, I. (2014). Do students' beliefs about writing relate to their writing self-efficacy, apprehension, and performance? *Learning and Instruction, 33*, 1–11.

Schensul, S. L., Schensul, J. J. & LeCompte, M. D. (1999). *Essential ethnographic methods: Observations, interviews, and questionnaires.* Oxford, UK: AltaMira Press.

Scott, T. (2008). Happy to comply: Writing assessment, fast capitalism, and the cultural logic of control. *Review of Education, Pedagogy and Cultural Studies, 30*(2), 140–161.

Stake, R. E. (2003). *The art of case study research.* Thousand Oaks, CA: Sage

Tedlock, B. (2003) Observation of participation and the emergence of public ethnography. In N. K. Denzin & Y. S. Lincoln (Eds.), *Strategies of qualitative inquiry* (2nd ed.) (pp. 151–172).Thousand Oaks, CA: Sage.

Tinto, V. (2003). Learning better together: The impact of learning communities on student success. In V. Tinto (Ed.) *Promoting student success in college* (pp. 1–8). Syracuse, NY: Syracuse University Press.

Wilson, N. & Bai, H. (2010). The relationships and impact of teachers' metacognitive knowledge and pedagogical understandings of metacognition. *Metacognition Learning, 5,* 269–288.

Yancey, K. B., Robertson, L. & Taczak, K. (2014). *Writing across contexts: Transfer, composition, and sites of writing.* Logan, UT: Utah State University Press.

Zawacki, T. M. & Williams, A. T. (2001). Is it still WAC? Writing within interdisciplinary learning communities. In S. H. McLeod, E. Miraglia, M. Soven & C. Thaiss (Eds.), *WAC for the new millennium: Strategies for continuing writing-across-the-curriculum programs* (pp. 109–140). Urbana: National Council of Teachers of English. Available at https://wac.colostate.edu/books/millennium/.

CHAPTER 11

METACOGNITION AND THE REFLECTIVE WRITING PRACTITIONER: AN INTEGRATED KNOWLEDGE APPROACH

Kara Taczak
University of Denver

Liane Robertson
William Paterson University of New Jersey

The eight habits of mind put forward in the *Framework for Success in Postsecondary Writing* (Council of Writing Program Administrators, National Council of Teachers of English, and the National Writing Project, 2011) suggest a balanced approach of the "intellectual and practical" in writing pedagogy. This balanced approach to writing studies is one we have previously advocated in our Teaching for Transfer (TFT) curricular model, which combines knowledge *about* writing with practice *in* writing to encourage students' transfer (Yancey, Robertson & Taczak, 2014). Focusing on both the conceptual and the practical involved in writing, students are able to develop the rhetorical knowledge that allows for effective analysis of writing situations and to develop what Anne Beaufort (2007) has referred to as the "conceptual framework" that enables the transfer of writing knowledge and practice (Beaufort, 2007). This conceptual framework helps students not only to learn to transfer, but also to approach writing with the active stance advocated by the *Framework*. For the purposes of this chapter, we focus specifically on the *Framework's* eighth habit of mind—metacognition—because recent scholarship (Beaufort, 2007, 2016; Taczak, 2015; Tinberg, 2015) indicates metacognition to be a key link to students' ability to develop the knowledge required for success when repurposed in other writing contexts.

Before we focus on metacognition, we must situate it within a construct of the ways students learn to become the self-aware writers we aim to shepherd. Metacognition is a lynchpin in a larger picture of writing development, and central to that development, and to our writing classes, is the transfer of writing knowledge and practice. We know from transfer research that students are not as successful at using their knowledge in new contexts when they have nothing to transfer into (Sommers & Saltz, 2004). When students have no context for further transfer, or perhaps don't *recognize* a context as one they might be able to transfer existing knowledge into, transfer often fails or is only partly successful. Further, for students to be able to transfer what they know about writing from one context to another, they have to understand not only the context for which their writing is destined, but also the context from which the knowledge is abstracted. In order to achieve high-road or mindful transfer (Perkins & Salomon, 1992), we suggest a model in which students utilize the abstraction of knowledge, the mindfulness, and the metacognition required for this kind of transfer (see also Beaufort, 2007, 2016). We refer to our model as *integrated knowledge*.

We use the term *integrated knowledge* to describe a robust approach to developing knowledge, including how writers understand what they know and how they know it, how they continue to build on what they know in school, work, and outside experiences through communities of practice, and how they use what they know in particular contexts and how they know it to be appropriate for that context. When this complex array of knowledge is integrated, and writers understand what they have as a resource or repertoire of knowledge capability, they can develop a greater sense of agency as writers. Self-agency for writers allows for continual development, for enculturation in communities of practice—defined as groups of people or communities made up of people who learn through shared experiences and information—(Lave & Wenger, 1991), and for successful utilization or repurposing of knowledge in multiple contexts.

An integrated knowledge model as we define it, includes (1) the concepts of cognition, metacognition, and reflection; (2) prior knowledge, attitudes, and beliefs students bring into their writing and that impact existing and new knowledge; (3) concurrent knowledge or experiential knowledge students develop in the workplace or other contexts outside of the classroom; and (4) dispositions that vary among individual students and which impact their learning. As instructors, our awareness of all these different types of knowledge that students have access to, helps us provide students with ways to think about and think with these types of knowledge. Central to our thinking, then, is that when cognition and metacognition are accessed together through reflection, students are able to assess themselves as writers, including their own understanding of these different types of knowledge, allowing them to adopt the active stance in their own learning advocated by the Framework.

Understanding this integrated knowledge model, or how students might access and make use of various types of knowledge as learners and writers, is valuable for both students and instructors to consider in writing courses. In this chapter, we'll discuss the ways in which students and instructors can tap into and make use of the integrated knowledge model as a way to help facilitate transfer. We will address the roles of cognition, metacognition, and reflection in students' writing development and in the teaching of writing. When these three concepts are defined and explored as interconnecting and unique parts of a writer's development, they contribute to writing instruction that aims at students becoming reflective writing practitioners—writers more equipped with the knowledge and practices necessary for future writing tasks. By developing such knowledge and practices that allow for transfer, students can better cultivate the habits of mind that lead to increased success in college.

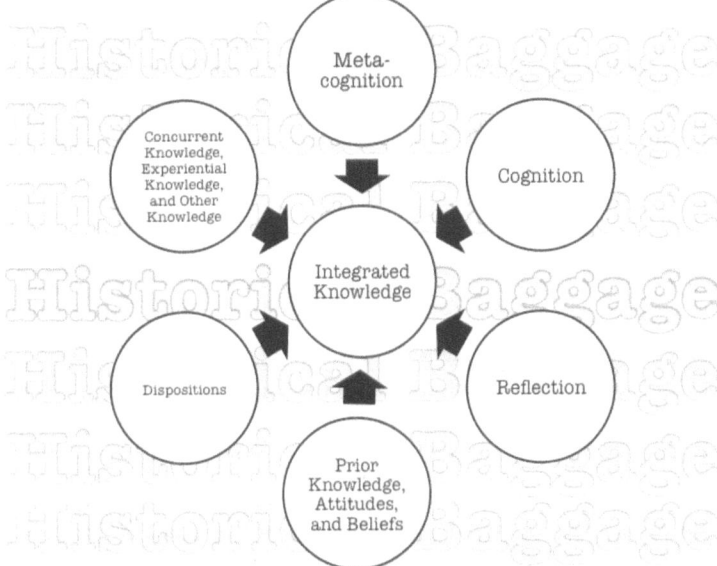

Figure 11.1. Integrated knowledge model.

COGNITION, METACOGNITION, AND REFLECTION: TOWARD INTEGRATED KNOWLEDGE

To fully understand what metacognition means for transfer, we must also discuss cognition and reflection because, as we note above, these three concepts contribute to the integrated knowledge development that can help students successfully transfer knowledge and practices to other writing contexts, and help them learn to become the reflective writing practitioners they need to be in order to continue to grow as thinkers and writers. All three of these concepts have been defined and redefined many times in our field, and in using these terms we draw upon a variety of disciplines including, but not limited to, education, psychology, linguistics, neuroscience, and philosophy, for example; for our purpose here, we draw upon what is most relevant to our model.

As reflective writing practitioners, students learn to develop the repertoire of integrated knowledge useful for future writing situations (whether that situation is for another college course, everyday writing practices, or a current or future job). The roles of cognition, metacognition, and reflection in students' writing development and in the teaching of writing, are interconnected; although different, each contributes toward a writer's development in cultivating the habits of mind suggested by the *Framework*.

When cognition, metacognition, and reflection are developed by students and understood by them as contributing to integrated knowledge, these concepts help foster growth in writing knowledge and practice that goes beyond mere awareness or ability. Understanding that integrated knowledge can be developed by considering all three of these concepts, along with other contributors to student learning, means that deeper conceptual mastery and greater capacity for agency in one's learning can be cultivated.

COGNITION

In 1966, The Dartmouth Conference effected change about how writing instruction in college was viewed, and as part of this conference, scholars looked at what research was suggesting about cognitive processes and their relationship to writing. Fifteen years later, and after a multitude of scholars had discussed, analyzed, and theorized about composing processes, Linda Flower and John R. Hayes (1981) presented their cognitive process theory of writing, which influenced much of our field's understanding about how students think through and about writing, having implications even today (for a more comprehensive historical overview of cognition in Writing Studies see Ellen Carillo's work in this volume). We know, and we have known for some time, that cognition (i.e., cognitive processes) is extremely important in writing. Research today on cognition expands upon how we understand it to include both "inside the skull" and "outside the skull" (to use Dylan Dryer's [2015] terms). This means that writing is "always a social and rhetorical act, [and] it necessarily involves cognition" (Dryer, 2015, p. 71). And we keep expanding this understanding with insights from neurology (and its many sub-fields):

> . . . insights from the social turn and insights from what some are calling the *neurological turn* appear to be converging, as can be seen in this recent definition from two cognitive researchers: "The writing process is supported by a single sys-

tem—the writer's internal mind-brain interacting with the external environment (including technology tools)." (Berninger & Winn, 2006, p. 108). (Dryer, 2015, p. 73)

Thus, cognition continues to impact our understanding of writing because "writing is a full act of the mind, drawing on the full resources of our nervous system, formulating communicative impulses into thoughts and words, and transcribing through the work of the fingers" (Bazerman & Tinberg, 2015, p. 74).

We know that writers draw on their cognitive processes, and Howard Tinberg (2015) explains how and when they do. He characterizes writers' cognitive processes in terms of the following actions they undertake:

- demonstrate an understanding of the question;
- deploy accurately and purposefully concepts, knowledge sets, and terms that reveal genuine expertise;
- meet the needs of their audience;
- fulfill the requirements of genre; or
- exhibit a control over language, grammar, and mechanics.

But as he also explains, this takes time and it requires that students use their metacognitive abilities as well (Tinberg, 2015, p. 76). This indicates that cognition and metacognition relate and connect together, and that how they connect together, and how students use them together, impacts writers' ability to successfully learn.

For the purposes of our chapter, and building on previous scholarship, we define cognition as the internal or external or social process of assimilating knowledge as a way to recognize what is happening in a particular writing moment (see also Taczak, 2015).

METACOGNITION

Metacognition has been defined simply as "thinking about thinking" (see, for example, Beaufort, 2007 or Berthoff, 1990). But the *Framework for Success in Postsecondary Writing* (CWPA et al., 2011) furthers this definition by referring to metacognition as "the ability to reflect on one's own thinking as well as on the individual and cultural processes used to structure knowledge" (p. 5). More recently, Howard Tinberg (2015) innovatively and accurately indicates that "metacognition is not cognition" explaining that "performance, however thoughtful, is not the same as awareness of how that performance came to be" (p. 75). Metacognition, as Tinberg describes it, has an important connection to writing, specifically to students' ability to reflect on their processes and their knowledge. Perhaps more significantly, and as the research team behind "Cultivating Constructive Metacognition: A New Taxonomy for Writing Studies" (Gorzelsky, Driscoll, Hayes & Jones, 2016) suggests, there's recent research further supporting the connection between metacognition and transfer that other scholars have identified (Adler-Kassner, Clark, Robertson, Taczak & Yancey, 2016; Beaufort, 2007, 2016; Nowacek, 2011; Reiff & Bawarshi, 2011; Taczak, 2015; Wardle, 2009). The Gwen Gorzelsky, Dana Lynn Driscoll, Carol Hayes, and Ed Jones study (this collection) argues for a specific type of metacognition—constructive metacognition (drawing upon Kathleen Blake Yancey's [1998] constructive reflection)—which is "a metacognitive move that demonstrates a critically reflective stance likely to support transfer of writing knowledge across contexts" (2016, p. 218) and more explicitly it calls for "reflection across writing tasks and contexts, using writing and rhetorical concepts to explain choices and evaluations and to construct a writerly identity" (Gorzelsky et al., 2016, p. 227). The Gorzelsky et al. study conveys the hope that constructive metacognition will "provide an important tool for helping students to cultivate metacognitive capacities that support writing development" and, as its authors conclude, helps to support the transfer of knowledge and practices (2016, p. 244).

While Gorzelsky et al.'s study focuses more on a specific type of metacognition than on metacognition overall, it does align with research reported by the National Research Council's volume *How People Learn*, which claims that "metacognitive approaches to instruction have been shown to increase the degree to which students will transfer to new situations" (Bransford, Pellegrino & Donovan, 2000b, p. 67). This reported success with transfer, according to *How People Learn*, is due to the idea that metacognition helps students become "more aware of themselves as learners who actively monitor their learning strategies and resources" (Bransford et al., 2000b, p. 67). Metacognition allows students to "monitor" their learning in different situations; this helps them "regulate" their own understanding of the situations which then helps them to be able to take this understanding and use it in other situations (Bransford et al., 2000b, p. 78).

As we suggest below, scholars and instructors alike often conflate metacognition and reflection, using the terms interchangeably in higher education to describe learning practices students need to be successful. However, as Kathleen Blake Yancey (2016) notes in her edited collection, *A Rhetoric of Reflection*, "As constructs, reflection and metacognition have some overlap, but they also are assigned different attributes and roles in supporting learning" (p. 6). We take a similar approach to reflection and metacognition: they are similar, yet distinct, and separate but interrelated, as we describe in the sections that follow.

Towards that end, we define metacognition as the ability to mindfully monitor and consider why specific choices were made in a particular writing moment, including, but not limited to, considering the different types of knowledge(s) learned before and acquired during that particular writing moment, and to be able to utilize that knowledge there and elsewhere.

REFLECTION

Definitions and perceptions of reflection across our field have varied widely, just as the concepts of cognition and metacognition are defined somewhat differently across our discipline. Also similar to metacognition and cognition, throughout the years, we have pulled from other fields to help us define reflection (e.g. Schön's *The Reflective Practitioner* [1984]). But definitions and, perhaps more importantly, perceptions of what reflection means with regard to writing, have little consensus among us. There is a perceived understanding that reflection is a staple of any writing classroom, and that students must reflect on writing in order to understand and improve. But beyond that, definitions have ranged widely. Throughout the last 30 years, reflection has been defined in different ways, from the pausing and scanning of one's work (Pianko, 1979) to meditation (Moffett, 1982) to the reframing of a problem through reflection-in-action (Schön, 1984) to changing and transforming (Berthoff, 1990) to helping students become active agents in their own education (Yancey, 1998) to silence (Belanoff, 2001) to using process descriptions to address "how real students argue" (Jung, 2011) to asking students to examine their own beliefs alongside their classmates (Sommers, 2011) to various others. Yancey (2015) recently suggested reflection is "both a central yet productively open term . . . needing better definitions and more sophisticated research" (p. 153).

As Jeff Sommers (2011) noted, reflection allows students to use their own language in ways that enable them to tap into and build on prior knowledge and experiences. Often reflection becomes an "inside the head" activity that does not require the act of writing—it's inductive. And as many of our students have mentioned, they *do* reflect: they reflect on their daily experiences; they reflect on the classes and college life in which they're engaged; and they reflect over the good and bad things that happen in their lives. The challenge for teachers of writing becomes getting students to broaden their notion of reflection so that they "recognize what they are doing in that particular moment (cognition), as well as consider why they made the rhetorical choices they did (metacognition). The combination of cognition and metacognition, accessed through reflection, helps writers begin assessing themselves as writers, recognizing and building on their prior knowledge about writing" (Taczak, 2015, p. 78).

It's also the case that *their reflections*, as the students phrase them, are different from the focused systematic activity we are advocating: a very specific type of rhetorical reflection similar to that suggested by previous researchers (Bransford, Pellegrino & Donovan, 2000a, 2000b; Perkins & Salomon, 1992; Taczak, 2011; Yancey, 1998) —that encourages two actions: (1) theorizing about writing, including writing identity, writing practices and processes, and knowledge about writing, and (2) putting learning into practice as a way to move forward in their writing ability (Taczak & Robertson, 2016). Thus, we define reflection as "a mode of inquiry: a deliberate way of systematically recalling writing experiences to [frame or] reframe the current writing situation" (Taczak, 2015, p. 73; also see Adler-Kassner et al., 2016). As Yancey explains, reflection involves thinking about what we've chosen to do in a writing situation in order to understand why we chose to do it, and that making sense of that choice improves our performance. But more importantly, "reflecting contributes to self-efficacy precisely because it helps us understand that we have learned (even if not always successfully); how we have learned; and how we might continue to learn" (Yancey, 2016, p. 8). Reflection helps students become self-aware, and as we noted above, it's the self-awareness that's helpful in guiding them to successful transfer.

Indeed, reflection has evolved, for many of us in writing studies, into a means by which students better understand how they are making knowledge about writing; by engaging in reflection students are able to learn from each writing context and its exigence in a way that aids their ongoing learning for writing contexts yet to come.

COGNITION, METACOGNITION, AND REFLECTION: OVERLAPPING, CONNECTED CONCEPTS

The complexity that surrounds these three concepts—cognition, metacognition, and reflection—stems from a rich and varied past. They bring with them what we refer to as "historical baggage" or past histories, experiences, issues, definitions, perceptions and understandings that affect the current disposition surrounding the concepts. Historical baggage is what we carry with us into the classroom as teachers, and what students also carry in and are influenced by. It affects how we teach and makes use of these three concepts in our classroom and affects how students comprehend using them inside their thinking and writing processes. Historical baggage influence what we do in the classroom and how our students respond to what we do in the classroom, and what they do in their own writing. Because of rich and varied pasts, historical baggage can be dichotomous: potentially positive or negative, both clear and unclear, seemingly isolated and yet systematic.

We argue that historical baggage *can* be a way to view how integrated knowledge is organized and accessed. For this to occur, though, cognition, metacognition, and reflection must be aimed for in teaching in intentional, overlapping ways. As our definitions of these three concepts suggest, we believe that they connect, creating opportunities to enhance transfer by encouraging cognition in a particular writing moment (whether it be internally, externally, or socially), while encouraging metacognition through mindful monitoring of rhetorical choices in a very deliberate way, recalling the past to reframe the current moment.

HABITS OF MIND: ORGANIZING AND ACCESSING KNOWLEDGE

As instructors of writing and advocates for teaching for transfer, we are always striving to employ effective instruction for students to engage in cognitive, metacognitive, and reflective practices. Throughout the field's history, we have explored each concept's relationship to writing—sometimes together and sometimes not—but it's clear, at various stages, these concepts have helped inform writing instruction and student writing processes (for example see Bazerman & Tinberg, 2015; Beaufort, 2007, 2016; Flower & Hayes, 1981; Gorzelsky et al., 2016; Reiff & Bawarshi, 2011; Taczak, 2015; Tinberg, 2015; Wardle, 2007; Yancey, 1998). However the redefining of these terms is what helps to make them more elusive: reflection, for example, has always been, as Kathleen Blake Yancey (1998) has stated, "slippery"; cognition, as Peter Khost suggests in this collection, can be a "mystifying term"; and Brianna Scott and Matthew Levy (2013) note that metacognition is a "fuzzy concept" (p. 121). Thus, we might argue that figuring out how (and understanding where) these three concepts connect and work within the writing classrooms presents some difficulties. In fact, others agree. Gorzelsky et al. (2016) argue that the field doesn't have "strategies for teaching [the specific components and subcomponents of metacognition], either individually or to promote metacognitive development that supports the transfer of writing-related knowledge across courses and contexts" (p. 217).

Adding to the complexity of these concepts is the fact that metacognition has been underrepresented in the writing classroom (often because it's not clearly understood) and, as we stated above, is sometimes conflated with reflection or mistaken for cognition. Often, we have heard the terms "metacognition" and "reflection" used interchangeably, as Yancey also suggests (2016, p. 6), as if they are perceived as one and the same. We argue to the contrary: they are not one and the same, and in fact offer two different, yet connected roles in the writing classroom. In order to promote transfer, both metacognition and reflection must be understood and taught as separate concepts, encouraged through different types of directed activities and assignments. As the Gorzelsky et al. study claims, "instructors need information on how to teach metacognitive components in ways that promote transfer" (2016, p. 218) and as we argued alongside Yancey in Writing Across Contexts (Yancey et al., 2014), the same is true for reflection.

These three seemingly important and grounding concepts in our field, specifically to our pedagogies and our ability to encourage transfer, carry with them historical baggage. As instructors and scholars, how do we respond to the past histories, experiences, issues, definitions, and understandings that comprise historical baggage and that affect the current dispositions surrounding cognition, metacognition, and reflection?

In the following sections, we outline our response to this question first in terms of the teaching of writing, and second, in terms of students' ability to use it as a way to become active, engaged reflective writing practitioners.

TEACHING OF WRITING

For teachers of writing, an understanding of how students use the knowledge they bring to the classroom, develop in the classroom, and develop concurrently while enrolled in our classes, is critical. Even more critical is an instructor's role in helping students develop the ability to transfer that knowledge to new writing contexts.

Although developing integrated knowledge, as we have outlined above, helps students understand how to organize what they are learning, it is the multiple contexts in which they learn and adapt knowledge that creates an environment in which that knowledge can move forward. From a frame or an awareness level to a more robust understanding, it is within multiple writing contexts that students develop a sense of agency they can use to approach writing and to gain a sense of where their writing fits within their other academic work as well as outside pursuits. Students learn in *communities of practice*, or shared circumstances, in which collaboration, over time, contributes to one's knowledge development. "Communities of practice are groups of people who share a concern or a passion for something they do and learn how to do it better as they interact regularly" (Lave & Wenger, 1991). One community of practice is the college writing classroom, but it doesn't exist in a bubble; it is influenced by or is a part of the larger communities of practice in the college environment, and the still larger communities of practice in which students are engaged concurrently, across college or in a workplace or volunteer role, or other aspects of life.

But these communities of practice don't exist merely because students work together in a writing classroom. A community of practice involves shared values for learning and engaging in its practices, which our writing classrooms don't necessarily emulate (Lave & Wenger, 1991; Wenger, 1998). In fact, many approaches to teaching writing, especially first-year writing, favor a dispersed array of content, such as process-based writing instruction or instruction focused on a particular theme, which are not representative of what is taught in other classrooms across the country or beyond (Robertson, 2011). Without a more unified model or a consensus approach to teaching writing, we don't create a community of practice of writing course classrooms. However, we can acknowledge the communities of practice that exist for our students and to which we can integrate our classrooms to some degree, or at least help our students to understand and access. For example, we can help students relate to their work in our classes the knowledge about writing that comes into play in a student's major discipline, or that student's job or internship for which she must perform some writing task. The student's knowledge can be integrated across those contexts; or rather she can learn to integrate her knowledge across all of her contexts for writing, as her writing knowledge and understanding of writing—in *each* context but also *about* context as a concept to consider in tailoring writing to situations or audiences—continues to develop. In other words, as she develops self-agency with her increasingly integrated knowledge from various contexts, she can increase her effectiveness at the decision-making that undergirds her repurposing of writing knowledge appropriately for each context she faces.

STUDENTS AS REFLECTIVE WRITING PRACTITIONERS

Building on earlier research on reflection (specifically Schön, 1984; Taczak, 2011; Yancey, 1998, 2015, 2016), we describe a reflective writing practitioner as primarily a problem-solver, or a writer who utilizes reflection in these ways: (1) to understand the rhetorical situation and what a writer needs to do in response to it, (2) to develop a reflective framework for approaching writing situations, and in so doing, (3) draw on integrated knowledge that informs the reflective framework, while (4) organizing and accessing their knowledge in a way that allows them to thrive in a writing context and within their own writerly identities.

Drawing specifically upon Donald Schön's theory (1984) on reflective practice for the professional and Yancey's theory of reflection for the writing classroom (1998), we characterize a reflective writing practitioner as someone who is continually exposed to different writing situations and develops, through those situations, a repertoire of knowledge that can be integrated and repurposed. This characterization allows for reflection as a theory, as a practice, and as a means for encouraging transfer.

The utility of one's ability to become a reflective writing practitioner is primarily that so many professions use reflection as part of their practices: artists, social workers, scientists, educators, just to name a few. Doctors, specifically surgeons, are one such example: they build reflection into their practice as a way to better understand why a surgical procedure might have gone wrong, when they attend regularly scheduled morbidity and mortality conferences (see Yancey, Robertson, and Taczak, 2014, pp. 120–121). Students in our writing classrooms can develop knowledge in the same way, to understand how writing works well in one context, perhaps not appropriately in the next context, and ultimately how to approach each context with a repertoire of knowledge that can be drawn upon for success at writing in a current context. As Yancey writes, through reflective practice, "we see similarities in difference; difference in similarity; affinity in juxtaposition and affinity as part of the whole; arrangement and rearrangement as means of discovery; ready mades and newly mades" which why it's critical for students to learn it (or extend their learning): it helps them see things such as "similarities in difference; difference in similarity" and so on (Yancey, K. B., personal communication, September 15, 2015). It provides a space for them as students (and later on as employees and workers) to make sense of what they are doing, why they are doing it, and what it means, and in this way reflection connects directly to cognition and metacognition.

To connect reflection to cognition and metacognition for students, we advocate for the reflective framework discussed in our recent publication (with Kathleen Blake Yancey), *Writing Across Contexts: Transfer, Composition, and Sites of Writing* (Yancey et al., 2014). Our three-pronged framework includes reflective theory, reflective activities, and reflective assignments, all of which create opportunities for students to use both cognition and metacognition (see also Taczak & Robertson, 2016). To expect this kind of development from students, reflection is a reiterative practice woven through the curriculum as a key term, one that is referred to explicitly and defined for the students through the reading of different key theorists and examples of the key term in practice. It is also fostered through different types of reflective activities and assignments that move the students toward becoming reflective writing practitioners. There are several moments in which students encounter "certain types of [writing] situations again and again," aiding this development (Schön, 1984, p. 60).

As reflective writing practitioners, students can develop the repertoire we mention above, which involves integrated knowledge and different experiences with writing. This means that their attitudes, beliefs, and understandings of writing are a part of their repertoire, too, because students define their experiences with writing based on these areas. Dana Lynn Driscoll (2011) argues that students' attitudes are an important part of their ability to successfully transfer knowledge. As well, we have previously argued along with Kathleen Blake Yancey (Robertson, Taczak & Yancey, 2012; Yancey et al., 2014) that prior knowledge impacts students' ability to successfully transfer in a multitude of complex and interesting ways. As scholars researching transfer argue, we must acknowledge students' past relationships with writing because it directly affects how they learn, what they learn, how they develop as writers, and what they can transfer forward (Bransford et al., 2000a, Driscoll, 2011; Perkins & Solomon, 1992; Robertson et al., 2012). The repertoire provides students with a list of capabilities connecting to their writing practices, allowing them to begin to make an *active* move in their understanding of writing: from simply writing as a means to fulfill an assignment and receive a grade, to writing as a means of thinking about rhetorical moves and attempting to enact these rhetorical moves in their writing and in future writings.

We create assignments and activities that ask students to *think* like reflective writing practitioners in hopes that it will lead to them *becoming* reflective writing practitioners. The emphasis must be on encouraging students to move from *thinking* to *enacting*. This move is challenging because students (and some instructors) believe that reflection happens naturally rather than developmentally. Some students may not be developmentally ready to engage in reflection of this kind, and some instructors mistakenly believe they already engage students in this type of and level of reflection. But as Donald Schön (1984) claimed, practitioners use reflection as a way to solve problems—the problem of composing/writing a text and the problem of defining composing/writing—two different problems, but two problems with similar goals: to figure out how to compose/write better and to figure out what it is she *is* composing/writing.

Therefore, the reflective writing practitioner uses reflection to understand who she is as a writer, a very challenging question for any writer. Who am I as a writer? What do I believe about writing? What do I understand about writing? What do I know about writing from previous experiences? How do I write/compose in different situations? Do I write the same way in all situations? How can I use what I learn from one context to the next? Exposing students to different activities and assignments involving this type of reflection helps them develop the repertoire needed to encourage transfer.

We argue that when reflection is taught in this intentional way (using the reflective framework from the Teaching for Transfer curriculum), students become active constructors of their own knowledge about effective rhetorical practices; they can become reflective writing practitioners, integrating knowledge across contexts. But we are arguing for a very specific type of reflection—one that connects cognition with metacognition in deliberate ways:

> a practice that serves as both process and product; theory and practice; before-the-fact activity, during-the-fact activity, and after-the-fact activity. This type of reflection includes reflecting

> both inwardly—through the act of thinking about writing practice—and outwardly—through the act of writing about those writing practices. Thinking about writing gets at the *why* of a writer's rhetorical choices, which allows for deeper reflection on the act of writing than reflecting only on the *what* of a writer's actions. Likewise, when reflection is practiced as only an after-the-fact activity or as merely looking backward on what has been written, the writer focuses primarily on *what has been written*. (Taczak & Robertson, 2016, pp. 43–44)

Later, when students who are reflective writing practitioners enter new rhetorical situations, they can not only transfer what they've learned appropriately to a new context, but also teach themselves what they don't already know about what is needed to construct effective rhetorical responses in these new situations. Reflective writing practitioners can transfer more readily because they understand how to make use of their repertoire of knowledge and practices of composing; they are aware of how to frame or reframe different composing situations.

A TEACHING FRAMEWORK: REFLECTION AND METACOGNITION

In some of our previous work together and in our work with Yancey (see Taczak & Robertson, 2016; Yancey et al., 2014;) we have suggested our TFT (Teaching for Transfer) curricular model as an approach that integrates knowledge about and practice in writing to encourage transfer. Here we suggest that further integrating knowledge (and practice as part of that overall knowledge) into the ways we approach the teaching of writing is also critical. Part of that curricular approach involves the reflective framework we suggest is necessary for a writer to become a reflective writing practitioner and this type of reflection is different from the common practice of reflection in the writing classroom, as discussed above. We see the role of reflection as one that is a systematic, reiterative approach to thinking about writing in ways that contribute to a student's understanding of not only the process of writing, but also the conceptual framework of writing knowledge they develop in a course specifically designed for metacognition and transfer. Of course, no writing class can guarantee delivery on such a promise, but it can be designed to foster these attributes as much as possible. If we understand and account for the integrated knowledge students might work with in our classrooms, we are much closer to achieving the systematic reflection, cognition, and metacognition that we hope our students can develop in order to transfer their knowledge and practices.

We're assuming here that transfer is the goal of all teaching of writing. We can't imagine why it wouldn't be; no matter one's stance on the content of a writing course or one's opinion on the best approach to teaching writing, we assume that all teachers of writing want their students to be able to utilize elsewhere what they learn in the writing classroom. Therefore, we won't argue for transfer here. We will argue, however, for the consideration that students' knowledge about writing is critical to their development as writers, and that instructing students in just the practice of writing is only one part of teaching them to become better writers.

Engaging students in understanding, utilizing, and repurposing all the types of knowledge they bring to our classrooms requires that we teach with a framework in mind. This teaching framework, like a student's reflective framework or framework of conceptual knowledge, should provide our students with direction for organizing their knowledge, not only from the course but also from outside. We know from the National Research Council's *How People Learn*, that the relationship between noviceship and expertise is important to understanding how students make use of what we teach them, and that part of what helps them move toward expertise is the ability to discern patterns of information, to organize the content knowledge they learn in ways that let them develop deep understanding, and to be able to access and repurpose knowledge appropriately in new contexts (Bransford et al., 2000a, p. 31). There are other factors as well, but the three just mentioned are relevant to providing a framework for our teaching that helps students develop integrated knowledge on the way to becoming experts.

We also know from research in writing transfer that students bring dispositions to their learning and writing in college. Defined by Dana Driscoll and Jennifer Wells (2012) as "qualities that determine how learners use and adapt their knowledge" (n.p.), dispositions are part of a much larger system of an individual's approach to thinking. Dispositions include but are not limited to intellectual ability, skill, capacity for learning, motivation, or inclination; rather, they are all of these attributes, coupled with the ways individuals might utilize them.

And we know from research that students bring prior knowledge to their learning that can act as both help and hindrance depending on whether they know what to do with that knowledge or where it might be appropriate to use. When students bring prior knowledge (as well as prior beliefs/attitudes/dispositions) to a writing class, they integrate it with new and other knowledge. This framework of prior and new writing knowledge, as well as concurrent knowledge they might be developing in other courses or outside contexts, help them make sense of their entire repertoire of knowledge. And when metacognition is engaged in doing so, it can ultimately enable students to transfer what they've learned to the writing contexts they'll encounter across the university and beyond.

Regardless of the types of knowledge or attitudes, etc., and the similarities or differences between them, the common thread throughout is the need for writing teachers to help students organize and make sense of what they know so they might use it effectively. This focus, we argue should be as much our role as teachers as the processes, ways of expression, and techniques for writing long represented in our field.

Students are enculturated as learners, taking cues experientially and through the influences of much more of their lives than we see in any one writing course. An effective teacher of writing must tap into these experiences, along with the prior knowledge, dispositions, and any other factors impacting students' approach to writing, by providing a framework for students that engages them in becoming reflective writing practitioners aiming for metacognition and, ultimately, transfer.

Teaching writing with such a framework means we need to help students see the big picture, not just the writing that works in our classrooms. We must help students understand similarities and differences, to see the patterns of meaning that experts understand, and to be able to make effective selections from their repertoire of integrated knowledge to repurpose in new contexts.

INTEGRATED KNOWLEDGE, METACOGNITION, AND THE REFLECTIVE WRITING PRACTITIONER

Helping students develop self-agency as writers, by encouraging them to utilize integrated knowledge, to work to become reflective writing practitioners, and to understand and develop the capacity for metacognition—this is the framework for teaching writing that will best represent our abilities and their potential. Key to developing self-agency is metacognition, via reflection. By becoming reflective writing practitioners, and by understanding how to integrate knowledge, students can develop the capacity for metacognition that will propel them toward self-agency. As they continue to develop toward self-agency, they will become better writers overall because they will be able to understand the choices available in each context, based on integrated knowledge they know how to access and utilize. As teachers of writing, we can and should help them develop their sense of agency, so they can continue on their own in developing greater self-agency, increased metacognition, and ultimately to transfer what they know appropriately across contexts as writers in college and throughout their entire lives.

REFERENCES

Adler-Kassner, L., Clark, I., Robertson, L., Taczak, K. & Yancey, K. B. (2016). Assembling knowledge: The role of threshold concepts in facilitating transfer. In J. L.

Moore & C. M. Anson (Eds.), *Critical transitions: Writing and the question of transfer* (pp. 17–48). Fort Collins, Co: The WAC Clearinghouse and University Press of Colorado. Retrieved from https://wac.colostate.edu/books/ansonmoore/.

Bazerman, C. & Tinberg, H. (2015). Writing is an expression of embodied cognition. In L. Adler-Kassner & E. Wardle (Eds.), *Naming what we know: Threshold concepts of writing studies* (pp. 74–75). Logan, UT: Utah State University Press.

Beaufort, A. (2007). *College writing and beyond: A new framework for university writing instruction*. Logan, UT: Utah State University Press.

Beaufort, A. (2016). Reflection: The metacognitive move towards transfer of learning. In K. Yancey (Ed), *A rhetoric of reflection* (pp. 23–41). Logan, UT: Utah State University Press.

Belanoff, P. (2001). Silence: Reflection, literacy, learning, and teaching. *College Composition and Communication, 52*(3), 399–428.

Berninger, V. W. & Winn, W. D. (2006). Implications of advancements in brain research and technology for writing development, writing instruction, and educational evolution. In C. McArthur, S. Graham & J. Fitzgerald (Eds.), *Handbook of Writing Research* (pp. 96–114). New York: Guilford.

Berthoff, A. E. (1990). *Sense of learning: The making of meaning*. Portsmouth, NH: Boynton/Cook.

Bransford, J. D., Pellegrino, J. W. & Donovan, S. (Eds.) (2000a). How experts differ from novices. In J. D. Bransford, A. L. Brown & R. R. Cocking (Eds.), *How people learn: Brain, mind, experience, and school: expanded edition* (pp, 31–50). Washington, DC: National Academies Press.

Bransford, J. D., Pellegrino, J. W. & Donovan, S. (Eds.) (2000b). Learning and transfer. In J. D. Bransford, A. L. Brown & R. R. Cocking (Eds.), *How people learn: Brain, mind, experience, and school: expanded edition* (pp. 51–78). Washington, DC: National Academies Press.

Council of Writing Program Administrators, National Council of Teachers of English, and the National Writing Project (2011). *Framework for success in postsecondary writing*. Retrieved from http://wpacouncil.org/files/framework-for-success-post secondary-writing.pdf.

Driscoll, D. L. (2011). Connected, disconnected, or uncertain: Student attitudes about future writing contexts and perceptions of transfer from first year writing to the disciplines. *Across the Disciplines, 8*(2). Retrieved from https://wac.colostate.edu/atd/articles/driscoll2011/index.cfm.

Driscoll, D. L. & Wells. J. M. (2012). Beyond knowledge and skills: Writing transfer and the role of student dispositions. *Composition Forum,* 26 Retrieved from http://compositionforum.com/issue/26/beyond-knowledge-skills.php.

Dryer, D. (2015). Writing is (also always) a cognitive activity. In L. Adler-Kassner & E. Wardle (Eds.), *Naming what we know: Threshold concepts of writing studies* (pp. 70–74). Logan: Utah State University Press.

Flower, L. & Hayes, J. (1981). A cognitive process theory of writing. *College Composition and Communication, 32*(4), 365–387.

Gorzelsky, G., Driscoll, D., Hayes, C. & Jones. E. (2016). Cultivating constructive metacognition: A new taxonomy for writing studies. In J. L. Moore & C. M. Anson (Eds), *Critical transitions: Writing and the question of transfer* (pp. 217–250.). Fort Collins, CO: The WAC Clearinghouse and University Press of Colorado. Retrieved from https://wac.colostate.edu/books/ansonmoore/.

Jung, J. (2011). Reflective writing's synecdochic imperative: Process descriptions redescribed. *College English, 73*(6), 628–647.

Lave, J. & Wenger, E. (1991). *Situated learning: Legitimate peripheral participation.* Cambridge, UK: Cambridge University Press.

Moffett, J. (1982). Writing, inner speech, and meditation. *College English, 44*(3), 231–246.

Nowacek, R. S. (2011). *Agents of integration: Understanding transfer as a rhetorical act.* Carbondale, IL: Southern Illinois University Press.

Perkins, D. N. & Salomon, G. (1992). Transfer of learning. *International encyclopedia of education, 2*, 6452–6457.

Pianko, S. (1979). Reflection: A critical component of the composing process. *College Composition and Communication*, 30(3), 275–278.

Reiff, M. J. & Bawarshi, A. (2011). Tracing discursive resources: How students use prior genre knowledge to negotiate new writing contexts in first-year composition. *Written Communication, 28*(3), 312–37.

Robertson, L. (2011). *The significance of course content in the transfer of writing knowledge from first-year composition to other academic writing contexts.* PhD diss., Florida State University.

Robertson, L., Taczak, K. & Yancey, K. B. (2012). Notes toward a theory of prior knowledge and is role in college composers' transfer of knowledge and practice. *Composition Forum, 26*. Retrieved from http://compositionforum.com/issue/26/prior-knowledge-transfer.php.

Schön, D. A. (1984). *The reflective practitioner.* New York: Basic Books.

Scott, B. M. & Levy, M. G. (2013). Metacognition: Examining the components of a fuzzy concept. *Educational Research, 2*(2), 120–131.

Sommers, J. (2011). Reflection revisited: The class collage. *Journal of Basic Writing, 30*(1), 99–129.

Sommers, N. & Saltz, L. (2004). The novice as expert: Writing the freshman year. *College Composition and Communication, 56*(1), 124–149.

Taczak, K. (2011). *Connecting the dots: Does reflection foster transfer?* (Doctoral dissertation). PhD diss., Florida State University.

Taczak, K. (2015). Reflection is critical in the development of writers. In L. Adler-Kassner & E. Wardle (Eds.), *Naming what we know: Threshold concepts of writing studies* (pp. 78–79). Logan, UT: Utah State University Press.

Taczak, K. & Robertson, L. (2016). Reiterative reflection in the twenty-first-century writing classroom: An integrated approach to teaching for transfer. In K. B. Yancey, (Ed.), *A Rhetoric of Reflection* (pp. 42–63). Logan, UT: Utah State University Press.

Tinberg, H. (2015). Metacognition is not cognition. In L. Adler-Kassner & E. Wardle (Eds.), *Naming what we know: Threshold concepts of writing studies* (pp. 75–76). Logan, UT: Utah State University Press.

Wardle, E. (2007). Understanding "transfer" from FYC: Preliminary results from a longitudinal study. *WPA: Writing Program Administration, 31*(1–2): 65–85.

Wardle, E. (2009). "Mutt genres" and the goal of FYC: Can we help students write the genres of the university? *College Composition and Communication, 60*(4): 765–89.

Wenger, E. (1998). *Communities of practice: Learning, meaning, and identity*. Cambridge, UK: Cambridge University Press.

Yancey, K. B. (1998). *Reflection in the writing classroom*. Logan, UT: Utah State University Press.

Yancey, K. B. (2015). Reflection. In P. Heilker & P. Vandernberg (Eds.), *Keywords in Writing Studies* (pp. 150–154). Logan: Utah State University Press.

Yancey, K. B. (Ed.). (2016). *A Rhetoric of reflection*. Logan, UT: Utah State University Press.

Yancey, K. B., Robertson, L. & Taczak, K. (2014). *Writing across contexts: Transfer, composition, and sites of writing*. Logan, UT: Utah State University Press.

CHAPTER 12

SEEING IS BELIEVING: RE-PRESENTATION, COGNITION, AND TRANSFER IN WRITING CLASSES

Marcus Meade
University of Virginia

Transfer, as a cognitive process that recognizes the interrelations of genres, is really an act of seeing (Nowacek, 2011). It describes the recognizing of similarities between contexts, which means seeing the boundaries between contexts as constructed, malleable, and fluid (Tuomi-Gröhn, Egenström & Young, 2003). Transfer is the making and remaking of boundaries in ways that make them capable of being transgressed. As an example, consider the boundaries between a learning context, such as a FYC course and a novel context such as a history course. To transfer from the former to the latter would require the ability to see similarity between those contexts, meaning one would need to conceive of the boundary between them as transgress-able rather than impenetrable—if one conceives of a boundary between them at all. Of course, some writers see more similarity than others, which means transfer isn't simply a matter of innate similarity between learning contexts and novel contexts but a matter of one's ability to *see* similarity between contexts. To teach for transfer, then, is to teach a particular way of seeing, a way that comes as the result of malleable and transgress-able cognitive boundaries.

Writing-related transfer theorists often discuss the boundaries between contexts, disciplines, and genres, but rarely the cognitive boundaries within individuals. But a conception of cognition as socially situated acknowledges the fact that boundaries that exist socially exist within individuals, as well, as a result of our intertextual nature (Fleckenstein, 1999). These boundaries impact the seeing of individuals and thus, impact the capacity to transfer. In fact, the boundaries between writing contexts are easily conceived of as boundaries within individuals rather than objective boundaries in the social landscape. Mark Johnson (1987) referred to the boundaries that make up our seeing as "image schemata," the cognitive blue prints people use to make meaning of and give meaning to the world. Terttu Tuomi-Gröhn, Yrjö Engeström, and Michael Young (2003) argued that transfer should be conceived primarily as an act of boundary-crossing and believed that transfer necessitates "significant cognitive retooling" (p. 4). Rigid, solid boundaries, which resist manipulation and transgression, inhibit transfer, while malleable boundaries make transfer possible and engender a type of seeing that views new contexts in terms of potential similarities rather than objective differences.

Writing-related transfer research often discusses the importance of the ability to see similarity between contexts, which is really the ability to make cognitive boundaries malleable. Scholars commonly hold that writers who transfer do so because they can see similarities between contexts, while those who do not fail to see similarities. In a study of dispositional thinking, David N. Perkins, Shari Tishman, Ron Ritchhart, Kiki Donis, and Al Andrade (2000) found sensitivity, defined as the ability to notice occasions to enact a behavior, to be the most important aspect of engaging thinking dispositions. David W. Smit (2004) noted that "expert writers learn to see analogies, to see similarities and differences between old and new genres and old and new contexts; novices don't often recognize the similarities between old and new genres and contexts in order to apply what they do know" (p. 134). More recent studies complicated Smit's ideas a bit by finding that students sometimes see similarities and the opportunity to transfer but don't find it necessary to meet their goals (Wardle, 2007, p. 73), or they see similarities and transfer but are unable to successfully show their transfer (Nowacek, 2011). Still, writing-related transfer theorists agree that the ability to see similarity is the primary determinate of transfer. With this, they are implicitly viewing difference and similarity not as separate and objective states, but as symbiotic ways of seeing that conceive of difference as the potential for similarity and similarity as the potential for difference.

If this seems odd, that's because it is—by modern standards anyway. And really, modern standards and modern ways of seeing lie at the heart of transfer as an issue. Anthony Giddens (1990) defined modernity at its simplest as, "modes of social life or organisation which emerged in Europe from about the seventeenth century onwards and which subsequently became more or less worldwide in their influence" (loc. 79). Giddens went on to explain that though capitalism and industrialization are primary focal points for many scholars of modernity, rationality is the "keynote" underlying the major theories of modernity (Giddens, 1990, loc. 212). Modern organizational schemata, with rationality, efficiency, and production as their driving logics, gave rise to the issue of transfer in the first place when modern society and modern universities became increasingly divided into specialized disciplines with specialized genres (Russell, 1991).

A conception of transfer that pushes into paradoxical understandings of similarity and difference and malleable cognitive schemata contradicts modernity's emphasis on rationality. Modern society organizes itself in terms of rationality, making similarity and difference wholly separate so that things do not contradict themselves. This increases efficiency and decreases dissonance, which aids the modernist push toward universal order and control (Holton & Turner, 1989, p. 69). Modernity is based in rationality and cannot abide irrational constructs, which is problematic for transfer and any conception of learning that acknowledges the importance of cognitive dissonance. Transfer is the transformation of boundaries so that which was once different might become similar, i.e., what was once a part of a foreign context can be made a part of the subject via its similarity to previous contexts. A wholly modern mind is likely to see a novel context as objectively different and refrain from disturbing the cognitive boundaries that prevent transfer.

In its quest to rationally order society, and the individuals who make it up, modernity turns to the modern spectacle as its tool. The modern spectacle, as defined by Guy Debord (1983), is a force of modernity that works to order and reorder human experience and relationships through mediating images. What might have been a face-to-face conversation becomes an email chain. What might have been a dialogue about the expectations of an assignment becomes an assignment sheet or a writing prompt. What might have been a conversation about the genre conventions typical in a given discipline becomes a stack of model texts. David R. Russell (1991) saw the increase in disciplinary divide as correlated to the increase in mediated relationships in American work places (p. 4). This makes mediation a key component of human relationships or as Debord put it, "The spectacle is not a collection of images, but a social relation among people, mediated by images" (1983, section 4). The modern spectacle demands a relationship of boundaries that both connect and disconnect, severing the wholeness of human experience and replacing it with the efficiency and static opacity of mediation. It reorders society as a series of mediated relationships, in which "Everything that was directly lived has moved away into representation" (Debord, 1983, section 1). Debord's absolutism may be hyperbolic, but in a world inundated with mediating images—much more so than in Debord's time—the presence of the modern spectacle is as apparent as the screen sitting in everyone's pockets, and it is the modern spectacle that develops a social schema of division, separation, and solidity internalized by individuals.

A society ordered by the modern spectacle works in the interest of modernity and can help achieve many aims modern society deems positive. Not only does it increase a certain type of efficiency—both cognitively and socially—it also provides a certain type of access. Establishing a boundary disconnects two entities, but it also connects them in certain ways, as those entities now share a boundary. Consider the proliferation of online education as an example. It provides access to education for those who may not otherwise have it by solving certain resource issues. It simultaneously connects people who are separated by geography while placing a boundary between them. Online education connects people in a certain way even if it doesn't provide the type of education many writing instructors feel is vital, one based on the human interaction felt in the classroom. Walter Benjamin (1939/2003) considered a similar issue in work on the impact of cinema. He wrote that cinema, unlike theater, replaces the eye of the audience member with the eye of the camera. Someone watching a film is not empathizing with the actor or the character being portrayed but rather is empathizing with the camera (pp. 259–260). The mediating image, the representation, fragments the wholeness of this human experience, and as a result, an experience that was once dynamic is made static. Or, as Baz Kershaw (2003) put it, "it [spectacle] deals with the human in inhuman ways" (p. 594).

Debord (1983) and Benjamin (1939/2003) focused on the social and political implications of spectacle, an important issue for educators—and especially writing teachers—to take up. But there's a second implication of their work that is often ignored—the impact of the modern spectacle on individual cognition. If we live in a society of spectacle, as Debord insisted we do, surely it impacts our individual cognition. Fleckenstein (1999) argued for a conception of individuals she termed the "somatic mind," "mind and body as a permeable, intertextual territory that is continually made and remade" (p. 281). This is supported by Johnson's (1987) conception of the body—and its relation to the physical world—as integral to the making and remaking of image schemata. What Fleckenstein's and Johnson's work tells us is that what exists in our social and physical realities is internalized as the blueprints of our cognition; our corporeal interaction makes and remakes our cognitive schemata. The modern spectacle, as a force that orders our social relations with mediating images, is a schema built of static boundaries. Mediating images have no agency; they are not malleable; they cannot manipulate themselves. I submit that in a society of spectacle, internalized cognitive boundaries—image schemata—are less malleable, less fluid, and less transgress-able than they might otherwise be.

Robert Kegan (1994) attempted to describe the demand modernity places on the cognition of individuals. In doing so, he describes a traditional view of one's consciousness as solidified and concrete as second-order consciousness. As part of our second-order consciousness, we develop a solidified sense of self, a distinction from others, and a sense that things may be grouped together in classes or sets he called "durable categories" (Kegan, 1994, pp. 21–23). This model explains the way in which we recognize and understand the distinctness of genres. The next phase of our development (third-order consciousness), the one many adults ask adolescents to take on and the one teachers ask students to take on when they ask them to transfer, Kegan associated with the development of "cross-categorical knowing," the ability to understand one's self as a durable category in relation other durable categories—people, groups, communities, disciplines (1994, pp. 24–25). Kegan, like Johnson, saw orders of consciousness as ways of ordering and making meaning of one's experiences. He viewed "abstraction" and "generalization"—terms often used in place of transfer—as an act of third-order consciousness, and though his view would see a lack of transfer as the lack of development of third-order consciousness. Kegan attaches third-order consciousness to modernism; however, I would argue that elements of modernity, such as the modern spectacle, inhibit cross-categorical knowing and the development of third-order consciousness by encouraging the internalization of impermeable boundaries. Although it's true that third-order consciousness often develops as people age, Kegan makes clear that it does not occur automatically and is highly contextual. Instead, it is either prompted or not by social influences, and the factors of our highly mediated world often allow people to remain within the boundaries of the second order.

The modern spectacle impacts the formation of our image schemata. It shapes our cognition in such a way that makes boundaries less malleable, less bothered to consider contradiction, more determined to quiet dissonance. We see and make meaning through a modernist lens meant to work most efficiently, an ideal measured by standards of efficiency constructed by modern logics. The modern mind sees with eyes trained to look most efficiently, and the most efficient way to interact with a novel context is to not interact with it at all or to interact with it in a representational and efficient way. To interact representationally does not require full engagement; it doesn't require someone to consider a novel context in relation to who they are; it simply demands that someone consider what they can represent. I'm always struck when students speak of writing instruction as if the goal is to find the correct codes to place in a text and get a particular grade. Modernity—and the internalized perspective of the modern spectacle—encourages this view, what Elizabeth Wardle (2012) calls an "answer-getting" disposition. It's much less efficient—much harder—to connect a novel context with one's identity and open the potential for transfer. Writing teachers see this daily, as they see students who never attempt to see the ways in which writing might share similarities with other aspects of their lives, the ways in which writing already is a part of their daily lives. Instead, many students are simply looking for the codes necessary to please the teacher and earn a certain grade.

Playing their part in the modern spectacle, teachers construct mediating images to make this work more smoothly—grading rubrics, assignment sheets, and model texts. Students may transfer some base knowledge and skills attached to their identity as a literate person or the components necessary to interact representationally, but they too rarely look beyond what they need to interact at a representational level. This is not meant as a condemnation of students' and teachers' ways of seeing; a condemnation of modern people for having modern ways of seeing makes no sense and neglects the ways in which everyone—myself included—is complicit in the forces of modernity. Rather, it is an explanation of why people within our modern society of spectacle tend to interact in the ways they do with novel contexts. Novice writers struggle to see similarity because our modernist gaze has us seeing new contexts through the internalized lens of the modern spectacle. This lens makes transfer very difficult, especially the transfer of dispositions and habits of mind, because our cognitive boundaries are not malleable enough to transfer. The boundaries between contexts, which are really boundaries within us, remain solid, fixed, rigid, and often unnoticed.

TRANSFER IN THE AGE OF SPECTACLE

Because early scholarship on writing-related transfer was an outgrowth of genre studies, it conceptualized writing-related transfer as an issue of genres and the inherent differences between them and focused more heavily on the social aspect of cognition. Genre and transfer scholars were exploring the realization that most of what was taught in FYC courses, or general writing skills instruction, was never transferred to other disciplines (Petraglia, 1995; Russell, 1995). From this inquiry, genre theory developed a new conception that understands genre as socially situated, culturally and ideologically influenced, momentarily stable, and continually evolving (Bazerman, 1988; Devitt, 2004; Smit, 2004). Russell (1995) characterized the issues of genre through the use of activity theory, and as Jessie Moore (2012) made clear, writing-related transfer research is typically focused on one of the three components of an activity system: subject, meditational means, and object(ive). Russell's ultimate conclusion, as well as Smit's, is that significant transfer of the knowledge and skills often taught in FYC is not likely because genres arise as part of their specific activity systems. The conditions of those systems cannot be recreated outside of them, and even if they could, writing teachers could never hope to learn the specifics of so many different activity systems.

Early writing-related transfer scholarship, heavily influenced by genre studies, locates transfer primarily as a social act. It is based in a social cognitive theory that saw transfer as entirely dependent on the similarity between learned and novel contexts (Bransford, Pellegrino & Donovan, 2000). Under this conception, contexts are objectively similar or dissimilar, and transfer will or won't occur based on their similarity. This places the locus of transfer outside the individual and locates it within the context. As a result of this social-epistemic view, early writing-related transfer theorists focused heavily on the social elements of activity theory—the meditational means and the object(ive)—rather than the subject as an individual. To study transfer at this time was to study the ways in which students construct meditational means to meet objectives. Transfer research was less focused on the individual's orientation to the object(ive) itself or how the individual felt about or identified with the object(ive). Individual cognition was subsumed under socially situated cognition, which echoes Debord's (1983) notion that the modern spectacle makes the individual invisible within the social.

As a consequence of its preoccupation with meditational means and object(ive)s, writing-related transfer scholarship often focuses primarily on the transfer of knowledge and skills (Driscoll & Wells, 2012), elements that are more easily represented via mediating images than dispositions, habits of mind, motivations, identity, or values. Though genre theory acknowledges the human elements that give rise to genres, it subsumes the individual within the social, and the objects of sociality and the means by which the individual is social—the representations of the individual's knowledge and skills—become the focus of study. Put simply, genre studies understands the importance of the subject in the creation of genres, but transfer theorists still focus primarily on what is more capable of being represented—knowledge and skills. Much of the research associated with meditational means and object(ive)s comes from 2007 or earlier, while none of the research focused on the subject as an individual comes from before that point (Moore, 2012).

A shift toward a look into the subject as an individual began in 2007 when Wardle included dispositions as a part of her inquiry into transfer. Her inclusion of dispositions was at the forefront of emerging scholarship that views transfer as an "individual act of cognition" (Nowacek, 2011, p. 29). Since then, scholarship from Wardle (2009, 2012), Mary Jo Reiff and Anis Bawarshi (2011), Nowacek (2011), and Dana Lynn Driscoll and Jennifer Wells (2012) spoke to the notion that learners' dispositions and habits of mind are essential components of transfer. Intuitively, this makes sense. Those who orient themselves to a given context in negative ways (dispositions) are unlikely to enact the positive habits of mind necessary to transfer. The National Council of Teachers of English, Council of Writing Program Administrators, and National Writing Project's *Framework for Success in Postsecondary Writing* (2011) identified openness as an important habit of mind for success in post-secondary writing; Arthur L. Costa (2008) identified it as an important habit of mind for success generally. It's hard to imagine someone transferring all the useful knowledge and skills possible if they have not first transferred openness to a given context . . . or curiosity . . . or persistence. Without the enactment of certain habits of mind, certain knowledge and skills will be left behind. And it's hard to imagine someone being open, curious, or persistent if they do not first have certain dispositions that might enact those habits. Students who display what Wardle (2012) called an "answer-getting" disposition aren't likely to enact curiosity in contexts toward which they have an answer-getting disposition. As a result, they are unlikely to engage the knowledge and skills curiosity often engages: good question asking, good critical thought, good research skills, etc.

Different writing-related transfer researchers have identified different dispositions important to transfer. Reiff and Bawarshi (2011) identified "boundary-guarding" and "boundary-crossing" students (p. 325), with boundary-crossers being students who engage in deliberate transfer of prior genre knowledge and boundary-protectors accidentally transferring prior genre knowledge with greater potential for negative transfer. Wardle (2012) identified students as having "problem-exploring" and "answer-getting" dispositions. Those with answer-getting dispositions want the answer quickly and efficiently; they are less open to curiosity, exploration, or multiple answers and perspectives. Those with problem-exploring dispositions are curious, reflective and willing to engage with multiple possibilities. Wardle added that formal education in the United States—an education system steeped in the modern spectacle—encourages and fosters answer-getting dispositions. The most extensive look at dispositions that help facilitate writing-related transfer came from Driscoll and Wells (2012) who identified four dispositions important to writing-related transfer: expectancy-value, self-efficacy, attribution, and self-regulation. Expectancy-value is the belief that one will obtain some value from a given context. Self-efficacy is the belief that one can be effective in a given context. Attribution is the belief that outcomes are the result of one's actions. And self-regulation is the ability to set goals and regulate one's path toward those goals—essentially, the ability to remain disciplined. Whether or not these dispositions—and not some others—are *the* dispositions necessary for writing-related transfer is still unknown, but they seem, at the very least, to be a good start at understanding what dispositions must be brought to a given context in order to facilitate greater transfer of knowledge and skills.

Although recent research in writing-related transfer has focused on dispositions, researchers have yet to dig into habits of mind that might facilitate transfer or be transferred. In part, this is because it's difficult to distinguish between dispositions and habits of mind; they are not exactly the same things, but they aren't wholly different. In fact, Driscoll and Wells (2012) listed some dispositions Costa (2008) considered habits of mind; which is to say, no one has constructed a definitive list of dispositions and habits of mind or clearly distinguished between the two. As I see it, dispositions are the way people orient themselves to a given context. They are not the content of learning, but they help facilitate learning and the application of learning (Driscoll & Wells, 2012). Habits of mind are more active. Because of that, I conceive of habits of mind as the enactment of different dispositions. Habits of mind happen as a result of a person's disposition. For example, a person with a problem-exploring disposition relative to a given context is curious about that context. Curiosity is the habit of mind enacted by those with a problem-exploring disposition. Both occur as part of our cognition, but I view one (habits of mind) as a result of the other (dispositions).

The society individuals inhabit impacts their dispositions and habits of mind, as it does all cognitive functions. Our somatic minds are an intertextual territory made and remade as the result of our interaction with the world. In a society of spectacle, our somatic minds—and the image schemata of them—are constructed for solidity and rigidity, not malleability and transgression. Wardle (2012) implicated formal education in the production of students with answer-getting dispositions, but formal education is just a reflection of the society that created it. The modern spectacle shapes our seeing—our cognition—in a way that cultivates dispositions and habits of mind conducive to the internalized schema of the modern spectacle. That means more students with answer-getting and boundary-protecting dispositions. It means an expectancy-value based solely on modernist ideals like career goals and economic achievement, as Driscoll and Wells' student Julie expressed. And it means students who see representations of ability (grades) as the ultimate goal, not the type of engagement necessary for transfer, learning, or success in post-secondary writing, as Wardle (2007, p. 73) found.

Two primary solutions emerged as a result of the early inquiry into genres and transfer. 1) Scholars encouraged universities to construct and support WID programs (Beaufort, 2007; Russell, 1995; Smit, 2004). This approach respects the differences between genres and the disciplines that construct them and relieves writing teachers from their un-tenable roles as multi-disciplinary experts. 2) Scholars encouraged writing programs to teach rhetorical knowledge and/or meta-knowledge about writing (Russell, 1995; Wardle, 2009). This approach sees possibility for rhetorical knowledge and meta-knowledge to transfer in useful ways and gives writers a language with which they can discuss writing in all genres. Both of these are sensible approaches. But with recent evidence on the importance of dispositions and habits of mind to successful transfer and success in post-secondary writing, it's important to develop a dispositional model of teaching for transfer. In the final section, I build on existing models of teaching for transfer to construct a model meant to facilitate the transfer of the dispositions and habits of mind necessary with particular attention to the subversion of the modern spectacle.

A DISPOSITIONAL MODEL OF TEACHING FOR TRANSFER

A model of teaching for transfer must work to subvert the impact of the modern spectacle, which means working to make and remake cognitive boundaries (image schemata) in ways that make them more malleable, more capable of being transformed and transgressed. To do this, writing teachers must ask students to confront the boundaries that exist within them. They must ask students to reflect on their past relationships with writing, understand their current writing selves, and imagine their writing futures. Smit (2004) explained that expert writers see analogies between genres and contexts, a position supported by Perkins et al. (2000). Writing teachers interested in teaching for transfer must teach novice writers to see as experienced writers see, to be sensitive to analogies between genres and contexts. This means writing teachers must teach students to engage certain dispositions and habits of mind in writing contexts, ones that are more conducive to seeing analogies. In essence, a dispositional model of teaching for transfer teaches students *to be* writers as opposed to teaching them *how to* write or *about* writing. Or rather, it teaches them to understand themselves as part of the constant process of becoming that is being a writer. This form of being engenders a way of seeing that transgresses the boundaries between contexts and within individuals. It accepts pluralism and embraces inquiry. Basically, it holds the dispositions identified as important for writers by writing-related transfer researchers and enacts all the habits of mind listed in the *Framework*'s statement.

Current models of teaching for transfer understand the importance of seeing. Nowacek (2011) introduced the idea of teaching students to become "agents of integration," which she defined as students capable of both perceiving and conveying to others the connections between contexts (p. 38). Nowacek's model addresses the difficulties of asking students to transfer within highly specialized universities with structures that often discourage transfer. As a result, she developed a framework based on "seeing" and "showing." Students who could both see the opportunity for transfer and show that they had made that connection would be agents of integration (2011, p. 40). While I agree with Nowacek's assertion that seeing is the key to transfer, and I think her findings on the importance of identity in transfer are particularly impactful, I believe her interest in "showing" as a key to being an agent of integration may undermine the type of seeing necessary for transfer. Nowacek's model serves as a middle-ground that allows students to meet the demands of modern institutions while recognizing the interrelations of genres (transferring), but never considers that those demands—the necessity to show—might be what's undermining transfer in the first place. An institution built on the modern spectacle encourages students to interact representationally and holds a view of intelligence based entirely on ability that can be represented (knowledge and skills) rather than a view of intelligence that includes dispositions, values, motivations, identity, etc. Consequently, the completion of writing tasks—the showing—becomes an act of finding the right combination of symbols within that activity system rather than engaging dispositions necessary to make connections and significantly transfer.

Kathleen Blake Yancey, Liane Robertson, and Kara Taczak (2014) developed a model of teaching for transfer that asks students to reflect in ways that might connect knowledge and skills from prior contexts to novel contexts. In doing this, they attempt to address the ways in which students see both their prior experiences and their current contexts. This model relies heavily on structured reflection and the development of meta-cognition through the teaching of key terms and concepts. It is heavily influenced by research from Wardle (2009) and the importance of teaching students "about writing" (p. 782). Although the Yancey, Robertson, and Taczak model of teaching for transfer fosters meta-cognition, an important aspect of transfer, it's emphasis on reflection provides opportunities only to see the past, and it's not clear how this is meant to help writers see similarity moving forward, though it seems Yancey et al. are cognizant of the importance of attempting to cultivate a way of seeing new contexts, as they included a prompt in their final assignment that asks students to imagine a future in which their new theory of writing might be applied (2014, p. 75). Still, Yancey et al. focused heavily on the transfer of knowledge and skills.

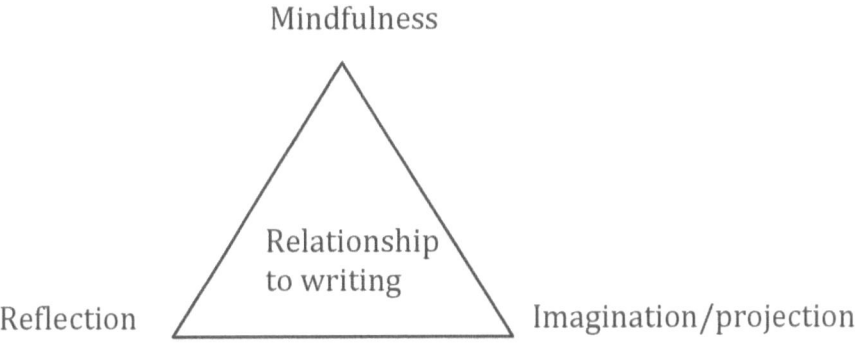

Figure 12.1. Model derived from Nowacek and from Yancey, Robertson & Taczak.

Models from Nowacek (2011) and Yancey et al. (2014), while they have certain components that address cognitive orientations that prevent transfer, do not fully confront and address these orientations. They touch on practices like reflection, but never put together a method that acknowledges the import role dispositions and habits of mind play in the reshaping of boundaries. I propose a model that builds on those from Nowacek (2011) and Yancey et al. and asks

241

students to explore their relationship to writing, what constructed it, what impacts it currently, and what it might look like in the future, in order to increase their sensitivity to seeing analogies. This model asks students to consider their dispositions and habits of mind, but more importantly it asks them to see as writers see and to understand that they are writers and they will always be writers; it is simply up to them to craft their conception of themselves as writers. This model is based on the incorporation of three components centered on the students' relationships with writing: reflection, mindfulness, and imagination or projection.

These components, taken as a whole, provide the opportunity to trace the history of students' dispositions and habits of mind related to writing, analyze their current dispositions and habits of mind related to writing, and image potential future dispositions and habits of mind related to writing. This model is built on an understanding of past, present, and future as inherently linked and repositions the locus of transfer within the individual. It calls for a comprehensive look at the social factors that crafted their relationship to writing and allows them to imagine multiple futures in which their relationship could be different. Most importantly, though, it asks students to see as writers see by reflecting on the elements that constructed the current moment, analyzing the conditions of the current moment, and imagining potential futures in which elements of the current moment and past moments will re-emerge.

Each of these components has a place in this model for a specific reason and both reflection (Yancey, Robertson & Taczak, 2014) and mindfulness (Perkins et al., 2000) have been explored as components of teaching for transfer or dispositional thinking before.

REFLECTION

Yancey et al. (2014) found that student transfer is often based on access to prior knowledge and what they call the students' "point of departure," meaning where students are and how they see themselves as writers based on previous feedback from others. They pointed to the importance of reflection as a way to access prior knowledge that might be useful to current contexts and used reflection as a key practice of their "Teaching for Transfer" course. The notion of a "point of departure" implies that being a writer is a state of being that's constantly in flux, and Yancey et al. conceptualize useful reflection as cognizant of that constructed nature of that point. This is the key to the type of reflection, which Yancey et al. reiterate in their contributions to this collection as well. Many students are given feedback like grades and as a result develop dispositions toward writing contexts that inhibit transfer and learning. A reflection of one's past relationship with writing needs to see writing identities, or "points of departure" not as where the student definitively is or was, but as a position the student occupied within a particular activity system—high school or grade school or social media. It's important to a dispositional model of teaching for transfer that reflection be the act of understanding the past and present as subjective and constructed rather than objective and fixed.

Mindfulness

Mindfulness sometimes takes on a connotation of the spiritual or mythical, but I use the term as nearly synonymous with awareness. As I see it, mindfulness is the capacity to understand all the things that make up a context, to be in the moment in a way that sees the past and future as joined in the present. This means seeing old and new contexts as joined within one's individual experience. As Perkins et al. (2000) explained, "Mindfulness is associated with a sense of personal agency and efficacy as well as a belief in a constructed and conditional reality, whereas mindlessness is more associated with a commitment to absolutes" (p. 284). For these reasons, mindfulness is a key component to a dispositional theory of teaching for transfer. The sense of agency mindfulness gives students to construct their realities is a key component in seeing contexts as conditional and thus seeing analogies.

Imagination/Projection

Johnson (1987) identified imagination as the force that makes and remakes our cognitive schemata, meaning it has an outsized role to play in transfer. Imagination, as he sees it, gives coherence to our cognition by shaping and ordering cognitive schemata in useful ways. It is the bridge between our bodied experience and our cognitive order. It allows us to make connections to novel contexts, as it "gives us image-schematic structures and metaphoric and metonymic patterns by which we can extend and elaborate those schemata" (Johnson, 1987, p. 169). Imagination, then, is that thing that determines the malleability of our cognitive schemata—our internal boundaries. Johnson's theory of imagination is important to conceptions of transfer because it understands the role of projection in creating "novel meaning" (1987, p. 165). To see analogies is to draw connections between previous contexts and novel contexts; this is a projection of one's self—experiences, knowledge, skills, dispositions, habits of mind—into a new context to make connections. Without imagination—without the ability or inclination to project into new contexts—analogies remain unseen. Put simply, we may be able to chalk up an inability to transfer to a lack of imagination.

A dispositional model of teaching for transfer may be enacted in different ways, as long as it includes aspects of the three components and an explanation of how they are connected. I have enacted it differently with different classes, using in-class writing and discussion, creative writing exercises, readings and discussion, debates, etc. Another example might be having students consider their own reactions to a newly assigned writing project in the moment of having those reactions and discussing those feelings, what made them, and where they might lead. What's most important is that the teacher be mindful when implementing the model, as well. It would be easy to implement it in ways that undermine its effectiveness, by relating to students through texts they produce (mediating images). Reflection, mindfulness, and projection mean very little if they're done in ways that are merely representational, merely done to achieve grades. A dispositional model of teaching for transfer is meant to account for the rigid cognition encouraged by modernity and implemented by the modern spectacle. To simply lean on mediating images or downplay the human element in this model's implementation would negate its purpose. When I have students' journal about their previous-day's experience with writing, they do it in class, and then, we discuss it. I never have them turn it in, and make very clear at the beginning of class that it will never receive a grade. I refuse to make this exercise another representational interaction, and I tell them why. When I have them imagine futures for their relationships with writing—sometimes weekly, sometimes less frequently—we discuss those futures, what makes them feel that way about their future, and what another version of that future might look like. We also discuss what it would take to make those futures realities, and I encourage my students to image the wildest, most-outlandish futures they can from time to time because I want them to stretch the boundaries not color within them. Then, we can laugh together when we conceive of a way to make wild, outlandish futures a reality. A dispositional model of teaching for transfer is useless if it is subsumed within the practices of modernity. Each component needs to be undertaken as part of a dialogue that encourages sincerity in the process and a real, human connection based on an inquiry into one's identity.

REFERENCES

Bazerman, C. (1988). *Shaping written knowledge: The genre and activity of the experimental article in science*. Madison, WI: University of Wisconsin Press.

Beaufort, A. (2007). *College writing and beyond: A new framework for university writing instruction*. Logan, UT: Utah State University Press.

Benjamin, W. (2003). The work of art in the age of its technological reproducibility. In H. Eiland & M. Jennings (Eds.), *Walter Benjamin: Selected writings, vol. 4,*

1938–1940 (pp. 251–283). Cambridge: Belknap Press. (Original work published 1939.)

Bransford, J. D., Pellegrino, J. W. & Donovan, M. S., (Eds.). (2000). *How people learn: Brain, mind, experience, and school.* Washington, D.C.: National Academy Press.

Costa, A. L. (2008). Describing habits of mind. In A. L. Costa & B. Kallick (Eds.), *Learning and leading with habits of mind: 16 essential characteristics for success* (pp. 15–41). Alexandria, VA: Association for Supervision and Curriculum Development.

Council of Writing Program Administrators, National Council of Teachers of English & National Writing Project (2011). *Framework for success in postsecondary writing.* Retrieved from http://wpacouncil.org/files/framework-for-success-postsecondary-writing.pdf.

Debord, G. (1983). *Society of the spectacle.* (F. Perlman, Trans.). Detroit, MI: Black & Red. (Original work published in 1967.)

Devitt, A. J. (2004). *Writing genres.* Carbondale, IL: Southern Illinois University Press.

Driscoll, D. L. & Wells, J. (2012). Beyond knowledge and skills: Writing transfer and the role of dispositions. *Composition Forum*, *26*. Retrieved from http://compositionforum.com/issue/26/beyond-knowledge-skills.php.

Fleckenstein, K. S. (1999). Writing bodies: Somatic mind in composition studies. *College English*, *61*(3), 281–306.

Giddens, A. (1990). *The consequences of modernity* (Kindle DX version). Retrieved from Amazon.com.

Holton, R. J. & Turner, B. S. (1989). *Max Weber: On economy and society.* London: Routledge.

Johnson, M. (1987). *The body in the mind: The bodily basis for meaning, imagination, and reason.* Chicago: University of Chicago Press.

Kegan, R. (1994). *In over our heads: The mental demands of modern life.* Cambridge, MA: Harvard University Press.

Kershaw, B. (2003). Curiosity or contempt: On spectacle, the human, and activism. *Theatre Journal, 55*(4), 591–611.

Moore, J. (2012). Mapping the questions: The state of writing-related transfer research. *Composition Forum*, 26. Retrieved from http://compositionforum.com/issue/26/map-questions-transfer-research.php.

National Research Council. (2000). *How people learn: Brain, mind, experience, and school* (Kindle DX version). Retrieved from Amazon.com.

Nowacek, R. S. (2011). *Agents of integration: Understanding transfer as a rhetorical act.* Carbondale, IL: Southern Illinois University Press.

Perkins, D., Tishman S., Ritchhart, R., Donis, K. & Andrade, A. (2000). Intelligence in the wild: A dispositional view of intellectual traits. *Educational Psychology Review, 12*(3), 269–293.

Petraglia, J. (1995). Introduction: General writing skills instruction and its discontents. In J. Petraglia (Ed.), *Reconceiving writing, rethinking writing instruction* (pp. xi–xvii). Mahwah, NJ: Lawrence Erlbaum.

Reiff, M. J. & Bawarshi, A. (2011). Tracing discursive resources: How students use prior genre knowledge to negotiate new writing contexts in first-year composition. *Written Communication, 28*(3), 312–337.

Russell, D. (1991). *Writing in the academic disciplines: A curricular history.* Carbondale, IL: Southern Illinois University Press.

Russell, D. (1995). Activity theory and its implications for writing instruction. In J. Petraglia (Ed.), *Reconceiving writing, rethinking writing instruction* (pp. 51–77). Mahwah, NJ: Lawrence Erlbaum.

Smit, D. W. (2004). *The end of composition studies.* Carbondale, IL: Southern Illinois University Press.

Tuomi-Gröhn, T., Egenström, Y. & Young, M. (2003). From transfer to boundary-crossing between school and work as a tool for developing vocational education: An introduction. In T. Tuomi-Gröhn & Y. Egenström (Eds.), *Between school and work: New perspectives on transfer and boundary-crossing* (pp. 1–15). Oxford, UK: Pergamon.

Wardle, E. (2007). Understanding transfer from FYC: Preliminary results of a longitudinal study. *Writing Program Administration, 31*(1–2), 65–85.

Wardle, E. (2009). "Mutt genres" and the goal of FYC: Can we help students write the genres of the university?. *College Composition and Communication, 60*(4), 765–789.

Wardle, E. (2012). Creative repurposing for expansive learning: Considering "problem-exploring and "answer-getting" dispositions in individuals and fields. *Composition Forum, 26.* Retrieved from http://compositionforum.com/issue/26/creative-repurposing.php.

Yancey, K. B., Robertson, L. & Taczak, K. (2014). *Writing across contexts: Transfer, composition, and sites of writing* (Kindle DX version). Retrieved from Amazon.com.

CHAPTER 13

"DID YOU EVER TAKE THAT TEST YOURSELF?" FAILED KNOWLEDGE TRANSFER, PEER-TO-PEER PEDAGOGIES, AND THE *FRAMEWORK* HABITS OF MIND AS TWO-WAY STREET

Steven J. Corbett with Jeremy Kunkel
Texas A&M University-Kingsville

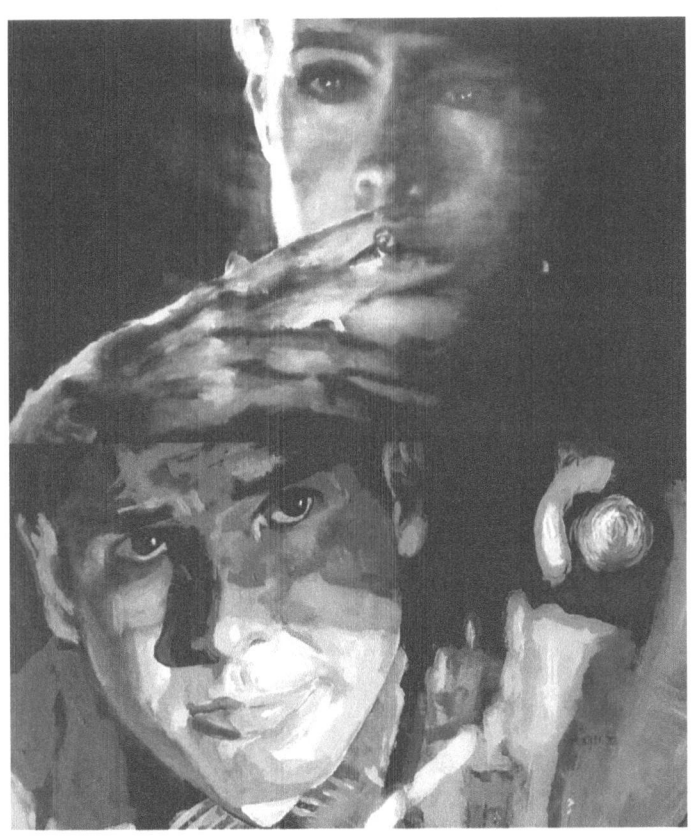

Deckard tests Rachel. (Original acrylic on canvas by Jeremy Kunkel [2016])

There's a scene from one of my favorite films, *Blade Runner* (1982), where Deckard (played by Harrison Ford) administers a test to Rachel (played by Sean Young) to measure and assess if she is a replicant (android) or a human being. Rachel, though performing quite well for much of the test, ultimately "fails" to prove human. Later, while confronting Deckard at his home, Rachel asks, "You know that Voight-Kampff test of yours? Did you ever take that test yourself?"

I believe Rachel asks a crucial question that we as teachers and tutors of writing should be asking ourselves at least every so often, if not every day. Are we holding ourselves up to the same rigorous standards as our students? Are we practicing what we preach enough? In a November 2011 exchange on the WPA listserv, prominent figures in the field debated the slippery question of whether the habits of mind called for in the Council of Writing Program Administrators, National Council of Teachers of English, and National Writing Project's (2011) *Framework for Success in Postsecondary Writing*—curiosity, openness, engagement, creativity, persistence, flexibility, responsibility, and metacognition—can or should be measured or assessed. Several respondents replied with dismay at the idea of such motivational terms being put under the scrutiny and micro-management of assessment. In a passionate reply, Chris Anson (2011) wrote,

> If we're going to assess anything, maybe we should start by looking at the conditions in which students are supposed to learn. A student can bring all the curiosity and creativity in the world into a classroom, but it won't help much if what she encounters there is an uninspired, poorly designed course taught by an ill-informed, unreflective dolt who dislikes students as much as the job of teaching (or just spends every hour lecturing "facts" to students in the manner of Gradgrind). (para.13)

Anson pinpoints an important consideration for all writing teachers/coaches: the fact that these habits of mind should apply just as much to instructors as they do to students. If we ask students to exercise curiosity, then it is only fair to ask: are we curious as instructors and how do we express that curiosity? Same for openness, engagement, creativity, and all the other terms. Identification in teaching and learning demands a two-way street in attitudes, habits, and actions. And if we fail to identify with our students in ways that motivate—and model ways for—them to perform optimally, we've failed them ... and ourselves, whether in the classroom or during one-to-one conferences.

Kenneth Burke often drew on George Herbert Mead's concept of "attitude as incipient action" (especially as discussed in Mead's 1934 *Mind, Self and Society*) in writing about human motivation (see, for example, 1973/1941, pp. 1, 10–11, 168–169, 379–382; 1945, pp. 235–247, 294; 1969/1950, pp. 50, 90–95). The habits of mind (Figure 13.1), while undergirding student incipient actions toward writing, should just as importantly be habits that inform our goals, attitudes, and actions as instructors of writing, especially if we want any of those habits of mind to facilitate knowledge transfer. This chapter will explore how and why both student and instructor attitudes toward writing need accounting for in any conversation about the theory, practice, or assessment of teaching and learning performances. I'll begin with a discussion of current writing research in knowledge transfer—particularly discussions of discourse communities and individual dispositions in moments of failed transfer in academic writing performances (e.g., Beaufort, 2012; Donahue, 2012; Driscoll & Wells, 2012; Wardle, 2012; Yancey, Robertson & Taczak, 2014; and, also in relation to threshold concepts, Anson, 2015, pp. 210–212; Downs and Robertson, 2015, pp. 112–113). I'll move on to focus on how experimenting with and studying peer-to-peer pedagogies, especially studies of successful and failed tutorial performances in both discipline-specific and developmental general-education writing courses (e.g., Corbett, 2015a; Mackiewicz & Thompson, 2015), can aid writing teachers and tutors in our attempts to model and scaffold salutary habits of mind for the benefit of our students and ourselves. I'll conclude with implications for one-to-one, small-group, and classroom teaching. This essay will highlight why looking in the mirror, and recognizing any inevitably human blemishes, must be the first step of a transfer-friendly pedagogical praxis.

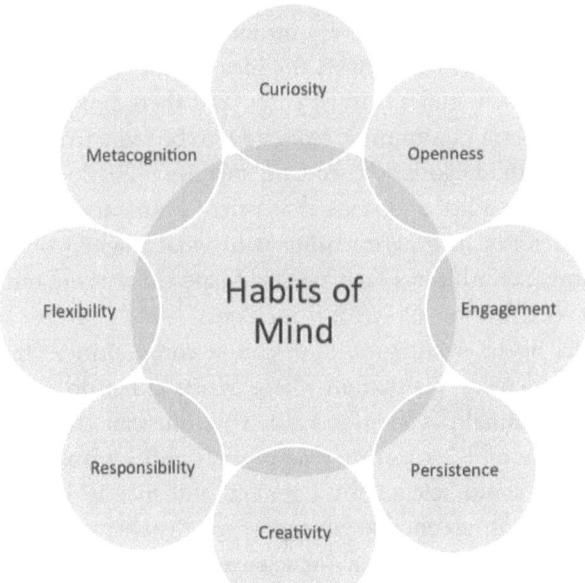

Figure 13.1. Framework habits of mind.

FRAMEWORKING FAILED KNOWLEDGE TRANSFER: DISCOURSE COMMUNITIES, INDIVIDUAL DISPOSITIONS, AND PERFORMANCES OF SELF

If we seek to account for ways to synthesize theories of failed knowledge transfer with theories of identity performance, we can realize a more robust lens with which to analyze the vagaries of applying the *Framework* habits of mind to our instructional practices and research. A discussion of negative and positive transfer provides a useful place to start. Athletes, dancers, actors, cooks, etc., spend countless hours watching, considering, and critiquing their own and their peers' performances—good and bad. In a notably cogent article, Christiane Donahue (2012) offers a review of the literature on writing and transfer drawn from education, psychology, sociology, and composition studies. Although much has been made about the power of metacognition in the successful transfer of learning from one situation to another (Donahue, 2012, pp. 154–156), we know relatively little, especially in composition studies, about what phenomenon might contribute to failed moments of knowledge transfer. Learning procedures without an understanding of the accompanying underlying concepts, a-contextualized learning, and the learner's pre-existing conceptions can all interfere with and prevent successful transfer.

The frequently used, somewhat problematic, concept of "discourse communities" is just one variable to consider in relation to failed/negative knowledge transfer. Donahue claims that the very notion of a discourse community in itself can lead to failed transfer because the idea of "the university as a discourse community into which students must enter, and then disciplines as more specialized versions of that community, seem now to be reductive and overly linear understandings of the negotiation students take on" (2012, p. 157). Donahue goes on to discuss studies and texts that offer "boundary-crossing" scenarios as productive exercises in experimenting with what might work in this situation versus another. Kathleen Blake Yancey, Liane Robertson, and Kara Taczak (2014)—with their notion of "critical incidents"—offer further unpacking of negative transfer in the negotiation of discourse communities. The authors define a critical incident as "a situation where efforts either do not succeed at all or succeed only minimally" (2014, p. 120). They illustrate this concept through the extended study of Rick, a first-year physics and astrophysics major, who struggled to write about science for a general audience in his writing course, then failed to write an acceptable lab report for his chemistry professor based on what he learned from writing about science for a more general audience. In short, Rick's struggles between two discourse communities involved complicated trial-and-error negotiations between genre, audience, prior knowledge, and his own developing self-efficacy and motivation (cf. Anson, 2015). Ultimately, Rick learned—through persistence and accepting responsibility for his own learning—to make moments of failure opportunities for growth and improvement. In a parallel example, Anne Beaufort describes some of the issues she failed to fully account for, in terms of positive knowledge transfer, in the sample curriculum and pedagogy suggestions of her 2007 longitudinal study College Writing and Beyond. Like Yancey et al., Beaufort reported on a student Tim, who much like Rick, left his freshman writing course believing he had learned strategies for writing applicable to the other discourse communities he would subsequently encounter. Yet, as Beaufort describes, Tim failed to come to terms with the multifarious communicative situations he faced, and apparently took much longer in his realization of the complex nature of discourse communities. Beaufort relays what finally had to occur for Tim to begin to realize some sense of how all the communicative pieces might come together for him to experience success, his first professional job with an engineering firm. Clearly, learning from failure can work for some people better (and faster) than others (as Yancey, Robertson & Taczak, 2014 also report, p. 135; cf. Brooke & Carr, 2015; Anson 2016; Downs & Robertson, 2015).

While the concept of discourse communities can account for a lot of the socio-rhetorical reasons why we might experience a critical incident, we also need to consider more personalistic and individualistic variables. Dana Driscoll and Jennifer Wells (2012) argue that individual dispositions—like motivation, values, self-efficacy, and self-regulation—need to be accounted for much more in transfer research. Importantly, this attention would bring the *Framework* habits of mind to center stage. For example, in considering the value of a more individually focused lens for Beaufort's student Tim discussed above, the authors observe:

> While Beaufort's study focuses on Tim's perceptions of his discourse communities, she does not focus on the dispositional aspects Tim has that may be causing those perceptions (such as locus of control, motivation, etc.). Beaufort also does not discuss anything about Tim as a person outside of the educational setting. (Driscoll & Wells, 2012, para. 14)

Turning our lens toward the personal and individual might nudge us to ask different types of questions regarding Tim's critical incidents. Could there have been personal reasons that caused some of the trouble Tim had in negotiating in and between the discourse communities of first-year composition, history, and engineering? Too many commitments like a job, family, or illness might have played a part. Simple lack of motivation and effort may have been a culprit. Neglect of any of the *Framework's* habits of mind—lack of curiosity, openness, engagement, persistence, creativity, flexibility, responsibility, and/or metacognition—may have contributed just as much to Tim's critical incidents as forces outside his individual dispositions. Perhaps by the time Tim finally saw the "end" of his education, when he finally succeeded in landing a professional engineering job, all the dispositional pieces came together (or started to come together) more synergistically with that particular discourse community. A concept Driscoll and Wells build into their disposition theorizing is the theory of attribution, which can help us begin to make connections between individual agency and motivation and the outside force of discourse communities. Simply put, attribution theory deals with how much control a person believes they have over a situation, how much the cause of success or failure is a result of their own actions or circumstances beyond their control (Turner, 2007; also see Babb & Corbett, 2016). Drawing on Pierre Bourdieu's concept of "*habitus*," Elizabeth Wardle (2012) speculates that perhaps fields themselves warrant attribution consideration for frequently inculcating students with problem-solving attitudes and dispositions at the expense of problem-exploring dispositions. The author believes that this dichotomy forces students into a "psychological double-bind" that can result in confusion and failure. In many ways, then, the students we discussed above with Yancey et al. (2014), Beaufort (2012), and Driscoll and Wells (2012) are understandably facing both immense socio-rhetorical as well as psycho-rhetorical forces they are doing their best to negotiate in the quest to survive the critical incidents, and the accompanying chance of a failed performance, we all must inevitably face.

Finally, and to further complicate this analytical frame, we would do well to remember the eminently quotable Erving Goffman's (1959) words from *The Presentation of Self in Everyday Life*: "We must be prepared to see that the impression of reality fostered by a performance is a delicate, fragile thing that can be shattered by a very minor mishap" (p. 56). Goffman suggests the ways in which socio-rhetorical actors, rather than simply "attempting to achieve certain ends by acceptable means," also "can attempt to achieve the impression that they are achieving certain ends by acceptable means" (1959, p. 250). Elsewhere, in the later work *Forms of Talk* (1981), Goffman analyzes the consequences of failure to execute a successful performance. He explains how the very awareness and prospect of social control is a powerful means of social control, causing social actors to make preemptive moves (right or wrong) to avoid the stigma of failure at all costs (cf. Clark, this volume, on the role of neuropsychology and genre in the performance, choice, and development of students' cultural identities). The plurality, often ambiguity, of control lends itself to the drama of human communication—including failed communicative performances—and adds yet another layer to the many variables (Figure 13.2) that can help us make sense of the vagaries of successful and failed knowledge transfer.

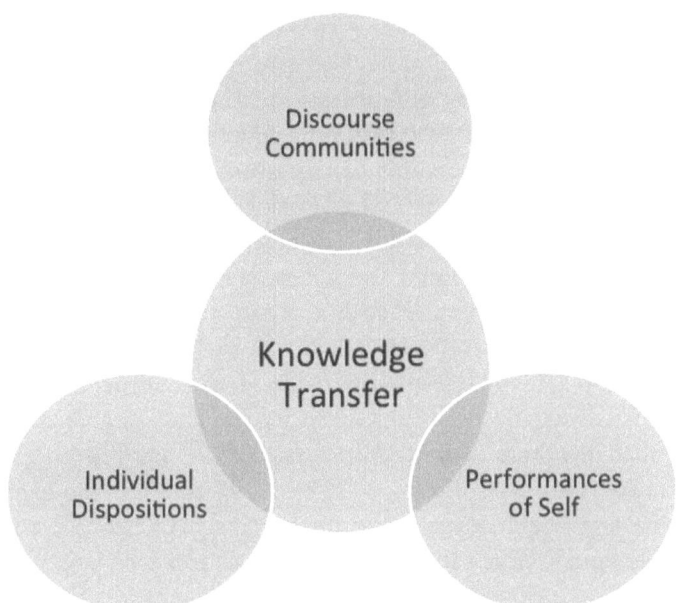

Figure 13.2. Overlapping socio-cognitive elements of knowledge transfer.

Writing center theory and practice offers a rich site for the discussion of successful pedagogical performances and knowledge transfer (e.g., Bromley, Northway & Schonberg, 2016; Devet, 2015; Driscoll, 2015; Nowacek, 2011). Yet, looking back over the course of the past few decades, one can also trace a pattern of reporting failed (or, at least, problematic and unsatisfying) tutorial performances (e.g., Corbett, 2015a; DiPardo, 1992; Nicolas, 2005; Severino, 1992; Sherwood, 1996). Jo Mackiewicz and Isabelle Thompson (2015) (echoing arguments made in the past in the works of Kenneth Bruffee and Muriel Harris) have recently suggested the value of studying tutoring strategies for all teachers of writing: one-to-one tutoring offers students abundant opportunities to experience more individualized feedback on their writing performances, greater interactivity and agency in their own learning, and more opportunities to express their thoughts and concerns about writing. Granted, studies like Bradley Hughes, Paula Gilliespie, and Harvey Kail's (2010) analyses of the reflections of 126 former tutors from three institutions touts the salutary skills and habits of mind students immersed in peer-to-peer learning can take with them from those experiences—including stronger listening and analytical abilities; values, skills, and abilities vital to family and professional relationships; and increased confidence in their writing and communication abilities—these studies can make it seem like peer tutors experience nothing but success. But teachers of writing can also learn a lot about what possible teaching strategies might cultivate and instantiate good teaching habits of mind by studying both successful and less-successful examples of peer tutors in action, especially when tutors are positioned in the immensely complex problem-exploring situation that arises when they are connected more closely with writing courses and curriculum.

Several writing fellows practitioners report on compelling conflicts during the vagaries of authority and method negotiation peer tutors must face when connected directly with a disciplinary writing course (e.g., Lutes, 2002; *Across the Disciplines*, 2008). Jean Marie Lutes offers an example of the tricky liminal space writing fellows must perform within, arguing that in their role as writing fellows, tutors are often concerned with living up to the role of "ideal tutor." She reports how a writing fellow, Helen, resorted to a more directive style of tutoring when she noticed students getting closer to the professor's expectations. Helen concluded that this more intimate knowledge of the professor's expectations, once she "knew the answer" (2002, p. 250, n. 18) made her job harder rather than easier to negotiate. It places peer tutors in the sort of dichotomous psychological double-bind Wardle (2012) spoke of above. This double-bind can affect tutors working more closely with students in developmental general education writing courses as well.

Barbara Liu and Holly Mandes (2005) and Melissa Nicolas (2005) describe how certain adjustments had to be made to methodological direction and control when tutors were moved into the developmental writing classroom—a location where the *habitus'* of the students they found themselves working more closely with may not have adequately equipped them with the dispositions and performance-savvy needed for mainstream academic success. Liu and Mandes would soon come to realize that when tutors are circulating in the classroom, in their zeal to help, they can all too easily "invade the writer's comfort zone" treading "a thin line between help and invasion" (2005, p. 91). Nicolas (2005) also points to the fact that this arrangement requires students to meet with tutors, rather than the typically optional writing center meeting. In her "Cautionary Tale" we see the difficulty in tutors moving from a more writing center-like setting to an instructional setting that demands that they experience closer communicative contact and negotiation with teachers and students in the classroom. This new arrangement puts tutors in situation where they may be struggling to apply what they have been taught about helping students take greater agency and interactivity in their own learning to this new and different instructional context. Nicolas reports how this caused authority and role confusion in the tutors. One tutor explained how, even though she tried to downplay her authority while working with students, still "they just always seem to look at me or toward me.... They like to be told what to do.... It's kind of confusing. It's sort of like a balancing act where you try not to be in it too much but try to be there, but it's like you're not there. It's hard" (Nicolas, 2005, p. 120). And just as classroom teachers either learn to balance levels of control and directiveness, questioning and listening, or just letting students run with ideas, tutors and students develop a heightened sense of these instructional moves. The tutor's willingness either to oblige the student or not is not always an easy choice to make. It is the psychological double-bind that underscores each move the tutor makes whether tutoring one-to-one or collaborating in the classroom. But studying how tutors approach these problem-situations, how they dance the habits of mind and attitude necessary to realize success (or suffer failure), can offer much to any writing teacher's ongoing learning and development.

ALL-TOO-HUMAN NARRATIVES OF PEER-TO-PEER SUCCESS AND FAILURE: T9 VS. JULIAN

Two recent, book-length studies of tutoring strategies respectively offer an illuminating narrative of success and a cautionary tale of tutors interacting more closely with students and instructors ripe for comparative scrutiny: Mackiewickz and Thompson's (2015) study *Talk about Writing: The Tutoring Strategies of Experienced Writing Center Tutors* and Steven Corbett's (2015a) *Beyond Dichotomy: Synergizing Writing Center and Classroom Pedagogies.*

IMPRESSIONS OF REALITY FOSTERED BY A FAILED PERFORMANCE: JULIAN

Corbett (2015a), following related research threads on peer-to-peer teaching and learning, including peer tutoring (e.g., Corbett, 2011a; 2013; 2015b) and peer review and response (e.g., Corbett, 2015c; Corbett, LaFrance & Decker, 2014) offers case studies of one-to-one tutorials in the writing center and small-group peer response workshops in the classroom in developmental first-year courses at two universities. Corbett comparatively analyzes the interactions of participants through multi-method, RAD research methods that include discourse analysis of tutorial transcripts, field observations, interviews and follow-up interviews, and participant journals. Attempting to build a frame for the comparative analyses of one-to-one tutorials and peer-response-group interactions, the author provides a macro- and micro-analytical frame (Figure 13.3). The macro-frame, drawn from Muriel Harris' (1995) "Why Writers Need Writing Tutors," offers an overarching rhetorical framework for how tutors can help writers. Tutors can: (1) encourage student independence in collaborative talk, (2) assist students with meta-cognitive acquisition of strategic knowledge, (3) assist with knowledge of how to interpret, translate, and apply assignments and teacher comments, and (4) assist with affective concerns. The micro-frame focuses on the linguistic features and cues of collaborative talk including: types of questions, discourse markers, fillers, overlaps, pauses and silences, forms of address, modal auxiliary verbs, and qualifiers. For the sake of comparative relevance, I will focus my analyses on the unsuccessful one-to-one tutorial performances, highlighted in the study, of one experienced, senior peer tutor—Julian.

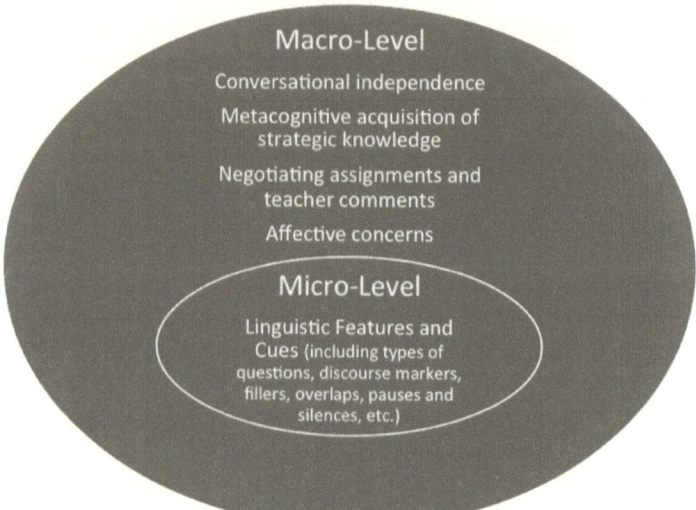

Figure 13.3. Corbett's (2015) Frame for analyzing one-to-one tutorials and peer-response-group interactions.

Julian's six tutorials all took place in the eighth week of the term. They all revolved around a major paper in which students were asked to analyze and make an argument about the rhetoric, ideology, usefulness, and feasibility of one of the topics from George W. Bush's 2006 State of the Union Address, topics including the No Child Left Behind Act; the war in Iraq; and immigration, especially the U.S./Mexican border. His six sessions averaged 36 minutes, with the longest lasting 53 minutes and the shortest 22 minutes. Careful analysis helps illustrate Julian's most salient negative tutorial pattern—the fact that he talks too much while allowing relatively much less student talk-time (or, concurrently, tutor listening-time). Couple this with the fact that he often talks a lot before he has heard the entire student's paper, and we are often left wondering why he is talking so much, often in the abstract, about the student's ideas and writing.

In session four, Julian works with a highly reticent student who is having obvious trouble negotiating the assignment. I quote this excerpt at some length because it illustrates the extreme that Julian can go to in his verbosity, in his domination of the session:

Julian: Yeah okay just get specific with it. Do you think we need to follow President Bush's plan because it affects everybody? How does it affect everybody? Like what's at stake? Like security? Like what else? What are the issues at play?

Student: I don't know.

Julian: That's cool. Just make a note for yourself or something. I just think about it because that's the kind of stuff I read. That idea makes sense right? Just kick it around. One thing to do is if you're totally like it's not coming to you forget about it for a while because it looks like you've got a good structure of your body paragraphs right? And this last sentence suggested like talking a little about there are many clear facts like what are you talking about? See where you can end up in your conclusion like ultimately we'll only need to listen to Bush and be ready to do this because these things are like why do we need to? What is President Bush saying that we need to do these things for right? So he says that we need to do this because ABC right? Do we need to do for AB and C if he's right if he's correct right? Where Bush says what we need is for AB and C and you look at that and he is right we do need to do it for these reasons one of those can be your stakes because that's what you're talking about right? You just need to introduce them in a general way. I know I'm rambling but I'm trying to say that the topics are the central ideas of your body paragraphs. You can sort of like generalize about them; just sort of go back and connect them to claim.

Student: Yeah. [5 Second Pause]

Julian: That's got to actually do a lot. When I get stuck on opening paragraphs like I'll just because I don't know I don't know how the writing process goes for you but you my intro paragraph takes me and my claim takes me about as much time as writing half of my body paragraphs, so sometimes I'll write by pulling my quotes and I'll write the central paragraphs and then in writing them I'll be like oh I do have something to say in like my conclusion. I'll, I'll go back and generalize to make a claim.

Student: All right.

Julian: I'm talking a lot, like let me ask you a question. You guys have talked about rhetorical analysis right? So what do you think about the rhetorical analysis you have so far on Bush in this first and second paragraph?

Student: I don't know what rhetorical means. (Corbett, 2015a, pp. 61–62)

In this striking example, Julian, granted, is faced with an incommunicative student whose inability to grasp the assignment makes Julian's job tough. But when Julian's first barrage of questions is met with "I don't know," it only spins him on more rambling. And he knows he is rambling, which causes him to actually slow down and ask a question that leads him to figure out the student does not understand the idea of rhetorical analysis. This seems promising. Yet rather than ask some questions that might get the student thinking, allow time for a response, and maybe even write some notes, notice how Julian will ask a question, then answer it himself (ironically, almost like a "rhetorical" question). Repeatedly, as evidenced in the above passage, and continuing throughout this session, Julian asks "does that make sense?" The student invariably responds curtly with "yes," "yeah," and "I think so." Julian also uses the tag question "right?" ubiquitously. Examples like this appear repeatedly in Julian's tutorial transcripts. We hear repeated instances of Julian asking a question, not waiting or allowing enough pause for student response, then moving on to offer extended stretches where he tries hard to offer useful suggestions.

In his sixth tutorial, Julian's actions suggest that though he is metacognitively aware of his rather "inauthentic" listening habit, the problem is indeed a deep one. At the very beginning of the session, the student says "she [Anne] gave us this peer review thingy." As if she hadn't said a word, Julian responds: "How is your week going?" They never return back to the student's initial utterance.

A Writing Fellow Gets It Right: T9

Mackiewicz and Thompson (2015), following related research threads by Thompson and colleagues (e.g., Mackiewicz & Thompson, 2013; Thompson, 2009; Thompson et al., 2009), offer detailed empirical methods and analyses of one-to-one tutor talk. In contrast to Corbett's study (2015a) discussed above, Mackiewicz and Thompson set out with the express goal of detailing the strategies of highly successful tutorials: conferences evaluated by the students and tutors as "highly satisfactory (five or six on a six-point scale)" (2015, p. 2). Their analytical frame also approaches one-to-one tutorials from both the macro- and micro-level (Figure 13.4). They analyze 10 video-recorded one-to-one tutorials at three macro-levels: opening, teaching, and closing. At the micro-level they analyze these same tutorials in great depth via three cat-

"Did You Ever Take that Test Yourself?"

egories of tutoring strategies: instruction, cognitive scaffolding, and motivational scaffolding. For the sake of comparative analyses, I will focus especially on the tutoring strategies of a student who started out as a tutor in the writing center as an undergraduate and later became a writing fellow as a graduate student—Tutor 9 (T9).

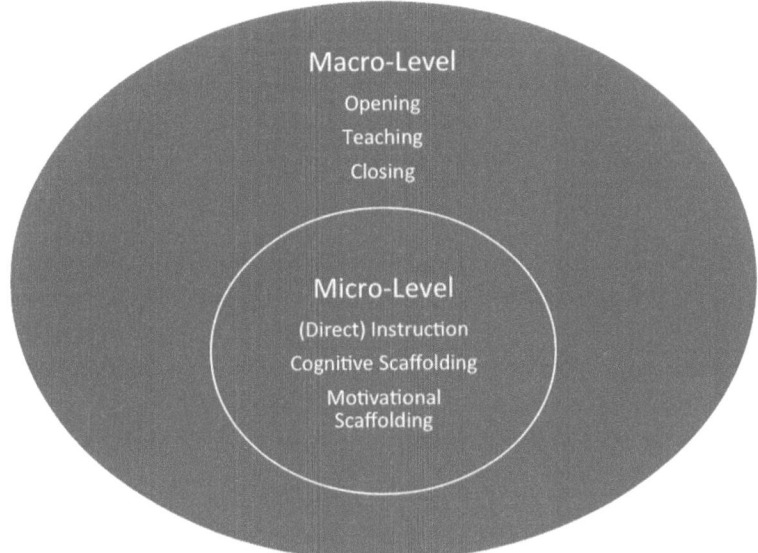

Figure 13.4. Mackiewicz and Thompson's (2015) frame for analyzing one-to-one tutorials.

Mackiewicz and Thompson compare four tutorials from T9, two with undergraduates while T9 herself was an undergraduate tutor in the writing center, and two tutorials with an undergraduate student years later when T9 was a graduate writing fellow attached to a business writing course. In terms of direct instruction (strategies like telling, suggesting, and explaining) the authors found that T9 was much more likely to use the explaining strategy in her tutorials as a writing fellow than during her tutorials at the writing center: about 45% in her fellow tutorials vs. 20% in writing center tutorials. The authors attribute the high level of direct instruction to the fact that T9, in her writing fellow role, was a much more direct intermediary between the students and the instructor and thus more obligated to explain aspects of genre and assignment negotiation. In terms of cognitive scaffolding (strategies like demonstrating, hinting, and prompting) the authors found that T9 was much more likely to use the strategy of "responding-as-a-reader-or-a-listener" in her writing center tutorials than in her writing fellow tutorials: about 23% in her writing center tutorials vs. about 7% in her writing fellow tutorials. The authors attribute the high level

259

of this strategy in the writing center tutorials to the fact that, even though T9 was familiar with the genres those students were writing in, she understood the assignments and the instructor's intentions for the assignments as much as possible. And in terms of motivational scaffolding (strategies like showing concern, praising, and using humor), rather than the major factor in the tutorial strategy of showing concern being influenced by T9's role as a writing center tutor or writing fellow, the major factor ended up being how familiar she was with the student. T9 was much more likely to show concern for students she was unfamiliar with than students she had worked with before: about 35% for unfamiliar students vs. about 10% for familiar students. The authors attribute this finding to T9's sense of her responsibility for helping students persevere in meeting the responsibilities of the assignment.

And yet, despite the fact that T9 experienced success on all fronts, Mackiewicz and Thompson offer a word of caution on just how easily the pedagogical problem of asserting perhaps too much control during an instructional moment can manifest. In the following brief excerpt of T9 working with Student 12 (S12), T9 exhibits a moment of appropriating the student's paper with directive instruction blended almost seamlessly with cognitive scaffolding and motivational scaffolding:

> **T9**: [Reading.] "Coca-Cola offer a variety of distribution channels, including, colon, vending machines, various supermarkets, and department stores." I don't know if I would say "various."
>
> **S12**: O.K.
>
> **T9**: But "supermarkets and department stores."
>
> **S12**: O.K.
>
> **T9**: And then you would start like a regular sentence. O.K. And I like this a lot. I like that you've expanded here. I think that's very good. (Mackiewicz and Thompson, 2015, p. 164)

While this may seem a very minor offense, the authors claim this moment may have crossed over the fine line of tutor-control by potentially neglecting S12's input into the reason she used the word "various." Yet, we have to acknowledge the fact that this session with S12 involved a revised draft of this paper, which had already undergone a conference with T9. So T9 was responding to a work that was much closer to a final draft. It would thus make more sense that T9 might feel more compelled and pedagogically freer to offer such a fine-grained and directive suggestion.

DISCUSSION

Comparing these two tutorial performances—trying to determine factors that contributed to the success of one and the failure of the other—is without a doubt a very complex undertaking. Thinking more about the overlapping contexts of these situations will help. T9 had much more of an understanding of the course and the expectations of the instructor, as well as much more thorough training and experience that prepared her for success in that particular discourse-community role. Mackiewicz and Thompson (2015) detail the elements of that training including: acting as a mentor for inexperienced tutors, receiving extensive training in the genres often discussed in business writing (p. 53; cf. Clark, this volume; Gorzelsky et al., this volume), and staying in close communication and collaboration (even to the point of collaborating on assignment design and evaluating document drafts) with the instructor of the course (p. 157; cf., Corbett, 2015a, especially pp. 99–129; Robinson & Hall, 2013; Soliday, 2011). In stark contrast, Corbett reports that Julian did not develop either salutary rapport with students nor have much of an understanding of what was going on in the course. While T9 was performing the role of almost a co-instructor, Julian's sense of himself as "reserved advisor" and the gross lack of communication between him and the instructor of the course (Anne) combined to co-construct this cautionary tale of failed knowledge transfer. Julian did not stay in regular communication, enough to know the nuances of Anne's expectations very well. Yet in all his interactions with students, he still tried hard to stay within what he felt were her expectations (primarily via assignment prompts and what students were *telling* him they thought Anne wanted). Anne felt that the lack of communication was all her fault and repeatedly, during the interviews Corbett reports on, expressed regret for not interacting more closely with Julian. But she also intimated that she felt students and Julian did not get to know each other well enough on an individual basis to enable Julian to move past his nondirective "reserved advisor"—that he had learned during his peer tutor training—approach toward a method that might take into account the more individualistic needs and dispositions of each student. Students never saw the habits of mind like responsibility or flexibility exhibited by Julian nearly to the extent they experienced it with T9 (or several of the other tutors from Corbett's study as well).

Still, I find great value in Julian's cautionary tale, value that points to the growth and development of writing center studies as a (sub)field that can make important contributions to the study of knowledge transfer and habits of mind. Like Lauren Fitzgerald and Melissa Ianetta (2012), I "take it as a sign of writing center studies' increasing sense of its own identity, as well as its increasing security as a field of study, that we can admit such 'failures' and then move on to create productive, important knowledge from these events" (p. 9). Julian's lack of pedagogical flexibility in his method was not even helped by his metacognitive awareness of his unhelpful habit of talking to the point of ranting with students. This fact suggests just how tricky it can be not only to advocate for a "non-directive conferencing style" (Hall & Hughes, 2011, p. 32) when preparing faculty and peer tutors to transfer what they know when they work more closely together with student writers in disciplinary writing courses or developmental gen-ed writing courses, but also how the vaulted notion of metacognition can sometimes prove hard to socio-cognitively corral in order to aid in transfer (cf. Anson, 2016; Driscoll, 2015).

MORE (OR LESS) HUMAN THAN HUMAN: CONCLUSION

> Memories . . . You're talking about memories.
>
> — Deckard, *Blade Runner*

One of the greatest lessons I continue to try and stay as metacognitively alert and flexible about as a teacher-and-learner of writing is the importance of balancing direct instruction and cognitive scaffolding—while staying attuned to the motivational scaffolding that can enhance identification, motivation, and knowledge transfer. While I know I have not always been successful in every attempt, I believe continuing to develop and hone this balancing act is perhaps my deepest responsibility, as well as the single most important pedagogical concept transferable between and among my instructional methods like classroom, small-group, and one-to-one instruction.

As I mentioned above, Hughes et al.'s (2010) analyses of the reflections of 126 former tutors from three institutions suggests some promising skills and habits of mind students immersed in peer-to-peer learning can transfer from those experiences, including: stronger listening and analytical abilities; values, skills, and abilities vital to family and professional relationships; and increased confidence in their writing and communication abilities. If *all* students were to experience systematic, iterated peer-to-peer pedagogical (including peer response groups and instructor-facilitated small-group conferences) activities in all of their writing-intensive courses, vertically in their curriculum from the time they were freshman to their senior year, and then on to those continuing in graduate and professional schools and programs, they could get their share of transferable communicative skills and values. Research and practice involving peer tutors, like T9 and Julian, more closely attached to writing courses offers insights into how peer tutors act when they are more or less expected to possess some sort of authority, some kind of hybrid teacher-student aptitude and responsibility.

This closer alignment with students' zone of proximal development offers intimate gazes into how students a bit closer to true "peer" status negotiate feedback strategies. An understanding of the strategies that can encourage students to negotiate when and how to do more talking, questioning, or listening can add much to any writing teacher's—no matter what level of experience—own ongoing negotiation and performance between discourse communities, individual dispositions, and habits of mind (like the kind of longitudinal faculty development reported in Condon et al., 2016). When we (as a discourse community or as individuals) choose to actively and thoughtfully gaze at our reflection in the mirror, what we see and how we feel about it can be scrutinized, compared to what others see, and gradually revised. Then, as the image of ourselves grows older, perhaps we can reflect back and remember from a wiser point of view. I sometimes wonder if Julian learned anything valuable from his experience, anything useful for his communicative habits of mind. I believe I, and perhaps others who have read his cautionary tale (or similar ones), have.

People have varying degrees of communication styles—some appear introverted and reticent, others outgoing and verbose. But it seems that all people like to feel that their interlocutors, especially during pedagogical moments, are listening to and valuing what they have to say. Staying open and curious about studies of writing tutors attempting to navigate the vagaries of interpersonal communication, like the ones we touched-on above with T9 and Julian, can aid in teacher's attempts to metacognitively and persistently develop flexibility and balance while interacting with students of various personality types and communicative styles and manners. The one thing all writing center and peer tutoring philosophies have in common is the belief in the primacy of the affective/motivational scaffolding aspect of peer-to-peer pedagogies. The most transferable pedagogical concept I've ever heard (attributed to various people, including Maya Angelou) is that people will not always remember what you said or did, but they will never forget how you made them feel. I recently had a student with a learning disability tell me she had to perform a writing sample given to her by her psychologist. She said the feedback was very negative and made her feel like a bad writer. In contrast, she said the experiences in our course, including the bonding with her group-mates, made her feel like a good writer. As fellow instructors of writing, I know you've heard and experienced similar stories. . . . Providing a pedagogical environment wherein students feel comfortable and confident enough to take some agency in their own (and to some degree their peers') learning *experiences* becomes the crucial first step (e.g., Corbett & LaFrance, 2013) in order for everyone to perform the teaching and learning of the types of cognitively demanding writing tasks I assign (e.g., my [2011b] contribution to the "Framework Representative Curricular Resources").

Let's return for a moment to the set of *Blade Runner*, where we started this chapter. Having failed the test, and subsequently learning that she was not human, Rachel experienced a life-jolting realization. When she asks Deckard, "Did you ever take that test yourself?" he does not reply because he has fallen asleep. When students—almost always implied—ask us the same question, I hope we are wide awake, listening carefully, and keep trying to remember the importance of offering a human-as-possible reply.

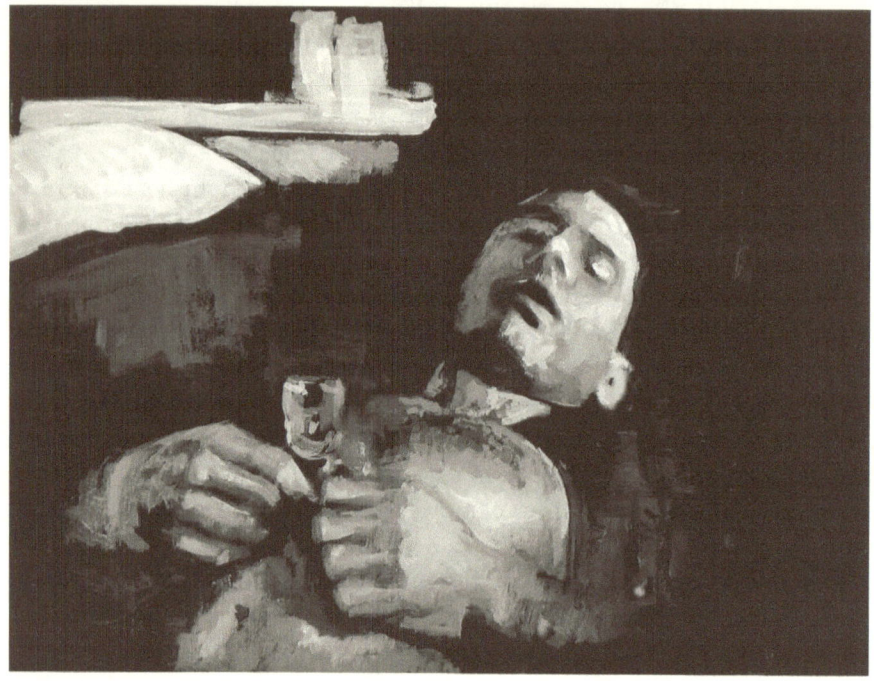

Closing Image. Deckard Falls Asleep. (Original acrylic on canvas by Jeremy Kunkel [2016])

REFERENCES

Anson, C. M. (2011, November 8). Re: measuring the habits of mind. WPA Listserv. Retrieved from https://lists.asu.edu/cgi-bin/wa?A1 = ind1111&L = WPA-L.

Anson, C. M. (2015). Crossing thresholds: What's to know about writing across the curriculum? In L. Adler-Kassner & E. Wardle (Eds.), *Naming what we know: Threshold concepts of writing studies* (pp. 203–219). Boulder, CO: Utah State University Press.

Anson, C. M. (2016). The Pop Warner chronicles: A case study in contextual adaptation and the transfer of writing ability. *College Composition and Communication, 67*(4), 518–549.

Across the Disciplines, 5 (2008). Special issue, Rewriting across the curriculum: Writing fellows as agents of change in WAC. B. Hughes & E. B. Hall (Eds.). Retrieved from https://wac.colostate.edu/atd/fellows/index.cfm.

Babb, J. & Corbett, S. J. (2016). From zero to sixty: A survey of college writing teachers' grading practices and the affect of failed performance. *Composition Forum, 34.* Retrieved from http://compositionforum.com/issue/34/zero-sixty.php.

Beaufort, A. (2007). *College writing and beyond: A new framework for university writing instruction.* Logan, UT: Utah State University Press.

Beaufort, A. (2012). College writing and beyond: Five years later. *Composition Forum, 26.* Retrieved from http://compositionforum.com/issue/26/college-writing-beyond.php.

Bromley, P., Northway, K. & Schonberg, E. (2016). Transfer and dispositions in writing centers: A cross-institutional mixed-methods study. *Across the Disciplines, 13*(1). Retrieved from https://wac.colostate.edu/atd/articles/bromleyetal2016.cfm.

Brooke, C. & Carr, A. (2015). Failure can be an important part of writing development. In L. Adler-Kassner & E. Wardle (Eds.), *Naming what we know: Threshold concepts of writing studies* (pp. 62–64). Boulder, CO: Utah State University Press.

Burke, K. (1945). *A grammar of motives.* New York: Prentice Hall.

Burke, K (1973/1941). *The philosophy of literary form: Studies in symbolic action.* Berkeley, CA: University of California Press.

Burke, K. (1969/1950). *A rhetoric of motives.* Berkeley, CA: University of California Press.

Condon, W., Iverson, E. R., Manduca, C. A., Rutz, C. & Willett, G. (2016). *Faculty development and student learning: Assessing the connections.* Bloomington, IN: Indiana University Press.

Corbett, S. J. (2011a). Using case study multi-methods to investigate close(r) collaboration: course-based tutoring and the directive/nondirective instructional continuum. *The Writing Center Journal, 31*(1), 55–81.

Corbett, S. J. (2011b). Communicating an important topic or idea in your field. *Framework for success in postsecondary writing assignment database.* Council of Writing Program Administrators, National Council of Teachers of English & National Writing Project. Retrieved from http://wpacouncil. org/communicating-an-important-topic

Corbett, S. J. (2013). Negotiating pedagogical authority: The rhetoric of writing center tutoring styles and methods. *Rhetoric Review, 32*(1), 81–98.

Corbett, S. J. (2015a). *Beyond dichotomy: Synergizing writing center and classroom pedagogies.* Fort Collins, CO: The WAC Clearinghouse and Parlor Press. Retrieved from https://wac.colostate.edu/books/dichotomy/.

Corbett, S. J. (2015b). Learning disability and response-ability: Reciprocal caring in developmental peer response writing groups and beyond. *Pedagogy: Critical Approaches to Teaching Literature, Language, Composition, and Culture, 15*(3), 459–475.

Corbett, S. J. (2015c). Great debating: Combining ancient and contemporary methods of peer critique. *Kairos: A Journal of Rhetoric, Technology, and Pedagogy, 19*(2). Retrieved from http://praxis.technorhetoric.net/tiki-index.php?page = PraxisWiki%3A_%3AGreat+Debating.

Corbett, S. J. & LaFrance, M. (2013). It's the little things that count in teaching. *The Chronicle of Higher Education*. Retrieved from http://chronicle.com/article/Its-the-Little-Things-That/141489/.

Corbett, S. J., LaFrance, M. & Decker, T. E. (Eds.). (2014). *Peer pressure, peer power: Theory and practice in peer review and response for the writing classroom*. Southlake, TX: Fountainhead Press.

Council of Writing Program Administrators, National Council of Teachers of English & National Writing Project (2011). *Framework for success in postsecondary writing*. Retrieved from http://wpacouncil.org/files/framework-for-success-postsecondary-writing.pdf.

Deeley, M. (Producer) & Scott, R. (Director). (1982). *Blade Runner* (Motion picture). US: Warner Brothers.

Devet, B. (2015). The writing center and transfer of learning: A primer for directors. *The Writing Center Journal, 35*(1), 119–151.

DiPardo, A. (1992). "Whispers of coming and going": Lessons from Fannie. *The Writing Center Journal, 12*(2), 125–144.

Donahue, C. (2012). Transfer, portability, generalization: (How) does composition expertise "carry"? In K. Ritter & P. K. Matsuda (Eds.), *Exploring composition studies: Sites, issues, and perspectives* (pp. 145–166). Logan, UT: Utah State University Press.

Downs, D. & Robertson, L. (2015). Threshold concepts in first-year composition. In L. Adler-Kassner & E. Wardle (Eds.), *Naming what we know: Threshold concepts of writing studies* (pp. 201–219). Logan: Utah State University Press.

Driscoll, D. L. (2015). Building connections and transferring knowledge: The benefits of a peer tutoring course beyond the writing center. *The Writing Center Journal, 35*(1), 153–181.

Driscoll, D. L. & Wells, J. (2012). Beyond knowledge and skills: Writing transfer and the role of student dispositions. *Composition Forum, 26*. Retrieved from http://compositionforum.com/issue/26/beyond-knowledge-skills.php.

Fitzgerald, L. & Ianetta, M. (2012). From the editors. *The Writing Center Journal, 32*(2), 9–10.

Goffman, E. (1981). *Forms of talk*. Philadelphia: University of Pennsylvania Press.

Goffman, E. (1959). *The presentation of self in everyday life*. New York: Doubleday.

Hall, E. & Hughes, B. (2011). Preparing faculty, professionalizing fellows: Keys to success with undergraduate writing fellows in WAC. *The WAC Journal, 22*, 21–40.

Harris, M. (1995). Talking in the middle: Why writers need writing tutors. *College English, 57*(1), 27–42.

Hughes, B., Gillespie, P. & Kail, H. (2010). What they take with them: Findings from the peer tutor alumni research project. *The Writing Center Journal, 30*(2), 12–46.

Liu, B. L. & Mandes, H. (2005). The idea of a writing center meets the reality of classroom-based tutoring. In C. Spigelman & L. Grobman (Eds.), *On location: Theory and practice in classroom-based writing tutoring* (pp. 87–100). Logan, UT: Utah State University Press.

Lutes, J. M. (2002). Why feminists make better tutors: Gender and disciplinary expertise in a curriculum-based tutoring program. In P. Gillespie, A. Gillam, L. F. Brown

& B. Stay (Eds.), *Writing center research: Extending the conversation* (pp. 235–237). Mahwah, NJ: Lawrence Erlbaum.

Mackiewicz, J. & Thompson, I. (2013). Motivational scaffolding, politeness, and writing center tutoring. *The Writing Center Journal, 33*(1), 38–73.

Mackiewicz, J. & Thompson, I. (2015). *Talk about writing: The tutoring strategies of experienced writing center tutors.* New York: Routledge.

Mead, G. H. (1934). *Mind, self, and society: From the standpoint of a social behaviorist.* Chicago: University of Chicago Press.

Nicolas, M. (2005). A cautionary tale about "tutoring" peer response groups. In C. Spigelman & L. Grobman (Eds.), *On location: Theory and practice in classroom-based writing tutoring* (pp. 112–125). Logan, UT: Utah State University Press.

Nowacek, R. S. (2011). *Agents of integration: Understanding transfer as a rhetorical act.* Carbondale, IL: Southern Illinois University Press.

Robinson, H. M. & Hall, J. (2013). Connecting WID and the writing center: Tools for collaboration. *The WAC Journal, 24*, 29–47.

Severino, C. (1992). Rhetorically analyzing collaborations. *The Writing Center Journal, 13*, 53–64.

Sherwood, S. (1996). Apprenticed to failure: Learning from the students we can't help. *The Writing Center Journal, 17*(1), 49–57.

Soliday, M. (2011). *Everyday genres: Writing assignments across the disciplines.* Carbondale, IL: Southern Illinois University Press.

Thompson, I. (2009). Scaffolding in the writing center: A microanalysis of an experienced tutor's verbal and nonverbal tutoring strategies. *Written Communication, 26*(4), 417–453.

Thompson, I., Whyte, A., Shannon, D., Muse, A., Miller, K., Chappell, M. & Whigham, A. (2009). Examining our lore: A survey of students' and tutors' satisfaction with writing center conferences. *The Writing Center Journal, 29*(1), 78–105.

Turner, J. H. (2007). *Human emotions: A sociological theory.* New York: Routledge.

Wardle, E. (2012). Creative repurposing for expansive learning. *Composition Forum, 26.* Retrieved from http://compositionforum.com/issue/26/creative-repurposing.php.

Yancey, K. B., Robertson, L. & Taczak, K. (2014). *Writing across contexts: Transfer, composition, and sites of writing.* Logan, UT: Utah State University Press.

SECTION V: STUDENT VOICES: RESEARCHING SELF-PERCEPTIONS, DISPOSITIONS, AND PRIOR KNOWLEDGE

CHAPTER 14

RESEARCHING HABITS-OF-MIND SELF-EFFICACY IN FIRST-YEAR COLLEGE WRITERS

Peter H. Khost
Stony Brook University

I do not think of myself as someone who studies cognition but rather metacognition.[1] I mention this because I suspect that I'm not alone in feeling more drawn to the latter than the former of these concepts, and it may be worth exploring why. For starters, *cognition* can be a mystifying term. At times the word just seems to mean *thinking*; at other times it entails emotions, non-emotional affect, and even assimilated social influences. So this word that denotes the thinking of a single person can also paradoxically connote the opposite of thinking and involvement of other people. But *metacognition* doesn't appear more inviting to comprehension. After all, this word encompasses its already confusing root term and further complicates it with a prefix meaning *among*, *with*, *after*, or *beyond*. This turns out to be a troublesome set of prepositions.

On the one hand, when we become aware of our thoughts, our perception might be said to be *among* or *with* those thoughts (i.e., together with them); this makes it difficult to distinguish cognition from metacognition. In such a state of mutual company, cognition appears to be knowable. Ann Berthoff (1984) seems to assume as much in her refrain "thinking about thinking" (p. 743), which was my first point of entry into metacognition per se. On the other hand, becoming aware of our thoughts indicates our perception's state of being *beyond* or *after* those thoughts (i.e., separate from them); this makes it difficult *not* to distinguish cognition from metacognition. As Howard Tinberg (2016) recently put it, "Metacognition is not cognition. Performance, however thoughtful, is not the same as awareness of how that performance came to be" (p. 75). When Linda Flower and John R. Hayes (1981) introduced their cognitive process theory, it

---

1   My study has been supported by grants from the Conference on College Composition and Communication Research Initiative, the Council of Writing Program Administrators, and the Stony Brook University Fine Arts, Humanities, and Social Science Initiative. Special thanks to Faina Shmulyian, Jiyun Elizabeth Shin, Gordon Levites, and Henry P. Khost, Jr. for their invaluable research and statistical assistance.

didn't take very long for scholars to argue that we cannot directly access cognition without altering it through the act of observation (Pierstorff, 1983, p. 217), a theory that suggests that cognition is unknowable.

I am not prepared to survey related debates in epistemology, but I do have ideas on why I feel more at home with metacognition than cognition, and why that matters. For some of today's emerging compositionists, scholarship on writing and cognition may seem somewhat passé—a pre-social-turn relic—if not also foreign (think fMRI labs). I confess that for me the pairing of cognition and writing has sometimes been just a vague metonym for a minor rite of historical coverage in grad school, not an everyday concern in my own classrooms. By contrast, *metacognition* and its cognates, especially *mindfulness*, appear to be everywhere these days, both in and outside of academe. We encounter metacognition playing important roles in genre theory, activity systems, transfer studies, writing about writing, and of course the *Framework for Success in Postsecondary Writing* (CWPA et al. 2011). Even my first-year writers regularly accept the task of demonstrating "metacognition" in their portfolio cover letters without bristling particularly.

So it may be that familiarity through exposure is why I feel more drawn to metacognition than to cognition. This possibility strikes me as important because, if it is true of others, then the arguably greater freshness and lesser resistance or baggage associated with metacognition, relative to cognition, could allow contemporary writing scholars easier passage into this general area of study, and potentially afford them more effective applications of their findings. In other words, that troublesome prefix, *meta-*, might be a ticket for cognition back into the mainstream of writing studies, or at least for something like cognition to come closer to the equivalent of a mainstream in today's increasingly specialized discipline. This could be promising especially for writing scholars pursuing deeper ties with the sciences and publics.

Where I see my present work in this scheme is closer to an experimental than a theoretical end of a spectrum, along which I believe there is need and room for a diversity of approaches. I began a study in 2013 that investigates possible effects of prompted metacognition on self-efficacy in first-year writing (FYW) students. The focus of this reflection is on the habits of mind of the *Framework* (CWPA et al., 2011): creativity, responsibility, engagement, metacognition, persistence, curiosity, openness, and flexibility. I want to better understand these habits' potential to counterbalance some habituated effects of high-stakes testing and test prep on American students, namely: the *suppression* of traits such as creativity, engagement, and curiosity. Irene Clark's excellent chapter in this volume deepens my faith in my study design, which originated in only an intuition of "neuroplasticity," whereby the forming of new habits in FYW may replace old ones formed by tests that are ironically administered in the name of college readiness. Readers may be familiar with Carol Dweck's (2006) version of this kind of neuroplasticity called "growth mindset," whereby innate intelligence and capability are developed through determined practice. I have chosen to examine self-efficacy rather than performance itself in order to avoid assessing students' habits of mind, and also because positive correlations are known to exist between writing self-efficacy and performance. This chapter will explain my study's design and selected results, but first I offer a review of relevant literature to justify my focus on self-efficacy, to familiarize readers with the concept, and especially to invite further research in this area.

I want my study to inspire writing teachers to habituate students' metacognition on their habits of mind, and to effectively promote this practice beyond their classrooms in whatever forms may be locally or individually appropriate—whether that be humanistic (Johnson, 2013), posthumanistic (Boyle, 2016), or otherwise. In order to increase our impact on popular opinion and secondary curricula that are facing Common Core State Standards-aligned tests, proponents of the Framework would do well to publicize valid and reliable research in addition to other forms of evidence. If taken literally and in the vein of social science, as I take it, the phrase *empirical research* indicates a systematic pursuit of understanding based on experiment or practice, not a quest for immutable Truth. Furthermore, *statistical significance*—a measure of reliability, or reproducibility, or the chances that a studied effect is well beyond random—technically identifies an experimental finding that is not definitive proof itself but is potentially meaningful and deserving of confirmation by other researchers (Frost, 2014, Guideline 2 section; Nuzzo, 2014, Out of Context section). A significant finding is potentially only one piece of a large puzzle that requires a very gradual putting together, as Charles Bazerman notes in this volume.

I take such literal and limited approaches to the use of empirical evidence. Yet I still see value in such research in the present case not only for fighting with fire the testing industry's ample psychometric data, but also for projecting a kind of self-scrutiny that is becoming of professionals who seek better public understanding and respect. If we want students, parents, and high schools to value metacognition on the *Framework*'s habits of mind, then we ought to present a variety of convincing evidence in support of this practice, including the use of valid and reliable research. The next section provides important context and precedents.

SOCIAL COGNITIVE THEORY AND WRITING SELF-EFFICACY

Social cognitive theory (SCT) is a model of human agency that is closely associated with Stanford psychologist Albert Bandura. SCT aims to predict some human behavior by measuring people's perceptions about their ability to complete a given task (Bandura, 1986, p. 18; 1997, pp. 2–3). Specifically, according to the social cognitive view, behavior is not fixedly sourced by people's biological condition any more than it is the creation of a truly random and internal thought process; rather, behavior is the gestalt result of a three-part dynamic whose equally operative components are "behavior, cognitive and other personal factors, and environmental events" (Bandura, 1986, p. 18). This is known as a "triadic reciprocality," a type of reciprocal determinism in which the model's constituent parts each determine the quality of their counterparts and so forth in a positive feedback loop (Bandura, 1986, p. 23). By "determinism" Bandura means each part contributing to the operation of the other two, not an inevitability to human behavior.

SCT rejects any conceptual insolvency in its simultaneous assertions that behavior is reciprocally determined and that freedom in human agency is real (Bandura, 1997, p. 7). As Bandura (1997) explains, "Freedom is not conceived negatively as exemption from social influences or situational constraints. Rather, it is defined positively as the exercise of self-influence to bring about desired results" (p. 7). It is this capacity for "self-influence" to impact a person's behavior that warrants SCT's orientation around perception of their own efficacy in making predictions about future behavior (Bandura, 1986, p. 20; 1995, pp. 2–3). This self-influence guides behavior because information that an individual may have about the reasonability of performing an action does not immediately compel subsequent engagement in it; instead, this information "becomes instructive only through cognitive processing of efficacy information and through reflective thought" (Bandura, 1997, p. 79).

Operationally defined, "perceived self-efficacy is a judgment of one's capability to accomplish a certain level of performance" (Bandura, 1986, p. 391). This is an important metric to consider when attempting to predict or influence behavior because research on people's perceptions of their efficaciousness in performing a given task shows that these perceptions determine whether or not the people try to complete the task, how often they do so, how much effort they put in, how much effort they expend in the face of related difficulty, their feelings of reward or success at the task's conclusion (feelings that encourage or discourage subsequent behavior), and their feelings before and during performance of the task (Bandura, 1986, pp. 393–394; 1995, p. 2; 1997, p. 3). A person's efforts in completing a task can be more a function of what that person perceives about their own capability than a result of what is actually true about their capability (Bandura, 1995, p. 2).

Self-efficacy beliefs originate from four sources: mastery experiences, vicarious experiences, social persuasion, and physiological/emotional states (Bandura,

1986, p. 399; 1995, pp. 3–4; 1997, p. 79). The first source, mastery experience, is the sum total of any personal memory or experience a person has with completing a given task (Bandura, 1986, p. 399; 1995, p. 3; 1997, p. 80). Research has been unequivocal about the primacy of mastery experience as a contributor to a person's self-efficacy beliefs, in that no other researched source has been shown to influence a subject's perception of self-efficacy more than the direct knowledge of what it is like to attempt to complete the task at hand (Bandura, 1977, pp. 195–196; 1986, p. 399; 1995, p. 3; 1997, p. 80; Pajares, Johnson & Usher, 2007, 113).The second most influential source of an individual's self-efficacy is vicarious experience, meaning the observed or otherwise modeled behavior of a person other than the individual him or herself, performing the given task (Bandura, 1977, pp. 197–198; 1986, pp. 399–400; 1995, pp. 3–4; 1997, p. 86). The third most significant source of self-efficacy belief is verbal/social persuasion, which is when someone other than the subject tries to convince the subject that he or she has the requisite efficacy in whatever skills are needed to complete a task (Bandura, 1977, p. 198; 1986, pp. 400–401; 1995, p. 4; 1997, p. 101). The last and least influential source of self-efficacy belief is the subject's emotional or physiological state, which is the feeling that the subject perceives both viscerally and affectively in the moment when they are expected to complete the task at hand (Bandura, 1977, pp. 198–199; 1986, p. 401; 1995, pp. 4–5; 1997, p. 106).

THEORETICAL CONTESTATIONS OF SELF-EFFICACY

A recurrent trope in self-efficacy literature is the need to differentiate the central construct of SCT from other constructs. The most commonly cited example is that of outcome expectancies, meaning the expectations an individual has about the consequences that would follow from engaging in a behavior (Bandura, 1997, pp. 125–126; Schunk, 1990, p. 3). Proponents of SCT note that an individual's expectations about outcomes that follow from engaging in a task are different from that individual's expectations about their ability to take the task to completion in the first place (Bandura, 2006, p. 309; Pajares, 1997, p. 5; Schunk, 1990, p. 4). Others see a circular logic in this separation of perceived outcomes of task completion from the perceived willingness to engage in it, since the former inevitably influences the latter (Pajares, 1997, p. 6). SCT supporters respond by noting that if perceptions of self-efficacy for a given task and expectancies about the outcomes of completing said task are indeed linked, then self-efficacy would be the dominant construct since "one cannot conjure up outcomes without giving thought to what one is doing and how well one is doing it . . . foresight requires a causal ordering" (Pajares, 1997, p. 6). Many researchers claim to have statistically shown through experimentation that self-efficacy remains a stronger predictive construct than outcome expectancy when it comes to writing (Pajares & Johnson, 1994, p. 325; Shell, Colvin & Bruning, 1989, p. 96; Shell, Colvin & Bruning, 1995, p. 395, 397; Zimmerman, 2000, p. 84).

Another disagreement pertains to terminology. SCT supporters complain of the repeated presentation of constructs such as self-esteem or self-concept as self-efficacy. The numerous facsimiles of self-efficacy include: self-concept of ability, performance expectancies, perceptions of competence, perceptions of task difficulty, self-perceptions of ability, ability perceptions, perceived ability, self-appraisals of ability, perceived control, and subjective competence (Pajares, 1996, p. 550; 1997, p. 10). The argument is that these psychological traits are too global to be relevant to self-efficacy perceptions because self-efficacy is always a particularized and context-dependent measure of task confidence that cannot be generalized to the degree achieved by these expansive self-estimates (Bandura, 2006, pp. 307–308; Pajares, 1996, pp. 560–561; Pajares & Johnson, 1994, p. 323; Zimmerman, 2000, p. 84). Many supposed publications about self-efficacy beliefs are critiqued by SCT proponents as failing to establish the requisite standard of task-specificity (Pajares, 1996, pp. 550–551; 1997, p. 7; 2003, p. 148).

TRENDS IN WRITING SELF-EFFICACY RESEARCH

There is ample research on the topic of self-efficacy as a predictor of writing ability. This is not surprising given that Bandura himself describes writing as a task that is quite dependent on the internally iterative thought processes that self-efficacy beliefs moderate:

> The act of writing is a familiar example of a behavior that is continuously self-regulated through evaluative self-reactions. Writers adopt a standard of what constitutes an acceptable piece of work. Ideas are generated and rephrased in thought before they are committed to paper. Provisional constructions are successively revised until authors are satisfied with that they have written. The more exacting the personal standards, the more extensive are the corrective improvements. (1978, p. 350)

This sentiment is echoed in published results of self-efficacy research on the construct's power to be predictive of writing performance. Postsecondary students who score highest on inventories of writing self-efficacy beliefs in studies earn better grades on essays than students with lower self-efficacy scores (Hetthong & Teo, 2013, p. 162; McCarthy, Meier & Rinderer, 1985, p. 468; Pajares, 1996, pp.

552–553; Pajares, 2003, pp. 144–145; Zimmerman & Bandura, 1994, p. 856). Explanations for such a phenomenon echo the self-evaluative hypothesis by reporting results that show students who frequently score low on both writing assignments and measures of their efficacy beliefs in writing may be succumbing to an internalized helplessness that undermines the level of effort they put into such work (Lavelle & Zuercher, 2001, pp. 376, 383).

In addition to the strong predictive power of writing self-efficacy to larger school populations, research has also examined how well the construct applies to populations varying by specific demographic factors. A study of postsecondary students distinguished by ethnicity found that students from different cultural or socioeconomic strata maintain different beliefs about the causal relationship between belief and performance in writing tasks when compared to a white, middle-class sample—though only beliefs were studied; no experimental data on how these perceptions affected in-situ writing performance was collected (Murphy & Shell, 1989, p. 7). A later pilot study at a technical college aimed to examine whether instruction that was modeled around SCT and the increase of self-efficacy beliefs for writing performance could serve as an intervention for academically at-risk black and Hispanic students found that it yielded an 80% pass rate compared to the 60% pass rate produced by a control group of students who took the traditionally structured course offered by the school (Campillo & Pool, 1999, p. 6).

Other studies on writing self-efficacy have controlled for age in attempting to examine the behaviorally predictive dimensions of the construct. A study found that between ages 7 and 8, students confused social conformity and high levels of effort with academic skill and that it is not until ages 10–12 that they begin to demonstrate concept-specific perceptions of different academic abilities such as actual proficiency in math or reading (Paris & Newman, 1990, pp. 89–90). At this point, results from various studies diverge. An initial study documented that writing self-efficacy beliefs increase with grade level from elementary school to high school, mirroring the students' total improvement in cognitive processing over time (Shell et al., 1995, p. 395). A later study showed writing self-efficacy beliefs declining in students transitioning between elementary school and middle school before crystallizing at that point for the entirety of high school, making middle school a prime target for interventions (Pajares et al., 2007, p. 115).

Another area in which results have been mixed pertains to the role that writing self-efficacy plays in postsecondary students for whom English is a foreign language. Recent studies examining smaller sample sizes of these students have found evidence that self-efficacy beliefs do indeed predict future writing performance, nationality notwithstanding (Hashemnejad, Zoghi & Amini, 2014, p. 1049; Hetthong & Teo, 2013, p. 159). Yet a slightly older project with an unusually large sample of students, which aimed to study self-efficacy and writing center visitation, found that a cohort of international students who scored lower on writing self-efficacy scales received much better grades in writing than their domestic counterparts did. The authors of this study speculate that the international students' self-awareness of their need to compete in class with native English speakers—reflected in their low self-efficacy scores—drove them to visit the university writing center more often. Writing center visitation was the only variable that predicted later writing performance across both international and domestic cohorts in the publication (Williams & Takaku, 2011, pp. 12–13).

Gender, as a demographic variable, has also produced observable trends in this literature. Initial publications on the topic identified that girls report higher writing self-efficacy than boys do through middle-school (Pajares, 2003, p. 148; Pajares et al., 2007, p. 115); however, an analysis of such results found that a gendered quality to the predictive power of writing self-efficacy became statistically insignificant when the students' prior academic success was factored in (Pajares, 2003, p. 149). Additionally, by the time students reach the postsecondary level, gendered qualities to their self-efficacy beliefs may have dissipated, as studies of this demographic variable at the later stages of schooling fail to find any relationship between gender and the predictive power of self-efficacy in writing performance (Hashemnejad et al., 2014, p. 1049; Williams & Takaku, 2011, p. 13).

PEDAGOGICAL APPLICATIONS

Collectively, this body of research on self-efficacy's predictive power has led SCT researchers to propose many pedagogical recommendations for improving students' writing performance. The most frequent and agreed-upon of these is a recommendation to replace or supplement the conventional first-day diagnostic essay with a survey of students' perceptions of their writing self-efficacy. The rationale here is to avoid measuring performance without insight into effort (Bandura, 1995, p. 215; McCarthy et al., 1985, p. 470; Pajares et al., 2007, p. 328; Zimmerman & Bandura, 1994, p. 858). Another suggestion based on this research is to focus student conferences on short-term rather than long-term goals since SCT research has shown proximal goals to elicit greater student effort than distal goals do, which can seem abstract. Also process-oriented goals positively correlate with improved academic performance as compared with control groups who receive product-oriented goals in conferences or had no conferences at all (Campillo & Pool, 1999, p. 4; Schunk, 1990, pp. 4–6). Other SCT researchers use their results to call on administrators to endow primary and secondary teachers with greater authority over curriculum, eschewing what Pajares refers to as "lockstep" and "scripted" approaches to literacy instruction that send students to college with low writing self-efficacy beliefs and prejudice against their own abilities to learn (McLeod, 1995, p. 380; Pajares et al., 2007, p. 116).

The aggregate message from research on SCT is that self-efficacy is indeed a predictive construct for writing performance. This includes a large number of studies across decades, subject populations, and experimental designs, though measured effects have fluctuated with each of these variables. Evidence suggests that principles of SCT can yield a significant effect on improving the performance of writing students; however, as with all empirical research, the studies reported here require further analysis in order to achieve greater validity and reliability status.

MY RESEARCH STUDY

Research Design

From spring 2013 to spring 2015, I conducted a study using online survey-based rating scales and free response questions with the aim of identifying potential effects of regularly prompted metacognition on FYW students' habits-of-mind self-efficacy regarding specifically their academic writing. The basis of evidence is comparisons of pre- and post-semester self-rating scores from (1) a test group that received bi-weekly metacognitive "treatments" about the habits of mind between the pre- and post- surveys over a semester, (2) a comparison group that received placebo treatments prompting metacognition about subjects other than the habits of mind, and (3) a control group that received no intervening treatments of any kind. All three groups were extremely well matched with each other at the outset of the study, and they showed equivalent course satisfaction at the end.

Subjects during this period included students at a flagship public doctoral highest-research-activity university in the northeast US. What is reported below represents a small selection from my available data, which my limited resources and time have enabled me to work on so far. This includes various analyses made of responses from 16 test groups between spring 2013 and spring 2015. The 103 participants in this subject pool include 62 freshmen, 25 sophomores, 11 juniors, four seniors, and one subject with an unknown class status.

After receiving human subjects research certification and IRB-approval, I recruited teachers of different sections of the same FYW course, awarding a stipend for their efforts in facilitating my blinded study. To minimize the potential influence of facilitating teachers on results, I worked only with instructors who taught no fewer than two sections of the same FYW course in the given semester, designating at least one of their sections as a test group and at least one as a comparison group (unbeknownst to teachers and students). The control group, which took only first and last week surveys, was drawn from a general call to other sections of the same FYW course.

The study's treatments consisted of five-minute freewriting sessions and related Likert scale questions that defined the given habit of mind or placebo topic. These occurred roughly bi-weekly over a 15-week semester, totaling seven installments between the pre- and post- surveys in the first and last weeks of each term. Subjects' incentive—beyond any intangibles they may have inferred as resulting from metacognitive exercises—was a chance to win a $50 Amazon.com gift card randomly awarded to a study participant at the end of each semester. Facilitating instructors were strictly forbidden from coercing participation, and they never knew which of their students was involved in the study or not. Those who declined to participate were asked to freewrite inconspicuously in a private forum while participants used the study's online surveying forum.

Limitations

Because my study took place in the "natural" context of FYW classrooms rather than a controlled setting, it needed to be as unobtrusive of class time as possible; hence, the limitation to only bi-weekly intervals and five-minute sessions. Furthermore, because my IRB required that participation in the study be optional, several related potential effects on the subject pool must be acknowledged. For one thing, there could be a self-selection bias, in that results reflect only those students who chose to participate in the study. Attrition is another factor. Effects could not be measured in subjects who began the study but did not finish it. Nor did I include data from subjects who missed more than one of the seven treatments. So my selection criteria required completion of the first and last week studies and completion of at least six of the seven intervening sessions.

Untrackable enrollment fluctuations over each semester and the impossibility of documenting attendance exactly across so many sections of FYW force me to have to estimate the participation rate among recruited subjects at 41% (using baseline of 17 students per section capped at 20). Limited resources also restricted the number of participating sections, with a total of 30 between spring 2013 to spring 2015. I paused the study in spring 2014 to analyze initial findings and decide on how to proceed. In proceeding, the only adjustment made was to subsequently guide subjects' free response "treatments" with specific prompts, which had previously been open. This change accounts for fluctuation in the base size in some calculations because 83 participants were given a "guided" prompt, and 20 were given an "open" prompt for explaining their answers generally (see Figure 14.1).

MEASURES

First-Week Survey

Habit of mind measures. These measures assessed the extent to which participants believed they possessed each of the habits of mind as academic writers ("Regarding your academic writing, how curious/responsible/flexible/engaged/open/creative/persistent do you think you are?"). Participants responded on a 5-point scale ranging from *not at all* to *extremely* (e.g., curious).

End of Semester Survey

Habit of mind measures. Identical habit of mind measures from the first-week survey were given to participants in or near the last week of the semester.

Course satisfaction. Participants were also asked in this survey to rate their overall satisfaction with the course. Participants responded on a 5-point scale.

Mid-Semester Survey

Habit of mind importance measures. Of the 103 participants, 83 received three questions that assessed the extent to which they believed each habit of mind is important (if at all) for achieving their intention, addressing an audience, and communicating in a context with regard to academic writing. This adjusted treatment prompt is derived directly from the *Framework*'s description of rhetorical knowledge, which is distinguished as the very "basis of good writing" and elaborated as "the ability to analyze and act on understandings of audiences, purposes, and contexts in creating and comprehending texts" (CWPA, et al., 2011, p. 6). Participants responded again on a 5-point scale. A mean score of these three measures was also calculated to establish an average importance value. The *Framework*'s eighth habit of mind, metacognition, was not included in the mid-semester surveys because of the would-be confounding effect of prompting and then measuring the occurrence of metacognition.

FINDINGS

Preliminary findings suggest that the modest classroom treatment in my study shows some effectiveness in improving students' habits of mind self-efficacy with regard to their academic writing. Week 1 to week 15 self-rating scores from test group sophomores, juniors, and seniors provide statistically significant evidence that the bi-weekly five-minute metacognitive sessions did correlate with improved habits of mind self-efficacy, as a whole, and in five of eight of the individual habits. This effect was not found in test group freshmen or in the control group. The placebo group showed gains, but these were not significant in any of the habits except metacognition, perhaps predictably, given the metacognitive study treatment. There was also a very high degree of positive correlation between the improvements of the test group's self-efficacy ratings and their overall course satisfaction, $p = .007$ (p meaning the probability the effect is by chance, i.e., less than 1% here). This means it is very likely that feeling efficacious about their habits of mind is related to students' satisfaction with their FYW course.

First-Week Habits of Mind Ratings as Predictors

A series of regression analyses was conducted to predict each of the three mid-semester importance ratings (i.e., achieving intention, addressing audience, communicating in context), average importance rating, and the word count in the free response question from each of the habit of mind ratings in the first week. The same types of analyses were conducted to predict course satisfaction and each habit of mind rating at the end of the semester.

Curiosity. Findings suggested that first-week curiosity rating was a significant predictor of achieving intention measure, $p < .05$, such that increase in curiosity rating was associated with increase in perceived importance of curiosity in achieving intention. This finding remained significant even when academic year in college was controlled for. In other words, regardless of their year in college, subjects' curiosity ratings in the first week were positively associated with the importance they assigned to curiosity in achieving their intention in academic writing. First-week curiosity rating was also a significant predictor of word count, $p < .01$, such that as curiosity rating increased, the more participants wrote about the importance of curiosity mid-semester. This association was significant even when controlling for participants' year in college.

Openness. Findings suggested that first-week openness rating was a significant predictor of word count, $p < .05$, such that as openness rating increased, the more participants freewrote about the importance of openness in mid-semester. However, this association was no longer significant when controlling for participants' year in college.

Creativity. Findings suggested that first-week creativity rating was a significant predictor of communicating in context rating, $p < .05$, such that creativity rating predicted greater perceived importance of creativity in communicating in a context in academic writing. This association remained significant even when controlling for year in college.

Persistence. Findings suggested that first-week persistence rating was a significant predictor of the addressing audience measure, $p < .01$, such that persistence rating predicted greater perceived importance of persistence in addressing an audience in academic writing. This association remained significant even when controlling for participants' year in college.

Course Satisfaction as a Predictor. A series of regression analyses was conducted to predict each of the habit of mind ratings at the end of the semester from course satisfaction ratings, while controlling for the corresponding first-week habit of mind ratings. Findings showed that course satisfaction was a significant predictor of responsibility, engagement, and creativity at the end of the semester, while controlling for first-week responsibility, engagement, and creativity ratings, respectively, $p < .001$ for responsibility; $p < .001$ for engagement; $p < .05$ for creativity. In other words, the more participants were satisfied with the course overall, the more responsible, engaged, and creative they felt at the end of the semester in terms of their academic writing, even when controlling for their first-week measure of each of the corresponding habit of mind. Course satisfaction also predicted flexibility and persistence ratings at the end of the semester, while controlling for first-week flexibility and persistence ratings (respectively); however, these associations were just outside the 95% significance level, $p = .06$ for flexibility and $p = .06$ for persistence.

Average Importance Ratings of Habit of Mind as Predictors. A series of regression analyses was conducted in which the average importance ratings of each of the habits of mind from the mid-semester survey were entered as the predictors and the outcome variables were free response word count from the mid-semester survey as well as course satisfaction and habit of mind ratings at the end of the semester. Corresponding first-week habit of mind ratings were controlled for in the analyses. Findings showed that the average importance rating for openness was a significant predictor of openness at the end of the semester, while controlling for first-week openness rating, $p < .05$, such that increase in average importance rating for openness was associated with increase in openness rating at the end of the semester.

Moreover, the average importance rating for engagement was a significant predictor of free response word count for engagement, $p < .01$, such that the more participants believed that engagement is important for achieving their intention, addressing an audience, and communicating in context, the more they wrote about engagement.

Change in Habit of Mind Ratings as Predictors. Habit of mind ratings from the end of the semester were subtracted from the first-week habit of mind ratings to establish a change score for each habit of mind. Regression analysis was used to predict outcome variables from each of the change scores. Findings showed that changes in ratings of responsibility, engagement, and creativity significantly predicted course satisfaction at the end of the semester, $p < .01$ for responsibility; $p < .01$ for engagement; $p < .05$ for creativity, such that increase in each of these habit's ratings from week 1 to the end of the semester was associated with greater course satisfaction.

QUALITATIVE ANALYSIS

Differences in Frequency of Personal Singular Pronoun Usage

A multivariate analysis of variance (MANOVA) was conducted to examine differences in the number of personal singular pronouns used by participants who were guided in their mid-semester survey free responses to write about the habits of mind specifically in terms of achieving intention, addressing audience, and communicating in a context, compared with participants whose free response prompts were open (e.g., "write freely for five minutes about your curiosity in your current work in this course"). The independent variable was the type of free response prompt (guided vs. open) and the dependent variables were the number of personal singular pronouns used in the responses for curiosity, responsibility, openness, creativity, persistence, flexibility, and engagement. Findings showed that the overall MANOVA was significant, indicating that there are differences between the two groups on the number of personal singular pronouns used in the seven written responses, $p < .001$. More specifically, as Figure 14.1 shows below, follow-up analysis of variance (ANOVA) tests indicated that participants whose free response prompt was open used more personal singular pronouns than those did whose free response was guided, and these differences were statistically significant.

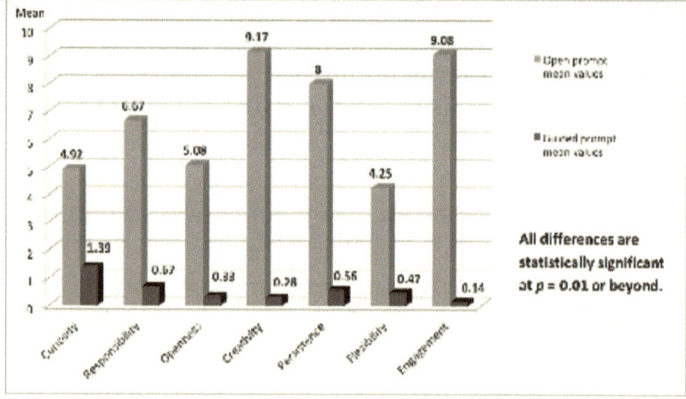

Figure 14.1. Means (i.e., averages) of singular pronouns used in open and guided free response prompts.

Content of Free Response Writing

Each response was coded based on the content of the writing by an individual coder (1 = about the habit of mind in terms of achieving intention, addressing audience, or communicating in context, 2 = about habit of mind in terms of writing or the course in general, 3 = about the habit of mind in college in general, 4 = about the habit of mind in life, 5 = no mention of the habit of mind). Another coder independently coded the responses for two out of seven habits (flexibility and engagement). Inter-rater agreement was high with Kappa = .85, $p < .001$ for flexibility and Kappa = .94, $p < .001$ for engagement. Only the first coder's coding was used for data analysis, following Rodolfo Mendoza-Denton, Geraldine Downey, Angelina Davis, Valerie Purdie, and Janina Pietrzak's (2002, p. 904) precedent.

A series of ANOVA was conducted to examine whether the content of the writing for each habit of mind predicted course satisfaction at the end of the semester. Only the responses that mentioned the habit of mind were included in the analyses (i.e., response coded 1–4; n = 88). Findings showed that content for creativity predicted course satisfaction at the end of the semester, $p = .05$. Follow-up Bonferroni tests showed that there was a marginally significant difference in course satisfaction between those who wrote about habits of mind in terms of writing or course in general, $M = 3.31$, $SE = .15$, and those who wrote about habits of mind in life, $M = 4.14$, $SE = .3.12$, suggesting that participants who wrote about the habit of mind in life reported higher course satisfaction than those who wrote about the habit of mind in terms of writing or course in general. However, this was just outside the 95% significance level, $p = .06$. Content of writing for other habits of mind did not yield significant results.

DISCUSSION

There are at least three categories for potential considerations of findings from my study of metacognition: research, rhetorical, and pedagogical. The least tenuous seems to be research, namely the call for more of it, given the great need to supplement my modest efforts, and the unfortunately incipient state of empirical research on the *Framework* in general. For example, I would like to see inquiries of any kind connected to why my first-year students' self-efficacy scores did not increase as they did for sophomores, juniors, and seniors, especially since the freshmen indicated higher end-of-semester course satisfaction, which was positively correlated to the test group's self-efficacy scores. This seems pertinent because the *Framework* targets incoming and pre-college students. By contrast, initial self-efficacy in flexibility and engagement predicted no outcomes across all levels in the data I have reported. What might account for the difference? Are these habits less personal or more abstract than the others? Furthermore, why were the habits of responsibility, engagement, and creativity bundled as a trio in my study in several significant findings related to course satisfaction?

Also, what can be made of the notable differences yielded by prompting or not prompting students to reflect on the habits in terms of rhetorical situation, as seen in Figure 14.1? Although the actual number of personal singular pronouns in subjects' free responses may not be important in itself, the stark difference in quantities registered by "guided" versus "open" responses does seem to be telling. For one thing, if you want FYW students to open up about themselves regarding the habits of mind, as opposed to about the habits more abstractly, then it seems the more open-ended your prompt, the better. But does this hold true over a longer freewriting session? Would the same stark contrast appear in spoken rather than written testimonies? More investigation seems warranted in all of the above areas.

Another reason to conduct research in this area is to make rhetorical uses of one's findings. My study shows that the more students value being engaged in rhetorical situations the more willing they are to write about their engagement. This might seem obvious, but 1) we now have statistically significant evidence that this is so, and 2) this suggests that all metacognition is not the same. Students seem to resist reflecting on unengaging writing tasks and to embrace doing so on engaging ones. So when we look to students' metacognition, say in a portfolio cover letter or on a college application or placement essay, we may not be getting a clear enough picture of what they would say under circumstances of better engagement with their audience, purpose, and context. Another rhetorical use of my findings might acknowledge the strong positive correlation between habits of mind self-efficacy and course satisfaction. Especially convincing is evidence of the predictive power of FYW course satisfaction on responsibility and engagement (both measured at a 99.9% confidence level). This knowledge could inform such administrative concerns as course completion, time to degree, and retention rates. For example, researchers might derive insights into increasing students' course satisfaction, and therefore retention and completion rates, by learning more about and supporting what engages them as academic writers and how they derive and manifest their senses of responsibility.

At this stage we should be wary of definitive pedagogical prescriptions based on these initial empirical investigations, but we can certainly more confidently take next steps in our classrooms and make a point of studying them. For example, my subjects whose initial self-efficacy rating in curiosity was high considered achievement of their intentions in academic writing to be more important than others did; these same students also wrote more about curiosity than others did. So let's explore ways to get students reflecting more and earlier on their curiosity. That could double as a diagnostic step and a potential rhetorical boon, given the correlation between curiosity and achieving one's intention, which is at the heart of most FYW courses. Similarly, my study found initial self-efficacy in creativity to predict the perceived importance of communicating in a context. With this in mind, anyone responsible for teacher training or shaping curriculum in writing—perhaps especially where habituating high-stakes tests and test prep are concerned—may want to reconsider the effects their programs have on creativity, and the influence that may have on students' perceptions of writing in contexts. College-level writing tends to require close attention to the rhetorical situation, so promoting students' creative approaches to real writing contexts seems an advisable preparatory method to consider in secondary programs, where this practice may not be as prevalent.

As a starting point for any number of future experiments, my study results importantly show that even by means of a very minimal stimulus, focusing students' metacognition on the *Framework*'s habits of mind is likely to increase their self-efficacy as academic writers. Furthermore, SCT tells us that this should increase benefits to students' performance outcomes. Teachers who may wish to adapt my methods for their future instructional purposes can obviously increase the frequency and intensity of the metacognitive treatment as they see fit to do. They can also change the nature of the treatment, for example, from rating scales and free responses to discussions or small writing assignments. Whatever they do, I hope these innovators will report on their adaptations and thereby continue to advance our metacognition about metacognition.

REFERENCES

Bandura, A. (1977). Self-efficacy: Toward a unifying theory of behavioral change. *Psychological Review, 84*, 191–215.

Bandura, A. (1978). The self system in reciprocal determinism. *American Psychologist, 33*, 344–58.

Bandura, A. (1986). *Social foundations of thought and action: A social cognitive theory.* Englewood Cliffs, NJ: Prentice-Hall.

Bandura, A. (1995). Exercise of personal and collective efficacy in changing societies. In A. Bandura (Ed.), *Self-efficacy in changing societies* (pp. 1–46). New York: Cambridge University Press.

Bandura, A. (1997). *Self-efficacy: The exercise of control.* New York: Freeman.

Bandura, A. (2006). Guide for creating self-efficacy scales. In F. Pajares & T. Urdan (Eds.), *Self-efficacy beliefs of adolescents* (pp. 307–337). Greenwich, CT: Information Age Publishing.

Bergen, B. (2012). *Louder than words: The new science of how the mind makes meaning.* New York: Basic Books.

Berthoff, A. (1984). Is teaching still possible? Writing, meaning, and higher order reasoning. *College English, 46*(8), 743–755.

Boyle, C. (2016). Writing and rhetoric and/as posthuman practice. *College English, 78*(6), 532–554.

Campillo, M. & Pool, S. (1999). Improving writing proficiency through self-efficacy training. Retrieved from ERIC database. ED 432 774.

Council of Writing Program Administrators, National Council of Teachers of English & National Writing Project (2011). *Framework for success in postsecondary writing.* Retrieved from http://wpacouncil.org/files/framework-for-success-postsecondary-writing.pdf.

Dweck, C. (2006). *Mindset: The new psychology of success.* New York: Random House.

Flower, L. & Hayes, J. (1981). A cognitive process theory of writing. *College Composition and Communication, 32*(4), 365–387.

Frost, J. (2014). Five guidelines for using p values. Retrieved from http://blog.minitab.com/blog/adventures-in-statistics/five-guidelines-for-using-p-values.

Hashemnejad F., Masoud, Z. & Amini, D. (2014). The relationship between self-efficacy and writing performance across genders. *Theory and Practice in Language Studies 4*(5), 1045–1052.

Hetthong, R. & Teo, A. (2013). Does writing self-efficacy correlate with and predict writing performance? *International Journal of Applied Linguistics & English Literature, 2*(1), 157–167.

Johnson, K. (2013). Beyond standards: Disciplinary and national perspectives on habits of mind. *College Composition and Communication, 64*(3), 517–541.

Lavelle, E. & Zuercher, N. (2001). The writing approaches of university students. *Higher Education, 42*(3), 373–391.

McCarthy, P., Meier, S. & Rinderer R. (1985). Self-efficacy and writing: A different view of self-evaluation. *College Composition and Communication, 36*(4), 465–471.

McLeod, S. (1995). Pygmalion or golem? Teacher affect and efficacy. *College Composition and Communication, 46*(3), 369–386.

Mendoza-Denton, R., Downey, G., Davis, A., Purdie, V. & Pietrzak, J. (2002). Sensitivity to status-based rejection: Implications for African American students' college experience. *Journal of Personality and Social Psychology, 83*(4), 896–918.

Murphy, C. & Shell, D. (1989). Reading and writing beliefs for ethnic students: Relationship of self-efficacy beliefs, causal attribution, and outcome expectancy to reading and writing performance for ethnically diverse college freshmen. Retrieved from ERIC database. ED 347 497.

Nuzzo, R. (2014). Scientific method: Statistical errors. *Nature, 506,* 150–152.

Pajares, F. (1996). Self-efficacy beliefs in academic settings. *Review of Educational Research, 66*(4), 543–578.

Pajares, F. (1997). Current directions in self-efficacy research. In M. Maehr & P. Pintrich (Eds.), *Advances in motivation and achievement* (vol. 10) (pp. 1–49). Greenwich, CT: JAI Press.

Pajares, F. (2003). Self-efficacy beliefs, motivation, and achievement in writing: A review of the literature. *Reading & Writing Quarterly, 19,* 139–158.

Pajares, F. & Johnson, M. (1994). Confidence and competence in writing: The role of self-efficacy, outcome expectancy and apprehension. *Research in the Teaching of English, 28*(3), 313–331.

Pajares, F., Johnson, M. & Usher, E. (2007). Sources of writing self-efficacy beliefs of elementary, middle, and high school students. *Research in the Teaching of English, 42*(1), 104–120.

Paris, S. & Newman, R. (1990). Development aspects of self-regulated learning. *Educational Psychologist, 25*(1), 87–102.

Pierstorff, D. (1983). Response to Linda Flower and John R. Hayes, "A cognitive process theory of writing." *College Composition and Communication, 34*(2), 217.

Schunk, D. (1990). Goal setting and self-efficacy during self-regulated learning. *Educational Psychologist, 25*(1), 71–86.

Shell, D., Colvin, C. & Bruning, R. (1989). Self-efficacy and outcome expectancy mechanisms in reading and writing achievement. *Journal of Educational Psychology, 81*(1), 91–100.

Shell, D., Colvin, C. & Bruning, R. (1995). Self efficacy, attribution, and outcome expectancy mechanisms in reading and writing achievement: Grade-Level and achievement level differences. *Journal of Educational Psychology, 87*, 386–399.

Tinberg. H. (2016). Metacognition is not cognition. In. L. Adler-Kassner & E. Wardle (Eds.), *Naming what we know: Threshold concepts of writing studies* (classroom ed.) (pp. 75–76). Logan, UT: Utah State University Press.

Williams, J. & Takaku, S. (2011). Help seeking, self-efficacy, and writing performance among college students. *Journal of Writing Research, 3*(1), 1–18.

Zimmerman, B. (2000). Self-efficacy: an essential motive to learn. *Contemporary Educational Psychology, 25*(1), 82–91.

Zimmerman, B. & Bandura, A. (1994). Impact of self-regulatory influences on writing course attainment. *American Educational Research Journal, 31*, 845–862.

CHAPTER 15

DEFINING DISPOSITIONS: MAPPING STUDENT ATTITUDES AND STRATEGIES IN COLLEGE COMPOSITION

E. Shelley Reid

George Mason University

It was an epic fail.

Upon hearing this comment, delivered cheerfully by an unassuming engineering major, students in my Spring 2012 advanced composition class perked up. At the podium, Luke was pointing to a vivid slide of a car crash to explain his recent experience drafting an analysis essay for his art history class. (All student names are pseudonyms.) We were midway through my fifth semester of assigning students to "decode" the rhetorical strategies they had used in a previous writing task via a three-minute presentation, and I'd been proud of how well they had been able to apply our new language of rhetoric—audience and genre, disciplinarity and revision—to their earlier work. Luke was reasonably adept at this rhetorical analysis, but his personal narratives came alive and made his explanation seem more emotionally honest. The art history class, he said, had been a boring general-education requirement, the assignment had seemed confusing and irrelevant, and so as the writer he had had zero motivation, procrastinated too long, and thus wound up with insufficient time to complete the necessary research or to figure out a specific stance to take. An epic fail—not because of his skills, but because of his attitudes. Across the room students were grinning and nodding: these were truths they knew about writing, especially writing in school.

I admit I have come late and dubiously to considering writers' dispositions as discrete, maneuverable factors integral to their classroom learning and success—as situational, strategic, and relevant rather than innate and ineffable. Even today, I remain skeptical about the exhortations of the field's founding statement on dispositional learning, the 2011 *Framework for Success in Postsecondary Writing* (see O'Neill, Adler-Kassner, Fleischer & Hall, 2012). It seems to me self-evident that a writer's attitude affects how and how well he or she writes. But within an institutional learning context, what can it mean for writing teachers to give formal instruction towards, much less assess students on improving, these affective, even personal characteristics? And why should these approaches be featured instructionally in a class about writing: a class about paragraphs, arguments, and genres? Yet I have recently discovered that when I bring dispositional concepts into our discussions, students and I benefit from being able to talk more truthfully and completely about what writers do. Moreover, in analyzing four semesters' worth of students' writing about their dispositional approaches, I have concluded that students' ways of feeling and doing as writers—their recognition, emphasis, and integration of dispositional factors as related to their writing-learning—suggest some distinct pathways for improving writing instruction.

DEFINING DISPOSITIONS

Placing "disposition" into a larger conversation about "cognition" in composition studies is challenging. If we use one common distinction, dispositional attributes might be seen as oppositional to cognitive achievements, in the way that "affective" and "intellectual" achievements are often separated. In line with David Conley's (2007) distinction between "academic behaviors" and "key cognitive skills" (pp. 16, 12) the *Framework* separates dispositional "ways of approaching learning"—behaviors such as curiosity, openness, engagement, creativity, persistence, responsibility, flexibility, and metacognition—from more classroom-based, epistemological structures for writing learning such as "rhetorical *knowledge*" and "critical *thinking*" (O'Neill et al., 2012, p. 525, my emphasis). Yet perhaps disposition and cognition have some elements in common. Approaches such as creativity, persistence, and responsibility echo more general strategies posited by Arthur Costa and Bena Kallik's (2000) habits of mind, Albert Bandura's (1986) work on self-efficacy, Barry Zimmerman's (2002) arguments about self-regulated learning, and Carol Dweck's (1996) investigations of learners' mindsets. Because these scholars emphasize the way advanced learners employ their own *awareness* and *control* of attitudes to enhance their learning and performance, we may identify a link between emotional dispositions and the more general concept of metacognition or reflective practice (Downs & Wardle, 2007; Nowacek, 2011; Yancey, 1998). In such a reading, learners' dispositions are revealed through metacognition and thus should be read as complementary rather than opposed to learners' cognition.

Other researchers blur the boundaries further: Shari Tishman, Eileen Jay, and David Perkins (1993) discuss "thinking dispositions," while Carolyn L. Piazza and Carl F. Siebert (2008) argue that "affect may be linked to both social and cognitive factors" (p. 276). Dana Lynn Driscoll and Jennifer Wells (2012) similarly align disposition as *parallel to* cognition, especially considering conversations (e.g., Flower & Hayes, 1981) that use "cognition" as a shorthand for "individual" or "interior" work that occurs distinct from a social approach to learning. That is, Driscoll and Wells contrast their work with writers' dispositions to the activity theory-oriented work of composition scholars such as David Russell (1995): they note, "In some [social] definitions, the learner is someone to whom or through whom transfer happens rather than being the agent of transfer" (Transfer of Learning section, para. 1). Identifying writers' dispositions as both inherent and malleable, Driscoll and Wells argue that these attributes are crucial for learning and for transfer, and call for further research into these connections.

Measuring the effects of dispositions for writing students is challenging. Looking to the future, Dryer and Russell (this volume) point to promising developments in integrated research approaches such as neurophenomenology, modeled by Antoine Lutz, Lawrence Greischar, Nancy Rawlings, Matthieu Ricard, and Richard Davidson (2004) in their combined examinations of personal narratives and brain scans of meditating Nepalese monks; currently, however, most U.S. scholarship focuses primarily on social and educational factors. Some studies, particularly focused on pre-college writers, have demonstrated that a curriculum that emphasizes dispositional or self-regulatory approaches can have a positive effect on students' attitudes (Kear, Coffman, McKenna & Ambrosio, 2000; Parajes, 2003). At the college level, Charles MacArthur, Zoi Philippakos, and Melissa Ianetta (2015) demonstrate that a comprehensive self-regulated strategy curriculum—including information to support genre awareness, instruction in self-regulatory strategies such as goal setting and self-evaluation, and instructor modeling of writing strategy application (Harris & Graham, 2009)—results in improved persuasive writing by students. While this study is one of a very few to link some dispositional attributes to improved competency in written assignments, their comprehensive approach makes it difficult to pinpoint the influence of attitudinal changes alone, much less to understand how those changes interacted with the work of student writers.

So for now, the causal links between college students' dispositions and their writing performance remain largely unexplored; even correlations are only tenuously theorized, and scholars raise questions as quickly as they suggest options. For instance, Carol Severino (2012) posits that dispositional success does not necessarily associate with mastery of standard writing conventions; Kristine Hansen (2012) likewise argues that there is no reason to presume that writing education is a primary or even likely way to instill such habits into students' repertoires. We may also face concerns about student exclusion as Kristine Johnson

(2013) notes, because any course that assesses students on a personal trait not supported by their home communities may put them at an unfair disadvantage. Until we know more about how students gain dispositional proficiency and how their dispositions relate to other aspects of their writing learning or achievement, we will continue to have difficulty achieving the larger vision of the *Framework*, in which teachers "develop activities and assignments that foster the kind of thinking that lies behind these habits [of mind]" (O'Neill et al., 2012, p. 527). In this study, then, I take additional steps toward that knowledge, by tracking some of the ways students respond to direct requests to narrate their own writing dispositions, and by analyzing how they perceive their affective challenges and successes as being connected to their rhetorical, structural, and analytical work as writers.

STUDY DESIGN: TRACKING DISPOSITIONS

Data in this article come from students' writing in four sections of English 101: Composition that I taught—fall 2014 (two sections), spring 2015, and fall 2015—and from four assignments that students completed therein. The project was approved by my university's institutional review board, and all of the students whose work is considered here consented to participate in my research. In all, 44 students participated, though not all students completed all assignments. Nearly all were first-year college students; the group includes 25 women and 19 men. Although I did not track language or ethnicity, students were a typical mix for George Mason University, where 20–30% of students speak a language other than English as a home or first language, and just over 40% are non-white (*George Mason Factbook 2013–2014*).

One goal for me in these classes was to help students move away from a sense that people "get writer's block," a mystical affliction without clear remedy. I aimed to move us instead toward identifying a wider range of problems that writers need to solve. Especially following my experiences with students like Luke, I also encouraged students to draw connections among writing problems they didn't usually identify as related to "cranking out an essay," such as comprehension of information and managing their own attitudes. Thus, drawing in part on the work of scholars who advocate deliberately *teaching for transfer* (Beaufort, 2007; Taczak & Robertson, this volume; Wardle, 2007; Yancey, Robertson & Taczak, 2014) we regularly used the following framework of overlapping categories:

- *Rhetoric problems*: Challenges in identifying one's goal, meeting an audience's needs, adapting to a relevant genre

- *Knowledge problems*: Challenges in comprehending an issue, adapting to the breadth or depth of information needed, providing analysis and/or challenging assumptions
- *Process problems*: Challenges in generating and organizing text, working through the steps of inquiry and source evaluation, and/or revising and editing
- *Disposition problems*: Challenges in generating confidence or motivation, in managing time and resources, and/or in staying persistent, curious, or flexible.

Early in each semester, students read some short passages to help them become familiar with these terms. In addition, several of the assignment prompts cued students to remember or consider these categories (see Figures 15.1 to 15.4). Beyond that, however, we did not spend much formal class time defining these categories precisely or setting specific goals around them; indeed, in the case of the disposition problems, after a brief first-week discussion, we spent almost no class time analyzing the specific nature of the challenges in this category. My previous experience with the Decoder assignment had suggested that these students could generally gain a useful working knowledge of these concepts through repeated opportunities to consider and apply key terms to their own projects.

To gain this working knowledge, students completed a series of guided, graded metacognitive assignments, including the four Decoder-based tasks analyzed here as well as regular reflective writing about their major writing projects for the class. These assignments were evaluated primarily on completion; the projects analyzed for this study combined for just under five percent of students' final course grade. Because assignments were graded, some students may have represented their interest in or progress with particular writing strategies more positively than was actually the case. And since students were usually prompted to consider all four categories of writing problems, they may have discussed some challenges that they did not actually perceive as important during their writing process. However, since students were given their choice of multiple sub-categories, received credit for (and very little commentary from me on) all completed assignments, and were invited to represent successes or difficulties as they preferred, they faced relatively little external pressure on these assignments to provide "right" answers that differed substantially from their own experiences.

DECODER PREPARATION AND DECODER PRESENTATION

In the first half of the semester, students reflected on a writing task that they had completed elsewhere recently, for a class or outside of school, and used disciplinary terminology to "decode" the challenges they had faced while writing it. They were asked to respond to a series of questions as part of their initial information gathering (Decoder Preparation), and then to give a three-minute presentation to the class, using some sort of visual aid such as a PowerPoint or Prezi (Decoder Presentation), while their peers took notes. Students in these classes described their work on college application essays, awards banquet speeches, personal and professional emails, and high school research papers; among more wide-ranging tasks were those by an ROTC student who described presenting a quarterly report to her commander and an engineering major who described writing a one-act play.

Decoder Comparison Homework and Final Quiz

For a late-semester assignment, students were asked to choose any three of their peers' Decoder Presentations that they had taken notes on and reflect on what those reports told them about how writers work (Comparison). They completed a table comparing the writers' efforts in three categories of their choice (such as "Rhetoric Problems" or "Author's Biggest Challenge"), wrote a paragraph about any trends they might extrapolate from their chart (did writers have common difficulties or strategies?), and explained how they might use any of the three writers' experiences to address their own current or future writing challenges. Finally, for the first section of our last quiz, students were given a choice of three briefly described Decoder situations from the semester's presentations, and asked to explain how a writer who needed to complete one of those tasks might prepare for and address challenges (Quiz).

Collecting and Coding Dispositions

For this analysis, I collected electronic copies of participants' Decoder-cycle assignments. Generally, I set aside responses to introductory or framing questions (such as "What was your task and your audience?"), and instead selected responses to the questions that most directly requested students' thinking about writing strategy problems and dispositional challenges. In order to attend to relationships among writing problems, I looked at units of text in which students were intending to focus on a single writing problem: in some cases, a text unit was several sentences responding to a question (e.g., about disposition challenges); in other cases, a text unit was a single bullet point or sentence from a student's summary of multiple challenges. From the Decoder Preparation exercises I collected students' final conclusion statements as well as any statements they made in response to a middle section of questions prompting them to consider

Defining Dispositions

at least one problem in each of our four categories: rhetoric, knowledge, process, and disposition.

> **Rhetoric Problems:** *Answer at least one.*
> Say something about solving
> - the **audience** or **genre** problems of your document
> - the **evidence** problems in your document
> - the **presentation** problems in your document
>
> **Knowledge Problems:** *Answer at least one.*
> Say something about solving
> - the **breadth/depth** problems in your document
> - the **analysis** problems in your document
> - the **assumption** problems in your document
>
> **Process Problems:** *Answer at least one.*
> Say something about solving
> - the **inquiry** problems in your document
> - the **generation** problems in your document
> - the **organization** problems in your document
> - the **revision** problems in your document
>
> **Disposition Problems:** *Answer at least one.*
> Say something about solving
> - the **confidence** problems in your document
> - the **motivation** problems in your document
> - the **deliberate time and resource management** problems in your document
> - the **persistence** problems in your document
>
> **Conclusion Part A:** If you had to do this writing task again, how might you do it differently and/or better?
>
> **Conclusion Part B:** How is this task similar to another kind of writing task (in or out of school) that you or we might do in the future, and how could you (or the rest of us) use similar strategies to solve that writing problem?

Figure 15.1. Selected preparation prompts.

From those question sections I coded each response as a single entry, whether it was a few words or a longer paragraph. From the conclusion sections, each sentence was coded individually, since students used those sections to list multiple strategies and approaches. From the presentations, I collected text statements from the problem-focused sections of students' visual aids: each non-header bullet-point or slide section was coded individually, regardless of length (see Figure 15.2).

> In a 3–4 minute presentation, you will use key terms that advanced writers use to talk about writing, plus an assessment of your specific challenges and resources, to show how a writer might start to solve a writing problem.
>
> Instead of predicting how to solve an unknown problem, you'll use 20–20 hindsight to explain how you solved the problems in an earlier writing task.
>
> You may discuss a writing task from another (current or previous) class or a writing task from your workplace, community, or personal sphere. You should choose a task that's at least a little different from what others have presented on.
>
> Choose the most interesting information from your Prep Form to include in your presentation to the class. Your presentation must include some of your concluding information, especially "how is this task similar to another kind of writing task (in or out of school) that you or we might do in the future?"

Figure 15.2. Selected presentation prompts.

These presentations replicate selected material from students' Decoder Preparation assignments, but here students chose their own emphases, since they were under no requirement to include any particular element(s) except a transfer-focused concluding statement.

Student responses to the Comparison exercise came in two parts (see Figure 15.3).

From the tables comparing three presentations using three categories of the student's choice, each cell was coded as an individual unit, regardless of length, while each sentence in the reflective overviews of strategies was coded individually. Finally, students wrote three problem-solving quiz answers as short paragraphs (see Figure 15.4) and each of their answers for the third question, "explain a disposition problem," was coded separately.

Overall, these data from the Decoder sequence represent increasing latitude for student choice about what to focus on in their responses, and they show students moving from their own past experience toward more generalizable and future-oriented writing strategies.

> Put some categories into your 4x4 table. You can choose what categories to list, based on your notes; you can combine ideas into one category. For instance,
> 1. Writer's rhetoric problems
> 2. Writer's knowledge problems
> 3. Writer's process problems
> 4. Writer's disposition problems
> 5. Special challenges the writer faced
> 6. What the writer learned/recommended
> 7. Other category: you choose
>
> What can you say about whether these writers experienced common and/or different rhetoric, process, knowledge, and/or disposition problems? What are strong influences on or challenges for these writers? What seems easy for them?
>
> What are two or three lessons you can take and apply to your own current projects and/or future writing?

Figure 15.3. Selected comparison prompts.

> Choose ONE of the three writing tasks listed below. (You cannot choose a task you presented on to the class.)
>
> In your answers, feel free to be blunt: "One rhetoric problem could be because , so I / the writer should and work on ." You should use our class' specific problem solving language….
>
> For the task you've chosen, explain a disposition problem you/the writer could face and how you/the writer could adapt to it.

Figure 15.4. Selected quiz prompts.

Once all data were collected, individual responses were coded to identify the type(s) of writing problem to which students refer. Mentions of *strategic* writing problems were coded as rhetoric, knowledge, or process problems according to students' description of relevant challenges; these codes were applied based on how the entry matched the problem definitions as articulated above rather than only on whether the student named the challenge directly. In a few cases in which students mentioned more than one strategy, I coded for the first-mentioned one only. So, for example, the following three responses (quotations in this chapter retain student wording and syntax although I have corrected spelling errors) were all coded as "**rhetoric problems**" (audience, goal, genre):

> I had to **make sure that the audience was engaged** in what I was talking about. (Sandy)
>
> **I wanted to build myself up** but at the same time not sound too full of myself. (Evan)
>
> **I chose this genre because** when it comes to a lab report its main purpose is to inform someone of whatever your experiment was based on. (Helen)

I also coded separately for mentions of *dispositional approaches*, using codes for confidence, motivation, time management, and persistence, as well as an "other" category that included generalized mentions of "disposition problems" as well as other dispositions (flexibility and curiosity, for instance, were less frequently prompted and almost never written on). Again, codes were applied using the formal definitions rather than only by direct mention; in a few responses where multiple dispositions were mentioned together, I coded for the first mention. In the following three entries, the first is coded as <u>time management</u>, while the second is cross-coded as *confidence* and **rhetoric**:

> I also <u>had trouble finding the time to write the essay</u> when I was busy with other extra curricular activities and schoolwork. (Rachel)
>
> My *confidence at first was a little off* because of the thoughts that came to mind about the admissions office. **If I did not write this essay in a way that they would like it**, then I could possibly not be admitted to the school. (Akeem)

Finally, before the statistical analyses analyzing independence of variables were completed, responses that did not receive any disposition-related code were filtered out; since many questions asked about different strategies separately (see Figures 15.1 to 15.4), students didn't usually have a need to write about dispositional approaches. Thus from the initial set of over 2,000 responses, these analyses focus on about 20% of those responses ($N = 461$) in which students identified at least one dispositional issue.

THE INFLUENCE OF DISPOSITIONS IN STUDENTS' WRITING WORLDS

Part of my own initial skepticism about including disposition-education in a transfer-focused writing course arises from questions of relevance and timing:

in a course that already has too much to cover in 14 or 15 weeks, why should instructors take time to focus on generalized affective learning? Time turned out to be less of a factor than I had anticipated: students in this study required little prompting or support to begin addressing dispositional issues in ways that revealed direct connections to their own understanding of writing and of learning writing. For instance, in two years of teaching with this approach, I have never had a student protest against sharing stories about his or her writing dispositions: in fact, 42 of 43 of the public presentations in this study included a disposition mention, despite that element not being required. And while just over half of students had presentation slides that neutrally or positively identified a dispositional (Saeed: "Motivation was simple for me because I enjoyed the topic"), over third of the presenters used their formal slides to overtly identify a dispositional challenge as a personal failure. Evan does this in discussing an application essay: "I *had trouble* managing my time, it was really important to me but I kept putting it on the back burner for school [projects]" (emphasis added). Although I don't have recordings of the full presentations, my sense is that many of the students with neutral slides were also speaking in a self-critique mode, and that like Luke, they found these admissions were received well by their peers. While it may be true that "writing instruction inherently teaches students ways of being in the world" (Johnson, 2013, p. 536), my students already seemed immersed in these "ways of being" independent of my classroom instruction.

Students' dispositional comments also covered a lot of territory. In these four assignments, students mentioned disposition more often than any writing problem category except rhetoric (see Figure 15.5).

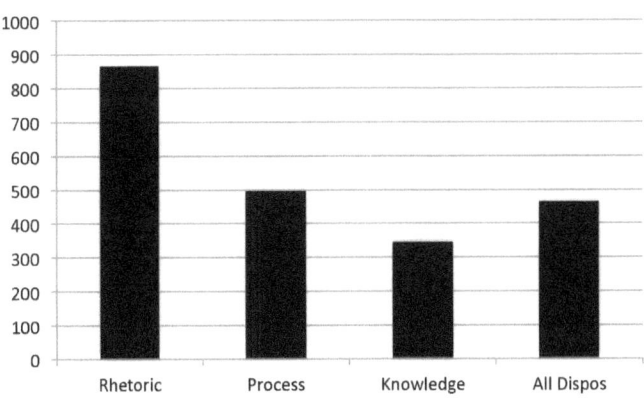

Figure 15.5. Number of responses.

Men and women wrote almost exactly as often about disposition factors and chose similar factors to mention; women were not, for instance, more likely to discuss confidence challenges than men. Although women students in these classes tended to produce more words overall, students in all assignments wrote at equal length about disposition approaches compared with their writing about disciplinary strategies such as rhetoric or process problems. Lastly, in the few instances in which students chose to identify a "most important challenge/lesson" or "hardest problem" outright (not just "this was difficult"), disposition challenges were identified about as often as all the other writing-strategy problems put together:

> Motivation for any assignment is the toughest part for me.
> Just getting started, but once I start it fairly easy. (Manuel)

In several ways, then, we see students moving easily to include dispositional factors in their reflective writing, despite having been provided very little relevant instruction.

Students didn't address all of the cued dispositions equally. Among the major disposition factors presented to them in class, students were most likely overall to choose or mention time management factors and least likely to choose or mention persistence factors (see Figure 15.6).

Figure 15.6. Number of disposition responses.

Confidence and motivation were chosen with similar frequency, and occasionally students described another disposition problem or just mentioned "disposition problems" generally. Without further data, I have only speculations about this distribution of responses. For these first-year college students, concerns about time management may be more familiar across a wide range of school or professional settings in which deadlines are common. Yet as I discuss below, students' explanations frequently complicate and connect writing problems, so a simple explanation—students are just overwhelmed in their first weeks of college, and thinking of nothing but time management—is unlikely to provide a complete answer. That said, it's likely that familiarity brings additional responses: fewer of the assignment prompts cued students to investigate issues of curiosity and flexibility as formal, changeable orientations toward their writing tasks, while the growing prevalence of time management descriptions in class presentations and informal discussions may have itself encouraged even further attention to that issue.

One exception to the time-management prevalence pattern comes in student responses on the Final Quiz, for which students were expected to anticipate the challenges that they or another writer might face in addressing a future writing task. Even though students' presentations on these topics were more likely to mention time management problems—and the quiz examples were drawn from those presentations—students' quiz descriptions were almost twice as likely to mention confidence as either time management or persistence. Some of that effect might be due to the inclusion in all four quizzes of a writing task that involved a spoken presentation, and thus we see more of students' anxieties about public speaking than about a writing project:

> A disposition problem the writer could face would be a lack of confidence. Giving a speech is already something that makes people nervous. (Nate)

And yet students were equally ready to identify confidence as a challenge for applications, analysis essays, and letters, and to predict other reasons why confidence might be a challenge:

> I may have issues dealing with confidence level. Again, this [topic] is something that I don't know much about so I might get discouraged if I don't find the information that I'm looking for. (Beth)

It's possible that this change in response proportions reflects students' sense that for a formal, exam-type setting, their general time management approaches don't seem as relevant within a college or professional writing scene. However, given that "I would manage/would have managed my time better" is such a common refrain in students' *looking-back* writings about how they could improve as writers, perhaps that reflective temporal distance is important. Perhaps we see here an echo of what self-regulation studies suggest: that students are generally aware of the concept that time (and other resources) can be managed, but they lack models for or consistent practice in *planning for time management* as they begin work on a writing project (MacArthur et al., 2015; Zimmerman, 2002).

In addition, while familiarity and cuing likely influenced student responses, discussion of dispositions sometimes emerged without specific prompting. For instance, in the Comparison homework, students could choose any categories to analyze; no specific disposition is listed in the prompt. In the lists of categories chosen, dispositions still make a showing (11 times), though they are eclipsed by choices of rhetoric (31) and process (19), among others. Rhetoric might have been perceived as a more "serious" or accessible category, and it also appeared at the top of the list of choices cued by the prompt. Yet as students discussed writing difficulties in more detail, disposition mentions increased. Overall, in the Comparison assignment, disposition discussions surface over 200 times, second only to mentions of rhetorical problems. Again we see that when left to their own choices, students frequently tell themselves and their peers' stories about their attitudes and approaches. The more we investigate how and when students identify dispositional factors in their own stories of writing, the more we may understand about general concerns of "writing anxiety" or "self-regulation" as they apply to our students' writing lives, and the better we will do at linking new strategies to students' prior knowledge.

COMPLEX INTERSECTIONS: TIME MANAGEMENT AND CONFIDENCE

Evidence that students are comfortable with discussions of dispositional challenges might alleviate our concerns about whether these conversations would divert time from other strategy discussions; Peter Khost (this volume) and Marcus Meade (this volume) have likewise reported high student engagement with metacognitive concepts such as imagination, curiosity, and openness even with relatively minimal intervention. However, this familiarity doesn't yet auger for addressing dispositions as a particularly necessary element of composition curriculum design (Johnson, 2013). One could argue that self-regulation and similar dispositional strategies would be better taught in "Introduction to Study Skills" courses, though some research suggests that to solidify long-term gains students need practice applying such strategies in the context of disciplinary classes (Karp et al., 2012). To believe that students' writing learning is enhanced by their awareness and/or application of dispositional strategies, we need better evidence that these particular cognitive approaches are associated with threshold concepts in writing studies. Students' responses in this study don't give us a causal relationship; however, they do reveal some crucial relationship patterns that can guide faculty in integrating dispositional awareness into our teaching. Participants were already primed to discuss their core writing strategies as intertwined with their sense of time management, confidence, and motivation.

Michael, for instance, sees research, drafting, and revision as fundamentally interwoven with time management, confidence, and motivation:

> Although I thoroughly enjoy learning and writing about the Revolutionary War, I had little motivation to write this because I was more interested on the tactical battlefield side then the propaganda side. Due to the lack of motivation in writing this I had low confidence in how I would do with it and I procrastinated a lot. Though by the fourth revision I had more motivation and confidence in myself because I had improved my first three drafts and I started to get fascinated by how writings conveyed their messages.

Over a third of responses coded as time management—and over half of responses coded for confidence—are also coded for rhetoric, process, and/or knowledge problems (see Figure 15.7).

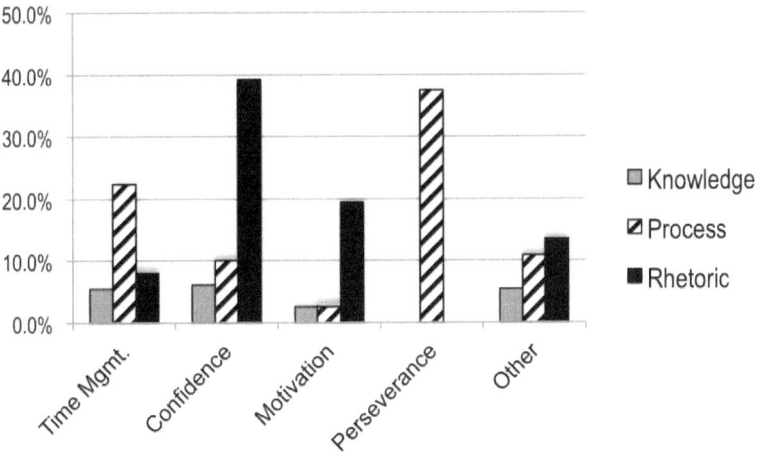

Figure 15.7. Percentage of responses in each disposition category cross-coded for a strategy.

Chi-square testing shows that among cross-coded responses, disposition choices overall are significantly related to strategy choices ($N = 461$, $\chi^2(15) = 79.07$, $p. < 0.0001$, Cramer's $V = 0.717$). Within those cross-codes, two patterns stand out as worth further analysis: a link between time management and process problems, and a link between confidence and rhetoric problems. Neither of these cross-code patterns should cause surprise, but each suggests a plausible route toward curriculum revision. (Although other trends shown in Figure 15.7 look interesting, motivation is statistically notable only for a lower-than-expected number of cross-codes overall, and there were too few perseverance responses to reach statistical significance.)

In the current study, 22.3% of comments coded as "time management problems" were cross-coded as "process problems," a significantly higher than expected rate ($N = 201$, $\chi^2(3) = 19.99$, $p < 0.001$, $\varphi = 0.32$). In hindsight, and from an instructor point of view, this link seems obvious, since we often teach writing processes *by way of time management.* That is, in order to foster students' awareness of threshold concepts such as *writing creates knowledge, revision is a central* and iterative process, and *writing is a social activity* (e.g., see Adler-Kassner & Wardle, 2015), we design and enforce deadlines to externally manage student writers' time. This is not always the same thing as teaching students to understand the underlying process-related threshold concepts about writing. So when students in this study—a population with strong high school preparation—show they have internalized a connection between writing process challenges and time-management challenges, that may be as much cause for concern as for satisfaction.

Granted, these students are using graded assignments to construct a vision of themselves as writers to share with classmates and their instructor, and so their perspective is likely to be more idealized and may reflect what they expect a writing instructor wants them to say. Some writers like Saeed begin an explanation with what sounds like a familiar litany:

> Managing my time was very difficult to do. I had wrestling practice and also I had a job so I was constantly busy.

They then shift to writing-process language in order to show how they are already employing additional coping strategies such as revision, as Saeed does here:

> I would be up late night working on this paper and trying to make even the smallest improvements.

Students also associate time management with other kinds of process moves, including generating and organizing material, focusing and conducting research, revising and editing:

> Time allowed for continuous ideas to flow. (Sabine)

> If I would have set aside time each day to interview at least three families then I would have been able to collect data faster so I could have time to write the essay. (Deeanna)

> I would give myself ample time again, but this time I would allow myself to make drafts, work on my process system and allow for mistakes. (Binah)

Reaching beyond students' ready idealism about how they'll do better next time, however, one conclusion here might be that their understanding of writing as iterative and multifaceted is limited by the time available: if they had time, they'd "allow themselves" to use multiple drafts or complete sufficient research, but when they don't, they don't. As writing teachers, we may be reinforcing this concept if we assign discrete process steps without appropriately involving students in the crucial decisions about how to choose ways to invest their time as writers.

Moreover, when we only discuss time management in crisis settings or punitive contexts (via late-work penalties, e.g.), we may increase writers' sense that they are stuck with a generalized and/or very personal bad habit. We would likely prefer that students understand that they are faced with a situational problem, one in which writers always need to be choosing the best possible responses from within constrained resources. After all, improving as writer isn't about suddenly having "enough time" or ceasing to procrastinate. Research shows that expert writers succeed in more accurately predicting the kinds of work that will take more or less time and choosing appropriate priorities for investing time and resources (Bereiter & Scardamalia, 1993). Thus as writing teachers we may have not just an opportunity but a reason to be more direct in discussing how writers self-regulate to manage time and resources. If students' prior understanding leads them to think of iteration, collaboration, review and/or revision as luxury options rather than inherent features of engaged writing, then they will need guidance to learn not just to "manage their time" (choosing how much time to allot) but to "manage their writing goals" within whatever time they can make available.

Similarly, the prevalence of "confidence" statements cross-coded as "rhetoric" seems obvious in retrospect but may present new avenues for instruction. Students in this study referred to rhetorical challenges in 39.2% of their statements about confidence, significantly more often than they referred to process or knowledge problems ($N=130$, $\chi^2(3)=36.90$, $p. < 0.0001$, $\varphi=0.53$). Typically, these statements took the form of linking confidence to the expectations of the known or anticipated audience:

> Confidence: . . . I was still nervous and unsure when applying into the program and writing this essay, for it is so highly competitive I wasn't sure what to expect. (Sherry)

> It was difficult for me to be confident writing about this topic to someone who was well versed in this field of knowledge. (Liesl)

As I noted above, the confidence-audience relationship patterns might be enhanced due to the number of spoken presentation assignments discussed in the Decoder sequence: several students like Patricia were "not confident in speaking in front of so many people." But that particular concern does not dominate the conversation about audience expectations, and students also linked their confidence levels to concerns about their own goals and/or to considerations of genre or style:

> Problems: Confidence—never wrote a philosophy style type paper of this length. (Cristian)
>
> My confidence was low coming into this project just because I wasn't where I should have been in the reading and I wasn't sure what I wanted to focus on yet. (Mark)
>
> I know how to clearly get my point across and I am very confident writing in this type of genre. (Anila)

In contrast to studies of writing anxiety or apprehension that have focused on how a student's inherent personality or skill levels affect overall individual self-efficacy (Cheng, 2004; Daly & Wilson, 1983), these responses suggest that—at least for these generally high-performing students—confidence is also rhetorical and social. The connection becomes even more interesting, from a curricular standpoint, when flipped. As writing instructors we invest intensely in having students come to understand that their writing should be purposeful and intended for a particular audience, without always addressing the ways that such intentionality may affect a writer's confidence. Even expert writers with high self-efficacy may encounter goals, readers, or genres that stress or distress them, and so writing problems don't always become more easily solvable when writers clearly identify their rhetorical situation. Unless we directly acknowledge how and why students who set aside an arhetorical task like a five-paragraph timed essay or an "all-about" research paper may struggle—because of a dispositional shift as well as because of any skill-level challenge—we risk losing students' faith in our proclamations. In both of these cases, our teaching of rhetoric and our teaching of process, we are telling students only part of the story if we fail to discuss dispositional challenges; if we consistently leave out parts of the story that they find most immediate, compelling, and/or reassuring, we may limit their abilities to fully integrate and transfer new knowledge.

MOVING FORWARD: DISPOSITION INSTRUCTION VS. DISPOSITION INTEGRATION

Assignments and instruction in the classes for this study were designed to enable students to gain awareness of and tell stories about how their dispositional approaches interacted with their school writing endeavors. Over the course of the semester, then, students engaged in the "meaningful practice" (Gorzelsky,

Hayes, Paszek, Jones & Driscoll, this volume) of identifying and monitoring component elements of complex writing problems. Students gained reasonable understandings of these components, including dispositional factors, with minimal prompting, and their responses suggest some ways we can and should heed the *Framework*'s call to adapt assignments so as to take advantage of this richer view of writing learning. However, these classes were not designed to formally follow up on students' dispositional learning. While students were frequently instructed in specific strategies for solving more conventional rhetoric, process, or knowledge problems—and their final projects were evaluated for competence in rhetorical adaptation, organization, and analytical power—students received very little instruction and no external assessment on any efforts they might be making to solve disposition problems, or any related improvements they might have made in their attitudes or texts. Scholars like Johnson (2013) argue that "Teaching habits of mind asks who writers should become and why they should become that way" and thus increases writers' agency and civic awareness (p. 527), and a growing body of work suggests that participating in integrated metacognitive exercises generally increases student success (Taczak & Robertson this volume; Winslow & Shaw, this volume; Yancey et al., 2014). But we do not have data to demonstrate that kind of causality for disposition-focused instruction. The question of whether writing students can and should be directly assessed on their dispositions—either their predilections for or their improvements in (writing-related) attitudes—remains open.

Assessment of such "ephemeral and personal habits of mind" may prove challenging, especially as we try to distinguish between students *acquiring* and students only *performing* these dispositions (Johnson, 2013). Conley (2007) proposes that we can assess general dispositional progress through "relatively straightforward" processes such as surveys that document students' self-reported integration of behaviors with academic assignments (p. 21). Although such instruments exist (see Piazza & Siebert's [2008] Writing Dispositions Scale), Conley argues that challenges remain in connecting such measures with other assessments of academic reasoning and content knowledge. As MacArthur et al. (2015) demonstrate, tying student improvement to a new disposition-aware curriculum is challenging, while identifying student writing success as linked to discrete elements of that curriculum such as persistence or motivation is very complicated. We don't have evidence yet that a particular level of proficiency in dispositions such as time management, confidence, motivation, or persistence is necessary for success in writing, and so we need additional research into how these attitudinal processes affect writers' progress.

In the meantime, though, results from this study indicate that as we teach strategies that we have long argued are crucial for proficient, flexible writers—

including threshold concepts such as the rhetorical nature of written communication and the need for a recursive, knowledge-generating writing process—we would do well to integrate deliberate discussions of related attitudes, and to do so with an integrated "enculturation" approach that returns agency to students rather than requiring particular performances (Tishman et al., 1993). If, as my students' responses demonstrate, college writers already believe or are quite ready to believe that dispositions are connected to their own work as writers, then we need to engage that prior knowledge as we strive to help them improve and to transfer new knowledge to other writing situations. Since we can present this more complete vision of writing without having to take much time away from our current assignments or lessons, we face little risk in adapting our instruction to integrate disposition concepts into our curricula. As we do so, we may find students to be more willing or even more able to adopt new, successful strategies as they solve ever-more-complex writing problems.

REFERENCES

Adler-Kassner, L. & Wardle, E. (Eds.). (2015). *Naming what we know: Threshold concepts of writing studies.* Logan, UT: Utah State University Press.

Bandura, A. (1986). *Self-efficacy: The exercise of control.* New York: Freeman.

Beaufort, A. (2007). *College writing and beyond: A new framework for university writing instruction.* Logan, UT: Utah State University Press.

Bereiter, C. & Scardamalia, M. (1993). *Surpassing ourselves: An inquiry into the nature and implications of expertise.* Chicago: Open Court.

Cheng, Y.-S. (2004). A measure of second language writing anxiety: Scale development and preliminary validation. *Journal of Second Language Writing, 13,* 313–335.

Conley, D. T. (2007). *Redefining college readiness.* Eugene, OR: Educational Policy Improvement Center.

Costa, A. L. E. & Kallick, B. E. (2000). *Discovering and exploring key cognitive strategies: A developmental series.* Alexandria, VA: Association for Supervision and Curriculum Development.

Council of Writing Program Administrators, National Council of Teachers of English & National Writing Project. (2011). *Framework for success in postsecondary writing.* Retrieved from http://wpacouncil.org/files/framework-for-success-postsecondary-writing.pdf.

Daly, J. A. & Wilson, D. A. (1983). Writing apprehension, self-esteem, and personality. *Research in the Teaching of English, 17*(4), 327–341.

Downs, D. & Wardle, E. (2007). Teaching about writing, righting misconceptions: (Re)envisioning FYC as intro to writing studies. *College Composition and Communication, 58*(4), 552–584.

Driscoll, D. L. & Wells, J. (2012). Beyond knowledge and skills: Writing transfer and the role of student dispositions in and beyond the writing classroom. *Composition*

Forum 26. Retrieved from http://compositionforum.com/issue/26/beyond-knowledge-skills.php.

Dweck, C. (1996). *Mindset: The new psychology of success*. New York: Random House.

Flower, L. & Hayes, J. R. (1981). A cognitive process theory of writing. *College Composition and Communication, 32*(4), 365–387.

George Mason University. (2014) *George Mason Factbook 2013–2014*. Retrieved from https://irr2.gmu.edu/factbooks/1314/Factbook1314.pdf.

Hansen, K. (2012). The *Framework for Success in Postsecondary Writing*: Better than the competition, still not all we need. *College English, 74*(6), 540–543.

Harris, K. J. & Graham, S. (2009). Self-regulated strategy development in writing: Premises, evolution, and the future. In V. Connelly, A. L. Barnett, J. E. Dockrell & A. Tolmie (Eds.), *Teaching and learning writing* (pp. 113–135). Leicester, UK: British Psychological Society.

Johnson, K. (2013). Beyond standards: Disciplinary and national perspectives on habits of mind. *College Composition and Communication, 64*(3), 517–541.

Karp, M. M., Bickerstaff, S., Rucks-Ahidiana, Z., Bork, R. H., Barragan, M. & Edgecombe, N. (2012). *College 101 courses for applied learning and student success*. CCRC working paper No. 49. New York: Columbia University, Teachers College, Community College Research Center.

Kear, D. J., Coffman, G. A., McKenna, M. C. & Ambrosio, A. L. (2000). Measuring attitudes toward writing: A new tool for teachers. *The Reading Teacher, 54*(1), 10–23.

Lutz, A., Greischar, L. L., Rawlings, N., Ricard, M. & Davidson, R. J. (2004): Long-term meditators self-induce high-amplitude gamma synchrony during mental practice. *Proceedings of the National Academy of Sciences 101*(46), 16369–16373.

MacArthur, C. A., Philippakos, Z. A. & Ianetta, M. (2015). Self-regulated strategy instruction in college developmental writing. *Journal of Educational Psychology, 107*, 855–867.

Nowacek, R. (2011). *Agents of integration: Understanding transfer as a rhetorical act*. Carbondale, IL: Southern Illinois University Press.

O'Neill, P., Adler-Kassner, L., Fleischer, C. & Hall, A. (2012). Creating the *Framework for Success in Postsecondary Writing*. *College English, 74*(6), 520–533.

Pajares, F. (2003). Self-efficacy, beliefs, motivation, and achievement in writing: A review of the literature. *Reading & Writing Quarterly: Overcoming Learning Difficulties, 19*(2), 139–158.

Piazza, C. L. & Siebert, C. F. (2008). Development and validation of a writing dispositions scale for elementary and middle school students. *The Journal of Educational Research, 101*, 275–285.

Russell, D. (1995). Activity theory and its implications for writing instruction. In J. Petraglia (Ed.), *Reconceiving writing, rethinking writing instruction* (pp. 51–78). Hillsdale, NJ: Lawrence Erlbaum.

Severino, C. (2012). The problems of articulation: Uncovering more of the composition curriculum. *College English, 74*(6), 533–536.

Tishman, S., Jay, E. & Perkins, D. N. (1993). Teaching thinking dispositions: From transmission to enculturation. *Theory Into Practice 32*, 147–153.

Wardle, E. (2007). Understanding transfer as generalization from FYC: Preliminary results of a longitudinal study. *WPA Journal, 31*(1/2), 65–85.

Yancey, K. B. (1998). *Reflection in the writing classroom.* Logan, UT: Utah State University Press.

Yancey, K. B., Robertson, L. & Taczak, K. (2014). *Writing across contexts: Transfer, composition, and sites of writing.* Logan, UT: Utah State University Press.

Zimmerman, B. J. (2002). Becoming a self-regulated learner: An overview. *Theory Into Practice, 41,* 64–70.

CHAPTER 16

MAPPING THE PRIOR: A BEGINNING TYPOLOGY AND ITS IMPACT ON WRITING

Kathleen Blake Yancey
Florida State University

As studies like those reported in *How People Learn* (*HPL*) (Bransford, Pellegrino & Donovan, 2000) make clear, prior knowledge contextualizes learning of all kinds. Sometimes, prior knowledge is a very good fit for the new learning; in such situations, there is a foundation on which the learner can build. Some other times, according to *HPL,* prior knowledge is a misfit: the learner's understanding is at odds with the new learning, and/or the learner's beliefs are in conflict with principles or theories grounding the new learning. Prior knowledge, of course, also shapes the ways that writers develop. We know, for example, something about writing process knowledge and about the ways that students draw on prior writing process knowledge for use in new writing tasks (e.g., Navarre Cleary, 2013), and about how both composing process knowledge and composing practices contribute to new composing processes that seem an assemblage of the old and new (e.g., Cirio, 2016). Likewise, research has demonstrated that school curricula influence composers: the research reported in *Writing Across Contexts* (Yancey, Robertson & Taczak, 2014) demonstrates that when provided with a curriculum rich with compositional content, students are more likely to draw upon that content, that writing knowledge, when they take on writing tasks in new rhetorical situations precisely because the content, with a set of key terms available as a framework for new tasks, is *usable* (Yancey et al., 2014). Put as a proposition, prior writing knowledge and practice is most valuable to writers when it seems usable.

A larger review of the research on transfer of writing knowledge and practice, however, as well as of research on composing processes and pedagogies, demonstrates that prior knowledge is more than simply knowledge, and that, as important, it is a much larger and more complex category than has been synthesized in the literature. As a review of the literature documents, the "prior" includes a diverse set of dimensions, including processes, knowledge, dispositions, beliefs, values, and affect, which students, and others, develop as they compose in writing situations both in and out of school, and which are also shaped by larger cultural forces (Wardle, 2012). Moreover, as some research shows (e.g., Roozen, 2010), the prior influences, sometimes extraordinarily, various choices and decisions—including about majors and even jobs—that students make as they continue developing as writers. This chapter, then, drawing on multiple case studies, begins to detail some of these dimensions of the prior, tracing in particular its influence on students' writing practices. I then conclude by suggesting that engaging students in the work of helping map the prior will assist us in understanding more fully both the prior and its multiple effects.

INVISIBLE SCHOOL-BASED CONTRIBUTIONS OF THE PRIOR TO STUDENTS' COMPOSING PRACTICES

When writing researchers refer to the prior, what they often mean is prior knowledge, which tends to stand in for a range of constructs, among them processes, dispositions, beliefs, knowledge, and points of departure, which, as *Writing Across Contexts* (Yancey et al., 2014) defines it, refers to an external indicator of quality—for example, a grade or test score—indicating to students how well they write and contributing to their sense of themselves as writers. Much of this research has focused on school contexts, but there is a corresponding line of writing research on the prior developed in non-school contexts—in workplace contexts, for example, as well as in contexts of everyday writing. Here, like Charles Bazerman (this volume), in exploring these dimensions of the prior—past writing processes, knowledge, and beliefs—I draw on multiple contexts and sites of composing simultaneously rather than treating them as separate sites of learning, in large part because, as we will see, writers do just that, repurposing what they learn in multiple sites for new writing tasks, regardless of whether these tasks and the prior processes and knowledge that writers call on are developed in school or out.

The focus on writing process in rhetoric and composition, of course, has a long history. Since the 1970s (and indeed somewhat before that time), faculty in rhetoric and composition have seen helping students develop an elaborated writing process as their primary curricular aim; as Richard Fulkerson (2005) argues, teaching writing as process is the single writing outcome postsecondary writing instructors agree on. It's also one that is responsive to entering students' needs. Considerable research—including that of Arthur Applebee and Judith Langer's and the University of Washington's SOUL study (2009; 2011)—demonstrates that students entering collegiate sites of academic writing bring with them an underdeveloped writing process, and for several reasons, among them the large number of students high school teachers teach, which precludes the critical mass of assigning and responding to writing that developing writers require; and the pervasive effects of testing, which collectively represents writing as a 45-minute single-draft activity. In the case of most entering college students, the research shows, the major prior school writing practice is a test-motivated, single-draft writing practice.

Even when in such a school environment, however, students may develop composing practices complicated in ways we cannot see, in ways that don't show up in the curriculum; as important, in such cases, what students construct as writing knowledge and what becomes writing practice varies considerably from what we see in curricula and research, as we learn from two students, each of whom illustrates how composing processes are shaped by prior experiences.

I interviewed Nicole, with her permission, as I inquired into how students make use of the prior, whatever it might be. What Nicole's experience shows is how students translate a common experience into a composing commitment informing their composing processes; in Nicole's case, this is a commitment she developed in school, although probably not in the way either the teacher or curriculum intended. More specifically, Nicole's commitment occurred in response to what Yancey, Robertson, and Taczak (2014) call a critical incident, "a failed effort to address a new task that prompts critical ways of thinking about how to write and about what writing is" (p. 143). Seen from one perspective, Nicole was the kind of student the literature reports, in her case a successful student who completed Advanced Placement English in high school as a single-draft writer, but who also found the format of a five-paragraph essay sufficiently flexible that she called on it for much of her composing in college. In fact, she called her AP class "training for the essay" and claimed that its format had provided (1) a throughline for her as she traveled from college class to college class, and (2) a flexible format that she could expand, adapt, and repurpose as needed.

Seen from another perspective, however, Nicole developed a writing process that now always includes a special feature: her unique contribution, a feature she added after a critical incident in the same AP English class. One of the AP assignments, Nicole had believed, would allow her to draw on material from pop culture as evidence for a claim she was making; her plan was to tap material from a favorite, the *Harry Potter* series. The teacher, however, required Nicole to draw on course material. Disappointed and a bit angry, Nicole didn't draw the same distinction between canonical and pop culture materials that the teacher did; she construed a different distinction, one between school material and Nicole's material. In other words, what the teacher excluded, according to Nicole, was Nicole herself and thus what seemed to Nicole to be the reason to write: to contribute something that is uniquely hers. This episode, which is a kind of critical incident, changed Nicole's process: from that point on, Nicole says, she has been committed to inserting or incorporating her own interests into *all* academic assignments. She likes, she says, "tak[ing] things that don't belong" and "sticking them in academic papers." Nicole's writing process, then, has been significantly shaped by two prior practices, one expected, one not. First, composing the AP essay has provided Nicole with a consistent and flexible genre-based framework for all her assignments, much as, though more successfully than, the writers studied by Mary Jo Reiff and Anis Bawarshi (2011). Second, at about the same time a critical incident prompts Nicole to design into her writing process her commitment, the consistent feature of incorporating her own interests, even when "they don't belong," which in many ways drives her future composing process.

The second student is Marie, who was profiled by Joe Cirio (2014) in his exploration of when and how students negotiate scoring guides. Like Nicole, Marie responds to a school directive about composing, but in an unanticipated way; in Marie's case, rather than seeing the rubric as an outline of audience expectations, she sees it as a design tool for writing. As Cirio explains, the scoring guide brokers what Marie understands as an exchange: the teacher's role is to provide the criteria used for grading an assignment, the student's role, and Marie's role in particular, to compose a text meeting those criteria. Such a view seems in some ways commonplace: writers often write explicitly to a set of criteria. In Marie's case, however, assignment criteria aren't goals to strive for, but rather directions for "build[ing] our papers":

> If we had a project, we would get a rubric with, like—it was, like, the grid. You'd get graded one through five. And if it was five, you had all the details. And, like, it'd be different for, like, presentation, wording, and all the stuff like that. And for my English class last year my teacher would give us, like, this really strict rubric about everything he was looking for, and if we had extra things we knew what kind of extra points we would get and where he would take away points and stuff like that. So, it was really easy to build our papers. (Cirio, 2014, p. 63)

The purpose of a rubric, according to those who advocate for them (see, for example, Turley & Gallagher, 2008), isn't to provide a blueprint for composing, but Marie's composing practice has repurposed the rubric for such use, especially because of its role in awarding the grade. With such a set of criteria/directions, Marie can "build" her texts. Thus, when asked what she hopes to see in a rubric, Marie is quite clear about the need for it to be specific: "I think something with details that—so we could get the best grade we could. So, stuff that showed specific details of what we actually needed to put in the paper and nothing that, like, left us questioning, like, "should I put this in my paper? Should I add this type of reference?'" (Cirio, 2014, p. 65). Moreover, Marie understands how very specific teachers' expectations can be: in describing a "bad rubric," she identifies vagueness as problematic:

> Sometimes teachers are really vague about the things that they want. They're just, like, "give me five sources." What kind of sources are they looking for? Or something like that. So, it's not, like, I don't want them to put, like, "give me five sources." But I want to be, like "do you want book sources, newspaper article?" Stuff like that. (Cirio, 2014, p. 65)

Marie's writing process, then, isn't merely informed by a rubric: it's driven by it. Put another way, in an interesting case of deixis—when a tool is repurposed to do a completely new task—Marie takes a tool intended to help students understand reader expectations and puts it to two other aims: (1) to define formal features of successful texts, and thus (2) to earn an *A*. Her writing process is oriented not to an assignment, but to the reward of a grade that the scoring guide accompanying it defines. Moreover, Marie's understanding of writing as an exchange, which oscillates between a belief about writing and a knowledge of it, is in perfect accord with her composing practice, one that isn't visible. Her prior experience with scoring guides, in other words, defines both her composing process and her understanding of composing.

More generally, what we see in these two writers is that prior writing experiences in school can influence, and even define, students' understanding of composing and can shape, and even distort, their writing practices. Moreover, without learning from students about their understandings and practices, faculty are less able to help them, precisely because they don't know that students' practices may be informed by episodes and desires important to the student but invisible to or deemed insignificant by the instructor; they don't know which conceptions of writing—the individual student's and the classroom's—are in dialogue; and they don't know when beliefs, some of them shifting into conceptualizations, motivate and direct composing practices.

THE ROLE OF THE PRIOR IN DIGITALLY MULTIMODAL COMPOSING PROCESSES

Much of what we know about writer development, of course, is predicated on models of writing and writing development that neglect technology, and yet as Jody Shipka (2011) suggests, technology of all kinds, ranging from pen and paper to wireless tablets, is at the heart of writing and of researching writing processes: "the main challenge facing process researchers today has to do with finding ways to trace the dynamic, emergent, distributed, historical, and technologically mediated dimensions of composing practices" (p. 36). And composers, as the next set of students illustrates, make very different uses of technologically facilitated composing practices: Nicole, whose writing practices were largely word-centric and who didn't identify a multimodal composing practice as such or draw on prior practice in her formal texts; Adam, who drew on composing knowledge and practice associated with a semi-professional interest in photography in creating a formal multimedia text; and Noreen, who created a multimedia text by drawing on her literacy not so much in writing, but rather in music, which as her major provided her with both knowledge and a set of practices to tap. Across these three accounts, what we see are some of the diverse factors influencing composers' use, or non-use, of the prior in digital multimodal composing: assignments, curriculum, and conditions of writing.

Nicole, the student whose writing always includes her own interests, was a double major, in Editing, Writing, and Media (EWM) and in Classics. In EWM, she completed the required courses, including the junior-level Writing and Editing in Print and Online (WEPO) course, where she, like all students in WEPO, composed in three spaces—print, screen, and network—and where she created a culminating networked electronic portfolio (Fleckenstein, Davis & Yancey, 2015). In WEPO, she thus wrote in a fully multimodal way, composing intentionally with layout, color, images, hyperlinks, and so on. Within a year of completing WEPO, Nicole was assigned a two-fold writing task in one of her classes in classics, an assignment with a strong visual component: (1) develop a catalogue of ancient seals based on replicas hosted in a special exhibit at the FSU Art Museum, and (2) analyze either their contributions to our understanding of the ancient world or the contributions of the Englishman responsible for discovering them, Sir Arthur Evans. Nicole reacted ambivalently to the assignment. On the one hand, she understood that the professor was "trying to give us an opportunity to do something more hands-on," and she thought it was "cool to handle them and look at all the detail." On the other hand, she believed that she didn't have sufficient background to do a good job, and she wasn't particularly invested in the task.

In the composing processes supporting her catalogue, Nicole worked multimodally, not because she understood working multimodally as a means of composing, despite her having taken WEPO, but rather because doing so contributed to a more efficient composing process. At the museum, Nicole made notes and took photos of the seals; taking photos of the seals, she said, saved time, since she would only need to go to the museum once, and they provided a record she could draw on, "just so that you could use them as a [photographic] reference." To verify the accuracy of her photo-based descriptions, she also checked "online sources to see the same seals: those sources told you if it was a palm leaf, but [this site was] written in German, so there were pictures that you had to match. I could see them more clearly; reference them more easily." Still, she didn't include photos in either the catalogue text, an excerpt of which is included here, or the formal text. When I asked Nicole why she had not included photos in either document (or both), she replied that including them is "maybe more of a digital or Internet kind of thing. In an academic paper, I hadn't expected it."

What we learn in this account of Nicole's is twofold. First, using a composing process clearly attuned to twenty-first century technologies, including use of a camera and the Internet, Nicole saves time and completes the assignment as efficiently as possible, but she doesn't understand this as writing. In other words, although she employed fully multimodal composing processes for her WEPO texts, Nicole doesn't draw on that prior practice for the composing in classics since she doesn't see any similarity between the processes she employed in the two classes, even tacitly. Second, she wasn't cued to include images in the final texts, and without being cued to include images in the formal writing for the catalogue or the larger project, Nicole didn't consider incorporating them, even when both documents seemed ideally suited for them and she had the images to use.

A good question is why Nicole doesn't draw on the prior composing practice and knowledge she developed in WEPO; another is why she relies on a photo-informed composing process, but doesn't include the images so important to that process in her formal texts. In the interview, Nicole hinted at answers responsive to both questions. She doesn't under-

> **K174/CMS VI.93.** Three-sided, elongated, red-brown cornelian. Kenna notes that he agrees with Evans about this being a royal seal.
>
> **A. From Kenna:** Seated cat, between its ears a *silphium* sign, on one side the leg sign, and on the other the snake. The gate sign is used as a base or exergue.
>
> **B. From Kenna:** A template in the center of the field, surmounted by a pronged instrument and the *silphium*. At each end of this face there is a panel of three palmettes springing from lunettes. This design shows a remarkable feeling for unity and economy. It has something of the quality of a fine Egyptian cartouche.
>
> **C. From Kenna:** Trowel, adze, wheel or rayed disk, flanked by a design which is a combination of four C-spirals in pairs, sometimes called bugles, and lunettes.

stand the use of the camera, for instance, as a part of her composing process, but rather as an independent time-saving activity. And that understanding accords with her own knowledge of genres, which categorizes "Internet" texts and academic texts separately: including photos, she says, "maybe more of a digital or Internet kind of thing. In an academic paper, I hadn't expected it." In other words, Nicole seems to have a theory about the kinds of texts that include photos, which is also a theory about the kinds of texts that do *not* include them, a theory or working knowledge that both WEPO and the Classics classes support. WEPO didn't help Nicole conceptualize writing capaciously: the intent of composing in the three spaces is, in part, to help students see the similarities in composing across those spaces, but Nicole seemed to see them as different, with one set of rules or conventions for print and a different set for the digital. Likewise, there was no cue in the classics assignment that she might include photos, so as she says, it simply didn't occur to her. More generally, then, what we see here is the dynamic relationship between prior writing knowledge and prior writing practice: what we know about writing from our prior experience, which in Nicole's case is about where photos do and do not belong in texts, shapes our practices and the texts we create.

ASSIGNMENTS, OTHER LITERACIES, AND PRIOR KNOWLEDGE AND PRACTICE

In the cases of Adam and Noreen, we see a different relationship between prior writing knowledge and practice, one based in writing tasks new to them and in knowledge and practice developed in whole or in part outside of English classes or even school itself. Both Adam and Noreen were composing a novel text, a remediation project requiring that they repurpose a print text for another medium, a kind of assignment that is a relatively recent addition to the suite of college writing tasks. Jay David Bolter and Richard Grusin's (1999) *Remediation*, which provides the theoretical foundation for such assignments, was published in 1999, and while some faculty have used remediation assignments for some time (see, for example, the reference to them in Yancey's "Composition in a New Key" 2004 CCCC Chair's Address [Yancey, 2004]), they are not yet standard fare in college composition (Beardon, 2016). Moreover, given the nature of the assignment—the same material provides invention for two different texts composed for two different media—the assignment itself may have played a role in their use of the prior. In addition, in composing their remediation projects, both Adam and Noreen tapped prior literacies developed *outside* of the writing classroom to help them respond to these novel writing situations. Their respective assignments also differed somewhat, as did their use of the prior: in Adam's case, the project allowed him to decide which media he wanted to use, while Noreen's assignment asked her to translate a narrative across media, from print to digital or the reverse, so for her both genre and medium were prescribed.

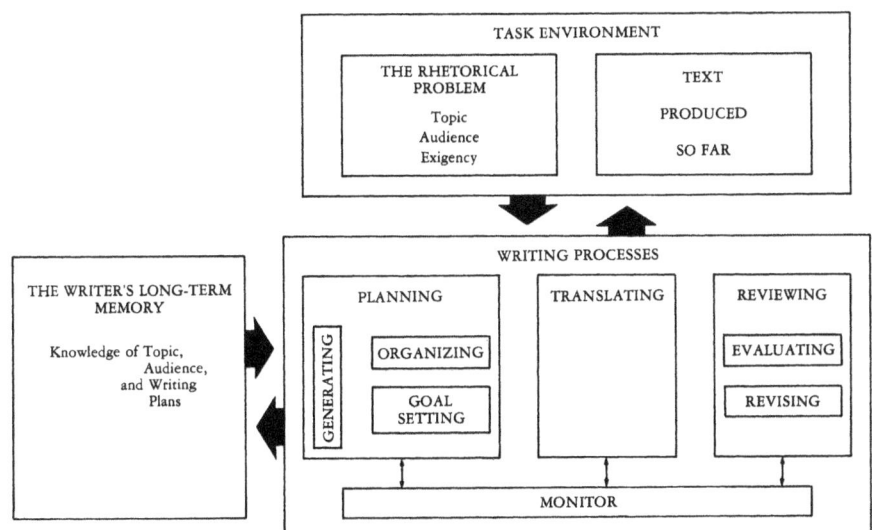

Figure 16.1. Structure of the writing model

As Bret Zawilski (2015) explains in his study of cross-media transfer of writing knowledge and practice, Adam's composing process itself, in the context of this remediation project, diverges considerably from accounts in the literature, at least in its materiality and inclusion of writing technologies. For example, as Charles Bazerman (this volume) suggests, like other models of its time, the Flower and Hayes' account of composing, visualized here, is limited, in this case providing (only) a mental model of composing; more recent accounts of composing (e.g., Pigg, 2014) are much fuller, often highlighting the materiality and technology entailed in current composing practices, as quick description of Adam's composing emphasizes:

> [Adam] props a tablet next to his laptop computer, pulling up his original print project—a newsletter defining visual rhetoric and simultaneously exploring the complexity and influences of modern electronic dance music. On the tablet, he navigates to an online magazine, considering how he might frame his text in a similar way. His hands move back and forth between the two devices, browsing through texts and gathering raw materials. While the tablet continues to display model texts, Adam shuffles through windows on the desktop

> of his computer, opening documents in Word and InDesign while searching through his personal photography both on his computer and on the digital photography platform Flickr. (Zawilski, 2015, p. 2)

Composing for Adam, as we see here, is neither exclusively putting pen to paper nor exclusively putting fingers to the keyboard or screen: rather, it's a materially rich process involving, in addition to paper, multiple networked devices, multiple software packages, and a collection of his own photography.

Indeed, it was his own photography and his photographic practices that informed Adam's remediation project, which began with his four-page print newsletter defining his key term visual rhetoric and which hosted three articles: one defining visual rhetoric, another addressing the ways the visual represents electronic music, and the last pointing to graffiti. He was happy to write this newsletter on visual rhetoric precisely because it allowed him to draw on his passion for photography and incorporate some of his own photographs into the text. For the remediated text, Adam's overall intent was to remediate the newsletter into an online magazine modeled on one of his favorites, *Game Informer Magazine*. Put another way and as Zawilski (2015) explains, given Adam's prior reading and writing on the Web, the models of networked texts he'd already been exposed to played a large role in how he conceptualized the composition task (pp. 89–80), a point that Doug Brent (2012) makes as well in studying students writing in internships. In his context, Adam drew on two versions of the prior: in the first instance, on the process he had used earlier and on material that he had also used previously; in the second instance, on a network-informed knowledge of community that complicated the assignment for him.

In creating the online magazine, Adam wanted to include images as he had for the print newsletter, but the ones he wanted to use for the remediated text were blurry, so he faced a choice: search online for new ones, or simply draw from his own archive of photographs on Flickr. He decided to use his own photos, a practice that linked to that used for the newsletter, though here his use of the prior was twofold: a practice he had successfully used; and material that he had earlier collected for whatever purpose and archived. In this sense, drawing on his prior practice and material made the task somewhat easier. The online magazine he chose as a genre, however, complicated his task; in this case, the prior was knowledge-based. Adam designed the newsletter so that it would circulate in two communities, the community of the class, of course, but also an online community, and it was this latter community that he thought should take priority since it had a "realness" to it that the classroom community did not. As Zawilski explains, "The community of Medium.com itself served as a second environment, and Adam needed to consider how his text would circulate within that environment," especially since "Adam . . . saw a real value to the work he was producing" (2015, p. 126). Moreover, questions around this dual community led to a related complication when it came time for peer review of drafts: while Adam's peers were also composing texts that would circulate on the Web, theirs were social media texts and thus short-form, so that Adam's, which was long-form, seemed odd to them.

Whereas many of his classmates were creating short remediations through social media platforms, Adam had to account for their feedback (namely that his text was too long) alongside an awareness that the length was called for by the conventions of the community in which his text was circulating. [According to Adam,] "And it [was] a gamble because, you know, the piece is still on the Internet. So it's still a part of that community. But I was presenting it and creating it for the purpose of the classroom . . . there was a sacrifice that was made and a decision that had to be made regarding the genre and how I presented it" (Zawilski, 2015, p. 119).

Interestingly, though for different reasons, Adam finds himself in a similar situation as Marie: both of them find their writing more complicated because of an assignment, the specifics accompanying it, and/or their interpretation of it. In Marie's situation, as described above, her school writing tasks were more complicated because instead of thinking about what each task might require, she approached each one with rubric in hand, using a statement of reader expectations, a scoring guide, as a blueprint for "building" the text. Put another way, a teaching device, the scoring guide, was put to another use, one not appropriate for it, a problem that school unintentionally created when it introduced the rubric. Likewise, in Adam's case, the assignment, in allowing audiences outside of school, which is a strategy the field applauds, put him in something of a bind: should he play by the school conventions, especially as enforced by his peers, or should he play by the conventions of the discourse community that were part of his prior knowledge but not that of his peers?

Noreen's remediation project exemplifies another aspect of the prior, in her situation the role of prior knowledge, especially as located in key concepts, and their effect in composing. Like Adam, Noreen was composing a remediation text, hers originating in very specific kind of literacy narrative, as Michael-John DePalma (2015) explains: students were asked to "compose both a written essay and a digital story that explore a critical moment in their literacy development, a turning point in their ethical development, a shift in their sense of identity, or a change in their beliefs" (p. 620). Noreen enacted a story in print that "explored her emotional and psychological growth as an artist through the lens of Berlin's reconstruction after WWII" (DePalma, 2015, p. 621). A music major, Noreen finds in the digital story assignment, with its images and music, an appropriate opportunity to draw on her knowledge of music, which informs the planning and arrangement of both print and digital stories. For example, Noreen used concepts in music to help structure "the timing and the emphasis and the flow of the story" (DePalma, 2015, p. 624), a process and structure she understood as organic:

> In classical music things tend to happen in pairs. You have a primary thing, and you have a secondary thing. You have an antecedent, and you have a consequent. And so, with the structuring of the essay, I was very aware of that parallel. I'd always have something that goes back, like a counter-part before and after.

She continues:

> In music, you present an idea, and it oftentimes recurs later in the composition, and so you go, "Oh, that's where I heard that before! That's where that comes from." So it's very organic in music, and that's what I was thinking in this essay, as well. I was trying to make the ideas really organic. (p. 624)

Noreen used other concepts from music to achieve other purposes, for example both to structure and to provide rhythm to the text, including in her digital story "a technique in music composition called 'time-points'" (DePalma, 2015, p. 625), her intent in doing so to align music and image—the ending of the music marking the fading of the image—for a particular effect on the audience, a process that was so familiar to her that it felt "natural" (p. 626). In describing Noreen's use of music in her remediation project, DePalma appropriately emphasizes the integration of literacies such projects can invite, in Noreen's case her written literacy and her musical literacy providing the intersection for her stories. It's also worth noting, however, that Noreen's musical literacy is knowledgeable and sophisticated: she is a music major, and it shows—in her vocabulary, in her conception of structure, in her transfer of one set of strategies from music to the essay. The key terms, in fact, may be an important factor contributing to her use of the prior precisely because they are so familiar, and, as the research in *Writing Across Contexts* demonstrates, precisely because they provide a very specific vocabulary useful for describing both tasks and aims. More generally, it's a good question as to the role that the key terms play in activating prior knowledge.

Fully multimodal writing—moving beyond words only to include connections to photography, to art, to music, to design, and to other modalities—makes a wider set of prior knowledge and practices available to composers. In some cases, like Nicole's, a writing process may be unintentionally multimodal, and without the text itself benefitting from that process, in part because the prior acted to constrain rather than open up, in part because no cue signaled her that she might think about the text more capaciously. In other cases, like Adam's, assignments calling for digital multimodality make opportunities to tap the prior of homegrown literacies available even as they complicate the (classroom) writing situation. And still other writers, as we see in Noreen's account, in calling on other literacies, find in them a prior vocabulary useful for conceptualizing and enacting a text incorporating multiple modalities.

THE ROLE OF (PRIOR) PLACES TO WRITE IN SHAPING COMPOSING

The places where people write, from classrooms and dorm rooms to libraries and coffeehouses, are now also considered an element of composing, and though we don't know as much about writers' current practices as we'd like, especially given the influence of mobile technologies, we would expect that prior practices and knowledge would play a role here as well. Stacy Pigg (2014), for instance, has rendered the ways that connection to place is both weakened and strengthened through mobile technologies. Kim, one of the students whose composing Pigg profiles, explains this process: "Before I had the laptop, I had a desktop, so if I was writing, I had to be at home, I had to be at my desk. And I had to be, you know, in that space, which was a lot different. Using a laptop, I can take it anywhere" (2014, p. 259). For Kim, the coffee shop Gone Wired, one of several she frequents, is her composing place four days a week; this schedule gives her both the flexibility awarded by mobile technologies and the stability of a common writing place. Given that it is a public place, part of the task in composing there is managing distractions.

Distractions were not ordinarily a problem for Nicole, who mentioned where she wrote only once, in connection with the classics assignment. She didn't begin drafting the text until the a few days before it was due, so she was anxiously writing to and against the deadline. Accordingly, she used a strategy she had used before: she "spent 12 hours in Strozier [the campus library]" where she used one of the library's computers. And like Kim, critical to Nicole's completing the project was reducing distractions: the library, she said, was helpful in this regard because it could "put me in a work frame of mind." Taken together with Kim's account, what Nicole's episode suggests is twofold: first, that when writers are anxious, they return to composing places that helped them complete other tasks before in the hopes that such success will occur again; and second, that in the age of ubiquitous composing, maintaining distractions is an important component of composing.

Other students, however, are consistently intentional about where they write, and for some of them, as Jacob Craig's (2016) research demonstrates, identifying that physical place is an exercise of the prior, as we see in the case of Lily. An EWM major, Lily claims that finding a hospitable place to write is a crucial part of her composing process; she wants her composing place to offer physical features matching those of the first place she found success as a writer. Her use of this prior, in other words, involves a kind of replication: identifying a specific kind of composing place that iterates places where she composed successfully before.

Lily's first writing place was inside the Boston home where she grew up: a three-seasons porch with comfortable furniture, windows, light, and through the windows, "a scene [with] a lot of trees in the background," a place often filled with the sounds of people she loves, the "hustle and bustle" of the "4–5 people living in it" (Craig, 2016, p. 108). She appreciates both the light and the noise: interestingly, for her, unlike Kim and Nicole, the noise doesn't distract, but rather helps her focus, as she says: "I like working with hustle and bustle around, because I can focus" (Craig, 2016, p. 108). When she enters college, Lily finds a place replicating this first place and calls it her "sanctuary," one that as Craig describes, includes windows, furnishings, and friends, but as Lily explains, she's not sure how aware she was of this reiterative composing practice until her interview with Craig:

> I like studying at this house, because it reminds me of where—back home. It's actually like a 2 story house that used to belong to a family. And I have a couple of friends who bought it together. They're friends that I've become good friends with that live here. So, I feel comfortable enough to sit on the couch and work for hours. I think honestly, looking back and reflecting on it. It's interesting how I composed this [current text] and composed back home like with the computer on the arm of the chair and looking out the window because that's exactly what I did here sub-consciously. (Craig, 2016, p. 183)

Place is thus another factor that influences composers, sometimes, as in Nicole's case, on an as-needed basis, and other times as a replicating practice, tacitly or explicitly.

MAPPING THE PRIOR

As all these accounts make clear and as Bazerman suggests in this volume, "aspects of writing that are less visible, lost in the recesses of minds and feeling" can play a large influence in how writers compose. As this chapter demonstrates, such invisible aspects influence the ways students like Nicole and Marie, in translating teacher directions, create new composing processes; and the ways fully multimodal assignments invite in students' other prior knowledge and practice, as in the case of Adam and Noreen; and the ways places sponsor composing practices for just-in-time or continuous composing. Likewise, we know about these invisible composing practices and uses of prior knowledge and practice through student accounts, and it is through such accounts that practices and uses of the prior might become more visible, that we might learn more. Toward that end, I here suggest three approaches we might consider as we continue to map composers' uses of prior composing knowledge and practice.

Students' beliefs often influence students' knowledge of composing. Marie, for instance, believes that writing functions as an exchange between teacher and student and that rubrics provide a blueprint for "build[ing] texts." Similarly, Nicole believes that all her writing should include a part of her: that good writing, even academic writing, is personally inclusive. Clearly, there is a relationship between beliefs and knowledge: what we believe sometimes becomes what we know, or stands in for what we know; and beliefs-becoming-knowledge shape what we do. One approach to investigating the relationships of students' beliefs, knowledge, and practices is, of course, located in asking them, a pedagogical approach Jeff Sommers (2011) has outlined. On the first day of class, Sommers shares the beginnings of three sentences—I believe writing . . . ; I believe revising . . . ; and 1 believe writing courses . . .—and asks students to complete the sentences and to share their responses (2011, p. 103). They do so, and thus begins a semester-long, collective consideration of what students believe about writing, revising, and writing courses. Asking students, perhaps individually or perhaps in focus groups, to engage wwith questions like these, especially over time, might help us begin to trace the dynamic relationship between beliefs, knowledge, and practices.

A second, more structured approach to exploring students' prior writing knowledge and practice is to frame an inquiry by using a revised version of Bloom's Taxonomy. Sharing with them this revised version, as visualized here, would focus students' thinking about ways they define writing and might identify prior knowledge and practices. What, students would be asked, are facts about writing? How do they know these? How are these different than beliefs, if they are? What are the writing concepts that they know? That they use? What practices do they engage in, and why? What role, if any, does reflection (Yancey, 1998, 2016) play? And what connections across these dimensions do they make, and why? The value of such a taxonomic approach is that it would provide a framework for inquiry such that aspects of the prior are sorted and can then be connected. Put another way, this taxonomy could produce a very specific kind of map of the prior.

The Knowledge Dimension	Remember	Under-stand	Apply	Analyze	Evaluate	Create
Facts						
Concepts						
Processes						
Procedures						
Principles						
Metacognitive						

Figure 16.2. The Knowledge Demensioni—major types and subtypes.

Yet a third approach is to employ the method devised by Erin Workman, which is to ask students on the first day of class to identify their key terms for writing and to map them so that their relationships are made visible. Although Workman's project is oriented to ways that the Teaching for Transfer curriculum can support students' transfer of writing knowledge and practice, her approach, or one similar to it, could be used for research purposes. It would be useful to know how students conceptualize writing by reference to key terms, to learn how they structure such terms, to ascertain if some structures are more sustainable and/or productive in terms of use, and to continue to inquire into the role that key terms, as we saw in the case of Noreen, do or do not play in making prior knowledge available for use.

There is, of course, much more to learn about the prior than this chapter has been able to address, but one observation we can make on the basis of the evidence presented here is that the prior, even when it only taps knowledge, practices, and beliefs, is much more complex and sophisticated than is commonly understood. Moreover, given that much of it is invisible, it is impossible—without asking students—to know what they think writing is, or what practices serve best. As evidenced here, however, and with students' help, we can continue to explore and to map more accurately this important but under-researched area.

REFERENCES

Applebee, A. & Langer, J. (2009). What's happening in the teaching of writing? *English Journal, 98*(5), 18–28.

Applebee, A. & Langer, J. (2011). A snapshot of writing instruction in middle schools and high schools. *English Journal, 100*(6), 14–27.

Beardon, L. (2016). *Favorable outcomes: The role of outcomes statements in multimodal curricular transformation.* Retrieved from http://diginole.lib.fsu.edu/islandora/object/fsu:366031/datastream/PDF/view.

Bolter, J. D. & Grusin, R. (1999). *Remediation.* Cambridge, MA: MIT Press.

Bransford, J. D., Pellegrino, J. W. & Donovan, M. S. (Eds.) (2000). *How people learn: Brain, mind, experience, and school: Expanded edition*. Washington, DC: National Academies Press.

Brent, D. (2012). Crossing boundaries: Co-op students relearning to write. *College Composition and Communication, 63*(4), 558–593.

Cirio, J. (2014). *The promise of negotiation: Situating rubrics in the fourth wave of writing assessment*. (Master's thesis). Retrieved from http://diginole.lib.fsu.edu/islandora/object/fsu%3A185364.

Craig, J. (2016). *The past is awake: Situating composers' mobile practices within their composing histories*. (Doctoral dissertation). Retrieved from http://diginole.lib.fsu.edu/islandora/search/catch_all_subjects_mt%3A(World%20Wide%20Web).

DePalma, M. J. (2015). Tracing transfer across media: Investigating writers' perceptions of cross-contextual and rhetorical reshaping in processes of remediation. *College Composition and Communication, 66*(4), 615–642.

Fleckenstein, K. S., Yancey, K. B. & Davis, M. (2015). A matter of design: Context and available resources in the development of a new English major at Florida State University. In G. Gibberson, et al. (Eds.), *Writing majors: Eighteen program profiles* (pp. 175–190). Logan, UT: Utah State University Press.

Flower, L. & Hayes, J. (1981). A cognitive process theory of writing. *College Composition and Communication, 32*(4), 365–87.

Fulkerson, R. (2005). Composition at the turn of the twenty-first century. *College Composition and Communication, 56*(4), 654–687.

Navarre Cleary, M. (2013). Flowing and freestyling: Learning from adult students about process knowledge transfer. *College Composition and Communication, 64*(4), 661–687.

Pigg, S. (2014). Emplacing mobile composing habits: A study of academic writing in networked social spaces. *College Composition and Communication, 66*(2), 250–276.

Reiff, M. J. & Bawarshi, A. (2011). Tracing discursive resources: How students use prior genre knowledge to negotiate new writing contexts in first-year composition. *Written Communication, 28*(3), 312–337.

Roozen, K. (2010). Tracing trajectories of practice: Repurposing in one student's developing disciplinary writing processes. *Written Communication, 27*(3), 318–354.

Shipka, J. (2011) *Composition made whole*. Pittsburgh, PA: University of Pittsburgh Press.

Sommers, J. (2011). Reflection revisited: The class collage. *Journal of Basic Writing, 30*(1) (Spring), 99–129.

Turley, E. D. & Gallagher, C. W. (2008). On the "uses" of rubrics: Reframing the great rubric debate. *English Journal, 97*(4), 87–92.

Wardle, E. (2012). Creative repurposing for expansive learning: Considering "problem-exploring" and "answer-getting" dispositions in individuals and fields. *Composition Forum, 26*. Retrieved from http://compositionforum.com/issue/26/creative-repurposing.php.

Workman, E. (2016). *Visualizing transfer: Using mapping exercises to learn about students' writing knowledge and practice*. (Doctoral dissertation). Florida State University, Tallahassee, FL.

Yancey, K. B. (2004). Made not only in words: Composition in a new key. *College Composition and Communication, 56*(2), 297–328.

Yancey, K. B. (1998). *Reflection in the writing classroom.* Logan, UT: Utah State University Press.

Yancey, K. B. (Ed.) (2016). *A rhetoric of reflection.* Logan, UT: Utah State University Press.

Yancey, K. B., Robertson, L. & Taczak, K. (2014). *Writing across contexts: Transfer, composition, and sites of writing.* Logan, UT: Utah State University Press.

Zawilski, B. (2015). *When all that is old becomes new: Transferring writing knowledge and practice across print, screen, and network spaces.* (Doctoral dissertation). Retrieved from https://oatd.org/oatd/record?record=oai%5C%3Afsu.digital.flvc.org%5C%3Afsu_273628.

AFTERWORD
REFLECTION: WHAT CAN COGNITIVE RHETORIC OFFER US?

Linda Flower
Carnegie Mellon University

As this volume richly illustrates, the intersection of writing and cognition has been a site of fresh discovery, contention, and changing paradigms. Unlike some areas of inquiry shaped by strong disciplinary conventions and methodologies, writing studies are often stimulated by the situated challenges posed by real writers and diverse contexts. Consider the challenges raised in this volume, from working with a disability or transferring knowledge across genres, to understanding the value of "practice" or actually teaching metacognition. A second feature of research at this crossroad has been its highly eclectic and interdisciplinary nature, using (and championing) diverse methods, explanatory metaphors and analogies, from the perspectives as apparently inimical as critical theory and neurobiology. Is crossover work a strength or a mistake? We have not always agreed.

Given these situated challenges and the sometimes competing responses that turn up at the intersection of writing and cognition, I want to focus on two contributions *cognitive rhetoric* can make. One is the way its distinctive *cognitive* perspective on the activity of writing can give writers themselves a unique level of data-based access to the complexity of their own performance, merging inquiry with learning. At the same time, cognitive rhetoric's *rhetorical* perspective encourages us to see the meaning of "writing and cognition" as a contested historical construction—one which reflects the reception, in English and composition studies, of unfamiliar psychological paradigms from modeling and statistics in argument, to the new use of fMRI data. As with any disciplinary shift, this is partly a story of growth in understanding and a matter of "acceptance." Change may mean moving beyond unsophisticated ways of reading arguments outside one's discourse or it may be the outcome of perceived competition among those discourses for significance in the field. So this volume also offers us a social/cultural picture of an evolving field, as Dylan Dryer and David Russell (this volume) put it, at 35 years of age.

THE RHETORIC OF INQUIRY IN WRITING AND COGNITION

The intersection of writing and cognition is a place where multiple research frameworks talk with and at each other, each bringing its own assumptive base, loaded concepts, and methods. This can, of course, pose a challenge to communication across such differences. The Hayes-Flower *model* of the composing process first proposed in 1980, expanded and revised through 2012, is a good example (Flower & Hayes, 1981; Hayes, 2012; Hayes & Flower, 1980). In cognitive psychology a model, when instantiated in a detailed computer program, offers a way to test an information processing hypothesis about what people did (or in other cases to show how to do it better). However, in the context of larger ill-defined problems such as writing or design, a model typically functions as a hypothesis designed to guide exploration. So the Hayes-Flower model—as a data-based, working hypothesis about critical dimensions of this cognitive process—was a launching pad for inquiry—into various questions. Its framework allowed for a productive use of disciplinary difference. A comparison (based on the name of the first author) also shows a difference in emphasis when a paper was directed to readers in educational psychology versus readers in rhetoric and composition, particularly in the choice to elaborate models or to uncover the role of strategic choice. (cf. the 1980 and the 1981 papers cited above, or two later studies on revision: Flower, Hayes, Carey, Schriver & Stratman [1986] and Hayes, Flower, Schriver, Stratman & Carey [1987]).

The generation of studies this working hypothesis launched started with building richer accounts of planning and revision which soon posed their own questions. If, for instance, planning was the rich, multi-modal process these early studies suggested, would more experienced writers do it differently, with a different repertoire of strategies (a standard expert/novice question in educational psychology) (Flower, Schriver, Carey, Haas & Hayes, 1992)? And when these revealing differences did turn up, one wondered: was a novice performance a question of merely don't or can't? Maybe expert performance on college tasks, for instance, depended primarily on genre knowledge, or acculturation to academic discourse, or perhaps on processes below the level of consciousness? So subsequent studies tried to tease this out, by offering writers gentle prompts to use "expert" moves seen in the earlier studies (e.g., to consider the possibility that a reader might disagree). I should emphasize that exploratory research also regularly reveals things you never thought to ask. As I will turn to later, this particular sequence of digging deeper opened up a new line of inquiry into the process and pedagogy of collaborative planning.

Working from a psychological paradigm in which a model is a tool for inquiry produced some interesting consequences for interpretation in composition studies. In the discourse of modeling, this framework, its visual diagram of *planning, translating, revising,* represented broad, but distinguishable categories of cognition, embedded, most importantly, in a highly recursive process—that invited investigation. But for some readers it was easy to conflate these complex theoretical spaces with the familiar stage model of prewrite/write/rewrite or with the popular "classroom process" (freewriting, peer review, etc.) criticized by Arthur Applebee (1986) in "Problems in Process Approaches" as a set of teacher-sequenced, obligatory activities oblivious to goals in writing (pp. 95–96). Perhaps more problematic for the reception of a "model," were the assumptions triggered by an empirical paradigm itself. For some readers rooted in a humanist tradition, such research was viewed through the history of empiricism, inseparable from a positivistic stance to knowledge shrunken to what statistics could describe—and a threat to the study of English. Cognitive and educational researchers on the other hand were working out of a different interpretative frame in which protocol data was "only data" awaiting interpretation that meets evidentiary demands. Statistical significance was merely another form of argument—a test in which the difference you observed may or may not reveal "truth," but at $p < 0.05$ it was not random or likely to have occurred in more than five times in a hundred. The paradigm one brings to reading such research can clearly dictate strikingly different interpretations (Flower, 1997). (A small example: in informal surveys with my rhetoric students on reading articles with data, they report typically skipping over the tables with numbers.)

Another social consequence of this intersection of disciplinary voices will be the politics of paradigm shifts. In 1980, English was undergoing a seismic shift, as writing discovered its theoretical roots in classical and contemporary rhetoric and composition was being liberated from the pedestrian practice of the freshman "theme." Cognitive rhetoric contributed to this energy with a new focus on the writer as a thinker. In the process model noted above, social context was acknowledged but not explored, subsumed in the standard psychological concept of the task environment. However, as the popularity of the metaphor "turn" implies, there is a certain trendiness in some scholarly circles in which a new idea must dominate or dismiss another perspective to prove its significance. Following the impressive rise of cultural criticism in literature, the "social turn" in composition journals put a good deal of energy into constructing a simplified binary conceptualization of writing as being a "social process" *rather than* a cognitive one (which was often represented in terms of a reductive, usually positivistic body of assumptions).

The irony of course, is that there is no such cognitive/social split in people, much less in the act of writing. The split lies first in our necessarily chosen vantage point and focal interest (writers in action, or broader social forces, or genre conventions, etc.). Given the differing paradigms that necessarily attend each focus, reading such research will also require some effort to understand one another. A second source of this divide is the very real difficulty of studying how social, cultural, and cognitive forces actually do interact, in the acts of writing, learning and teaching, communicating, or social knowledge making. Research does tend to find strength in narrowness and the interactions we theorize are hard to study. Yet this is one of the great challenges many of the authors in this volume are trying meet in innovative ways.

My particular contribution to this volume's border crossing will draw in part from those studies that led me to study collaborative planning as an explicitly rhetorical form of problem solving. Observing writers themselves interpreting and responding to the context *they* envisioned, offered a way to study what I described as the construction of *negotiated* meaning, and propose a more integrated social/cognitive theory of writing (Flower, 1994). As a part of the broad inquiry this volume documents, the stance of cognitive rhetoric I will turn to offers a way understand this social, intellectual, and affective process in a way that highlights the strategic thinking and agency of writers themselves.

THE (META)COGNITION OF INQUIRY

It is often helpful to approach cognitive rhetoric as a capital D Discourse, in James Gee's (1989) sense of the term. Entering and drawing on a given Discourse entails us in a distinctive set of *"saying (writing)-doing-being-valuing believing combinations"* (Gee, 1989, p. 6). For instance, the notion of *task representation* from problem-solving research in cognitive psychology adds a powerful new dimension to how we think about the act of writing. Unlike the concept of *assignment* (which we are given) or a *genre* (whose established conventions a text tries to fit), this "saying (writing) . . . believing combination" imports assumptions and guides perception, thinking, and investigation down a particular path. It leads us, for instance, to envision an agent with a task to do in a context he or she must interpret, which in turn foregrounds the work of representation and construction, the work, in effect, of making up that task. Here assignments or genres are merely cues, that the writer as agent may or may not attend to, understand, or instantiate in the same way as the assigner or a different writer would. Perhaps more important are the assumptions this Discourse engages. We can expect for example, that because this representation is a *construction*—with its distinctive though often unacknowledged network of features, goals, priorities—it will lead to some marked differences in performance, including expert/novice or insider/outsider ones, as people carry out the task they have given themselves to do.

As a distinctive Discourse we can enter, cognitive rhetoric then prompts us to think of writing in terms of actions more than text, to think of writers in terms of a repertoire of strategies, habits or moves tied to age, experience, ability, or intention, and to see the writer as an agent, even with all the constraints of context. Choosing the writer or individual minds as one's focal point can of course be controversial when it evokes the literary legacy of romantic individualism or the dichotomies of the "social turn," both of which offer a somewhat impoverished Discourse for understanding interactions. Gee would argue that to understand one's own Discourse, one needs to know others, to be bi- or multi-discursive. Such flexibility allows us in order to read cognitive rhetoric or social constructionism, for instance, for their relative power as explanatory accounts or as ways to support complex human experience.

Rhetoric has traditionally stood at this individual/social intersection. With rhetoric as its root noun, cognitive rhetoric places us in the larger Discourse of classical and contemporary rhetoric, signaling a critical departure from individualistic, romantic paradigms. Even with its own split focus on text analysis versus performance, its writer/rhetor is always embedded in a social, historical context, engaged in a dialogic performance shaped by Aristotle's "available arguments" and tradition. Unlike the Discourses that foreground these social realities, the methods of cognitive rhetoric offer a distinctive (though not the only) way to study social context, conventions, or interactions *in action*—by tracking how they are interpreted and responded to by actual writers and learners.

Another way to account for what cognitive rhetoric can offer is to view the performance of writing as a social-cognitive-cultural activity, as Yrjo Engeström and other activity theorists would define it. Whereas discourse theory reflects the descriptive agenda of language studies, activity analysis identifies itself first as a research tool. Engeström (1996) has represented "the basic structure of an activity system" with two superimposed triangles in which its foundational trio—a Subject, Object (or Outcome), and a Community—exist in interaction with another trio of forces: Rules, Mediating Tools, and the Division of Labor (p. 67). Recognizing the influence of mediational means, for instance, has been a powerful addition to thinking about writing (e.g., about the shaping influence of computers vs typewriters, of generalized genre expectations vs. report templates, or of practices such as peer review). The "meaning" of Engeström's little diagram, however, does not lie in a theoretical elaboration of its key terms, but in its rather daunting implication: that to understand an activity system as a "system," you need to recognize—to investigate—each of these key elements. Moreover, the model asserts, important aspects of a social-cognitive-cultural, activity are likely to be in conflict with one another. In his figure, Engeström uses a zig zag line to trace "contradictions" within the system. The question in any given study (of a health care center or a traffic court) is just where those internal contradictions lie, since the points of disturbance in a given system are the sites where innovation and "expansive transformation" of an activity itself are likely to occur (Engeström, 1999, p. 27).

Analyzing writing as an activity, cognitive rhetoric suggests that six critical components (writer/performance+outcome/community, in conjunction with rules/tools/power) not only interact in ways we may not see, but that significant aspects of this activity are probably working in contradiction. For instance, the mediational tools a writer can call on may not be aligned with the institutional or disciplinary demands she faces. The genre expectations of knowledge display that an economics student mastered for college papers will misfire when her readers are paying for a consulting report. In fact, the most striking finding in the planning studies noted above was the constant role conflict played in this process and how discovering those points of contradiction and conflict often opened up a place for transformative understanding. So by analyzing writing as a social cognitive activity, cognitive rhetoric can uncover patterns of thinking and strategic choices that have a traceable effect on performance (from how a task is represented to how a new mediational tool such as argument mapping is actually used). It reveals not only sites of conflict but problematic hidden logics on which a writer may be operating. And it offers a set of methods for inquiry suited to multiple forms of inquiry, to which I would like to now turn.

COGNITIVE INQUIRY AS AN EDUCATIONAL PRACTICE

Perhaps one of the most unusual things cognitive rhetoric affords is its direct transfer into teaching and learning—as both practical advice and a practice of inquiry. It is not surprising of course that studies of cognition as problem-solving, designed around expert/novice comparisons could be directly applicable. My own enthusiasm for cognitive research was initially sparked by the work John R. Hayes was doing with designers, revealing the thinking behind what was often treated as an art based on un-transferrable talent; research he then transferred into his very popular psychology course on Problem Solving in multiple domains. At the time my problem was how to develop a new writing program for CMU's MBA students. Given their math and engineering backgrounds, the reigning current-traditional focus on style and genre, much less the use of expressive writing (emerging then in composition) was unlikely to earn credibility in this fast track environment. It was with this jointly motivated curiosity about what effective writers were actually doing that Dick Hayes and I began our exploratory collaboration.

From a psychological point of view, one of the most interesting outcomes of this early research was that 1980 model of the composing process. From a rhetorical perspective, it was the discovery of the fascinating things both experts and novices did and why the difference mattered. Sometimes the teaching potential only slowly dawned on us. For instance, it was becoming clear that experienced writers used planning to develop a larger, interconnected set of broader rhetorical goals, which they often tested by simulating a reader's possible response. And they actively considered alternative textual conventions, e.g., "Do I want to argue this point here, or maybe just use a suggestive example?" (Flower et al., 1992). This raised the question about novices: is their performance a matter of "can't or don't"? The series of sophomores who came to my office for the study generously bought into the fiction that our computer would actually write the paper for them, if they just planned out loud, in response to a series of questions, ranging from, "What is the point of this paper?" and "How are you going to show that?" to "Well, what if someone said, 'I don't believe that'" or "Could you imagine a different type of introduction." In short, they were invited to do the sort of rhetorical thinking we saw in experts. And in fact they could do sophisticated things—when prompted.

However, the penny actually dropped when these "subjects" (fulfilling their subject pool requirement), asked me if their roommates could come and do the study too. We had chosen students from Dick Hayes' course so we could ask them to plan around a real paper that was due, on a topic where they all had comparable topic knowledge. Yet, this rather lengthy and demanding planning session had turned out to be so helpful they were recommending it as way to write the paper. They were telling us that our prompts were in fact an effective performance enhancing tool. And we had the good sense to listen and translate them into the formal pedagogical practice of "collaborative planning" in which writers were actively prompted by partners to talk out (in many cases, figure out) their "key point, purpose, audience response, and use of textual conventions" for a paper at hand. And the tapes of these sessions—focused on this most demanding part of planning—turned out to be a rich source of data for us and the students (Flower, 1994, pp. 128–191).

This sequence of planning studies illustrates some different ways cognitive rhetoric supports pedagogy. In my own effort to teach problem solving strategies for writing, each new set of studies led to an expanded edition of a textbook I wrote (Flower, 1993). In my classes I noted that explaining and giving a name to a thinking strategy, in the way textbooks do, did indeed give many students a new sense of power and conscious choice over moves they may have even done without recognizing their value. However, other students who had little experience planning around a rhetorical purpose, needed that experience, in this case of responding to the live prompts of a planning partner. By, in essence, modeling the strategy to themselves they could reach that ah ha moment in learning.

These two accounts of using collaborative planning illustrate a traditional educational practice: teaching the results of our research to students. Yet perhaps one of cognitive rhetoric's most distinctive contributions is to a pedagogy in which students take over the reins of inquiry to develop their own strategic knowledge. Because much of the research in cognitive rhetoric works at the level of conscious attention, even if that awareness is fleeting or barely articulated, it has developed a set of methods that lets writers treat themselves as "subjects" in their own inquiry. When, for instance, students re-examine what happened in their own protocols, taped collaborative planning sessions, or reflections, they can not only compare local rhetorical choices to broader intentions or their own strategies to expert/novice patterns, they can read textual choices in the context of their plan and/or a partner's response to it. When writers can do a data-based retrospective analysis using prepared, research-style questions or pursuing serendipitous discoveries, they often uncover the hidden logic behind what they did or didn't do.

For want of a better name, we could call this methodical metacognition. As part of a course on the Cognition of Reading and Writing, students work with a small Student Research Guide that translates methods developed in formal research projects into (inexpensive) inquiry tools. Offering models for collecting, representing and analyzing data, it helps students use think-aloud protocols, collaborative planning episodes, retrospective reports, rhetorical reading, in-process probing, and critical incident self-interviews. Responding to the theory and predictions from their scholarly reading (e.g., from Bakhtin, Vygotsky and activity theory, to linguistic research on comprehension, to schema theory to writing studies), students then use these process-tracing methods to glimpse first-hand what both readers and writers may in fact be doing. For instance, how do the writers they observe deal with conflicts in their own plans, or how are readers (in a line by line rhetorical reading) actually interpreting one of the student's own texts? (A typically eye-opening experience.) More significant however, is the data they collect over the course of the term on their own extended process of producing an important piece of writing for some other class, internship, or project. Their study typically starts with self-interviews reviewing the germination of an idea or recent conversations with a teacher, mentor or friend, supported by notes, rhetorical/interpretive readings of the assignment, or comments, which lead to think aloud data or critical incidents interviews on selected episodes of planning, writing, or revision. Their final paper is an analysis of their own planning/writing/revision process, combining concepts from theory and research with their own data and self-analysis. The goal is "a strategic portrait" of their own experience.

The analytical methods of cognitive rhetoric, as it is important to emphasize, are themselves mediating tools in the sense activity theory describes. Standing between the social/cultural/cognitive process of a mind at work in its shifting contexts and their representation of it, these tools shape what a writer will see and will surely miss. Just like the theories students read and the discourse they are entering, these methods name and shed light on certain parts of this process. At the same time, they transform learning by supporting a distinctive kind of metacognition—one that is built on data-based reflection. And as students study themselves, the focus of their inquiry goes beyond questions that motivate published research, into posing questions that reflect their own needs, conflicts, self-discoveries, or the exigence this work posed for them. Moreover, when you (as a teacher/researcher) have the opportunity to compare your reading of such data with what the analyzing "subject" discovers, you recognize not only the powerful insights metacognitive analysis offers, but the advantage of combining both sorts of interpretation (Flower, 1994, pp. 236–291).

To briefly illustrate the kinds of learning this sort of data-based metacognition can elicit, consider some examples from two final Strategic Portrait papers that include data from the various methods students tried. Rain, drawing on a joint degree in architecture and linguistics, choose to track the construction of an important section of her master's thesis. Her provocative thesis starts simply enough: The technical/descriptive conventions of architectural proposal writing—which are designed to help readers *visualize* a building in space—are indeed used by professionals, as this excerpt of data from Rain's in-process probe of a professional architect reading a proposal illustrates.

Paragraph Number	Here the analyst's notes paraphrase & quote from the think aloud reading tape with her commentary in brackets*
¶1	The building is made of concrete and steel "although I don't *know* that" [Reader acknowledges that he is conjecturing, that this has not been stated.]
¶3	"Okay so now we're putting it in context, the building is on Madison Avenue, now we know that" [Reader is . . . "building" a knowledge base of the building.]
¶3	[For the first time, reader says "yes" in response to Q about whether he can mentally visualize the building at this point, and then proceeds to describe the building's form.]

* Note: *In place of a full transcription,* the Student Research Guide *suggested representing taped data with this combination of selected quotes, paraphrases, and commentary linked to cues for finding the section again.*

Rain however, wants argue for what she sees as a controversial alternative to this traditional discourse—for a proposal design that is adapted to real users, the non-technical readers and clients. The following data, excerpted from her early collaborative planning session shows her developing the precision of that goal (in response here to her partner, V's, prompts, such as, "So what's your key point?" Or "How might X respond?").

Counter	Speaker	Here the Speaker (Rain or V) is in quotes and the analyst's paraphrase or commentary in brackets.
1:09	R	"present a piece of text describing the building . . . how can writers describe architecture *best* "
1:35	R/V	[I'm wondering whether to write a "theory-based guide" for readers or writers.] V: "It's kind of the same thing in the sense that the guide for the readers is going to be ultimately what guides the writers."
5:55	R	[Discussing current architectural writing, the different purposes and audiences of the two kinds of writing]
6:20	R	"So maybe that means I wanna come up with ideas on how to translate, in a sense, the architectural way of writing into a narrative."
9:10	R	"The whole point is for the reader to . . . is trying to imagine the building" [goal to set the context of the reading]

But this plan—not to mention her goal to challenge a highly standard professional practice—presented some dilemmas. Taping a self-interview on a "critical incident" that that occurred along the way, Rain starts by noting the context for this incident:

0:05	"So I'm trying to investigate how I negotiated the discourses of architecture and academia."
0:57	"I had defined my own metrics of success and deliverables but didn't know what advisors expected or wanted."
1:35	[M-L (architecture advisor) suggested some artists and sources to look at (more research) while M (linguistics advisor) had said, don't do any more research, start writing.]
5:58	"I assumed that both . . . advisors had ideas about what they wanted from me." [I realize here that maybe their expectations weren't as specific as I had thought.]
7:53	"In the end it falls to me as my thesis to figure out what works Best." [Don't look for others to decide what the outputs and specifics are; self-define them. But then, I am the student, and they evaluate my performance. How do I know what they are looking for?]

In her final paper for the Process class (A Strategic Portrait of My Writing Process), Rain interprets these events as more generalizable and transferrable insights.

> There are several aspects of my process and resulting strategic methods that may be specific to this case study, though this is not to say that they will not work for other genres. First, I was writing academic, conceptual prose, different, for example, from the kind of text my thesis was proposing, which was concrete, descriptive, fiction-type text. I was also representing and responding to two very different discourse expectations: that of the academic thesis paper and the architectural thesis. I was also attempting to negotiate multiple discourses, mediating research from many different fields into one final thesis.

She concludes with a "Quick Reference Guide" for herself—a note on 10 particular strategies she discovered working well for her across data-gathering, planning, and writing, from seeking out experts for advice early on, to using nonsense words to keep the flow going when you need info or don't have the right word. It is an idiosyncratic set—not a theory—to be sure. But it reflects the value of *using* theory and methods to discover and articulate a new level of understanding about your own thinking, the discourse, the social context you are in and the question of transfer.

Sara, on the other hand, looks back over her data and constructs a narrative of initially unnoticed, quietly competing schemas, which she used to explain previous struggles. Her story ends, however, with a revealing insight into the way "affect" directly influenced her strategic choices. One of her strategies for writing this process paper itself was to consider the explanatory power different concepts from our course readings might offer this analysis. When she looks at her own "task representation" as a "schema," she notices: "I used to think that before I wrote a paper, my ideas and inferences and conclusions were already established in my head. I discovered that this rarely happens. As we will see, . . . "

Her story starts with a discussion with her Chaucer professor in which they agreed that an "interesting" paper would want to go beyond a simple comparison/contrast of two characters to a more specific idea.

> I also said off-handedly that I think there's something fishy about the Prioress, but I couldn't quite put my finger on it—something was just off about her. I reasoned that maybe with more research, I would have a better understanding of my feelings towards her. [The Professor] agreed, and said

> something that seems to have foreshadowed my whole writing process for this paper: write out your thesis/main argument right now, before you do any research, she said, and then research and write and realize that your perspective may change. This session with Peggy was really important in helping me understand myself as a strategic writer.

As Sara's story unfolds, she sees herself moving into a "knowledge-based" phase, guided by a familiar "schema."

> Because I dedicated a lot of time and effort to finding sources and listing somewhat objective information about the Wife of Bath [sic] and the Prioress, my schema for this writing task seemed to change. I completely forgot about looking into the "fishiness" of the Prioress, and I just went on comparing and contrasting the two characters in terms of [how they glossed the Scriptures]. I convinced myself that even if I didn't offer a profound insight to anything, it would still be kind of an interesting paper . . .
>
>   It was easier to choose a task representation that followed my schema of "a comparison paper" rather than construct a task representation where I would have to further build new connections to my schema of the two characters in *The Canterbury Tales* (this is what I was expected to do—and, of course, what requires a lot more cognitive effort).

She reports an epiphany and schema shift between the sixth and seventh draft when, in a self-interview, "I realized that Peggy has probably read all these articles I'm citing. I have to create my own voice." Sara's interpretation draws on a theoretical contrast between "knowledge-driven and constructive planning" from our readings. But her reasoning about the necessary trigger is a different claim (that was debated when she presented it in the class):

> That was when I went from knowledge-driven to constructive planning. I discovered that I could interpret the Prioress's character and tale *through* the Wife of Bathe [sic] (and that would help me uncover her fishiness!). . . . I believe that being stuck in knowledge-based planning for six drafts was necessary for me to reach a higher level of understanding. I don't think I would've thought that I could use the Wife of Bathe [sic] to interpret the Prioress if I hadn't listed all of the facts about both pilgrims to begin with.

Reflection: What Can Cognitive Rhetoric Offer Us?

It would be easy to look at the strategies Sara and Rain discuss as part of a growing repertoire of options suited to particular parts of a writing process or to solving a variety of knowledge-building or discourse demands. We might expect that more experienced writers have more of these in the store room and a better indexing system to call them up. This self-analysis gives them presence and a name. Sara's summation is a nice example:

> So, the problem for writing my Chaucer paper was going from choosing a task representation to *constructing* one. I discovered that this transition involves: going from knowledge driven to constructive planning, recognizing the audience (and moving to reader-based prose), and incorporating cognition and affect to make inferences about the context. Cognition plays another important role: it helps build a schema of a new task representation; it challenges you to not only use already well defined connections between points in your schema network, but to create new connections, make new inferences, offer a unique insight—and, in this case, to look at the Prioress from the perspective of the Wife of Bathe [*sic*].

However, when Sara's final self-interview explored the role of "affect," she also she got at one of the profound but less visible connections between cognition and rhetoric.

> When I was writing my first few drafts of just plain comparisons, for example, I was not hoping to impress my professor or offer an amazing insight in the field. In a retrospective interview, I said:

> "I wish I could say that I knew what I was doing—that I was laying down information first and then I knew I was going to interpret it in a unique way after I had everything written. But I don't think I was. I think I was just going to compare and contrast and write info that I found and I just reasoned that one mediocre grade won't kill me. . . . It wasn't until I thought about Peggy [my Professor], and how much I enjoy the class, and how I want to contribute something. So my respect for my professor's knowledge motivated me to offer a more insightful paper; not just a mediocre essay that didn't offer anything new."

From a theoretical perspective Sara has sketched writing as a social/cultural/cognitive activity loaded with affect. It is an action deeply tied not only to the

343

context of education, achievement, and academic discourse but also to personal relationships, her own self-image, and her goals and choices in a paper on Chaucer. And more to the point for her as a learner, these ideas have taken a live, richly instantiated, potentially memorable shape in terms of her own experience.

A pedagogy that incorporates a social cognitive process of inquiry is also an example of teaching for transfer. As Anson suggests in his case study of a failure to cross genres, transfer is difficult even when it is supported by metaknowledge of rhetorical strategies. An earlier volume called *Transfer on Trial* helps show why, especially in the cases James Greeno, Joyce Moore, and David Smith call the "transfer of situated learning" (1996). What transfers, they argue is not *knowledge* (abstract, symbolic, or propositional representations), but *knowing*. That is, knowing how to interact with people and things, how to participate in another activity by being able to perceive the "affordances" of both situations, to recognize critical features and see parallels (pp. 99–100).

As Rain would say, the power of narrative is to let us put ourselves into a space, walk around and do things. Engaging with writing as a social cognitive process draws us into the space theory can provide, helping us imagine the interactive, interpersonal activity in which writing takes place. And as an educational practice, its methods and ideas are available to both researchers and students.

REFERENCES

Anson, C. (2016). The Pop Warner chronicles: A case study in contextual adaptation and the transfer of writing ability. *College Composition and Communication, 67*(4), 518–549.

Applebee, A. N. (1986). Problems in process approaches: Toward a reconceptualization of process instruction. In A. R. Petrosky & D. Bartholomae (Eds.), *The teaching of writing* (pp. 95–113). Chicago: National Society for the Study of Education.

Engeström, Y. (1996). Developmental studies of work as a testbench of activity theory: The case of primary care medical practice. In S. Chaiklin & J. Lave (Eds.), *Understanding practice: Perspectives on activity and context* (pp. 64–103). Cambridge, UK: Cambridge University Press.

Engeström, Y. (1999). Activity theory and individual and social transformation. In Y. Engeström, R. Miettinen, R.-L. Punamäki (Eds.), *Perspectives on activity theory* (pp. 19–38). Cambridge, UK: Cambridge University Press.

Flower, L. (1993). *Problem-solving strategies for writing in college and community*. New York: Harcourt Brace Jovanovich.

Flower, L. (1994). *The construction of negotiated meaning: A social cognitive theory of writing*. Carbondale, IL: Southern Illinois University Press.

Flower, L. (1997). Observation-based theory building. In G. A. Olson & T. W. Taylor (Eds.), *Publishing in rhetoric and composition* (pp. 163–185). Albany, NY: State University of New York Press.

Flower, L. & Hayes, J. R. (1981). A cognitive process theory of writing. *College Composition and Communication, 32*(1), 365–387.

Flower, L., Hayes, J. R., Carey, L., Schriver, K. & Stratman, J. (1986). Detection, diagnosis, and the strategies of revision. *College Composition and Communication, 37*(1), 16–55.

Flower, L., Schriver, K. A., Carey, L., Haas, C. & Hayes, J. R. (1992). Planning in writing: The cognition of a constructive process. In S. P. Witte, N. Nakadate & R. D. Cherry (Eds.), *A rhetoric of doing: Essays on written discourse in honor of James L. Kinneavy* (pp. 181–243). Carbondale, IL: Southern Illinois University Press.

Gee, J. P. (1989). Literacy, discourse, and linguistics: Introduction. *Journal of Education, 171*(1), 5–17.

Greeno, J., Moore, J. & Smith, D. (1996). Transfer of situated learning. In D. Detterman & R. Sternberg (Eds.), *Transfer on trial: Intelligence, cognition, and instruction* (pp. 99–167). Norwood, NJ: Ablex.

Hayes, J. R. (2012). Modeling and remodeling writing. *Written Communication, 29*(3), 369–388.

Hayes, J. R. & L. Flower (1980). Identifying the organization of writing processes. In L. Gregg & E. R. Steinberg (Eds.), *Cognitive processing in writing: An interdisciplinary approach* (pp. 3–30). Hillsdale, NJ: Lawrence Erlbaum.

Hayes, J. R., Flower, L., Schriver, K., Stratman, J. & Carey, L. (1987). Cognitive processes in revision. In S. Rosenberg (Ed.), *Advances in applied psycholinguistics, Vol II: Reading, writing and language processing* (pp. 176–240). Cambridge, UK: Cambridge University Press.

CONTRIBUTORS

Charles Bazerman is a Distinguished Professor at the University of California Santa Barbara. He has recently been designated Doctor Honoris Causa by the National University of Cordoba, Argentina, one of the first universities in the Americas.

Ellen C. Carillo is Associate Professor of English at the University of Connecticut and the Writing Program Coordinator at its Waterbury Campus. She teaches courses in composition and literature, and is the author of *Securing a Place for Reading in Composition: The Importance of Teaching for Transfer* (Utah State University Press, 2015).

Irene Clark is Professor of English, Director of Composition, and Director of the Master's option in Rhetoric/Composition at California State University, Northridge. Her articles have appeared in *College Composition and Communication, Writing Program Administration, Composition Forum*, the *WAC Journal*, the *Writing Center Journal*, and the *Journal of General Education*.

Steven J. Corbett is Director of the University Writing Center and Assistant Professor of English at Texas A&M University-Kingsville. He is the author of *Beyond Dichotomy: Synergizing Writing Center and Classroom Pedagogies*, and co-editor of *Peer Pressure, Peer Power: Theory and Practice in Peer Review and Response for the Writing Classroom*.

Dana Lynn Driscoll is Associate Professor of English at Indiana University of Pennsylvania, where she teaches in the Composition and TESOL doctoral program. Her scholarly interests include writing centers, writing transfer, RAD research methodologies, writing across the curriculum, and writing assessment.

Dylan B. Dryer is Associate Professor of Composition Studies at the University of Maine. His research has won the Kenneth A. Bruffee (2014) and Richard Braddock (2013) Awards. Current projects include corpus-based approaches to identifying novice teachers' construct-representations and an attempt to reconcile rhetorical and cognitive constructs of genre.

Linda Flower is Professor of English at Carnegie Mellon University. She has written on cognitive rhetoric (*The Construction of Negotiated Meaning: A Social Cognitive Theory of Writing*), supporting urban engagement (*Community Literacy and the Rhetoric of Public Engagement*), and holding community think tanks, "Difference-Driven Inquiry" in *RSQ*.

Gwen Gorzelsky is Executive Director of The Institute for Learning and Teaching (TILT) and Professor of English at Colorado State University. She has published articles in *College Composition and Communication, College English, Reflections, JAC, JAEPL,* and other venues. Her research interests include writing instruction, learning transfer, metacognition, and literacy learning, particularly uses of literacy for personal and social change.

Carol Hayes is Assistant Professor of Writing at George Washington University where she serves as Writing Center Deputy Director. Her research interests include writing centers, first-year writing, and on the transfer of writing skills from one context to another (such as high school to college, or first-year writing courses to writing performed in disciplinary courses).

John R. Hayes is Professor Emeritus of Psychology at Carnegie Mellon University has been a pioneer in introducing cognitive psychology in writing research publishing multiple articles, chapters, and books. He currently supports the open-access *Journal in Writing Research*, including a biannual award for outstanding quantitative or qualitative empirical research in writing.

Alice S. Horning is Professor of Writing & Rhetoric/Linguistics at Oakland University, where she has taught business writing, first-year writing and served as program administrator. Her work has appeared in the major professional journals; forthcoming is her co-edited volume, *What is College Reading?* from ATD Books.

Edmund Jones is Associate Professor of English at Seton Hall University where he is researching knowledge transfer in writing. His other interests include directed self-placement, computer-based assessment of essays, self-efficacy and other self-beliefs in relation to writing achievement, and integrating assessment across the campus.

Peter H. Khost is Assistant Professor at Stony Brook University. His book *Rhetor Response* is forthcoming from Utah State University Press. Khost received grants from CCCC and CWPA to study student writers' habits of mind. He is founding chair of CWPA's Task Force for Publicizing the *Framework for Success in Postsecondary Writing*.

Marcus Meade is a doctoral candidate and lecturer at the University of Nebraska-Lincoln and co-director of the Writing Lincoln Initiative. His scholarly work has appeared in *College Composition and Communication*.

Patricia Portanova is Associate Professor of English at Northern Essex Community College where she teaches writing and communication. Her research focuses on writing with distractions, multilingual student writers, and service learning. Her work appears in the collection *Linguistically Diverse Immigrant and Resident Writers* and the forthcoming *Social Writing/Social Media*.

Joseph Paszek is Assistant Professor, Director of the Writing Program, and Director of the Writing Center at the University of Detroit Mercy. He received his doctorate in rhetoric and composition from Wayne State University in 2016 for his project that investigated student values and perceptions of core curriculum writing courses.

E. Shelley Reid is Associate Professor of English and Director of the Center for Teaching and Faculty Excellence at George Mason University. Her work on teacher preparation, mentoring, and writing education appears in *Composition Studies, College Composition and Communication, Pedagogy, Writing Program Administration*, and *Writing Spaces*.

Dirk Remley is Professor of English at Kent State University, where he teaches professional writing courses including business writing and technical writing. He has authored books on cognitive neuroscience and multimodal rhetoric pertaining to instructional messages as well as persuasive messages.

J. Michael Rifenburg is Assistant Professor of English at the University of North Georgia where he directs first-year writing and leads workshops on faculty writing through UNG's Center for Teaching, Learning, and Leadership. His book *The Embodied Playbook: Writing Practices of Student-Athletes* is forthcoming from Utah State University Press.

Liane Robertson is Associate Professor at William Paterson University of New Jersey. Her current research explores writing transfer across multi-institutional contexts, especially the role of transfer-oriented content in writing curricula. Her recent work is featured in *Writing Across Contexts: Transfer, Composition, and Sites of Writing* and *Naming What We Know: Threshold Concepts of Writing Studies*.

Duane Roen is Professor of English at Arizona State University, where he serves as Dean of the College of Integrative Sciences and Arts, Dean of University College, and Vice Provost. His current projects focus on applications of the Framework for Success in Postsecondary Writing and on family history writing.

David R. Russell is Professor of English at Iowa State University. He has published widely on writing across the curriculum (WAC), international writing instruction, activity theory and genre theory. He is the author of *Writing in the Academic Disciplines: A Curricular History*, numerous articles, and co-editor of four collections. He also edits the *Journal of Business and Technical Communication*.

Phil Shaw is a lecturer in the Rochester Institute of Technology's University Writing Program. He teaches first-year writing and basic writing courses which foreground writing about writing, metacognition, identity, and institutional power. Phil's interdisciplinary interests and research includes psychology and cognitive science as they apply to learning and student-teacher connections.

Kara Taczak, Teaching Assistant Professor, teaches writing courses and advises first-year students at the University of Denver. Her publications have appeared in *Composition Forum, Teaching English in a Two-Year College*, and *Across the Disciplines*; she received the 2015 *CCCC* Research Impact Award and the 2016 *CWPA* Book Award for her co-authored book, *Writing Across Contexts*.

Contributors

Jen Talbot is Assistant Professor at the University of Central Arkansas, where she teaches courses in the Writing major and the First-Year Writing program. She studies feminist and institutional rhetorics; her writing can be found in *Works & Days*, *JAC*, and *Feminist Rhetorics and Science Studies* (forthcoming).

Bonnie Vidrine-Isbell conducts interdisciplinary research as a doctoral candidate at the University of Washington, specializing in bilingual brain studies and second language pedagogy. She has taught English as a Second and Foreign Language for ten years in Washington State, Louisiana, Thailand, Spain, and Belize.

Dianna Winslow is Assistant Professor of English at Rochester Institute of Technology. She teaches Writing and Rhetoric with a focus on community of practice knowledge creation and transfer. She has written articles on rhetorics of food system advocacy, public memory, and the applicability of translingual theory to signed languages.

Kathleen Blake Yancey, Kellogg Hunt Professor of English and Distinguished Research Professor at Florida State University, has served as President of NCTE and Chair of CCCC. Currently, she leads "The Writing Passport Project," a multi-institutional transfer-focused research project. She has authored/co-authored of over 100 articles and book chapters and authored/edited/co-edited 14 scholarly books.

www.ingramcontent.com/pod-product-compliance
Lightning Source LLC
Chambersburg PA
CBHW060512080526
44586CB00012B/460